COMPUTER MUSIC

SYNTHESIS, COMPOSITION, AND PERFORMANCE

CONSULTING EDITOR: GERALD WARFIELD

COMPUTER MUSIC

SYNTHESIS, COMPOSITION, AND PERFORMANCE

Charles Dodge

Brooklyn College of the City University of New York

Thomas A. Jerse

Signal Analysis Division of the Hewlett-Packard Company

SCHIRMER BOOKS
A Division of Macmillan, Inc.
NEW YORK

Collier Macmillan Publishers
LONDON

Schirmer Books
A Division of Macmillan, Inc.
866 Third Avenue, New York, N.Y. 10022

Collier Macmillan Canada, Inc.

Library of Congress Catalog Card Number: 83-18773

Printed in the United States of America

printing number
2 3 4 5 6 7 8 9 10

Figure 2.9 is reproduced from *The Acoustical
Foundations of Music*, 2nd Edition, by John Backus,
by permission of W.W. Norton & Company, Inc.
Copyright © 1977, 1969 by W.W. Norton & Company, Inc.

Library of Congress Cataloging in Publication Data

Dodge, Charles.
  Computer music.
  Includes index.
  1. Electronic music—Instruction and study.
2. Musical instruments, Electronic. I. Jerse.
Thomas A. II. Title.
ML1092.D54 1984   789.9′9   83-18773
ISBN 0-02-873100-X

CONTENTS

CHAPTER 8
Composition with Computers   265

CHAPTER 9
Real-Time Performance of Computer Music   323

PREFACE

Computer music activity has proliferated in recent years. It has grown from its somewhat specialized origins as an interdisciplinary subfield of electronic music, digital signal processing, and experimental music to occupy an increasingly central position in the technologies of professional recording and home audio, as well as electronic music synthesis and composition. The expanded use of digital electronics in music is likely to continue; what we are now experiencing may be only the beginning of an era in which computer technology predominates in all aspects of the reproduction and synthesis of music.

The purpose of this book is to provide the musician with an entry into the three main fields of computer music—*synthesis*, *composition*, and *performance*. The material is presented in such a way that a person with little background in mathematics or engineering can be brought to the point where he or she can comprehend the evolving developments in the computer music field.

The text is divided into four parts. Chapters 1 and 2 present the fundamentals of computer music: computers, digital audio, and psychoacoustics. The second part, chapters 3 through 7, details the many techniques of sound synthesis and modification. The third part, chapter 8, covers the application of the computer to composition. The final part, chapter 9, describes performance practices and compositional approaches that have been used in live performance of computer music.

Because computer music is multifaceted, we have designed the book to be used in several ways. When read in the normal sequence, the diligent musician with little or no previous experience in computer programming or electronic music synthesis will develop a basic level of understanding over the entire range of the field.

In a classroom situation, the instructor could begin with the first three chapters to build the fundamentals of computer music systems, psychoacoustics, and synthesis. At this point, various synthesis techniques can be selected from chapters 4 through 7 in any order. This material, of course, would be supplemented by the user's manual for the synthesis system available to the students. Both chapters 8 and 9 may be presented independently of the psychoacoustic and synthesis topics. The instructor may wish to skip certain of the more technical sections in the chapters on synthesis, such as the final section of both chapters 4 and 6 and the final three sections of chapter 5.

The home computer user, already acquainted with the principles of computer system organization and programming can start with section 1.3, *Software for Computer Music*, and learn the fundmentals of digital audio systems. After this initial reading, the reader might focus on the psychoacoustics and synthesis chapters (2–7), computer-aided composition (chapter 8), or computer-music performance (chapter 9), depending on his or her particular interests and applications.

A composer of music for either acoustic instruments or electronic sounds can read this book with an eye to its implications for the composition of music. Once again, the interests of the reader will determine the particular parts of the book to be read. In addition to reading the chapter on computer-aided composition (chapter 8), a composer might concentrate on the sections in chapters 3 through 7 concerning compositional applications of particular sound-synthesis techniques. Chapter 9 also contains descriptions of a number of compositional applications of real-time performance in computer music.

When writing about computer music, it is especially difficult to strike a balance between generality and direct application to a specific system. We have chosen to present in flowchart form the designs for particular computer-generated sounds, rather than limit the book's usefulness to any single sound-synthesis language or system. With the aid of the appropriate user's manual, the reader can implement the flowchart designs into the sound synthesis language on an available system.

In addition, the appendix contains computer programs for most standard synthesis algorithms. While this collection of algorithms does not constitute a complete sound synthesis language, it can assist the reader in gaining a more detailed technical understanding of the algorithms and also serve as a basis for developing other synthesis algorithms. The reader without access to a synthesis language can use the appendix and the examples in sections 1.3A and 3.6 as starting points in developing synthesis software.

All the computer programming examples in the book are written in the FORTRAN language. Selecting a language proved to be a difficult task fraught with compromises. The decision to publish the routines in FORTRAN was based on various considerations, including FORTRAN's widespread use, its relative efficiency of execution on many systems, and the great familiarity of many computer programmers with FORTRAN. Some readers will want to translate the FORTRAN routines into other programming languages. This should be reasonably simple due to the short length and relative linearity of the programs. However, the way in which subprograms are passed data and store intermediate results is quite different in some languages. Therefore, the translator must check these procedures carefully.

A number of individuals donated considerable amounts of their time in assisting the authors to write this book. Katharine Schlefer Dodge helped the authors both in the organization of their thoughts and the expression of their ideas. Her attention to the book provided the impetus and focus for the project. Without her help on the first draft of the manuscript, the book would not have been written.

Johan Sundberg, professor in the Department of Speech Communication and Music Acoustics of the Royal Institute of Technology in Stockholm, aided tremendously in the formulation of the both the chapter on psychoacoustics and the sections of chapter 6 concerning the synthesis of the singing voice. His advice was always willingly offered and invariably enriched our work.

Preface

A number of computer music professionals read the first draft of the book and made helpful suggestions for strengthening it. These included Lejaren Hiller and his student Charles Ames of the State University of New York in Buffalo; William Buxton of the University of Toronto; and Steven Haflich of the Experimental Music Studio at the Massachusetts Institute of Technology.

John Chowning of the Center for Computer Research in Music and Acoustics at Stanford University was extremely generous with his time in explaining the intricate detail of his composition, *Stria*. Similarly, composers Roger Reynolds, Morton Subotnick, Charles Wuorinen, Larry Austin, Jon Appleton, Paul Lansky, and John Melby were each most helpful in editing the commentary on his computer music.

Joseph DiMeo, our student at Brooklyn College and the C.U.N.Y. Graduate Center, programmed all the instrument designs of the book, first into MUSIC 360 and later into MUSIC 11, thereby proving that a reader could actually program the instrument designs from the flowcharts and descriptions in the text. Other students of computer music at Brooklyn College diligently and patiently provided feedback on various drafts as the book evolved.

Stephen Bown, member of the technical staff of Hewlett-Packard, Santa Rosa, graciously assisted with the section on digital noise generators.

David Warrender, president of Euphonics in Sebastopol, California, painstakingly reviewed several early versions of the manuscript and his thoughtful comments resulted in numerous improvements.

Finally, we would like to acknowledge the full cooperation of our employers. The Hewlett-Packard Company granted a leave of absence to one of us (Jerse) to take the position of Technical Director of the Brooklyn College Center for Computer Music for the academic year 1979–1980. It was during that year that this book began to take form. The authors also gratefully acknowledge the use of Hewlett-Packard facilities for word processing the text and generating many of the figures by computer.

The Conservatory of Music at Brooklyn College and its director, Dorothy Klotzman, also provided necessary support for this project. Not only has the school supplied the Center for Computer Music with personnel and equipment necessary to make it a place where the full-range of computer-music practice could be studied and taught, but, in addition, the Conservatory's progressive attitude toward music has fostered a flourishing musical environment in which computer music plays an important role.

Charles Dodge
Thomas A. Jerse

COMPUTER MUSIC

SYNTHESIS, COMPOSITION, AND PERFORMANCE

1

FUNDAMENTALS OF COMPUTER MUSIC

1.1 Computers

Regardless of the specific purpose to which it is applied, a computer performs two basic functions: it rapidly performs a sequence of instructions (a program), and it stores and recalls large amounts of information (data). A computer may be characterized by its speed of operation, the types of instructions it can execute, and the capacity of its memory.

The term "hardware" refers to the electronic equipment that forms a computer system. The amount and type of electronic circuitry that constitutes the hardware determine the capabilities of the computer. Most computer users are generally not concerned with the inner workings of the machine. The user ordinarily becomes aware of the hardware only when it limits the types of tasks the user wants performed; that is, when the hardware does not operate rapidly enough to perform a task within a desired period of time or when the computer's memory is too small to contain needed programs or data.

The term "software" refers to the programs that a computer can perform or execute. Computer systems have large collections of programs that perform a variety of tasks. An essential part of the software of a computer system is a group of programs known as an operating system. The operating system assists the user in creating new programs and otherwise smooths the interaction of the user with the hardware. Without an operating system, the computer hardware would be so difficult to use that its utility would be severely limited.

Software is valuable only if its instructions can be executed by the hardware. In the same way, computer hardware represents only the potential capability of the computer; without software, it can do nothing meaningful. Therefore, the acquisition of computer hardware is only the beginning. Development of software is, on most systems, the means for accomplishing the desired tasks. It is a long-term, on-going process. (More about software will be discussed later.)

Figure 1.1 diagrams the functional arrangement of a computer system. The central processing unit (CPU) is the nerve center of the computer. It controls the operation of the system by interpreting the instructions of a program and executing them. The types of instructions available include mathematical and logical operations as well as instructions for the movement of information. These instructions

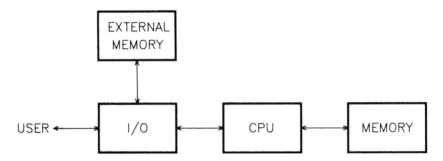

FIGURE 1.1   The functional arrangement of a computer system.

may also make decisions based on data that is either stored in the computer or received from external devices. This capability greatly extends the usefulness of a computer beyond that of a calculator.

The memory holds both programs and data. It is divided into distinct locations in which items of information are stored. A unique numerical address distinguishes each memory location. The CPU stores information by "writing" a numerical value into a specific memory location; it retrieves information by "reading" a stored value. The numerical value represents either a program instruction (e.g., "add two numbers") or a datum such as a number, a character, an attribute of a sound, or anything else the programmer determines. However, no matter what it represents, the stored entity is in numerical form.

When a computer begins operation, the CPU is given the address of the memory location containing the first program instruction. (This may simply be the result of the operator's pushing the "start" button.) Execution begins from that point. Subsequent instructions are taken from successive memory locations unless an instruction directs the CPU to "branch" to another instruction elsewhere in memory. During the execution of any instruction, references may be made to other memory locations for storage or retrieval of either data or further instructions.

The example program of figure 1.2 adds the numbers found in memory locations 104 and 105 and stores the result in location 106. Figure 1.2a shows the contents of memory before the program starts. Note that the contents of the first four locations are interpreted as instructions, and the contents of the last three locations (starting with location 104) are interpreted as data. The first instruction causes the contents of location 104 (1230) to be loaded into a specific place in the CPU called a register. A register is a special memory location that can be used by the CPU more easily than main memory. The next instruction brings the contents of location 105 (3017) into the CPU and adds it to the data already in the register (the contents of memory location 104). The register holds only the result of the addition (4247); the two original numbers are no longer present inside the CPU. Next, instruction 102 moves the result into location 106 for storage. Finally, instruction 103 halts the program and the memory contains the values shown in figure 1.2b.

The numbers contained in locations 100 through 103 are the numerical codes for the instructions. The left-most digit of the code determines the instruction type. "0" means stop, "1" means load, "2" means store, and "3" means add. The right three digits of the code indicate the memory location to be used in the operation. (The stop instruction does not use the memory, so the right three digits of

Address	Contents	Meaning
100	1104	LOAD 104
101	3105	ADD 105
102	2106	STORE 106
103	0000	STOP
104	1230	DATA
105	3017	DATA
106	0000	DATA

a) Before execution

Address	Contents	Meaning
100	1104	LOAD 104
101	3105	ADD 105
102	2106	STORE 106
103	0000	STOP
104	1230	DATA
105	3017	DATA
106	4247	DATA

b) After execution

FIGURE 1.2   Contents of a computer memory before and after execution of example program.

instruction 103 have no meaning.) This method of instruction representation was invented for the purpose of the example. The format and codes used in actual computers vary widely among computer product lines.

The stored program gives the computer the flexibility to perform a large set of diverse tasks because the program can be changed rapidly by changing the contents of the memory. In the earliest computers, the program and data did not share the same memory, and so program changes were more difficult, sometimes even requiring alteration of the hardware. In the late 1940s, John von Neumann first incorporated the idea of utilizing the same memory for both data and instructions. This represented a milestone in computer design, because it permitted instructions to be treated as data. Programs could be written to generate other programs thereby greatly facilitating the translation of the programmer's ideas into instructions for the computer. (See section 1.2.)

The smallest unit of information that a computer can recognize is the bit. A bit can be represented by the position of an electronic switch inside the computer hardware. A computer switch, like a light switch, can assume only one of two states, off or on. Thus, a bit can assume only one of two states, usually denoted 0 and 1 (hence, the name bit is a contraction of the term binary digit). Each memory location is composed of a group of bits, enabling the location to store a datum that can assume more than two values. The pattern of the bits determines the contents of a location. For example, two bits can assume four unique patterns: 00, 01, 10, and 11. Thus, a memory location made up of two bits will contain one of four distinct values. In general, n bits can assume 2^n unique states. The number of bits per location varies among computer product lines. The most popular approaches use an even power of 2, such as 8, 16, or 32.

The byte is used almost universally to measure memory capacity. Nearly all manufacturers define a byte to be a group of 8 bits. A byte, therefore, can assume any of 2^8 or 256 unique states. The amount of memory found inside a computer can vary from very few to more than a million bytes. An instruction may occupy from one to several bytes. Many machines use variable-length instructions: instructions whose length varies with their purpose. This obviously makes for more efficient use of memory since simpler instructions need not occupy the same amount of memory as more complex ones. The number of bytes used to store a datum also varies. For example, one byte is used to store a single character such as the letter "G." In this case, the actual contents of the byte is a numerical code which has been agreed upon by programmers to represent "G." The most widely-used coding standard is known as ASCII (American Standard Code for Information Interchange). It consists of a set of 128 numerical codes that represent alphanumeric characters, punctuation marks, and special control codes such as carriage return. The 8-bit pattern 01000111, for example, is the ASCII code for the upper case of the letter "G."

Numerical values generally take from one to eight bytes depending on their format and the precision with which they are stored. The way in which numbers are represented in a computer can have significant effects on the quality of computer-generated sound. We will discuss these effects in section 1.5 and other places throughout the text. Here, we will introduce the two most widely used formats: integer and floating-point.

We are all familiar with the decimal number system which is so named because it is based on the number 10. It is also called a positional number system, because the value of an individual digit in a group of digits depends on its position relative to the other digits. Each position is worth 10 times as much as the position to its right. For example, the number 247 is evaluated as

$$(2 \times 10^2) + (4 \times 10^1) + (7 \times 10^0) = 247$$
$$(2 \times 10 \times 10) + (4 \times 10) + (7 \times 1) = 247$$
$$200 + 40 + 7 = 247$$

The same approach applies when evaluating a group of bits. Because the binary number system is based on the number 2, each position in the group is worth twice as much as the position to its right. Thus, the binary number 1001 is evaluated as

$$(1 \times 2^3) + (0 \times 2^2) + (0 \times 2^1) + (1 \times 2^0) = 9$$
$$(1 \times 2 \times 2 \times 2) + (0 \times 2 \times 2) + (0 \times 2) + (1 \times 1) = 9$$
$$8 + 0 + 0 + 1 = 9$$

Table 1.1 shows the decimal equivalents of some binary numbers. This binary format for representing numbers in a computer is called integer representation, because only whole numbers can be represented. The number of bits used determines the available range of integers. Generally 16 bits (two bytes) are used to store integers. When both positive and negative numbers are provided for, this gives a range of -32768 to $+32767$. When a larger range of integers is needed, four bytes are ordinarily used.

1 = 1	10000 = 16
10 = 2	100000 = 32
11 = 3	1000000 = 64
100 = 4	10000000 = 128
101 = 5	100000000 = 256
110 = 6	1000000000 = 512
111 = 7	10000000000 = 1024
1000 = 8	100000000000 = 2048
1001 = 9	1000000000000 = 4096
1010 = 10	10000000000000 = 8192
1011 = 11	100000000000000 = 16384
1100 = 12	1000000000000000 = 32768
1101 = 13	10000000000000000 = 65536
1110 = 14	100000000000000000 = 131072
1111 = 15	1000000000000000000 = 262144

TABLE 1.1   Some Binary-to-Decimal Equivalents

Many applications of computers require a range of numbers greater than that made possible by even a four-byte integer format. For this reason, floating-point representation was developed. A number such as 824.68 can be written as

$$824.68 = .82468 \times 10^3$$

where the mantissa is .82468 and the exponent is 3.

The exponent, 3, signifies the number of places that the decimal point had to be shifted to the left in order to be in front of the first digit. The other half of the floating-point number, .82468, is known as the mantissa. A number with a magnitude less than .1, such as .068514, can be represented as

$$.068514 = .68514 \times 10^{-1}$$

The negative exponent indicates that the decimal point must be moved to the right in order to be in front of the first non-zero digit. A computer stores a floating-point number as a separate mantissa and exponent. A power of 2 or a power of 16 is generally used rather than a power of 10, but the principle is the same. The floating-point data format provides for the representation of a larger range of numbers than the integer format. However, the CPU performs mathematical operations involving floating-point numbers considerably more slowly.

Generally, four bytes are used to store a floating-point number, split approximately into one byte for the exponent and three bytes for the mantissa. The number of bits used for the mantissa determines the number of significant digits represented in the mantissa. The use of three bytes (24 bits) gives a resolution that is equivalent to approximately seven decimal digits. When greater accuracy is needed, more bytes are appended to the mantissa.

Input/output (I/O) devices provide the means for communication between the computer and its users. These devices, often called peripherals, interface (connect) with the CPU and convert the electronic signals inside the CPU into a form that can be interpreted by the user. Conversely, peripherals are also used to change physical actions of the user into electronic signals. The most common I/O device, the data terminal, allows the user to type instructions to the computer and to receive messages originating from the CPU. Today most data terminals display information as video on the screen of a cathode ray tube (CRT) similar to ones found in television sets. A graphics terminal enables not only text to be displayed but also line drawings. Utilizing the appropriate peripherals, the computer can communicate with its users through a wide variety of visual, aural, and tactile means. Chapter 9 details many of the I/O devices that have been used for music. Certain types of I/O devices enable a computer to exchange information with other computers and other types of digital hardware.

Another widely used class of I/O equipment is the mass-storage device. These devices form the external memory of a computer system. They hold programs and data that are not currently being used by the CPU. The storage medium is most commonly magnetic, such as a disk or a tape. External memory is usually larger than internal, running into hundreds of millions of bytes on some disks. With removable media, such as digital tapes and some disks, the computer's memory is limited only by the number of tapes and disks available. Removable media also enables the transportation of information between computer systems.

The contents of external memory is normally organized into files. A file may contain a program, a collection of data, or both. The length of a file is determined by its contents. To execute a program that is stored in external memory, the CPU incorporates the program into the main memory by "loading" the appropriate file. Data files may contain any type of information. A program can instruct the CPU to transfer a particular data file into the main memory for use in its operations. For example, a program can be written to take a data file containing a description of musical sound and, utilizing the appropriate I/O devices such as those described in section 1.5, convert the data into sound.

Although technological advances are making the distinctions less clear, computers are often classified into three general sizes: mainframe computers, minicomputers, and microcomputers. A mainframe computer is large, fast, and expensive. At most educational institutions and businesses, at least one mainframe computer forms the basis of a computer center. Minicomputers were originally developed for scientific laboratory applications. They are somewhat slower and generally have less memory than mainframe computers, but they are smaller and more accessible. Many centers have been able to reserve a minicomputer exclusively for applications to music. Microcomputers were made possible by the invention of the microprocessor, which is the central element of a computer on a single integrated circuit or chip. In the past three decades, the advances made in miniaturizing electronic circuitry have been truly dramatic. Once a single, relatively simple computer occupied a large room and consumed enormous amounts of power. Today one can purchase any of a number of small, portable microcomputers that consume very little power, yet outperform the giant computers of thirty years ago. The key to such advances has been the development of large scale integrated (LSI) circuits—tens of thousands (in some cases hundreds of thousands) of electronic devices deposited on a tiny rectangular chip of silicon that is smaller than a thumbnail. The small size and relatively low cost of the microcomputer has greatly expanded the availability of computing resources. Although microcomputers generally offer lower execution speed and less memory capacity than the other types, they have been successfully employed for a great many purposes.

1.2 Programming Languages

In theory, a computer can be programmed to perform any task that can be defined. Defining a task, however, can be extremely difficult. The programmer must determine a procedure (algorithm) that can be written as a sequence of instructions. Each step of the algorithm must be defined unambiguously, and there must be a clear path to the completion of the algorithm. The results of an algorithm are called outputs, and of course any useful algorithm must have at least one output. An algorithm may accept data (inputs) to use in determining the output(s), but inputs are not a necessity.

As an example of an algorithm, consider the procedure used by a beginning piano student to play a simple, single-voice piece.

1. Find beginning of piece.

2. Read first note.

3. Go to step 5.

4. Read next note.

5. Depress appropriate piano key on the appropriate beat.

6. Count duration in beats and release key.

7. Was this the last note?
    If yes, then go to step 8.
    If no, then go to step 4.

8. End of algorithm.

The output of this algorithm is the sound produced by the piano. The input to the algorithm is the data (notes) on the sheet of music. Finite completion of the algorithm is assured if there is a finite number of notes in the piece. This particular algorithm makes a decision, but this is not the case with every algorithm.

A programmer communicates algorithms to a computer by means of a programming language. The languages used are called artificial languages, as opposed to the natural languages of human communication. They differ from natural languages in that their structure and syntax are rigidly defined; that is, the programmer's intentions must be explicitly declared. Many different programming languages have been developed. The language selected for expressing a particular program depends on several factors: the type and complexity of the algorithm(s) to be communicated, the languages available on the computer system being utilized, the form of the data to be used by the program, and the programmer's familiarity with the available languages.

A computer can be programmed by entering directly into memory a list of numerical values (see figure 1.2) corresponding to the actual instructions to be performed. This approach is called machine-language programming, because it conforms directly with the internal configurations required by the machine. It is both tedious and time consuming. Moreover, it obscures the goal of the program because the programmer must not only define the operations on a more primitive level than that required by other languages, but he must express them in the cumbersome numerical equivalents of the instuctions. As a result, machine-language programming normally is used only by people who design and repair the hardware.

It is possible to communicate an algorithm to the computer through a language more intelligible to the user, if there is a program available to translate the encoded algorithm into machine-language for the computer. Nearly every computer system has such translating programs. When using a computer language, the programmer produces a written text of a program, enters it into the computer, and then invokes a translating program. Depending on the type of translator, the results of the translation are either executed immediately or stored in a form that can be executed on demand.

Programming languages are sometimes compared on the basis of their similarity to machine language. A low-level language is close to machine language. The most widely used low-level language is assembly language. Generally, one statement in assembly language will create a single machine-language instruction when translated. The set of machine instructions differs among computer product lines, and so a given assembly language program can be executed only on the type of machine for which it was written. The most effective use of assembly language is for communication of algorithms that must be executed with optimum speed and efficiency. Usually, only computer specialists write programs in assembly language.

Most programming is done in a high-level language. This allows the programmer to communicate in terms that are more or less familiar to the programmer and/or suited to the task at hand. The use of high-level languages confers several benefits, one of which is shorter program texts. For example, the following program fragment, written in the high-level language FORTRAN, calculates the average of two numbers.

```
X=12.4
Y=3.6
AVERAGE=(X+Y)/2.
```

After this portion of the program is run, the variable (see glossary) AVERAGE would be equal to 8. On most computers the operation of division, represented in the example by the symbol "/", requires the execution of a long sequence of machine-language instructions. Thus, the use of a high-level language has relieved the programmer from specifying much of the detail of the actual operation of the computer. Shorter program texts contribute to increased programming productivity and even increased accuracy. High-level languages also make it unnecessary for the programmer to be intimately familiar with the architecture of the system hardware.

Another important advantage of most high-level languages is machine independence. Machine-independent languages allow the same program to be transported between computers that have different machine languages (assuming that each machine has the appropriate translating program).

There are many high-level languages. Among the best known are FORTRAN, ALGOL, COBOL, Pascal, APL, BASIC, and C. Each language is optimized for solving specific classes of problems. For instance, FORTRAN and BASIC are optimized for algorithms that are best expressed algebraically, whereas COBOL is aimed at business applications such as record keeping and record searching. "Problem-oriented" languages have been invented that address a relatively narrow problem area. Such languages are closer to the actual tasks that need to be done and further from the demands of the computer. In these problem-oriented languages, the more cumbersome algorithms have already been written for the user by computer specialists. The remainder of the work can be programmed in a language that enables a more straightforward formulation of the task at hand. Numerous languages have been developed for music, and some of them will be discussed in sections 1.3 and 3.6.

Two basic methods are available for translating a program written in a high-level language into machine language: compilation and interpretation. The programs that accomplish these tasks are called compilers and interpreters, respectively. A compiler reads through high-level program text, written in a language such as FORTRAN, and generates another representation of the program in a lower-level (compiled) form. The compiled program is stored in memory, and the computer can then be instructed to execute it at any arbitrary time. The compiled program can be run as many times as desired without having to repeat the compilation process.

A compiler performs the tasks of program translation and execution as two distinct, sequential steps; an interpreter interweaves them. After an interpreter reads a statement from the high-level program text, it determines the exact set of machine instructions required to perform the operations indicated. Those instructions are then executed immediately, and the interpreter moves on to the next statement. Thus, instead of having a discrete compilation step, the translation process occurs throughout the execution of the program. Programs that are interpreted run much more slowly than compiled ones. Nevertheless, interpreters enjoy widespread use, in part because they make finding program errors easier. Sound synthesis programs generally perform an enormous number of calculations, and so are most commonly compiled.

To simplify their task, programmers often divide programs into a main program and one or more subprograms called functions or subroutines. A subroutine contains an encoded algorithm for accomplishing a specific task. A subroutine is employed in the following way. The CPU starts execution at the beginning of the main program. A subroutine is invoked by the execution of a program instruction that "calls" it. The address of the first instruction of the subroutine is loaded into the CPU. This causes the CPU to begin executing the instructions of the subroutine. When the subroutine is completed, the control of the CPU returns to the point in the program from which it was called. Thus, the same subroutine can be called from several different places in a program, or even from other subroutines. When a subroutine is called, the calling program may supply or *pass* data to be used in determining the actions of the subroutine. A datum passed to a subroutine is known as an argument or parameter.

Subroutines are an important part of most computer music programs. For example, sound synthesis programs generally divide the sound generating algorithms into separate subroutines. The parameters passed to the subroutines determine the character of the sound produced. (See section 1.3B and the chapters on sound synthesis.) In the area of computer-aided composition (see chapter 8), composers have used subroutines that perform particular tasks on musical passages such as transposing them.

A function is a special type of subroutine found in many computer languages. When a function is called, it is passed values that are used in calculating the value of the function. This result is returned for use in the calling program. For example, a function can be written to calculate the square of a number. In FORTRAN, this function would take the form:

```
FUNCTION SQUARE(X)
SQUARE=X*X
RETURN
```

X is the parameter that is passed to the function. The $*$ operator signifies multiplication. In the main program the function could be used in a statement such as the following.

```
V=SQUARE(5.0)
```

When this statement was executed, the variable V would take on the value of 25.

As noted in section 1.1, computer systems have an organized collection of software known as an operating system (OS), which makes it much easier for the user to interact with the hardware. An OS provides many useful services. For example, an OS contains the software for communication through I/O devices, such as programs that enable users to type in programs on a terminal. An OS also provides for the orderly transition of control of the CPU from one program to another, thus making it possible to link programs together. Another important service relates to the handling of the files stored in external memory. A user may create, store, edit, and use files just by typing simple commands to the OS. Without an OS, each user would have to write a complicated program to perform these tasks.

On small computers where there is just one user, the computer is devoted exclusively to executing the program that has been entered. When a system has many users, it is common for many programs to be submitted to the computer at once. In this case, the OS must serve as an arbiter between users, allocating computing resources so as to achieve the most efficient system operation possible. In addition, the OS must ensure that one program does not disturb another. The two principal approaches to the handling of multiple programs are batch processing and time-sharing. In batch processing, the programs are submitted as "jobs" that are executed sequentially. This technique is relatively simple to implement, but it prevents users from interacting with their programs during execution: A user cannot provide data to a program while it is running in batch mode. Time-sharing was developed to provide many users with the ability to interact concurrently with programs during the execution. In this mode, the OS allocates the sequential use of the CPU to each user's program for a small interval of time called a slice. During a slice, the CPU executes the program of the designated user, and any inputs received from that user are serviced. If the slices are short enough to permit a small time between successive services of a given program, each user will have the impression of having uninterrupted access to the computer.

1.3 Software for Computer Music

1.3A An Overview

Over the years, a large body of software has been developed to simplify the task of making music with a computer. Most computer music software falls into three categories: algorithms for sound generation, programs that assist the musician in composing with generated sounds and/or the sound of acoustic instruments, and programs that enable the performance of the composition using generated sounds. This division is based on traditional musical activity, but it is not the only possible model.

The most commonly encountered methods of realizing computer music are diagrammed in figure 1.3. The musician selects the algorithms for sound synthesis using software that aids in its specification. The musician also determines the use of those sounds by producing a score, often with the assistance of a score editing program or composing program. Performance practice in computer music encompasses a broad range of possibilities, from a computer-generated score played by acoustic instruments to a program that, during performance, combines a score in computer memory with the algorithms for sound synthesis to produce sound with no performance or compositional intervention. Notice that the methods shown in

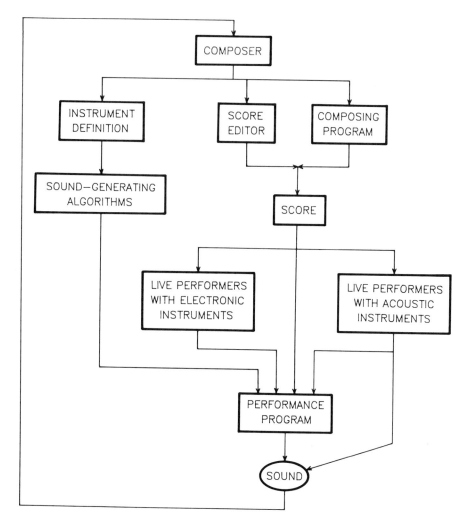

FIGURE 1.3 Ways in which composers make use of a computer.

the figure form a loop. The feedback that the musician receives from the performance can be applied to revisions of the composition just as in traditional composition.

When using the computer as a sound-synthesis medium, the musician determines the palate of sounds for a composition and then attempts to formulate the appropriate algorithms to generate them. Each of these algorithms, called instruments, produces a particular type of sound. A computer instrument need not be restricted to producing single tones at a time, but can be designed to generate any number of simultaneous parts, as well as long, evolving sounds. Each algorithm has inputs, known as parameters, that control various aspects of the sound produced. The number and type of these inputs are determined by the instrument designer depending on what the composition requires. Common parameters include acoustical attributes such as pitch, duration, amplitude, location, and controls on timbral aspects of the sound. (See section 1.4 and chapter 2.) The parametric values for a computer instrument come from data stored in the computer's memory or from a peripheral device actuated by a performer. Chapters 3 through 7 will present the principles of instrument design with illustrative examples.

Once the instruments of the computer orchestra are defined, the musician must describe how and when the instruments are to play. This ordinarily takes the form of a score—a list of musical events. Each event can be thought of as a "note," in the sense that it calls upon an instrument to perform, even though the event need not be a note in the traditional sense. For example, a single event might call upon an instrument that is designed to play several successive tones. The minimum specification of an event identifies the instrument that is to play and the time at which the event begins with additional parameters required by the instrument. Examples of score encoding in serval common music languages will be given below.

Once the score and the descriptions of the instruments have been entered into the computer, they can be combined by a performance program: a program that turns instructions and data into sound. Performance programs vary widely, depending on the hardware and the amount of manual intervention desired during performance. In chapter 9, various modes of live performance and many of the control devices used by performers will be discussed.

1.3B   Examples of Computer Music Languages

The first general-purpose program for sound synthesis was MUSIC 3 created by Max V. Mathews at the Bell Telephone Laboratories in the early 1960s. Its successor, MUSIC 4, was exported to a few American universities where computer music activity began to proliferate and new programs were devised to suit local circumstances. Figure 1.4 displays a "family tree" of the sound synthesis programs that have evolved since Mathews' earliest experiments in the late 1950s.[1] The geographical dispersion of the languages also indicates structural differences among them. The figure is roughly chronological from top to bottom.

The center of the tree shows the programs developed by Mathews and his group at Bell Laboratories. The branch on the right shows variants of MUSIC 4 that Godfrey Winham and Hubert S. Howe produced at Princeton University and the subsequent developments of that program: MUSIC 360 and MUSIC 11 by Barry L. Vercoe and MUSIC 7 by Howe. The branch on the left shows the music compilers MUSIC 6 and MUSIC 10 produced at Stanford University.

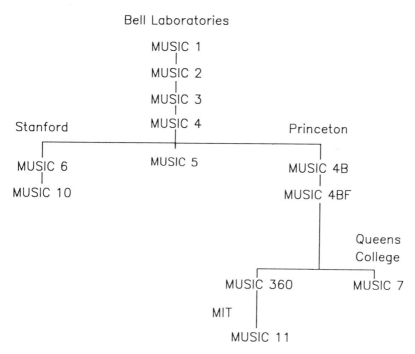

FIGURE 1.4   Family tree of sound synthesis languages. (*Adapted, with permission of the author, from the Musician-Machine Interface in Computer Music, by Stanley Haynes, Doctoral dissertation, University of Southampton, 1979.*)

All of the programs, with one exception, were designed for use on large, batch-oriented computer systems: MUSIC 11 was written for Digital Equipment Corporation's PDP-11 family of minicomputers. Of the batch-oriented languages, only MUSIC 5 and MUSIC 4BF were written in FORTRAN, enabling their use on any computer system with a FORTRAN IV compiler. All the others were designed to run on a particular family, or in some cases, model of computer. In some instances the languages are no longer in use because the computers for which they were written are obsolete.

Figure 1.5 illustrates the process by which all the MUSIC 4-type sound synthesis programs make sound. The first step (1a) is for the musician to create the orchestra by defining the instruments (following, of course, the rules of syntax for the particular language). Each instrument is designed to produce a particular type of sound and has input parameters that control various characteristics of the sound, such as duration, loudness, and pitch. Examples of several methods of instrument definition will be given in section 3.6.

The second part of step 1 (1b) is to provide input to the particular score editor associated with the system. With step 1, the musician's input to the sound synthesis process is complete. Steps 2 and 3 are performed by the computer without intervention by the musician. In step 2, the instrument definitions are translated into a machine language program, and the input from the score editor is compiled (if necessary) to put the score into the proper format for the processing of step 3. In step 3 the program actually "plays" the score on the instruments, thus creating the sound. The processing of a note of the score in step 3 consists of two stages: initialization and performance. At the initialization of a note, those values that are to remain fixed throughout the duration of the note are set, most often by obtaining

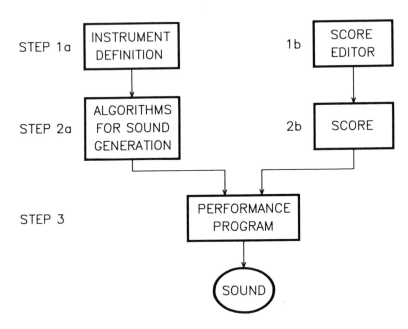

FIGURE 1.5   Process by which MUSIC 4-type languages make sound.

parameter values for that note from the score. During the performance of a note, the computer calculates the actual output corresponding to the sound.

Score input using lists of alphanumeric characters offers special difficulties for the musician. In a conventional musical score, time runs from left to right and musical detail is shown vertically. In a computer-music score, time runs from top to bottom with the musical detail on the horizontal dimension. Example 1.1 shows score input to MUSIC 11[2], MUSIC 5[3], and MUSIC 4BF[4] for the music in the example. Each line in the score input for each language consists of an alphabetic code (i, NOT, I) followed by numerical values. The alphabetic code denotes the type of statement (only statements that generate notes are shown), and the numbers represent parameter values that will be passed to an instrument. Each parameter resides in a "field" called a p-field. In example 1.1 all the coded examples make use of 5 p-fields. In the MUSIC 11 coding "1" is in the first p-field, "0" is in the second, "1" is in the third, etc. As you can see, the p-fields may vary in size, depending upon, among other things, the music-synthesis program being used.

The coding in our example assumes a rather simple computer instrument using only the parameters of instrument number, starting time, duration, frequency, and amplitude. Frequency and amplitude are acoustical attributes of tones corresponding to pitch and loudness, respectively. (See section 1.4 and chapter 2.) Pitch is specified in cycles per second. The choice of the amplitude value of 20,000 to represent the *mf* in the score is an arbitrary decision. The actual value would vary from system to system.

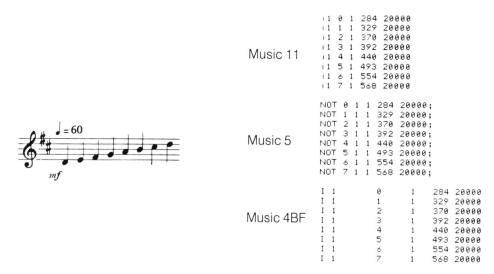

```
                                    i1  0  1  284  20000
                                    i1  1  1  329  20000
                                    i1  2  1  370  20000
                                    i1  3  1  392  20000
                Music 11            i1  4  1  440  20000
                                    i1  5  1  493  20000
                                    i1  6  1  554  20000
                                    i1  7  1  568  20000


                                    NOT  0  1  1  284  20000;
                                    NOT  1  1  1  329  20000;
                                    NOT  2  1  1  370  20000;
                                    NOT  3  1  1  392  20000;
                Music 5             NOT  4  1  1  440  20000;
                                    NOT  5  1  1  493  20000;
                                    NOT  6  1  1  554  20000;
                                    NOT  7  1  1  568  20000;


                                    I  1          0      1    284  20000
                                    I  1          1      1    329  20000
                                    I  1          2      1    370  20000
                Music 4BF           I  1          3      1    392  20000
                                    I  1          4      1    440  20000
                                    I  1          5      1    493  20000
                                    I  1          6      1    554  20000
                                    I  1          7      1    568  20000
```

EXAMPLE 1.1 Musical example and its coding in MUSIC 11, MUSIC 5, and MUSIC 4BF
for a simple instrument with five parameters.

The disadvantages of the score encoding shown in the above example are obvious:
too many keystrokes with too little visual or conceptual similarity between the
musical score and the computer score. Solutions to these problems (by more
efficient and intuitive score encoding) are shown below, but for certain kinds of
computer music—ones employing a few events played on complex instruments to
which many parameters are passed—this sort of coding is quite efficient. It is
precisely this kind of score that was used to good advantage for Variations 7–8 of J.
K. Randall's *Lyric Variations for Violin and Computer*.[5] Each "note" or event
consists of many parameter values which control the complex, evolving sonorities.
Since each event is so complex and extended, relatively few notes are needed to
create a very rich texture. In the Randall example only 12 notes are played in the
entire two-minute section of music; the notes, each 20 seconds long, enter singly
and overlap the succeeding note by 10 seconds.

A score preprocessor provides a useful facility for entering certain types of
music into the computer. It is particularly useful for music with many notes
intended to be played on relatively simple computer instruments. Score preprocessors enable the musician to express the notes of a composition in a sort of
shorthand. From this description, the preprocessor creates the note list in the
format required for input to the particular music synthesis program. Examples of
pre-processors are Leland Smith's SCORE for MUSIC 10, Alexander Brinkman's
Score 11 for MUSIC 11, and M.I.T.'s SCOT for MUSIC 11. Example 1.2 shows the
Score 11 text for the scale shown in Example 1.1.

```
        i1 0 8;
        p3 rh 4*8;
        p4 no d4/e/fs/g/a/b/cs5/d;
        p5 nu 20000;
        end;
```

EXAMPLE 1.2 SCORE 11 code for the scale of Example 1.1.

The first line of the example means that the passage is to be played on instrument number 1 starting at beat 0 and continuing for eight beats. (The first beat is always called beat 0.) The second line indicates a rhythm of 8 quarter notes. (The "p3" means the data is in parameter 3.) The third line is a sequential list of the eight pitches where the second 4 in the line indicates tones in the octave of middle *C*. Line 4 sets parameter 5 (amplitude) to a value of 20,000 for all notes.

Clearly, the sort of coding shown here is far superior to those of Example 1.1 both because it is much easier to type without making mistakes, and it bears a closer relationship to the actual notation of the music. Score 11 and other preprocessors often include additional features that make it possible to specify editorial changes to an entire subscore. That is, they provide the means for specifying, with a single command, the values for a given parameter on *all* notes of a particular passage. Example 1.3 shows a brief musical passage, its Score 11 coding, and the computer-generated MUSIC 11 score. Here, the musician is able to indicate the duration of all the two-second notes with a single statement.

```
i  1 0 10;
p3 nu 2;
p4 no c4/e/gs/a/fs;
end;

i1 0.000 2.000 8.00
i2 2.000 2.000 8.04
i3 4.000 2.000 8.08
i4 6.000 2.000 8.09
i5 8.000 2.000 8.06
end of score
```

EXAMPLE 1.3   SCORE 11 code and the computer-generated MUSIC 11 score for the musical passage shown.

The first line of the Score 11 coding indicates that the entire passage is for instrument number 1 (that is, the value of the first parameter of all following notes is 1), and that it begins at time 0 (that is, the starting time of the first note is 0) and the entire passage lasts for 10 beats. Note that the second parameter (p2) contains the starting-time indications for each note. This will be seen only in the computer-generated MUSIC 11 score. Line 2 specifies the duration (third parameter—p3) of all notes as two beats. (In the absence of any further input, the beat defaults to a duration of one second.) Line 3 sets the pitches of the five notes in the passage, and line 5 delimits the Score 11 input.

Example 1.4 shows another sort of subscore editing made possible in Score 11 and other preprocessors. Here the values for the duration, frequency, and amplitude for all notes are obtained by interpolation between limits specified in the Score 11 text. In our example, Score 11 obtains the 18 notes with only five lines of input. As before, Line 1 designates the instrument number for the notes, the starting time of the first note, and the duration of the passage. The "move" command in line 2 calls for a linear interpolation in the note durations, over five beats, from .75 to .05 seconds per note thus creating an accelerando. The third line

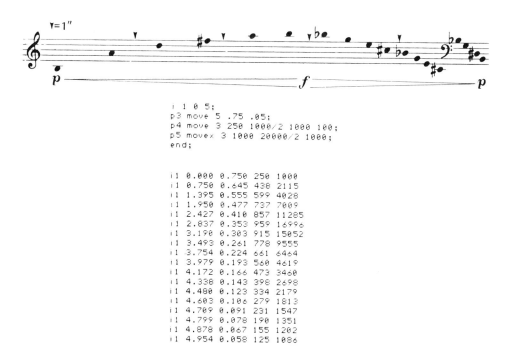

```
i 1 0 5;
p3 move 5 .75 .05;
p4 move 3 250 1000/2 1000 100;
p5 movex 3 1000 20000/2 1000;
end;
```

```
i1 0.000 0.750 250 1000
i1 0.750 0.645 438 2115
i1 1.395 0.555 599 4028
i1 1.950 0.477 737 7009
i1 2.427 0.410 857 11285
i1 2.837 0.353 959 16996
i1 3.190 0.303 915 15052
i1 3.493 0.261 778 9555
i1 3.754 0.224 661 6464
i1 3.979 0.193 560 4619
i1 4.172 0.166 473 3460
i1 4.338 0.143 398 2698
i1 4.480 0.123 334 2179
i1 4.603 0.106 279 1813
i1 4.709 0.091 231 1547
i1 4.799 0.078 190 1351
i1 4.878 0.067 155 1202
i1 4.954 0.058 125 1086
```

EXAMPLE 1.4   Demonstration of the interpolation commands of SCORE 11 showing the resulting score in both MUSIC 11 and music notation.

creates (non-tempered) frequencies for the notes by linear interpolation between 250 and 1000 cycles per second in the first three beats and from 1000 to 125 cycles per second over the next two beats. The "movex" command applies an exponential interpolation to the amplitude (fifth parameter—p5) of the notes, creating a crescendo for the first three beats and a diminuendo for the final two beats.

Certain score preprocessors such as Leland Smith's SCORE implement a feature for designating a string of pitches and/or rhythms as a musical "motive." After declaring a motive, larger units of music can be created by calling for concatenation and overlapping for the motive itself. In addition, reiterations of the motives can be made with such variations as transposition, retrogression, inversion, and the like. See section 8.2B for a discussion of compositional techniques in computer music using motivic manipulation.

Example 1.4 demonstrates the sort of flexibility that a score preprocessor can offer to a composer for creating passages that cannot be expressed with accuracy within the traditional notation system of metered rhythms and tempered frequency. Nonetheless, alphanumeric encoding of music can still seem quite foreign to the musician, and music notation is, after all, the most visually natural way to present many kinds of music. This approach, visual display of music notation on a video graphics display, has been taken successfully at a number of installations including Stanford University in conjunction with Leland Smith's SCORE program, the M.I.T. Experimental Music Studio, and the SSSP system of William Buxton at the University of Toronto.

At M.I.T. the pitch of the note is entered by pressing the key corresponding to the desired pitch on an organ keyboard. At the same time, the rhythmic value for the note is specified by pressing the appropriate button on a special-function box attached to the computer. The music notation is then displayed on a graphics terminal in the format of a musical score. Hard copy of the score is available from a printer. From the standpoint of ease of proofreading, systems using computer graphics to display scores in music notation are unbeatable. For a musician to proofread the notation and compare it with the music played electronically takes great advantage of skills acquired and perfected over years of the musician's training. In this approach, then, rather than requiring the musician to acquire new skills of a different type of score reading, the system reinforces and relies on skills already well developed. A variety of systems (some available commercially, such as the Synclavier) make music notation a standard part of the computer music system. Some will even print out in music notation scores of music improvised on the keyboard.

William Buxton and his colleagues of the Structured Sound Synthesis Project (SSSP) at the University of Toronto have extensively investigated the use of computer graphics to aid musicians in manipulating scores stored inside a computer.[6] The SSSP group has implemented several methods of score entry using three I/O devices: a graphics display, a digitizing tablet, and a slider box. A digitizing tablet is a flat surface upon which a stylus or other marking device is placed. The tablet senses both the horizontal and vertical position of the marker and relays this information to the computer. The position of the SSSP marking device on the digitizing tablet is shown by the position of a cursor (a "+") on the graphics display. The user can move the cursor around with the marking device in order to point at objects drawn on the display. The SSSP marking device contains push buttons that provide additional means of control. The slider box contains small, treadmill-like belts that can be moved with a finger. They transmit a measurement of the amount and direction of the motion to the computer.

The musical score is presented on the graphics display in one of several selectable ways. For example, in one method of score entry a portion of a piano keyboard is shown on the display. The musician specifies a pitch by moving the cursor to the desired key and pressing a button. The duration of the note is then indicated by moving the cursor vertically along the key to a place corresponding to the desired value and pressing the button again. The symbol in music notation for the selected note now appears on the screen in the appropriate place.

A problem inherent in any system that displays a score with computer graphics is that of score "navigation." Because only a small portion of a score can be shown on the screen at any one time, provision must be made for roaming around the score for the purpose of viewing or editing. In the SSSP system, the score can be scrolled horizontally in either direction by moving one of the sliders. This technique works well when the new section is not too far from the old. However, it can be quite cumbersome when the musician wishes to view a part of the score that is far removed from the section that is presently on display. To expedite this operation, the SSSP system implements a time-line mode: the entire score represented as a horizontal line with the position of the current display marked by brackets. The musician can then move the brackets to any point of the time-line in order to quickly arrive at a different part of the score which is then displayed on the screen.

Another valuable feature of the SSSP system lies in its facility for manipulating subscores. Some other programs for score editing allow an operation to be performed only on a single note. For instance, in order to transpose a phrase, the pitch of each note of the phrase would have to be changed individually. However, the SSSP editor enables the musician to specify the scope of any operation from a single note to the entire score. In this way, alterations to groups of notes, such as transposition in the example above, can be made with relative ease. Many subscore operations are possible including replication, temporal changes, settings of dynamics, and so on.

1.4   Measurement of Sound

Before discussing algorithms to generate sound, we must consider how to describe sounds in numeric terms. Sound is produced by a vibrating source. The vibrations disturb the air molecules that are adjacent to the source by alternately pulling apart and pushing together the molecules in synchronism with the vibrations. Thus, the energy in a sound produces small regions in the air in which the air pressure is lower than average (rarefactions) and small regions in which it is higher (compressions). These regions of alternately rarified and compressed air propogate in the form of a sound wave much in the same manner as the troughs and crests of an ocean wave. When a sound wave impinges on a surface (e.g., an eardrum or a microphone), it causes that surface to vibrate in sympathy with the wave. In this way acoustic energy is transferred from a source to a receptor while retaining the characteristic vibration pattern of the source.

The pattern of pressure variations in time produced by a sound is known as the waveform of the sound. Figure 1.6 illustrates the waveform of a simple tone. When the waveform is above the axis, there is compression; points below the axis indicate rarefaction.

Examination of the waveform in the figure reveals that it is made up of a repeating pattern. Such a waveform is called periodic. The smallest complete unit of the pattern is known as a cycle, and the amount of time occupied by a single cycle is known as a period (see figure 1.6). For sounds in the range of human hearing, waveform periods vary between approximately .00005 and .05 seconds. Two units of time found useful in acoustics are the millisecond (msec) which is one-thousandth (.001) of a second and the microsecond (μsec) which is one-millionth (.000001) of a second. Thus, the range above (.00005 to .05 seconds) can be alternatively expressed as 50 μsec to 50 msec.

The rate at which the cycles of a periodic waveform repeat is called the

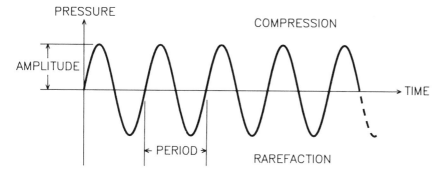

FIGURE 1.6   Periodic waveform.

frequency of the waveform. Frequency is measured in Hertz (Hz), formerly known as cycles per second. Frequency is the mathematical inverse of period, and so a waveform with a period of 1 msec has a frequency of 1000 Hz (i.e., there are 1000 repetitions of a cycle each second). A useful unit of measure for describing frequencies in the audio range is the kilohertz (kHz) which equals 1000 Hz. The range of human hearing is approximately 20 Hz to 20 kHz, although this varies somewhat among listeners and listening conditions. Frequency correlates physically with the perceived tone height, or pitch, of a sound so that tones with higher pitches have higher frequencies. (See section 2.2 for an explanation of the correspondence between pitch and frequency.)

Amplitude is the amount of change, positive or negative, in atmospheric pressure caused by the compression/rarefaction cycle of a sound. It is indicative of the amount of acoustic energy in a sound and is the most important factor in the perceived loudness of a sound. (See section 2.4.) Figure 1.6 illustrates the amplitude of the waveform shown. Amplitude is measured in Newtons per square meter (N/m^2),[7] that is, as a force applied over an area. The threshold of audibility represents an amplitude of approximately .00002 N/m^2. When this small amount of pressure change is compared with the average atmospheric pressure of nearly 100,000 N/m^2, the relatively high sensitivity of the ear becomes apparent.

A more meaningful characterization of the audible sensation associated with amplitude is the intensity of a sound. Intensity is a measure of the power in a sound that actually contacts an area such as the eardrum. It is proportional to the square of the amplitude. That is, if the amplitude of a sound doubles, the intensity increases by a factor of 4. Intensity is expressed as power applied over an area in Watts per square meter. The range of intensities that a human can perceive is bounded by $10^{-12}W/m^2$ at the threshold of audibility and 1 W/m^2 at the threshold of pain.

The intensity of a sound is perceived nearly logarithmically. This is one of the two principal modes of perception; the other is linear. A phenomenon is logarithmic if a change between two values is perceived on the basis of the *ratio* of the two values. In this case a change from .1 to .2 (a ratio of 1:2) would be perceived as the same amount of increase as a change from .4 to .8. Therefore, in the perception of acoustic energy, a reduction in the intensity of a tone from .1 W/m^2 to .01 W/m^2 will be judged to be similar to a reduction from .001 W/m^2 to .0001 W/m^2.

In the case of linear perception, the change between two values is perceived on the basis of the *difference* between the values. Thus, a phenomenon is perceived linearly if a change from .1 to .2 is judged to be the same amount of increase as a change from .7 to .8. Distance is a phenomenon that is usually perceived linearly.

The decibel (dB) is a unit of relative measurement used to compare the ratio of the intensities of two signals. The decibel is proportional to the logarithm of the ratio of two intensities and, therefore, is particularly well suited for the purpose of comparing the intensities of two sounds. The ratio of two signals with intensities I_1 and I_2, respectively, is given in decibels by:

$$10 \log_{10} (I_1/I_2)$$

By convention, a base-10 logarithm is used.

Although the dB was defined to compare the intensity of two signals, it has commonly come to be used to compare the amplitudes of two signals as well. The ratio in decibels of two signals with amplitudes A_1 and A_2, respectively, is given by:

$$20 \log_{10} (A_1/A_2)$$

This use of the decibel is only proper when the amplitudes are measured under the same set of conditions. For example, two signals of the same amplitude on two different computer music-synthesis systems could well have different intensities, and so the above equation could not be used correctly. In most cases on a single system, however, the dB is both a correct and convenient means of comparing amplitudes. For example, when an amplitude doubles, the increase corresponds to 6 dB.

The dB is sometimes used to give absolute measurement of acoustic intensity. Implicit in this kind of measurement is the existence of a reference sound pressure level to which the signal is being compared. In acoustics, the reference sound pressure level is taken as the threshold of audibility. A sound at that level has a value of 0 dB SPL, where SPL denotes "sound pressure level". Conversational speech has an intensity of approximately 60 dB SPL, while shouted speech is closer to 80 dB SPL. A sound at the threshold of pain has a level of 120 dB SPL, and so the range of audibility (120 dB) represents a ratio in amplitudes of one to one million.

The shape of a cycle of a periodic waveform has a large effect on the way it sounds. We will discuss waveshapes in more detail in section 2.6. At this point we will introduce the simplest and most fundamental pattern of vibratory motion, the sinusoid. The periodic waveform diagrammed earlier in this section (figure 1.6) is an example of a sinusoidal pattern. Its characteristically smooth shape shows no abrupt changes in pressure and there are no sharp points on the waveform. When the waveform is at a point near zero, it has a steep slope indicating that the pressure is changing quickly. At points near both the positive and negative peaks of the waveform, the pressure is changing more gradually resulting in the rounding of the tips of the waveform as shown. Sinusoidal oscillations in sound can be approximated with a struck tuning fork when the sound has almost died away; that is, the tines of the vibrating fork move up and down in a sinusoidal manner producing sinusoidal variations in air pressure. A perfectly sinusoidal sound waveform is difficult to generate by mechanical means, but electronic systems can generate very accurate sinusoids.

To gain an understanding of sinusoidal motion, consider the motion of the spoke in the wheel shown in figure 1.7. Suppose that the radius of the wheel (and,

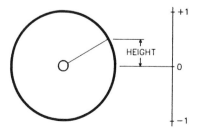

FIGURE 1.7   Measurement of the height of a spoke tip above the axle of a wheel.

hence the length of the spoke) is one. Let's measure the height of the tip of the spoke above the axle for various positions of the wheel. When the spoke is lying horizontally, it is at the same level as the axle, and so the height is zero. When the spoke points straight up, the height is one. When it points straight down, the height is −1, where the minus sign indicates that the tip is below the axle. Thus, for any position of the wheel, the height of the spoke tip always falls between −1 and +1.

Let the wheel rotate in a counterclockwise direction with a constant speed of 1 revolution per second. How does the height of the tip vary with time? Figure 1.8 shows the progress of the tip height as the wheel turns. Our experiment begins as the spoke points horizontally to the right, and so the initial height is zero. After 1/12 of a second (.083 seconds elapsed time) the tip reaches a height of .500. By 2/12 of a second (.167 seconds), the tip rises to .866, but the round shape of the

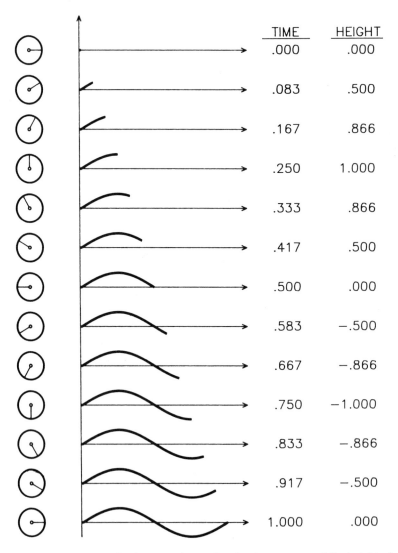

TIME	HEIGHT
.000	.000
.083	.500
.167	.866
.250	1.000
.333	.866
.417	.500
.500	.000
.583	−.500
.667	−.866
.750	−1.000
.833	−.866
.917	−.500
1.000	.000

FIGURE 1.8   Generation of a sine wave by tracing the time-pattern of the height of a spoke tip on a rotating wheel.

wheel causes the tip height to increase more slowly as the tip gets closer to the vertical position. The spoke arrives at a height of one at .25 seconds, thus completing one-quarter of a revolution. As shown in the figure, the tip height then begins to decrease, becoming zero at an elapsed time of .5 seconds when the spoke points horizontally to the left. The tip height then continues to decrease, taking on negative values. At .75 seconds elapsed time, the spoke points straight down and the tip height takes on its most negative value, −1. The tip then starts to rise, crossing the original horizontal position at 1 second as the wheel finishes one revolution. If the wheel continues to rotate at the same speed, the pattern will repeat itself with a period of one second and thus with a constant frequency of 1 Hz.

The pattern traced by the height of the spoke tip *versus time* is known as a sinusoidal waveform. It represents the purest form of motion because it is produced only when the wheel turns smoothly with a constant rate. If the wheel turns in some other way, such as speeding up and slowing down during the course of a revolution, the spoke tip would move in a more complicated pattern. We will discuss the analysis and implications of complex waveforms in section 2.6.

We can use the spoke-in-the-wheel analogy to introduce another attribute of waveforms, phase. Phase provides a means to mark a specific point on a waveform or to compare the positions of two waveforms relative to each other. A circle encompasses an angle of 360° and so the spoke in the wheel rotates through an angle of 360° during the course of one revolution. In one revolution of the wheel, the sinusoidal motion of the height of the spoke tip goes through one cycle. Therefore, one cycle of a waveform is said to include 360° of phase. Instead of plotting the waveform versus time, we can plot it versus phase as in figure 1.9. This method of waveform representation is independent of frequency, because frequency indicates the rate at which the phase of a waveform changes. It is often useful in computer music to consider a single cycle of a waveform only in terms of its phase.

The phase of a particular point on a waveform is measured as an angle from some reference position, most commonly taken as the point where the waveform has a value of zero and is increasing. On the wheel this corresponds to the spoke pointing horizontally to the right. When the waveform is at the reference point, it has a phase of zero degrees. At its peak, the waveform has a phase of 90°, which on

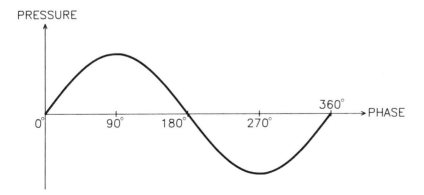

FIGURE 1.9   Representation of a waveform in terms of phase. One cycle of waveform encompasses 360 degrees.

the wheel can be visualized as the 90° angle formed between the spoke standing vertically and the horizontal reference position. When the waveform is zero and decreasing, the phase is 180° indicating that the waveform is midway through a cycle of 360°. At its most negative value, the waveform has a phase of 270°, and when it returns to its original value of 0, the phase is 360°, or equivalently 0° since the waveform is back to where it started.

Phase is also used to compare the relative position of two waveforms. One of the waveforms is chosen as a reference and the position of the other waveform is compared to it. For example, in figure 1.10, waveform A leads waveform B; that is, it reaches its peak amplitude before waveform B. (This might seem incorrect because B is shown to the right of A, but the horizontal axis is directly related to elapsed time so that points on the left happen earlier.) To quantify the relationship between waveforms, the distance between them is measured in terms of phase. In the figure, the difference between waveforms is 30°, and so waveform A is said to lead waveform B by 30°. Stated another way: The phase of waveform B with respect to A is −30°. A phase comparison of two waveforms is only meaningful when the waveforms have the same frequency or, in the more general case, when the ratio of the frequencies is an exact integer. A sinusoidal waveform that has a phase of 180° is exactly inverted from one with a phase of 0°. That is, when the 0° waveform has positive values, the 180° waveform has negative ones, and vice versa. The 180° waveform is often referred to in the literature as being "out of phase."

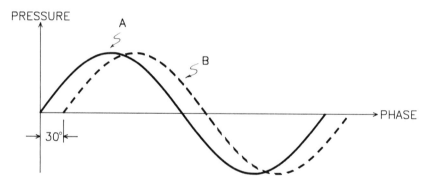

FIGURE 1.10   Phase comparison of two waveforms. Waveform A leads waveform B by 30 degrees.

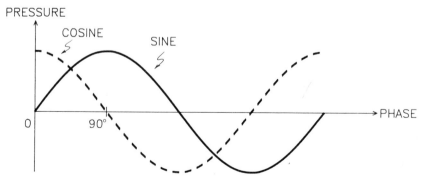

FIGURE 1.11   Cosine wave plotted relative to a sine wave.

There are two major types of sinusoidal waveforms: the sine wave and the cosine wave. They have the same shape; they differ only in phase. The reference phase for a sine wave is taken as the point where the waveform has a value of zero and is increasing. The reference point on a cosine wave occurs when the waveform is at its positive peak. Figure 1.11 plots a sine wave and a cosine wave on the same axis. Notice that the cosine wave leads the sine wave by 90°, and so the cosine wave has a phase of 90° with respect to a sine wave.

1.5 Digital Signals

How does a digital computer, designed to manipulate numbers, work with sound? Acoustical energy in the form of pressure waves can be converted into an analogous electrical signal by an appropriate transducer such as a microphone. The transducer produces an electrical pressure, called a voltage, that changes constantly in sympathy with the vibrations of the sound wave. To demonstrate that the voltage describes the sound received by the microphone, it can be connected to an amplifier driving a loudspeaker; in this way, the electrical signal may be converted back into sound and compared with the original. Because the change in voltage occurs analogously to the vibrations of the sound, the electrical signal is called an analog signal.

To change an analog signal into a form suitable for use by a digital computer, the signal must be converted into numbers. Two types of I/O devices link the digital computer with the analog world. These types are distinguished by the direction of transformation. Analog-to-digital (A/D) converters transform voltages into numbers, and digital-to-analog (D/A) converters transform numbers into voltages. Data converters are characterized by their precision and speed of conversion. The conversion process relies on the principle that at any point in time, an analog electrical signal can be assigned an instantaneous value by measuring its voltage. For example, it is possible to state that exactly 2.01 seconds after a certain sound began, the corresponding electrical signal had a value of .89 volts.

The analog voltage that corresponds to an acoustic signal changes continuously, so that at each instant in time it has a different value. It is not possible for the computer to receive the value of the voltage for every instant, because of the physical limitations of both the computer and the data converters. (And, of course, there are an infinite number of instances between every two instances.) Instead, the analog voltage is measured (sampled) at intervals of equal duration. The output of the sampling process is a discrete or digital signal: a sequence of numbers corresponding to the voltage at each successive sample time. Figure 1.12 shows a signal in both digital and analog form. Observe that the analog signal is continuous; that is, every point on the waveform is smoothly connected to the rest of the signal. The digital signal is not continuous because it consists of a sequence of specific values sampled at discrete times.

The amount of time between samples is known as the sampling interval or sampling period. Its inverse, the number of times the signal is sampled in each second, is called the sampling rate or sampling frequency (f_s) and is measured in Hertz (samples per second).

One might assume that the more samples taken of a phenomenon, the more accurately it could be represented—which suggests that anything less than an

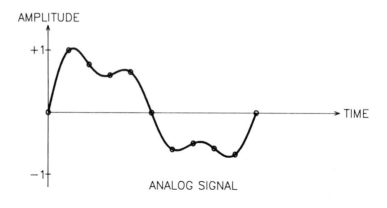

AMPLITUDE

+1

TIME

−1

ANALOG SIGNAL

{0,1,.77,.60,.65,0,−.59,−.49,−.57,−.67,0}

DIGITAL SIGNAL

FIGURE 1.12   Signal represented in both analog and digital forms. The dots on the analog waveform indicate the sampling points.

infinite sampling rate would cause some error in the digital signal. Fortunately, a mathematical analysis of the sampling process reveals that no error will be introduced by a finite sampling rate that is more than twice the fastest rate of change of the signal being sampled. That is, the chosen sampling rate must be faster than twice the highest frequency contained in the analog signal. Conversely, the highest frequency contained in the analog signal must be less than half the sampling rate. This maximum, $f_s/2$, is called the Nyquist (pronounced: "Nye-kwist") frequency and is the theoretical limit on the highest frequency that can be represented in a digital audio system.

To ensure that the frequencies in the analog signal are below the Nyquist frequency, an analog low-pass filter is placed before the A/D converter as shown in figure 1.13 (so that too high frequencies are filtered out). Similarly, a low-pass filter is connected to the output of the D/A converter to ensure that all the frequencies in the analog output signal are in the proper range. A filter separates signals on the basis of their frequencies (see chapter 5), passing signals of certain frequencies while significantly reducing the amplitudes of other frequencies. An ideal low-pass filter would permit frequencies below the Nyquist frequency to pass unchanged, but would completely block higher frequencies. Real low-pass filters, however, are not perfect, with the result that, in practice, the usable frequency range is limited to a little more than 40% of the sampling rate instead of the full 50%. Thus, a sampling rate of 40 kHz provides for a maximum audio frequency of slightly above 16 kHz.

The faster the sampling rate, the higher the frequency that can be represented, but the greater the demands on the speed and the power consumption of the hardware. The upper limit of human hearing is near 20 kHz, which implies a

FIGURE 1.13   The use of low-pass filters to prevent aliasing in a digital audio system.

sampling rate of 20 kHz/40% = 50 kHz, for full fidelity. However, many systems use lower rates due to economic restrictions.

To further understand the frequency limitations of a digital audio system, consider again the system diagrammed in figure 1.13. The computer has been programmed to transfer sample values from the A/D converter to the D/A converter as fast as they are taken. Thus, if the system works perfectly, the analog signal emerging from the output will be an exact replica of the analog signal applied to the input. Suppose a 10-kHz sinusoidal tone is sampled by the A/D converter at a rate of 40 kHz, as illustrated in figure 1.14. The resulting digital signal will be the sequence {1, 0, −1, 0, 1, 0, −1, 0,...}. When the digital signal is reconverted by the D/A converter, the low-pass filter smooths the signal so that a 10-kHz sinusoidal tone appears at the output. Why does the low-pass filter smooth the samples into a sinusoidal wave and not into something else, such as the triangle wave that would be made by connecting the sample values with straight lines? The low-pass filter places a restriction on the highest frequency of the analog signal that comes out of it. In the example, any waveform other than a sinusoid would contain frequencies that exceed the maximum frequency passed by the filter (see section 2.6). In the general case, there is one and only one analog waveform that will fit the

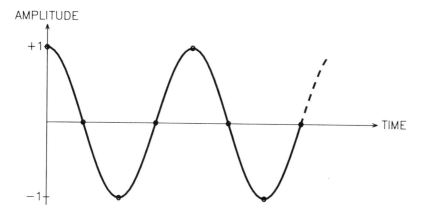

FIGURE 1.14   Sampling a 10-kHz sinusiodal tone at a 40-kHz rate.

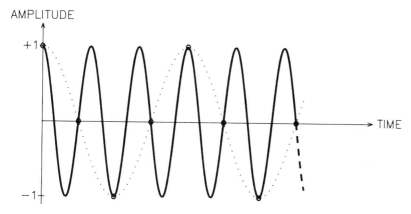

FIGURE 1.15   Sampling a 30-kHz sinusoidal tone at a 40-kHz rate. The samples also describe a 10-kHz sinusoid as shown by the dotted line.

sequence of numbers of a given digital signal and also contain no frequencies above the Nyquist frequency.

What would happen if there were no low-pass filter on the analog input and a signal were sampled that contained a frequency above the Nyquist frequency? Consider a 30-kHz sinusoidal tone sampled at a 40-kHz rate as in figure 1.15. The resulting digital signal of $\{1, 0, -1, 0, 1, 0, -1, 0, \ldots\}$ is the same as that of the 10-kHz tone shown in figure 1.14. Thus, when the digital signal is converted back to analog form, the output of the low-pass filter will be a 10-kHz sinusoidal tone. The 30-kHz tone has the same sample values as a 10-kHz tone, and so it is said to assume an "alias" at 10 kHz. Once a signal appears in a digital system under an alias, there is no way that it can be returned to its original frequency, because there is no way that the computer can determine whether a particular frequency is an alias or not. In a digital system, the alteration caused by the sampling process of frequencies higher than the Nyquist frequency is known as aliasing or foldover.

A low-pass filter at the input to an A/D converter effectively prevents aliasing in a digital signal simply by limiting the range of frequencies going into the converter. In the digital synthesis of sound, however, aliasing can occur in a more subtle way. Suppose that, on a system with a 40-kHz sampling rate, a user writes a program with the intention of producing a 30-kHz sinusoidal tone. The digital signal that the program would generate is identical to the sequence in the examples above, $\{1, 0, -1, 0, 1, 0, -1, 0, \ldots\}$, and therefore would be converted into a 10-kHz sinusoidal tone. Thus, in the computer synthesis of sound, the synthesis algorithms and their corresponding parameters are ordinarily specified in such a way that all frequencies produced by the computer instrument fall below the Nyquist frequency. (See section 3.4.) Certain composers, such as James Dashow, have made use of foldover to produce chordal structures.[8] Such a system requires the accurate calculation of the values of the aliased frequencies.

Let f_{in} be either a frequency applied to the input of an A/D converter or a frequency intended to be contained in a synthesized sound. For values of f_{in} between $f_s/2$ and f_s, the relationship between f_{in} and the actual frequency output (f_{out}) from the low-pass filter is

$$f_{out} = f_s - f_{in}$$

In this region of f_{in}, observe that f_{out} and f_{in} move in opposite directions. If a system with a 40-kHz sampling rate were programmed with the objective of producing an ascending glissando from 22 kHz to 39 kHz, the sound synthesized would actually descend from 18 kHz to 1 kHz.

Foldover occurs on every multiple of the sampling rate, and so frequencies higher than the sampling frequency will also cause unwanted responses. The general relationship is

$$f_{out} = |nf_s - f_{in}|$$

where n is an integer chosen for each value of f_{in} such that f_{out} is less than the Nyquist frequency. Thus, at a 40-kHz sampling rate, an output of 10 kHz would result from inputs of 10 kHz, 30 kHz, 50 kHz, and so on.

Another parameter that can affect the fidelity of a digital signal is the accuracy with which each sample is known. To explain these effects, we will first introduce two closely related concepts, dynamic range and signal-to-noise ratio. A character-istic that is a good indicator of the quality of any system that processes sound is dynamic range: the ratio of the strongest to the weakest signal that can exist in the system. Dynamic range is expressed in dB and a large ratio makes possible clear sounds. For a symphony orchestra in a typical concert hall, the dynamic range is measured as the ratio between the hall's ambient noise and the loudest orchestral sound. The ratio of amplitudes is generally around one to thirty-two thousand, or 90 dB.

The dynamic range of an electronic sound system is limited at the lower end by the background noise contributed by the electronic components and at the higher end by the level at which the greatest signal can be represented without distortion. Manufacturers specify the performance of their equipment under optimum condi-tions, and so the dynamic range available to someone listening to an electronic sound system will be smaller if the loudspeakers of the system are placed in a noisy environment.

A characteristic associated with dynamic range is signal-to-noise (S/N) ratio which compares the level of a given signal with that of the noise in the system. The term noise can take on a variety of meanings depending on the environment and even the tastes of the listener. In this context, it refers to the residual signal that is extraneous to the desired signal. In a concert hall, this would be the "background noise" that is always present, regardless of what is happening on stage. In electronic sound systems, noise generally takes the form of a hissing sound. A S/N ratio is expressed in dB and a large ratio indicates a clear sound. The dynamic range of an electronic system predicts the maximum S/N ratio possible; that is, under ideal conditions, the signal-to-noise ratio equals the dynamic range when a signal of the greatest possible amplitude is present. The ratio will be somewhat smaller on soft sounds. As an example, consider a digital sound system with a constant noise level and a dynamic range of 80 dB. The largest signal possible would have an amplitude 80 dB above the noise level, but a signal with a level 30 dB below the maximum would exhibit a S/N ratio of only 50 dB.

The S/N ratio of a good analog tape recorder can approach 70 dB, with improvement to nearly 90 dB possible through commercially available noise-reduction techniques. The S/N ratio of a digital audio system can be even greater. The performance of such a system is ordinarily determined by the resolution with which the data converters transform digital signals into analog and vice versa. When a conversion takes place, the analog signal is said to be quantized because in digital form it can be represented only to a certain resolution. For example, suppose that a D/A converter is capable of representing a signal in .001 volt steps. If a sample value were calculated as .01227 volts, it would be converted to .012 volts—an error of .00027 volts. The net effect of this type of error, called a quantization error, is the addition of some form of noise to the sound. The amount and audible effect of the quantization noise depends on the resolution of the converter and the type of signal being converted.

The resolution of many converters is measured in bits, corresponding to the size of the datum used to represent each sample of the digital signal. In the case, where the audio signal is constantly changing (as in most music), the dynamic range and hence, the best signal-to-noise ratio that can be achieved is approximately 6 dB/bit. For example, a system with 16-bit data converters has a dynamic range of around 96 dB. This means that the noise in the system will be 96 dB below a signal with the largest amplitude possible in the system. The noise level does not change with signal level, so that signals with amplitudes lower than the maximum value will exhibit less than the maximum S/N ratio. For instance, a sound with an amplitude of 40 dB below the maximum would have a S/N ratio of only 56 dB.

The nature of the audio signal helps to determine the audible character of the noise. In the case above, where the sound constantly changes, listeners generally perceive the quantization noise as the "hissing" normally associated with noise. On the other hand, when reasonably steady tones are produced, the quantization "noise" will usually sound more like distortion. Sometimes the frequencies produced by the distortion are aliased to yield sounds that are more objectionable than the 6-dB/bit S/N ratio would predict.[9]

In musical applications, the use of 12-bit data converters yields an audio quality roughly equivalent to that available from a good analog tape recorder without any noise reduction devices. The S/N ratio of a 16-bit system slightly exceeds the performance of the most advanced noise-reduction schemes for analog tape.

In recent years, the desire to minimize the amount of data needed to represent an audio signal has motivated a great deal of research into alternative schemes for digitally encoding sample values. Several techniques have been found that give a better dynamic range than the number of bits would indicate.[10] The most widely used of these approaches is the floating-point converter[11], which uses a special data format and circuitry to achieve a better S/N ratio on low-level signals.

The precision with which the computer represents sample values internally can also have an effect on the quality of the digital audio. Section 1.1 introduced the two numerical data formats, integer and floating-point. If the sample values are dealt with as integers, the number of bits used correlates with the S/N ratio as 6 dB per bit; floating-point numbers correlate with the S/N ratio as 20 dB per equivalent decimal digit.

The mathematical operations used to calculate samples can have a deleterious effect on the S/N ratio. When two numbers are combined by an arithmetic operation, a rounding error can result.[12] As an example, consider the floating-point product of 11.227×20.126, in a format that has an accuracy of only five digits. The result, 225.954602, when truncated to five digits becomes 225.95, an error of .004602. When using an algorithm that employs several multiplies to calculate each sample, the cumulative effect of such errors can be audible. To avoid this problem, programs working with audio generally use data formats that represent the samples with more resolution than the data converters. The number of additional bits or equivalent decimal digits necessary depends on the number and type of the mathematical operations used. The standard floating-point format found in most computer languages has enough resolution to accomodate most synthesis algorithms. On the other hand, the standard 16-bit integer format does not have enough resolution to take full advantage of the dynamic range available from a 16-bit D/A converter.

Another way that audio quality can be degraded is by generating signals that exceed the dynamic range of the system. In a D/A conversion system, the dynamic range is limited on the upper end by the maximum value that can be accepted by the data converter. For example, most 16-bit converters have a range from −32768 to +32767. A sample value given outside of that range will not be converted properly. When a digital signal describing a tone contains a single, out-of-range sample, a click will usually be heard during D/A conversion. When a significant proportion of the samples in the digital signal are out of range, severe distortion results. Therefore, in using algorithms to synthesize sound, the musician must choose parameters for the algorithm that ensure that all output samples fall within the range of the D/A converters used on the system. However, the sample values should be large enough to maintain a good S/N ratio.

1.6   The Use of a Computer in Audio Systems

A computer system can manipulate sound in several different modes of operation. The simplest of these is *digital recording* (figure 1.16a). The A/D converter transforms the incoming analog signal into digital form, and the computer stores this digital signal on an external memory device such as a disk or tape. For playback, the computer retrieves the stored signal from memory and sends it to the D/A converter for retransformation. Digital recordings have several advantages over analog ones. The recording medium stores numbers rather than an analog signal, and so offers superior noise performance and protects the sound more effectively against degradation during long-term storage. In addition, regardless of the number of generations removed, a copy of a digital recording maintains complete fidelity to the original.

The configuration of figure 1.16a can also be used for *signal processing*. Here the computer modifies digital signals before passing them to the D/A converter for reconversion. The modifications can be as simple as mixing the signal at the input

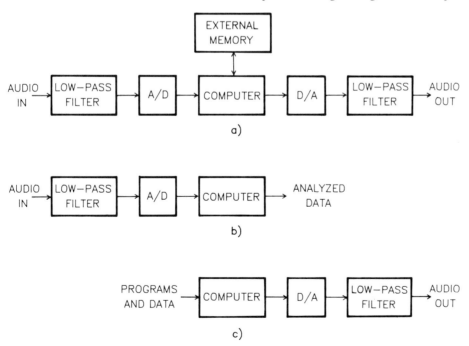

FIGURE 1.16   Configurations used in computer-audio systems.

with another digital signal previously stored in external memory. The use of a computer enables very complex operations such as removing the orchestral accompaniment from behind a singing voice. Other uses of the computer in this mode include modulation (chapter 3), filtering (chapter 5), and reverberation (chapter 7).

The computer can also be programmed to analyze signals (figure 1.16b). In this mode, the computer takes a digital signal and determines its characteristics mathematically. For example, a computer analysis can determine the frequencies contained in a sound and their corresponding amplitudes. Another kind of analysis can reveal the acoustical characteristics of a speech sound. The analytical capability of the computer makes it a powerful tool for the researcher in psychoacoustics. Chapters 2 and 6 will detail some of these applications. For the musician, analyses provide valuable information about acoustical processes and can be used as a basis for the synthesis of musical sounds.

The computer can also synthesize sound (figure 1.16c) by calculating a sequence of numbers corresponding to the waveform of the desired sound. In this mode, all that is required in addition to the computer is the D/A converter and its associated low-pass filter. This is the minimum configuration necessary to obtain computer-generated audio.

The name *direct digital synthesis* is given to the process of realizing sound by using digital hardware to calculate its waveform. Direct digital synthesis has several advantages over synthesis with analog hardware—accuracy, repeatability, and generality. The frequencies of the signals inside the computer are highly accurate, and so the frequencies and timings of the sounds produced can be precisely realized. The amplitudes can be accurately synthesized as well, because a precise numerical value can be attached to them. A related advantage is repeatability. Because of the accuracy of direct digital synthesis, every time the computer executes a given list of instructions and data, it will produce the same results. It is often desirable to introduce a certain amount of randomness within computer music (see sections 3.9 and 8.1). Digital synthesis gives the musician direct control over the degree and character of the randomness included.

The most important advantage of direct digital synthesis is its generality. Because any sound can be converted into a digital signal, it follows that any sound can be synthesized by using the appropriate algorithm to calculate its digital representation and then converting it. Thus, sounds produced digitally can, in theory, be arbitrarily complex and have any character. That is, the sound of one or a hundred symphonic instruments or of one or a hundred barnyard animals may be realized using the same general-purpose computer system.

One of the greatest challenges of digital synthesis is the determination of the algorithm to produce a desired sound. Chapters 3 through 7 will detail most of the current techniques. Many synthesis models are based on the analysis of natural sounds. Synthesis-from-analysis as this is called, can be used to reproduce the analyzed sound, but often musicians modify the analyses to produce new extensions of the original sound.

There are three rates associated with the process of sound synthesis: the sampling rate (described above), the calculation rate, and the control rate. In direct digital synthesis, the calculation rate is the speed at which the hardware calculates sample values. It is dependent on the type of machine and the particular algorithm.

The control rate is the speed at which significant changes in any sound-synthesis process occur. For example, the control rate in a simple program would be the rate at which the notes are played. In actual practice, there are usually several significant events during a sound. The control rate is much slower than the sampling rate and typically ranges from 1 to 1000 events per second.

When the calculation rate equals the sampling rate, a computer synthesizer is said to operate in "real-time". Without real-time operation, a computer-music system cannot be used for live performance. For the musician, real-time operation is preferable because it reduces the amount of time between instructing the computer and hearing the results (feedback time).

An interactive real-time system allows the user to modify the synthesis process as it takes place and to hear the results immediately. An example of an interactive situation is a digital synthesizer with a knob permitting the musician to adjust the tempo of a score in real-time. Interactive control over virtually every aspect of the performance process is theoretically possible, although the calculation speed of the hardware limits what can be done in practice.

To enable real-time operation, the computer must calculate each sample within a sampling interval. If the sampling frequency is 40 kHz, then there are just 25 microseconds between samples. If the computer averages one million operations per second (faster than most minicomputers), real-time algorithms are limited to those using 25 operations or less. Therefore, except for special examples, real-time synthesis is impractical with a general-purpose computer.

To achieve a calculation rate consistent with audio sampling rates, special-purpose digital hardware is attached to a host computer. This hardware executes a limited number of algorithms very quickly, with the host computer specifying (at the control rate) the calculations that are to be performed. The internal architecture of such a digital synthesizer usually places restrictions on the number and complexity of synthesis algorithms available. Thus, an increase in execution speed is often accompanied by a loss in potential generality in the number, type, and complexity of sounds that can be made. For a great many purposes, advantages of real-time operation far outweigh the loss of complete flexibility.

Practical hardware for real-time, direct digital synthesis was developed after the mid-1970s. Before then computer-synthesized sound was almost exclusively realized in a deferred mode of operation. This mode is used at installations where no real-time hardware is available or when the desired digital processes are too complex to be implemented on current real-time hardware. When the calculation rate is slower than the sampling rate, the calculated sample values must be stored in the computer's external memory. Upon completion of the calculation of a score, the stored sequence of samples can be converted in real-time. Use of the deferred mode greatly increases the feedback time to the musician. Depending on a variety of factors, it may be minutes or even days before the composer can hear the results.

The availability of "on-line" D/A-conversion facilities helps to minimize the waiting time. D/A converters are said to be on-line when they are attached to the same computer that calculates the sample values. The less desirable procedure of off-line conversion requires the calculated set of sample values to be physically transferred onto some medium, usually a digital tape, and then loaded onto another computer system outfitted with conversion apparatus. Sometimes a significant geographic distance separates the two computers and the digital tape must be mailed or otherwise transported to the conversion site. Fortunately, the decreasing cost of computers and data converters is making on-line conversion more commonplace.

Another undesirable characteristic of the deferred mode is the large amount of data storage necessary. For example, just one minute of stereophonic sound at a 40-kHz sampling rate is ordinarily represented by 9.6 million bytes, an enormous amount of data by any standard. As a result, musicians using this mode often realize their projects a small section at a time, employing analog tape to store intermediate results.

Computers can also be used in conjunction with analog hardware in a hybrid system. In such a system, the sound is actually synthesized by analog hardware, and the computer acts as a controller, providing the desired sequence of control voltages to the analog circuitry. The computer does not have to calculate samples, and so it can operate at the much slower control rate. Control voltages for the analog synthesizer are realized by connecting the computer to one or more D/A converters, but these in general can be slower and have fewer bits of resolution than those used for direct digital synthesis. Because a slower overall data rate is required from the computer, a microcomputer is generally used as the controller.

Analog synthesizers operate in real-time, but are less accurate and therefore do not produce results that are as well-controlled as those of direct digital synthesis. They also do not offer as much generality. Several of the synthesis techniques presented in this text cannot be fully implemented with practical analog hardware.

Notes

1.   Haynes, Stanley. "The Musician-Machine Interface in Computer Music." Doctoral dissertation, Southampton University, 1979.

2.   Vercoe, Barry L. *Reference Manual for the MUSIC 11 Sound Synthesis Language.* Cambridge, Mass.: Experimental Music Studio, M.I.T., 1979.

3.   Mathews, Max V. *The Technology of Computer Music.* Cambridge, Mass.: M.I.T. Press, 1969.

4.   Howe, Hubert S., Jr. *Electronic Music Synthesis.* New York: Norton, 1975.

5.   Randall, J.K. "Lyric Variations for Violin and Computer." Vanguard Records (VCS-10057), 1967.

6.   Buxton, W., Sinderman, R., Reeves, W., Patel, S., and Baecker, R. "The Evolution of the SSSP Score Editing Tools." *Computer Music Journal,* 3(4) 1979, 14–25.

7.   A few of these terms will not be used again in this text. They are presented here to aid the student in reading the professional literature.

8.   Dashow, James. "Three Methods for the Digital Synthesis of Chordal Structures with Non-harmonic Partials." *Interface,* 7, 69–94.

9.   Blesser, B. A. "Digitization of Audio: A Comprehensive Examination of Theory, Implementation, and Current Practice." *Journal of the Audio Engineering Society,* 26(10), 1978, 739–771.

10.   Blesser, "Digitization of Audio."

11.   Chamberlain, Hal. *Musical Applications of Microprocessors.* Rochelle Park, N. J.: Hayden, 1980.

12.   Rabiner, L. R., and B. Gold. *Theory and Application of Digital Signal Processing.* Englewood Cliffs, N. J.: Prentice-Hall, 1975.

2

THE ACOUSTICS AND
PSYCHOACOUSTICS OF MUSIC

Certain fundamentals of acoustics were introduced in section 1.4. Acoustics is the study of the physics and transmission of sound. It includes such concepts as frequency, amplitude, timing, spectrum, and location of sound. However, this study is not sufficient to describe the way things "sound." The workings of the ear, nervous system, and brain all affect our perception of sound. Psychoacoustics is the study of the way humans perceive sounds. Here the concern is with the subjective response to the sound in terms of its pitch, loudness, duration, timbre, and apparent location. Although the categories of psychoacoustics reflect the divisions of acoustics, there is, in fact, considerable interrelationship among them. For example, our sensation of pitch is time-dependent, and our perception of loudness varies considerably with frequency and timbre. This chapter will discuss pitch, loudness, duration, and timbre. Chapter 7 explores the role of location in the perception of sound.

The study of the literature of psychoacoustics can be a great aid in making computer music, but it must be remembered that the musician's ear is the final arbiter in determining how to use the computer as a musical instrument. Thus, the principles discussed below are offered as guidelines to help the musician take full advantage of the capabilities of the medium.

2.1 Sound and the Ear

Sound is received by the ear and processed by the auditory system, which extends from the outer ear to the cerebral cortex. The ear acts as a transducer, converting mechanical motion of vibration patterns to neural impulses. Figure 2.1 illustrates the important parts of this physical apparatus. When the sound reaches the ear, it travels down the external canal to the ear drum. Here it imparts its characteristic pattern of vibratory energy to the eardrum, which transmits the vibration to the ossicles, a chain of three bones: the hammer, the anvil, and the stirrup. The stirrup transmits the motion to a membrane called the oval window, causing a traveling wave to propagate in the fluid in the cochlea, which in turn stimulates the hairs on the basilar membrane. Nerves attached to these hairs transmit the stimulus to the brain. When periodic, sinusoidal vibrations at frequencies within the range of audibility reach the inner ear, they excite nerve endings at places on the basilar

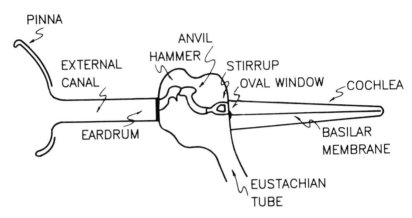

FIGURE 2.1   Schematic of the hearing apparatus of the ear. The cochlea is shown uncoiled for clarity.

membrane, proportional to the frequency of the tone.[1] The sensation of loudness is primarily determined by the amount of acoustical energy received by the ear.

2.2   Pitch

Pitch is our subjective response to frequency. It is the main sensation caused by the stimulation of nerve endings on the basilar membrane.

The approximate range of audible frequencies is between 20 and 20,000 Hz. The frequencies from 20 to 4000 Hz comprise the region of greatest perceptual acuity and sensitivity to change of frequency. This region occupies two-thirds of the basilar membrane; the remaining high frequencies contact only one third of it. Within the region of greatest acuity, discrimination of frequency for sinusoids is proportionately worse at low frequencies and becomes increasingly difficult the shorter the duration. It is independent of amplitude.

For the listener to detect a change in frequency of a single sinusoidal tone, the change must be greater than the "just noticeable difference" (JND) in frequency. It is postulated by some that the JND corresponds to some minimum spatial separation between points of stimulus on the basilar membrane. The exact value of the JND, like so many psychoacoustical determinations, varies from one listener to the next and according to the method of testing. For the statistically "average" individual, the JND for isolated sinusoids is 3% at 100 Hz and .5% at 2000 Hz.[2]

There is a nonlinear relationship between pitch perception and frequency: The stimulation on the basilar membrane occurs at points almost exactly proportional to the logarithm of the frequency. For higher frequencies, at least, when the frequency doubles, the distance between the points of stimulation on the basilar membrane changes by an approximately constant distance (circa 3.4 mm). Thus, listeners compare tones on the basis of the musical interval separating them—that is, on the basis of the ratio of their frequencies—rather than the difference between them. For example, the pitch interval of an octave corresponds to a frequency ratio of 2:1. We perceive this interval to be "the same" wherever it occurs in the frequency continuum. Figure 2.2 shows the frequencies of the piano keyboard. The piano keys are labeled with the notation for pitch used throughout this book: a

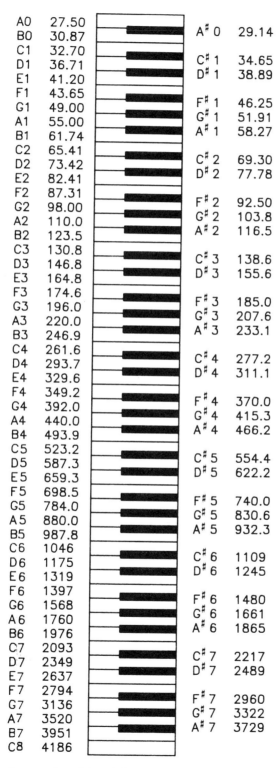

FIGURE 2.2   The frequencies of the pitches of the equal-tempered piano keyboard. (See section 2.3.)

pitch-class/octave notation where C4 designates middle C. Notice that the frequency of A3 (220 Hz) is exactly one-half the frequency of the tone an octave above, A4 at 440 Hz, which is one-half the frequency of A5 (880 Hz). Follow a chromatic scale up the keyboard from A3 to A4. Observe that there is not a constant frequency difference between any two adjacent tones; that is, to find the frequency of a tone, one cannot simply add a constant to the frequency of the previous tone. Section 2.3 shows several systems for determining the frequency relationships among tones.

In actual practice, listeners generally receive sounds that are much more complex than the single sinusoid described above. When a sound comprised of multiple sinusoids reaches the ear, the cochlear fluid responds by assuming a motion that is a combination of the vibration patterns of the component frequencies. In this case, the pitch or pitches to be perceived depend(s) not only on the values of the frequencies themselves, but also on the relationship among them.

One possible relationship among frequencies is that they are related harmonically; that is, that the frequencies are related as whole-number multiples. In this case, even though each tone stimulates a different spatial location on the basilar membrane, the perception will be of a single pitch at the "fundamental frequency." The fundamental is the frequency that is the largest common divisor of the harmonically related frequencies. Each of the sinusoids is called a harmonic or harmonic partial of the tone and is given a number based on its ratio to fundamental frequency. As an example, figure 2.3 shows a diagram of a complex periodic tone comprised of five harmonic partials. The fundamental frequency is 100 Hz, the second harmonic is at 200 Hz, the third harmonic is at 300 Hz, and so

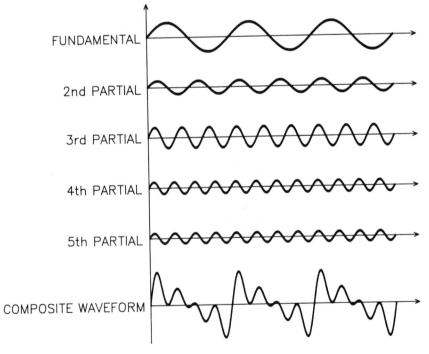

FIGURE 2.3   Complex periodic waveform and the five harmonic partials of which it is comprised.

on up to the fifth harmonic at 500 Hz. (For convenience, the fundamental may also be referred to as the first harmonic.) The figure shows how the harmonics add together to form the complex waveform.

Periodicity is thought to be a factor in our perception of a single pitch at the fundamental frequency when the multiple frequencies are harmonically related. As shown in figure 2.3, when harmonic partials add together, they form a periodic waveform that repeats at the fundamental frequency. One theory postulates that our hearing mechanism traces with time the pattern of repetition of the waveform to determine the period of the waveform. The listener then accepts the frequency corresponding to the measured period as the fundamental frequency.

In the region of approximately 150 to 500 Hz the fusion of harmonic partials into the sensation of a single pitch operates even when the fundamental frequency is absent.[3] The remaining partials continue to form a pattern of repetition at the frequency of their largest common divisor, that of the fundamental. Figure 2.4 shows two waveforms with the same fundamental frequency. The first (figure 2.4a) is comprised of partials one through seven; the second (figure 2.4b), of partials four

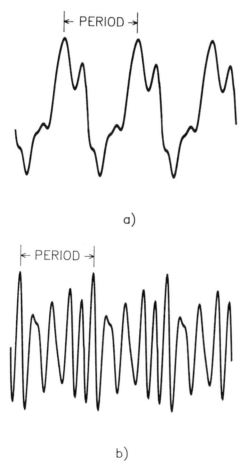

a)

b)

FIGURE 2.4   (a) Three cycles of a waveform containing harmonics one through seven. (b) Three cycles of a waveform containing only harmonics four through seven.

through seven. Notice that the period of the two waveforms is identical and therefore they will sound at the same pitch.

The situation can exist where two sinusoidal tones that are not harmonically related reach the listener at the same time with the same amplitude. If the frequency ratio of the two tones is sufficiently large, two distinct tones will be perceived. For instance, a tone at 111 Hz sounded with one at 1095 Hz will create the percept of two separate tones. If the frequency ratio of the two tones is very small, the listener will perceive a single pitch at the average of the two frequencies. For example, two sine tones at 219 and 220 Hz will be perceived to have the same frequency as a single tone at 219.5 Hz.[4] In addition, closely spaced tones produce a sensation of beating at a rate that is the *difference* between the frequencies of the two tones. Thus the two sine tones in the example cause a beating sensation of one beat per second. The beating is perceived as a periodic change of the amplitude of the resultant tone. Figure 2.5 illustrates this situation.

A phenomenon similar to the beating of two fused tones occurs when two tones are tuned close to an octave. The beating occurs at a rate corresponding to the difference between the frequency of the tone near the octave and the frequency exactly an octave above the lower tone. This "beating of mistuned consonances" disappears above around 1500 Hz.[5]

Beating between tones can also be observed, although much more weakly, when the difference between the two tones occurs at or near the interval of the pure fifth (3:2 in frequency ratio) or the pure fourth (4:3 in frequency ratio). For example, violinists tune the open strings by listening for beats between strings tuned a fifth apart.

The inclusion of non-harmonic partials in a sound ensures that, in most circumstances, beats will be heard. Beating can, in turn, help the tone to sound more lively. Section 3.12 includes a particularly good example of Jean-Claude Risset's compositional use of beats among the harmonics of complex tones which are tuned within a few hundredths of a Hz of each other.

Two pure tones will cause a beating sensation until the difference between their frequencies exceeds about 10 to 15 Hz. Within the region of beating lies the "limit of discrimination": a point at which the frequency separation of two tones is sufficiently large for the listener to perceive two separate tones. At separations just outside of the range of beating, there is a region described by acousticians as "tonal roughness." It is associated with the "critical band." The critical band is a measure

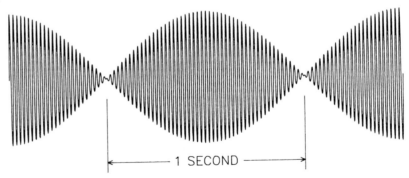

FIGURE 2.5   The waveform resulting from the addition of two sine tones at 49 and 50 Hz, respectively. Notice the beating at a rate of once per second.

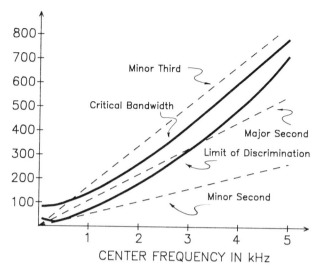

FIGURE 2.6 Critical bandwidth and limit of frequency discrimination as a function of center frequency. (*Based on* Introduction to the Physics and Psychophysics of Music *by Juan C. Roederer. Published with the permission of Springer-Verlag, Heidelberg.*)

of the ability of the ear to discriminate adjacent tones. For example, when the ear receives two closely spaced tones, there will be a certain amount of overlapping of the neurons stimulated on the basilar membrane. This causes the sensation of two tones to be more complex than it would be for tones with greater separations. The frequency difference between the tones at which the sensation abruptly changes is known as the critical band.[6]

The width of the critical band varies with frequency. It is a large percentage of the average frequency of two tones that are at low frequencies, and a small percentage for two tones of high frequencies. Figure 2.6 shows the change of width of the critical band with frequency. Above about 440 Hz, the width of the band is roughly constant at around one-fourth of an octave, i.e., around the musical interval of a minor third (around 19%). The fact that the critical band is a larger interval at low frequencies helps to explain the common usage of larger musical intervals in the bass register in most music. The width of the critical band plays a role in the perception of loudness and timbre, as well.

2.3 Tuning Systems

Most computer-music synthesis systems offer the musician complete freedom of choice with respect to tuning. This situation differs greatly from the fixed intonation of many acoustic and some electronic instruments. In the following section, we will describe the properties of four common systems for tuning: equal temperament, just intonation, meantone tuning, and Pythagorean tuning.

Equal temperament with twelve semitonal divisions of the octave is by far the most common system of musical intonation used today in Western music for keyboard instruments. In the general case of equal temperament, an interval I is divided into a number of intervals N all of equal size (that is, all having equal *ratios* of frequency). The expression for calculating the basic equal-tempered division, *i*, in the particular tuning system is $i=I^{1/N}$. (That is, *i* is the interval *I* raised to the one-over-*N*th power.) For the twelve-tone equal-tempered system, the basic division of the octave ($I=2$) is the semitone, and so $i=2^{1/12}$. Thus, two adjacent tones in this system tuned a semitone apart have a frequency ratio of 1:$2^{1/12}$, or 1:1.05946. The ratio for any interval in the system is $i=2^{m/12}$, where *m* is the number of semitones comprised in the interval. For example, the ratio for the equal-tempered perfect fifth (seven semitones) is 1:$2^{7/12}$, or 1:1.49828. Table 2.1 summarizes the frequency ratios for the intervals in twelve-tone equal tempera-ment. All equal-tempered intervals of the same size have the same frequency ratio, and thus, "sound the same." This fact enables the transposition of music in equal temperament to any pitch level without its becoming "out of tune."

To facilitate comparisons and measurements of tuning, the octave is divided into 1200 equal parts. The smallest division is called a cent, with a frequency ratio 1:$2^{1/1200}$, or 1:1.0005778. Thus, the octave is accorded 1200 cents, and the equal-tempered semitone has 100 cents; that is, $1200/12 = 100$. The perfect fifth of equal temperament comprises seven semitones and has 700 cents.

In the Pythagorean tuning system, the whole-number ratios of 3:2 (the pure fifth) and 4:3 (the pure fourth) are used to generate all the tones of a particular scale. For example, to generate the tones of the key of C, we create an upper tone, "G," at 3:2 in frequency to "C," then down to "D," a tone at the frequency ratio of 3:4 to "G," follows. The upper fifth to "D" is "A." "E," the lower fourth to "A," is followed by its upper fifth, "B." The octave of "C" is based on the frequency ratio of 2:1, and the final tone of the system, "F," is the lower fifth to the octave. Figure 2.7 gives the frequency ratios of the individual tones to "C" and to their neighbors. We can replicate the resulting scale in any octave to make a full gamut for musical use. Notice, however, that the scale has no sharps or flats. When we use the same method (3:2 frequency ratio) to generate all twelve tones, a 'comma,' or

	EQUAL TEMPERAMENT		PYTHAGOREAN		JUST		MEAN–TONE	
	Ratio	Cents	Ratio	Cents	Ratio	Cents	Ratio	Cents
Unison	1:1	0	1:1	0	1:1	0	1:1	0
Aug unis					1:1.055	92	1:1.045	76
Mi 2nd	1:1.059	100	1:1.053	90	1:1.067	112	1:1.070	117
Maj 2nd	1:1.122	200	1:1.125	204	1:1.125	204	1:1.118	193
Mi 3rd	1:1.189	300	1:1.185	294	1:1.200	316	1:1.196	310
Maj 3rd	1:1.260	400	1:1.265	408	1:1.250	386	1:1.250	386
P 4th	1:1.335	500	1:1.333	498	1:1.333	498	1:1.337	503
Tritone	1:1.414	600						
Aug 4th			1:1.404	588	1:1.406	590	1:1.398	580
Dim 5th			1:1.424	612	1:1.422	610		
P 5th	1:1.498	700	1:1.500	702	1:1.500	702	1:1.496	697
Mi 6th	1:1.587	800	1:1.580	792	1:1.600	814	1:1.600	814
Maj 6th	1:1.682	900	1:1.687	906	1:1.667	884	1:1.672	890
Aug 6th					1:1.778	996	1:1.747	966
Mi 7th	1:1.782	1000	1:1.778	996	1:1.800	1018	1:1.789	1007
Maj 7th	1:1.888	1100	1:1.898	1109	1:1.875	1088	1:1.869	1083
Octave	1:2	1200	1:2	1200	1:2	1200	1:2	1200

TABLE 2.1   Comparison of Frequency Ratios for Four Tuning Systems

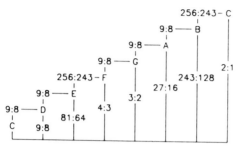

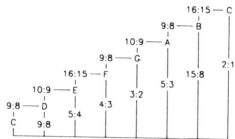

FIGURE 2.7

The frequency ratios of the tones to C and to their neigbors in Pythagorean tuning.

FIGURE 2.8

The frequency ratios of the tones to C and to their neighbors in just intonation.

disparity in intonation results. As an example, consider the cycle C, G, D, A, E, B, F♯, C♯, G♯, D♯, A♯, E♯, B♯. The frequency ratio between any two adjacent pitches is 3:2 and so the frequency of B♯ can be calculated by multiplying the frequency of the fundamental C by 3/2 twelve successive times. Therefore, the frequency ratio between the B♯ 12 fifths above the fundamental C and the fundamental is $(3/2)^{12}:1$ or 129.74634:1. The enharmonic equivalent of that B♯, namely C, is seven octaves above the fundamental C, a frequency ratio of $2^7:1$ or 128:1. Thus, there is a considerable difference in intonation between C and B♯. This "Pythagorean" comma, which has a frequency ratio of 129.74634:128 or 1.01364:1 (a disparity of 23.5 cents), is clearly audible.

In the system of just tuning,[7] we generate a scale with beat-free major and minor thirds (5:4 and 6:5, respectively) as well as pure fourths (4:3) and fifths (3:2). Figure 2.8 shows the frequency ratios of tones in a diatonic just scale to "C" and to their neighbors. One of the just system's great virtues is that some of its most frequently used triads (I, IV, and V) are all built of the beat-free ratios 4:5:6. One of its problems lies in the unequal size of the major seconds of the scale. As a result, certain intervals in the system create obvious beating. The diatonic just system can also include all twelve tones by dividing each whole step into two semitones. The problems are such that, for keyboard instruments, most compositional use of the system—in order to preserve a maximum of pure intervals—must employ diatonic pitch collections that avoid modulations to keys that are more than two sharps or flats away.

Meantone tuning represents something of a compromise between the Pythagorean and just tuning systems.[8] It results in major thirds that are slightly smaller than those of the Pythagorean system and minor thirds that are slightly larger. The fifths and fourths deviate from pure intervals, as well.

The scale tones of meantone tuning are generated by a cycle of fifths in which each fifth is lowered from its pure ratio of 3:2 by about 5 cents resulting in a ratio of 1.49533:1. This method of lowered fifths is used in extending the system to include sharps and flats, as well. Traditionally, the system included C♯, F♯, G♯, B♭, and E♭. In music with wider excursions of accidentals, the system begins to break down. One reason is the so-called "Wolf fifth" produced by the interval G♯ – E♭. It has 739 cents and is more than a third of a semitone sharp.

Table 2.1 compares the four intonation systems discussed. The composer of computer music freely chooses the intonation system according to the design and the demands of the music. Of course, the tuning for acoustic instruments may not always be in agreement with these schemes. Studies have shown that nuance in performance of vocal and instrumental music includes stretching the musical intervals in ways that do not conform to any standard intonation system.[9] For example, it has been observed that string players and choral groups tend toward the major thirds and minor thirds of Pythagorean tuning.[10] This is often due to the function of the pitches within the musical passage, and it is expected by listeners. The actual tuning of a tone may be varied for expressive purposes, as well.

Much computer music has been made using twelve equal-tempered divisions of the octave, but many different systems have been employed. For example, other tuning systems have been used in computer music by Carlton Gamer, Jon Appleton, John R. Pierce, and Gary Kendall—to name only a few. Section 4.11 examines John Chowning's *Stria*, which employs an entirely new system of interrelating frequencies in music—by equal-tempered divisions of a pseudo-octave made by projecting the golden-mean ratio (1:1.618...) over the frequency continuum.

2.4 Perception of Amplitude

The loudness of a sound is a measure of the subjective response to its amplitude. Loudness is strongly influenced by the frequency and spectral composition of the sound. Thus, the minimum detectable change in amplitude of a tone—its JND in amplitude—depends on both the spectral content and amplitude of the tone. Generally, in the musically relevant ranges of frequency and amplitude, the JND in amplitude for a sine tone is between .2 and .4 dB.[11] Figure 2.9 shows a comparison of the JND's for pure tones at 70 Hz, 200 Hz, and 1000 Hz.

Figure 2.10 displays the contours of a "Fletcher-Munson" curve. The contour lines represent the amplitude levels at which single sine tones of different frequencies sound equally loud. For example, figure 2.10 shows that near the threshold of audibility, in order for pure tones of 100 Hz and 1000 Hz to sound equally loud, the amplitude of the lower tone must be boosted by almost 40 dB.

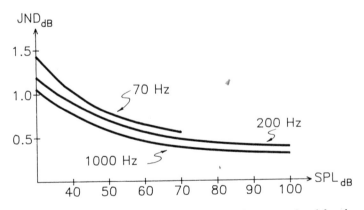

FIGURE 2.9   Just noticeable difference (JND) in sound pressure level for three frequencies. (*From* The Acoustical Foundations of Music *by John Backus. Published with the permission of W. W. Norton Co., Inc.*)

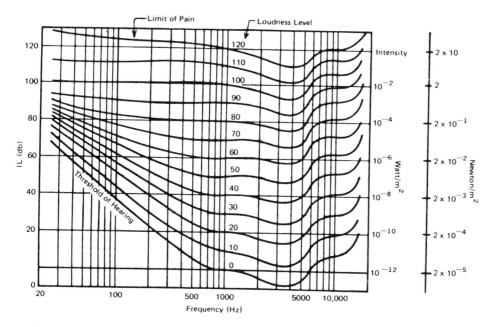

FIGURE 2.10   Fletcher-Munson diagram of equal loudness for tones of different frequencies. (*Reprinted from* Introduction to the Physics and Psychophysics of Music *by Juan C. Roederer with the permission of Springer-Verlag, Heidelberg and the Journal of the Acoustical Society of America.*)

The figure demonstrates that the ear is most sensitive to sound in the range from 250 to 3000 Hz, and that below 60 Hz and above 10 kHz the loss of sensitivity is considerable.

When the listener is presented with more than one tone, the perceived loudness varies with the frequency and amplitude relationships among the tones. This is a result of *masking:* the reduction in sensitivity to amplitude due to the fatigue of neurons on the basilar membrane. Thus, in the presence of a louder tone, a soft one may not be heard at all. The threshold of masking is defined as the amplitude level at which the softer tone disappears. It depends strongly on the frequency difference between the tones, on the amplitude of the louder tone and, to a lesser extent, on the frequency of the louder tone. Masking is particularly effective when the tones occupy the same critical band. In many cases a tone that has an amplitude of only 15 to 20 dB less than a stronger one will not be perceived. When the tones are close enough in frequency to cause beating the masking threshold is slightly reduced. For two loud tones outside the same critical band, the tone with the lower frequency more easily masks the upper tone. Low-amplitude sounds outside the same critical band do not generally mask each other.[12]

Masking occurs not only for simultaneous tones, but also for tones that occur in succession. Under many circumstances, the neuron fatigue caused by a louder, previous tone can affect our perception of a softer, subsequent tone.

Whenever a pure tone sounds with sufficient loudness, the ear creates "aural harmonics" not present in the tone. For example, a loud 1 kHz tone can produce sensations at 2 kHz, 3 kHz, etc. In addition, a pair of tones (with frequencies f_1 and f_2) causes the aural system to add other tonal sensations, "combination tones," that are combinations of the presented frequencies. The strongest additional sensation is a tone at the difference in frequency of the two tones (f_2–f_1). With complex tones, sensations occur at the differences in frequency between the fundamentals and all their harmonics. The most noticeable products are defined by the relationships of $2f_1$–f_2 and $3f_1$–$2f_2$. The sensation is fainter for higher harmonic numbers. For instance, the most significant additional sensations produced by two loud, complex tones at 150 Hz and 190 Hz, respectively, are heard at 40 Hz (f_2–f_1), 110 Hz ($2f_1$–f_2), 230 Hz ($2f_2$–f_1), 70 Hz ($3f_1$–$2f_2$), and 270 Hz ($3f_2$–$2f_1$).

2.5 Temporal Relationships

Time is a fundamental limitation on the ability to perceive pitch. When a tone sounds, a certain time must pass before the listener develops a sensation of pitch. The length of this time depends upon the frequency of the tone. In order to establish pitch, a listener must receive a number of cycles of a tone. Thus it takes a longer time to perceive the pitch of a tone at a lower frequency because that tone has a longer period. For example, a tone must last at least 40 msec at 100 Hz, whereas a tone at 1000 Hz must last only 13 msec.[13]

When a listener hears a sequence of tones, there are a number of ways in which it can be understood. The different modes of perception have important compositional implications. The way in which any individual sequence is perceived depends upon a number of factors: the rate at which tones are sounded, the pitch interval between tones, amplitude differences between tones, and timbral differences between tones, among others. The foremost determinant is the compositional context in which they are presented. While the results of scientific tests such as those described below are useful for determining general perceptual principles, the results can change with the experience and expectations of the listeners. For example, a theme or motive in a work, once well established, can be presented in ways normally thought to render it melodically incomprehensible and still be understood. The electronic works of Milton Babbitt contain examples of this effect.

In the examples that follow, we will consider sequences played on a single instrument with little variation in dynamic level. This will enable us to show more clearly the effect of both the rate at which the sequence is played and the pitch interval between members. The three primary ways of perceiving a sequence are: as a single line, as divided into multiple sublines, or as fused into a single sound.[14] In the first case, where the sequence is heard as a single line, it is said to evoke temporal coherence. The second case, where the listener partitions the sequence into two or more separate lines, is known as fission. The last case, where the sequence is played so rapidly that is forms a single audible entity, is known as fusion.

Consider a melodic line of eleven tones where the even-numbered tones and the odd-numbered tones are separated in register. As shown in figure 2.11a, at a rate of 5 or 6 tones per second, a listener would hear the sequence as a coherent succession. At a faster tempo—10 to 12 tones per second (figure 2.11b)—the high tones group together to form a separate stream from the low tones. At an intermediate tempo, around seven or eight tones per second, one can direct one's attention to any one of three percepts: a succession of alternating high and low tones, a stream of higher tones by themselves, or a stream of lower tones. At a high

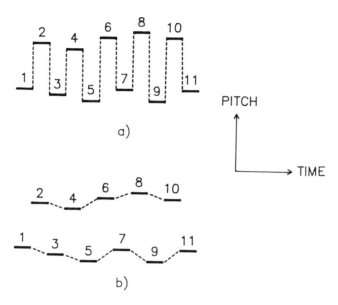

a)

PITCH

TIME

b)

FIGURE 2.11   (a) Perception of a sequence of tones sounded at five or six tones per second as temporally coherent. When the same sequence is played at 10 to 12 tones per second, fission can occur as shown in (b).

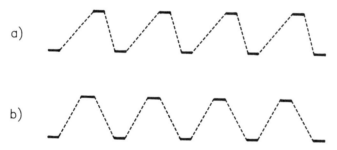

a)

b)

FIGURE 2.12   At high speeds and large melodic intervals, tone sequence (a) with uneven rhythms sounds like the tone sequence (b).

tempo (>20 tones per second), the listener will perceive the line as a "fusion" into a single complex sonority.

The size of the interval between the adjacent tones in the sequence will affect the speed at which the sense of temporal coherence gives way to fission. In the case of a trill, when the interval separating the two alternating tones is small, around one half step, the sequence evokes temporal coherence until the alternation rate is accelerated to beyond about twenty tones per second. One then hears a "fusion" of the two tones into a single sound. However, with a sequence of tones comprised of large intervals in the general range of a 12th, even at moderate speeds the listener can split the tones into successions by register.

Alternation of two tones at high rates can produce other effects as well. Consider the rapid alternation of two tones separated by a large interval: Even when the higher tones are not equidistant in time between the lower ones, the high and low tones will sound evenly spaced. Figure 2.12 illustrates this situation. The effect would be lost at small pitch intervals.

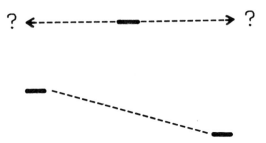

FIGURE 2.13   At large intervals and rapid speeds, it may be difficult to tell where in the three tone sequence the high note comes.

When a rapid, two-tone sequence is played at a small interval, a whole or half step, the order of the two tones is easily perceived. However, when the intervals are greatly increased, the situation becomes more complicated. To some listeners, the tones sound simultaneous, while to others, the order of the two tones is unclear. At high speeds where the tones jump between registers over large intervals, the listener loses the effect of a constant speed. The passage will appear to consist of subphrases proceeding at different rates.

The effect can be even more ambiguous in a three-tone sequence. Figure 2.13 illustrates very rapid sequences of three tones in which a wide registral span separates one tone from the other two. Even though the listener perceives the two tones in the same register as belonging to the same group, it may not be possible to determine the temporal order of the other tone.

2.6   Classical Theory of Timbre

Musical timbre is the characteristic tone quality of a particular class of sounds. Musical timbre is much more difficult to characterize than either loudness or pitch because it is such a diverse phenomenon. No one-dimensional scale—such as the loud/soft of intensity or the high/low of pitch—has been postulated for timbre, because there exists no simple pair of opposites between which a scale can be made. Because timbre has so many facets, computer techniques for multidimensional scaling have constituted the first major progress in quantitative description of timbre since the work of Hermann von Helmholtz in the nineteenth century.

Hermann von Helmholtz laid the foundations for modern studies of timbre in his book, *On the Sensations of Tone.*[15] This work contains a wealth of fundamental concepts necessary for the study of timbre. Helmholtz characterized tones as consisting of a waveform enclosed in an amplitude envelope made up of three parts: the attack, or rise time, the steady-state, and the decay, or decay time (figure 2.14). During the attack of the tone, the amplitude grows from zero to its peak. During the steady-state the amplitude is ideally constant. During the decay, the sound dies away. He concluded that sounds which evoke a sensation of pitch have periodic waveforms and further described the shape of these waveforms as fixed and unchanging with time. Helmholtz also established that the nature of the waveform has a great effect on the perceived timbre of a sound.

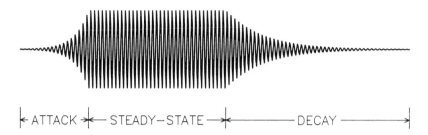

FIGURE 2.14   The three principal segments of a tone which takes the form of a simplified Helmholtz model.

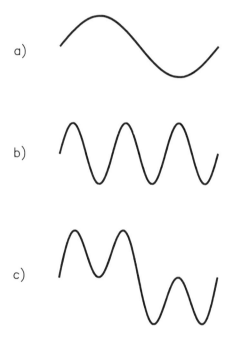

FIGURE 2.15   The addition of two sinusoids, a and b, to obtain the complex waveform, c.

   To determine which characteristics of a waveform correlate best with timbre, he made use of the work of Jean Baptiste Fourier who proved that any periodic waveform can be expressed as the sum of one or more sine waves. As an example, consider the two sine waves illustrated in figures 2.15a and b where the lower wave repeats with three times the frequency of the upper. If at every point in time (along the horizontal axis) we add the values of these waveforms together, the sum will be the entirely new periodic waveform drawn in figure 2.15c. Fourier showed that every periodic waveform is comprised of a unique set of sinusoids whose frequencies are harmonically related (see section 2.2). Thus, any waveform can also be described in terms of the sinusoidal components that it contains. Each sinusoid in the set is characterized by three parameters: frequency, amplitude, and phase relative to the fundamental (see section 1.4.). The first two parameters have a large effect on the perceived timbre of the sound. However, the phase relationships

among the sinusoids have only a minimal effect and will be discussed near the end
of this section. Spectral components are sometimes called the partials of the
waveform, and in the case of a harmonic spectrum, they can be called harmonics or
harmonic partials.

In the general case, Fourier demonstrated that any signal, regardless of
whether its waveform is periodic, can be described either by its pattern of
amplitude versus time (its waveform) or by its distribution of energy versus
frequency (its spectrum). Either form of this dual representation is sufficient to
describe the signal completely. Thus, it is common to speak of the two domains in
which a signal can be described: the time domain and the frequency domain.

The spectrum of a waveform is found mathematically by taking the Fourier
transform[16] of the waveform—a complex mathematical procedure, the specifics of
which are outside the scope of this text. However, it can be instructive for the
musician to develop a sense of the relationship between a sound's waveform and its
spectrum. Figure 2.16a illustrates the waveform of a square wave: a waveform that
spends 50% of the time at its most positive sound pressure and the other half at its
most negative sound pressure. The period of the waveform is denoted by T. The
waveform repeats at its fundamental frequency f_0 which is related to the period by
the equation that is shown in the figure. The spectrum of a square wave, shown in
Figure 2.16b, contains components that are odd harmonics of the fundamental. The
amplitudes of the components diminish with increasing harmonic number in

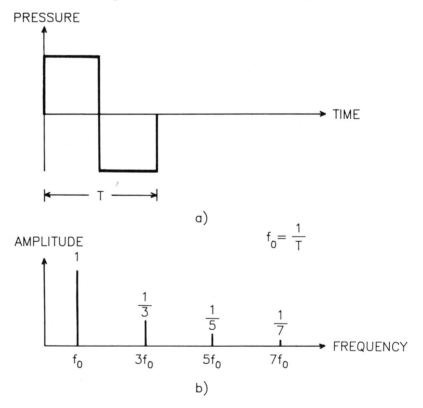

FIGURE 2.16   The waveform, a, and the spectrum, b, of a square wave. Each vertical bar
in b corresponds to a single spectral component.

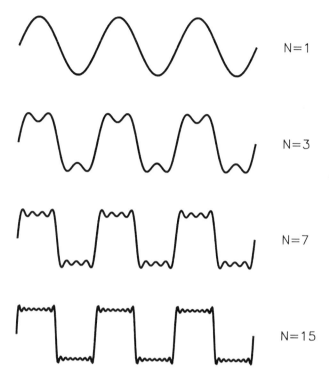

N=1

N=3

N=7

N=15

FIGURE 2.17 The waveforms produced by the addition of the first N partials of a square-wave spectrum.

proportion to the harmonic number. Thus, for example, the amplitude of the 7th harmonic is 1/7 of the amplitude of the fundamental. To demonstrate that this is indeed the spectrum of a square wave, we can build a cycle of the waveform by simple addition of the sound pressure patterns of the individual components of the spectrum. This process is called additive or Fourier synthesis. (Chapter 3 details this basic synthesis technique.) Figure 2.17 shows the results of adding the first N harmonics found in a square-wave spectrum for different values of N (i.e., the highest frequency found in the waveform is Nf_0). Observe that the higher the number of harmonics included, the more "square" the waveform becomes. Even after 15 harmonics are added together, the waveform is still not perfectly square. The reason for this is that the "perfect" square wave could exist only in a system allowing an infinite number of harmonics.

Figure 2.18 illustrates the waveforms and spectra of some other signals commonly encountered in analog electronic music studios. As might be expected, the spectrum of a sine wave is very simple. A sine wave has no harmonics, and so its spectrum contains energy only at a single frequency (figure 2.18a). Figure 2.18b shows a triangular wave and its spectrum, which contains only odd-numbered harmonics. The amplitude of the harmonics falls off with frequency in proportion to the square of the harmonic number. Thus, for example, the amplitude of the 5th harmonic is 1/25 of the amplitude of the fundamental. The spectrum of a sawtooth wave is shown in figure 2.18c. In this case, all harmonics are present and they diminish in direct proportion to the harmonic number. Figure 2.18d shows the relation between a pulse waveform, rich in harmonics, and its spectrum. The pulse

WAVEFORM   SPECTRUM

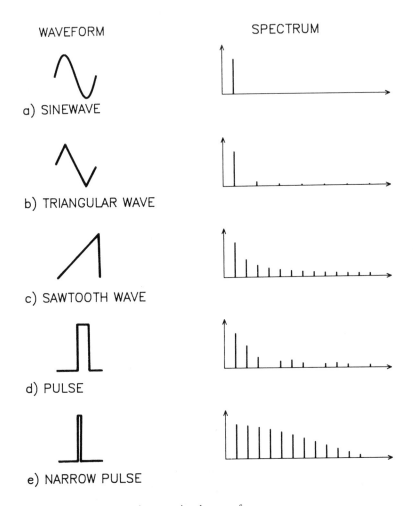

a) SINEWAVE

b) TRIANGULAR WAVE

c) SAWTOOTH WAVE

d) PULSE

e) NARROW PULSE

FIGURE 2.18   The spectra of some simple waveforms.

with the narrower width, shown in figure 2.18e, has an even richer spectrum, and hence, its energy is spread even more widely across the spectrum.

Helmholtz concluded that the spectral description of a sound has the most straightforward correlation with its timbre. As a result, almost every synthesis technique presented in this text will be concerned with the production of a signal with a specific spectral content, rather than a particular waveform. For instance, the qualitative description of "brilliant" or "bright" characterizes spectra that have a great deal of energy at high frequencies. The spectra produced by most brass instruments exhibit this trait. Sounds with extreme amounts of high-harmonic energy, such as the spectrum of the narrow pulse in figure 2.18e, sound "buzzy." A spectrum with little or no energy in the even-numbered harmonics characterizes the particular timbre that is produced by the clarinet in its low register. Most percussive sounds have spectra that are not even close to being harmonic. For example, the clangorous sound of a bell is the result of its highly inharmonic spectrum. In addition, research has shown that many pitched acoustical instruments exhibit spectra which are slightly inharmonic; that is, the overtones are slightly mistuned

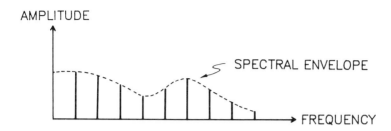

FIGURE 2.19   Graphical approximation of a spectral envelope from a spectral plot.

from exact harmonics. This causes the sensation of beating in the tone, contributing to its liveliness.

The spectral envelope of a sound is one of the most important determinants of timbre. The spectral envelope outlines the pattern of frequency distribution energy in a spectrum. The spectral envelope of a periodic waveform can be graphically approximated by connecting the tops of the bars in a plot of harmonic amplitude versus frequency. Figure 2.19 shows how a spectral envelope is approximated from a spectral plot.

Examination of the spectral envelopes of the waveforms most frequently encountered in both digital synthesis and acoustic-instrument tones shows them to be "band-limited." That is, there is a frequency above which the tones contain no significant amount of acoustic energy. (Of course, the ear is also a band-limited receiver because it can sense energy only within a certain frequency range.) The *bandwidth* of a sound is the width of the frequency region in which the significant components of a complex sound reside—one of a number of useful means of characterizing spectra. Spectra are often characterized by the steepness at which the energy in the spectrum decreases with frequency. This is known as the "rolloff" of the spectrum and is the slope of the spectral envelope. For example, the amplitude of the harmonics of a sawtooth wave (figure 2.18c) roll off in proportion to the harmonic number. Thus, the spectral envelope diminishes by a factor of 2 for each doubling in frequency. Recall from section 1.4 that halving an amplitude can be expressed as a reduction of 6 dB, and so the rolloff of a sawtooth wave is 6 dB/octave. In the triangular wave of figure 2.18b, the amplitudes of the harmonics roll off with the square of the harmonic number. In this case, doubling the frequency reduces the spectral envelope by a factor of .25 or 12 dB resulting in a slope of 12 dB/octave. Max Mathews and J. R. Pierce have observed that, "normal musical instruments tend to produce a spectrum which decreases faster than 6 dB per octave, but not as fast as 12 dB per octave."[17]

For synthesis of sound, we need a more detailed understanding of the relationships among fundamental frequency, spectrum, and timbre. If two tones with the same amplitude envelope and about the same fundamental frequency have identical relationships among their spectral components, their timbres will sound the same. However, if two tones of different fundamental frequencies have the same distribution of energy among their partials, often they will not be judged to have the same timbre. Our perception of timbral similarity is largely based on the presence of spectral energy in absolute-frequency bands. Therefore, the triangular wave in figure 2.18b will not have the same timbre in all registers. For a fundamental frequency of 50 Hz, the predominant energy of the triangular wave

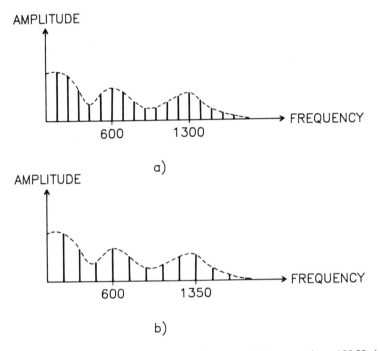

FIGURE 2.20   Spectra of tones with different fundamental frequencies—100 Hz in (a) and 150 Hz in (b)—exhibiting similar formant structures.

will be in the frequency region 50 to 450 Hz; a triangular wave with a fundamental frequency at 250 Hz will have most of its energy in the frequency region 250 to 2250 Hz.

Two tones with different fundamental frequencies which are judged to have similar timbres, will not have the same relationships among the amplitudes of the spectral components. Rather, their spectral envelopes will exhibit peaks of energy in the same frequency regions. In figure 2.20a, the spectrum of the 100-Hz tone has peaks around its sixth and thirteenth partials, i.e. around 600 and 1300 Hz. The 150-Hz tone (Figure 2.20b) has peaks around its fourth and ninth harmonics, in the same frequency regions as those of the 100-Hz tone. Given other similar characteristics, these two tones will be judged to have similar timbres. The spectral peaks in absolute frequency regions are called *formants*.

Human voices and most acoustic instruments exhibit formants in their spectra. Their characteristic sound results from a system consisting of an excitation source, such as vocal cords or a vibrating reed, and a resonating system, such as the vocal tract or a length of tubing. The resonating system causes the amplitudes of the partials occurring in certain frequency regions to be emphasized. This produces formant peaks in those regions which are related to the size, shape, and material of the resonating body. The same peaks will be present, in greater or lesser prominence, on all tones of the instrument, regardless of the fundamental frequency of the source. This explains why, in many instruments, different tones produced on the same instrument have a similar tone quality.

Figure 2.21 shows the resonances of a violin plate.[18] Notice that the resonance peaks on the violin are quite narrow. Vibrato on the violin, a quasi-periodic,

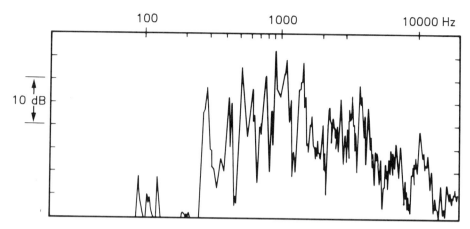

FIGURE 2.21   Response of a violin plate obtained with sinusoidal excitation. (*From "How the Violin Works" by C. M. Hutchins in* Sound Generation in Winds, Strings, Computers, *publication No. 29 of the Royal Swedish Academy of Music, edited by Johan Sundberg. Reprinted by permission of the editor.*)

relatively small change in frequency of the tone at a rate of 5 to 10 Hz, produces a very lively sound. The peaks and valleys in the curve illustrate the frequency regions at which the partials caused by the bowing action will be resonated or attenuated. This is because the resonances produce spectral changes by attenuating and emphasizing the harmonics passing through them at the vibrato rate.

Formant peaks bear a relation to the critical bands of frequency perception. Adjacent harmonics above about the fifth fall within the same critical band; therefore, the listener can judge only the relative acoustic energy present in a general region of the frequency continuum. The strengths of the individual harmonics within a critical band combine to produce the percept of a net amount of energy present in that band. Thus, when presented with a rich spectrum, a listener will usually be unable to detect the presence of a single, high-numbered harmonic other than to note its contribution to the net energy found within a particular critical band.

As stated above, each component in a harmonic spectrum is characterized not only by an amplitude and a frequency, but also by a phase measured relative to the fundamental. For example, in a spectrum made up of cosine wave components with the same phase, when the fundamental waveform reaches its maximum value, all the other harmonics are also at their peak.

The phase of the components directly affects the shape of the periodic waveform. Figure 2.22a shows a square wave approximated by summing 15 harmonics all of the same phase. Figure 2.22b shows the quite different waveshape that results from setting partials 3 and 5 to a phase of 180 degrees. (When the fundamental peaks, the third and fifth harmonics are at their most negative value.) Helmholtz observed that changing the phase of partials has, as a rule, a minimal effect on the perceived quality of the sound, even though the shape of the waveform can be radically different. Therefore, when repeated with the same frequency, the two waveforms in the figure would produce essentially the same timbre. Studies using computers to generate waveforms with spectra of arbitrary phase have confirmed that change in the phase of components produces a small

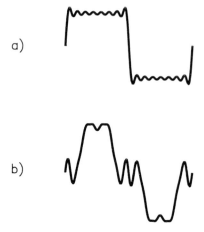

a)

b)

FIGURE 2.22   These two waveforms have the same spectral amplitudes but the phase between the partials is different. In (a) the square wave is generated with 15 partials, all of the same phase. In (b) the third and fifth partials have their phases opposite to the fundmental.

change in timbre (small in comparison with the result of changing the strengths of the harmonics). The greatest difference in timbre is between complex tones containing all sine or all cosine components and those containing alternate sine and cosine components. Still, the change in timbre is small; in one study it compared to changing the slope of the rolloff of the harmonics by between .2 and 2.7 dB per octave.[19]

2.7   Modern Studies of Timbre

The Helmholtz model of musical sound, a fixed waveform in an envelope, represents the most significant work done in the research of musical acoustics in the nineteenth century. Since then, researchers have determined a more accurate model of natural sound. Digital recording has enabled the modern researcher to show that the waveform (and hence the spectrum) can change dramatically during the course of a tone.

Almost all recent studies of timbre have been based on analysis by synthesis. With this method, the validity of any analysis can be tested by resynthesis.

As mentioned in section 2.6, the Fourier transform enables researchers to obtain the spectrum of a sound from its waveform. A computer technique which performs a Fourier transform on a digital signal is the Discrete Fourier Transform (DFT). The DFT is computationally intensive, but through a clever ordering of the computer operations involved in performing a DFT, Cooley and Tukey were able to reduce the number of computer operations significantly. Their algorithm is known as the Fast Fourier Transform (FFT).[20]

In his *Computer Study of Trumpet Tones* (1966). Jean-Claude Risset[21] employed an algorithm based on the FFT to gain information about the spectral evolution in trumpet tones. (The FFT by itself does not have sufficient resolution to accurately determine the spectrum of any arbitrary sound. However, if the fundamental frequency of the sound is evaluated prior to the application of the transform, the FFT can be made to estimate the harmonic amplitudes with relative precision. Other techniques, as described by Moorer[22], have also been used.) Where Helmholtz and other early researchers applied a Fourier transform to the steady-state portion of the tone, Risset "windowed" the samples of the trumpet tone. That is, the tone was analyzed by taking the Fourier transforms in successions of small groups of a few hundred samples. The typical window width for analysis—5 to 50 msec (i.e., 20 to 200 windows per second)—enables one to "view" the sound as a succession of short-term spectra. In this way, Risset was able to determine the time behavior of each component in the sound. He found that each partial of the tone has a different amplitude envelope. This clearly contrasts with the basic Helmholtz model in which the envelopes of all the partials have the same shape.

Risset drew the following conclusions from his analyses: The spectrum of a trumpet tone is nearly harmonic; the higher harmonics become richer as the overall intensity increases; there is a fluctuation in the frequency of the tone that is fast, small in deviation, and quasi-random; successively higher harmonics have slower rises to maximum amplitude during the attack; and there is a formant peak around 1500 Hz.[23]

Issues raised in Risset's interpretations of the trumpet analyses have been elaborated in subsequent studies. Risset observed that the evolution in time of the trumpet's spectrum plays an important part in the perception of the instrument's

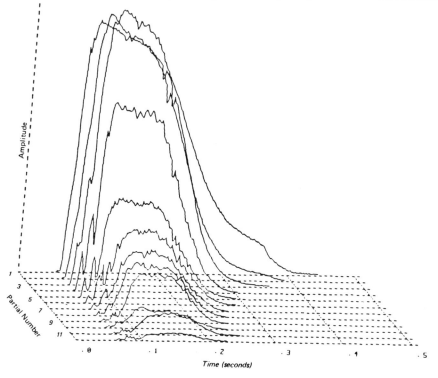

FIGURE 2.23   The amplitude progressions of the partials of a trumpet tone as analyzed by Grey and Moorer. (*Reprinted with the permission of the* Computer Music Journal.)

characteristic timbre. Others researchers following Risset have made systematic use of computer analysis to classify the spectral evolution of tones on a variety of instruments. James A. Moorer and John Grey have published computer analyses showing the evolution in time for spectra of a violin tone,[24] a clarinet tone, an oboe tone,[25] and a trumpet tone.[26] Figure 2.23 displays the spectral progression of a trumpet tone. Notice that no two partials have envelopes with the same shape. As Risset had found, the higher harmonics attack last and decay first. In addition to the amplitude progression, the analyses determined the frequency variation of each partial in the tone. It was found that the partials are rarely precise harmonics. The frequency of each partial fluctuates during the course of the tone, and this fluctuation can be particularly erratic during the attack of the tone. Resynthesis of the tone without the fluctuations in frequency produced a discernible change in the character of the tone.

The spectral progression shown in figure 2.23 contains a great deal of fine-grained detail—small fluctuations in the amplitude of a given harmonic. Can such data be simplified and still retain the character of the tone that was analyzed? To find out Grey, as Risset had done before him, approximated the amplitude variations of each partial with line segments, employing roughly eight segments per envelope. Using this simplified data, he was able to synthesize trumpet tones that were perceived to be virtually identical to the original recordings. Thus, the small, rapidly varying component of an amplitude envelope does not contribute significantly to the perception of timbre. Further, it was possible to approximate the frequency record of each partial with line segments and retain the character of the tone. In computer music, synthesis algorithms that directly recreate the partials of a tone (see section 3.7) generally use data stored as approximate line segments. This significantly reduces the amount of data required to represent a tone.

When viewing analyses such as those in the *Lexicon of Analyzed Tones*, it is important to be aware that resynthesis using the data is usually effective only within a small range of frequencies. For example, a tone based on the data but raised an octave from the original will most often not evoke the same sensation of timbre. Similarly, changing the duration often creates a different timbre. Further, patterns of spectral evolution differ markedly for differences in loudness. Risset has pointed out that, as the dynamic level increases, the higher partials of trumpet tones are raised in level relative to the other partials. For instance, the synthesis of a fortissimo tone taken from the analysis of a mezzo piano tone will generally exhibit the "volume-control effect." That is, the increase in loudness will appear to be imposed on the tone rather than the natural result of the physics of the musical instrument. Certain of the models for synthesis discussed in later chapters include provisions for change of spectral-evolution pattern with change of loudness.

When presented with a group of spectral components, a listener may or may not fuse them into the percept of a single sound. One of the determining factors is the "onset ansynchrony" of the spectrum which refers to the difference in entrance times among the components. For example, the slower rise times of the higher partials during the attack portion of a tone has been investigated by Grey and Moorer[27] and McAdams.[28] Grey and Moorer found that the onset asynchrony was typically in the range of about 20 msec. McAdams has found, for synthesized examples, that if the onset asynchrony of components exceeds 30 to 70 msec, the spectral components form a less-strong percept of fusion into a single sound.

Rudolph Rasch[29] has noticed a related phenomenon with regard to the synchronization of tones in chords in polyphonic music. He has found that a certain amount of asynchrony in starting times of chord tones actually improves our ability to perceive the individual tones while we continue to perceive the chord as a whole. Rasch has shown that the effect obtains best when the attacks of the tones are spread over a time span of 30 to 50 msec. Beyond that limiting amount of asynchrony, however, the tones no longer seem simultaneous. They are heard as appearing in a successive order.

The fluctuations in frequency of the various partials are usually necessary for the partials to fuse into the percept of a single tone. John Chowning[30] and Michael McNabb have demonstrated the importance of periodic and random vibrato in the perception of sung-vowel timbres. A demonstration tone first introduces the fundamental frequency, then adds the harmonics of the spectrum, and finally applies the vibrato to all the components. Chowning observes that it is only with the addition of the vibrato that the "tone fuses and becomes a unitary percept."

It is apparent that timbre is multidimensional. The perception of timbre involves correlating a number of factors of the tone, including the nature of the attack, the harmonic content, and the tuning of the partials. To some extent, the amplitude, pitch, and temporal aspects all contribute to our characterization of timbre. A number of researchers have sought a set of independent dimensions for timbral characterization. In recent years computer techniques for multi-dimensional scaling have aided in this research. For John Grey's study of timbre,[31] he recorded tones of 14 instruments and normalized them for identity in pitch, loudness, and duration. He then presented all possible pairs of the tones to listeners who were asked to rate the "relatedness" of the tones in the pairs. The responses were subjected to a three-dimensional scaling algorithm resulting in the three-dimensional timbral space shown in figure 2.24. (Other numbers of dimensions are possible.) A timbre space is a map of the relatedness of the tones. Tones appearing close together in the timbre space indicate listener judgement of their close timbral similarity.

Grey then examined the spectral analyses of the members of the timbral space and ascribed a salient characteristic to each of the dimensions. The x dimension (left to right) relates the synchronicity in the entrance and departure of the higher harmonics of the tones. In the winds (forward to left), there is often an entrance of harmonics in tandem; on the right (in the strings and flute), their entrance tends to be tapered.

The y dimension (up/down) correlates with the distribution of spectral energy. At the bottom of the figure, the muted trombone has the widest frequency spectrum (greatest richness); the ponticello string tone near the top has the narrowest spectral bandwidth.

Grey associates the z dimension (front/back) with the high-frequency, low-energy (often inharmonic) components in the attacks of the tones. Toward the back, the instruments that show such features—strings, flute, clarinets and saxes—are clustered. Toward the front are shown the instruments that have low-frequency inharmonicity and little or no high-frequency energy in the attack—bassoon, trumpet, and oboes.

In summary, the results of modern research into the nature of timbre offer valuable insights for the computer synthesist. Few "natural" sounds take the form

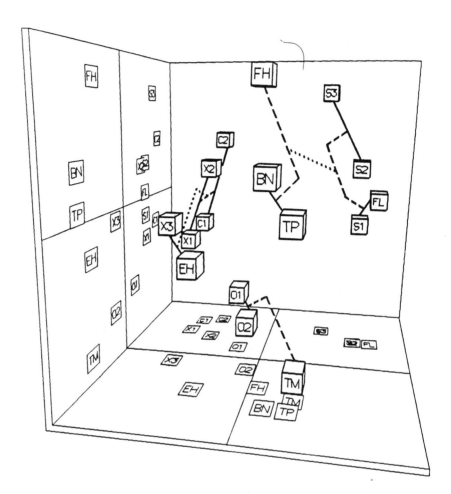

FIGURE 2.24 Grey's scaling of timbral relatedness into a three-dimensional space. (*Reprinted with the permission of John Grey.*)

of the classical model of an invariant waveform enclosed in an envelope. Instead, their spectral content varies substantially during the course of the tone. Listeners expect this characteristic in what they hear, and so an important key to synthesizing interesting sounds is the selection of algorithms that produce dynamic spectra.

Notes

1.   Roederer, Juan C. *Introduction to the Physics and Psychophysics of Music* (2nd ed.). New York: Springer Verlag, 1979, p. 21.

2.   Ibid., p. 23.

3.   Benade, Arthur H. *Fundamentals of Musical Acoustics*. New York: Oxford University Press, 1976, p. 66.

4.   Roederer, p. 27.

5.   Roederer, p. 39.

6.   Scharf, Bertram. "Critical Bands." In J. V. Tobias (ed.), *Foundations of Modern Auditory Theory* (Vol. 1). New York: Academic Press, 1970, pp. 157–202.

7. Backus, John. *The Acoustical Foundations of Music* (2nd ed.). New York: Norton, 1977, pp. 143–146.

8. Ibid., pp. 141–143

9. Roederer, p. 159.

10. Backus, p. 150.

11. Roederer, p. 81.

12. Backus, pp. 101–103.

13. Backus, p. 128.

14. Van Noorden, L. A. P. S. "Temporal Coherence in the Perception of Tone Sequences." Unpublished paper, Institute for Perception Research, Eindhoven, the Netherlands 1975.

15. Von Helmholtz, Hermann. *On the Sensations of Tone*. London: Longmans, 1885. (The original English translation by Alexander J. Ellis has been reprinted by Dover, New York, 1954.)

16. Bracewell, Ronald N. *The Fourier Transform and Its Applications* (2nd ed.). New York: McGraw-Hill, 1978.

17. Mathews, Max, and Pierce, John. "Harmonic and Non-harmonic Partials." *IRCAM Rapports 28*, 1980.

18. Hutchins, C. M. "Bowed Instruments and Music Acoustics." In Johan Sundberg (ed.), *Sound Generation in Winds, Strings, and Computers*. Stockholm: Royal Swedish Academy of Music, 1980.

19. Plomp, Reinier. *Aspects of Tone Sensation*. New York: Academic Press, 1976, p. 90.

20. Cooley, J. W., and J. W. Tukey, "An Algorithm for the Machine Computation of Complex Fourier Series." *Math Computation*, 19 (April), 1965, pp. 297–381.

21. Risset, Jean-Claude. *Computer Study of Trumpet Tones*. Murray Hill, N.J.: Bell Telephone Laboratories, 1966.

22. Moorer, James A. "On the Segmentation of Continuous Musical Sound by Digital Computer." Report STAN-M-3, Center for Computer Research in Music and Acoustics, Stanford University, 1975.

23. Morrill, Dexter. "Trumpet Algorithms for Computer Composition." *Computer Music Journal*, 1 (1), 1977, pp. 46–52.

24. Moorer, J. A., and Grey, J. M. "Lexicon of Analyzed Tones (Part I: A Violin Tone)". *Computer Music Journal*, 1 (2), 1977, pp. 39–45.

25. Moorer, J. A., and Grey, J. M. "Lexicon of Analyzed Tones (Part 2: Clarinet and Oboe Tones)". *Computer Music Journal*, 1 (3), 1977, pp. 12–29.

26. Moorer, J. A., and Grey, J. M. "Lexicon of Analyzed Tones (Part 3: The Trumpet)". *Computer Music Journal*, 2 (2), 1977, pp. 23–31.

27. Grey, John M., and Moorer, J. A., "Perceptual Evaluations of Synthesized Musical Instrument Tones." *Journal of the Acoustical Society of America*, 62, 1978, pp. 454–462.

28. McAdams, Steven. "Spectral Fusion and the Creation of Auditory Images." In Manfred Clynes (ed.), *Music, Mind, and Brain: The Neuropsychology of Music*. New York: Plenum Press, 1982.

29. Rasch, Rudolph. "Aspects of the Perception and Performance of Polyphonic Music." Doctoral dissertation, Institute for Perception TNO, Soesterberg, Netherlands, 1978.

30. Chowning, John. "Computer Synthesis of the Singing Voice." In Johan Sundberg (ed.), *Sound Generation in Winds, Strings, and Computers*. Stockholm: Royal Swedish Academy of Music, 1980.

31. Grey, J. M. "An Exploration of Musical Timbre." Doctoral dissertation, Stanford University, 1975.

3

SYNTHESIS FUNDAMENTALS

Sound synthesis is the generation of a signal that creates a desired acoustic sensation. This chapter begins with the fundamentals of signal generation and presents techniques of additive synthesis, modulation, and noise generation. Several example computer instrument designs are given along with compositional examples.

3.1 Computer Instruments and Unit Generators

In computer music, the term *instrument* refers to an algorithm that realizes (performs) a musical event. It is called upon by a computer program that is interpreting either a score stored in memory or the actions of a performer on a transducer. The instrument algorithm calculates the sample values of an audio signal using inputs, known as parameters, received from the calling program. For example, an instrument designed to play a single, simple tone might be passed parameters controlling the duration, frequency, and amplitude of the tone. Other parameters can be passed that affect other aspects of the sound. When designing an instrument, the musician determines the number and nature of the parameters to be passed. These are based on a choice of which attributes of the sound will be controlled *externally* during the generation of the sound. An instrument can also be designed to accept an audio signal in digital form as an input to be processed by the algorithm.

For both conceptual clarity and programming convenience, a complete sound-generating algorithm is usually divided into smaller, separate algorithms called *unit generators*. Each unit generator has input parameters and at least one output. Each performs a specific function of signal generation, modification, or combination. Most music languages express synthesis algorithms in terms of unit generators, using them as the building blocks with which instruments are made. The internal algorithm of each unit generator has been determined and encoded by the music-systems programmer. The musician's task is to interconnect the inputs and outputs of the unit generators to achieve the desired, overall synthesis algorithm. This is quite similar to the way in which instruments are realized on analog synthesizers by connecting (patching) various modules together. The unit generator is a useful concept because it minimizes the amount of knowledge of the inner workings of each algorithm required on the part of the musician, while retaining considerable flexibility for the construction of synthesis algorithms. Individual unit

63

generators and methods of interconnecting them will be demonstrated below in the explanation of the synthesis of specific sounds.

3.2 Signal Flowcharts

A signal flowchart, such as the example in figure 3.1, is a graphical representation of the way in which unit generators are interconnected to form an instrument. The symbols for the various unit generators will be given as they are introduced.

There are two basic rules that apply to the interconnection of unit generators: (1) An output of a unit generator may be connected to one or more input(s) of one or more other unit generator(s). Thus, an output can drive more than one input. (2) Outputs may never be connected directly together. The direct connection of outputs would result in an ambiguous situation if the unit generators provided conflicting numerical values. In the generalized unit generators of the example, the inputs go into the top of the symbol and the outputs come from the bottom of the symbol.

Outputs can be combined by mathematical operations. The most common

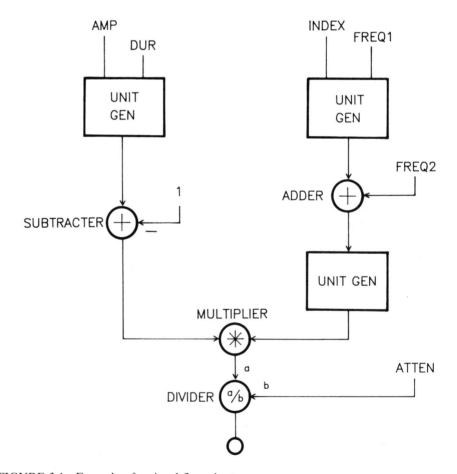

FIGURE 3.1 Example of a signal flow chart.

combinatorial operation is addition, represented in a signal flow chart by the symbol for the adder shown in figure 3.1. An adder has two or more inputs, denoted by arrows, and one output. The principal use of an adder is to mix signals together. The operation of subtraction also uses an adder. In this case, the *sign* of the subtrahend is reversed just before it enters the adder. This is indicated by a minus sign placed near the arrow connecting the subtrahend to the adder.

The signal flow chart shown in the figure includes a multiplier and a divider, as well. Multiplying a signal by a constant with a value greater than one increases the amplitude of the signal; this process is called amplification. The reverse process, attenuation, can be obtained through multiplying by a constant less than one. Multiplication and division generally take the computer substantially longer to perform than addition or subtraction; therefore, the instrument designer tries to minimize the number of these operations. The use of division requires special care. To avoid errors, the instrument designer must make certain that the divisor can never assume a value of zero. Such an error can be serious enough to cause the synthesis program to cease operation.

The parameters passed to an instrument are usually denoted in a signal flow chart by descriptive mnemonics. For example, the parameter that controls the amplitude of an instrument is often designated AMP.

Every instrument must have at least one output. The flow-chart symbol for an output is a small, empty circle located at the end the chart. There may be multiple outputs corresponding to a multi-channel audio system.

3.3   The Oscillator

The unit generator fundamental to almost all computer sound synthesis is the oscillator. An oscillator generates a periodic waveform. The controls applied to an oscillator determine the amplitude, frequency, and type of waveform that it produces. The symbol for an oscillator is shown in figure 3.2. The symbol inside the oscillator (WF in this case) designates the waveform of the oscillator. The symbol can be a mnemonic of a particular waveform or a drawing of one cycle of the waveform. The numerical value that is fed into the left input sets the peak amplitude of the signal. The numerical value applied to the right input determines the frequency at which the oscillator repeats the waveform. The frequency can be specified in one of two ways: (1) an actual number of Hertz, or (2) a sampling

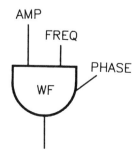

FIGURE 3.2   Flowchart symbol for an oscillator. The phase input is not often used.

increment. (Sampling increment, a number proportional to the frequency is explained below.) The input on the right side of the oscillator, PHASE, determines at which point on the waveform the oscillator begins. PHASE is usually not specified unless required for an explicit purpose. The output of the oscillator is a sequence of samples which forms a digital signal representing the waveform.

One method of implementing an oscillator algorithm specifies the waveform as a mathematical function of time. Thus, in order to generate a sine wave using this method, the algorithm would have to calculate the value of the mathematical function, sine, on every sample. This method (direct evaluation) for nearly any function is prohibitively slow.

For the sake of efficiency, most digital oscillators use a stored waveform: a waveform that is evaluated prior to the generation of any sound. The computer calculates the value of many points on a cycle of the waveform, and stores them in computer memory as a block called a wavetable. Thus, a wavetable consists of a long sequence of numbers, each corresponding to the value of successive points on the waveform. Once the waveform has been stored, the oscillator can generate sample values by simply retrieving values from the wavetable—a much faster operation for the computer than evaluating the waveform directly.

As an example, consider the wavetable in figure 3.3. It contains one cycle of a sine wave stored in 512 entries. Each entry is marked by an address, denoted in this case by the integers from 0 through 511. The oscillator algorithm maintains a numerical value, called the phase, which indicates the address of the entry currently in use. At the beginning of its operation, the oscillator is given an initial value of phase which denotes the first entry in the wavetable to be used. On every sample the oscillator algorithm obtains the current value of the phase (ϕ) and adds to it an

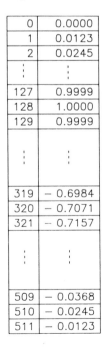

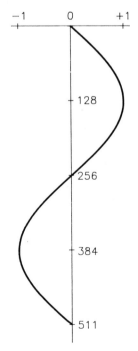

FIGURE 3.3   Wavetable containing one cycle of a sine wave.

amount that is proportional to the frequency of the oscillation. The new value of phase determines the entry used to calculate the next output sample. The amount added to the phase on every sample is called the sampling increment (SI): the distance in the wavetable between successive entries selected by the oscillator. When the value of the phase exceeds the number of the last entry in the table, it is "wrapped around" to a point near the beginning of the table by subtracting the total number of table entries from that phase. In this example, the number of the last entry in the table is 511. If $\phi=512$ after adding the sampling increment, then the oscillator algorithm would modify the phase so that $\phi=\phi - 512 = 0$, thereby returning phase to the first location of the table. Therefore, the oscillator algorithm can be thought of as scanning the wavetable in a circular fashion.

The two varieties of digital oscillator commonly encountered in computer music are the fixed sampling rate oscillator and the variable sampling rate oscillator. The remainder of this section describes the operation of the fixed sampling rate oscillator. See section 3.10 for a discussion of variable sampling rate oscillators.

Using the wavetable in figure 3.3, suppose that the sampling rate is 40 kHz and the oscillator is programmed to scan through the wavetable with a sampling increment of one; that is, one entry at a time. There are 512 entries in the table and the table contains one cycle, so it would take 512 samples to produce one cycle. Therefore, the frequency of the oscillator would be 40 kHz/512 = 78.13 Hz.

If a tone one octave higher is desired, the oscillator would be programmed to retrieve values from every other entry in the wavetable (SI=2). Because the oscillator would go through the wavetable twice as fast, there are half as many samples per cycle (256), and the frequency of the oscillator would be 40 kHz/256 = 156.25 Hz.

For a wavetable with N entries, to obtain a frequency f_0, the required sampling increment is

$$SI = N(f_0/f_s)$$

For example, if $N=512$ and the sampling rate (f_s) is 40 kHz, a 2.5 kHz signal would require a sampling increment of 32. That is, if the oscillator starts at entry zero in the wavetable, entries 0,32,64,... will be taken from the wavetable.

Of course, except for certain select frequencies, the sampling increment will not be an exact integer. For instance, with $N=512$, a 440-Hz tone at a 40 kHz sampling rate requires a sampling increment of 5.632. Suppose, in this case, that the oscillator starts at a phase equal to zero. On the first sample, it retrieves the waveform value from that location. On the next sample, the phase is 0+5.632=5.632. How does the oscillator treat a phase with a fractional part, if the entries in the wavetable are marked by integers? There are three techniques: truncation, rounding, and interpolation.

In truncation, the fractional part of the phase is ignored in determining the wavetable entry, so that in this case the value is taken from entry 5. To calculate the next phase, however, the oscillator includes in its addition the fractional part of the current phase. Thus, on the next sample, the phase is 5.632+5.632=11.264, causing the sample to be taken from entry 11.

When rounding is used, the entry taken is the value of the phase rounded to the nearest integer. Thus, for the example above, the first three wavetable values are taken from entries 0, 6, and 11, respectively. Rounding yields only a slightly more accurate waveform than truncation, and takes more computation time.

Of the three techniques, interpolation gives by far the most accurate approximation of the waveform. When a phase falls between two integer values, the waveform value is calculated as a combination of the two entries between which the phase falls. If, as above, the phase is 5.632, the oscillator algorithm interpolates the waveform value as a weighted average of entries 5 and 6. In this case, the phase is 63.2% of the distance between 5 and 6, so the waveform would be evaluated as the sum of 63.2% of entry 6 and 36.8% of entry 5. This process can be thought of as taking the waveform value on a straight line that connects the values of successive wavetable entries. Interpolation adds an extra multiplication to the oscillator algorithm and thus increases the amount of computation time.

The inaccuracies introduced in the waveform by any of the three techniques discussed previously evidence themselves as some form of noise or other unwanted signal in the sound. The amount and quality of the noise created depends on the waveform, on the table size, on the value of the sampling increment, and on the technique used. The larger the table size, the better the signal-to-noise (S/N) ratio. (See section 1.5.) Let k be related to the table size (N) by $k=\log_2 N$. For example, if $N=512=2^9$, then $k=9$. If the entries in the table are stored with sufficient precision to prevent significant quantization noise (see section 1.5.), the worst S/N ratio that can occur is given by the approximate expressions $6(k-2)$ dB for truncation, $6(k-1)$ dB for rounding, and $12(k-1)$ dB for interpolation.[1] Neglecting for a moment the S/N ratios of the data converters, an oscillator using a 512-entry table, for example, would produce tones with no worse than 42, 48, and 96 dB S/N ratios for truncation, rounding, and interpolation, respectively. The noise level resulting from a fractional sampling increment varies directly with the amplitude of the signal. Thus, S/N ratio due to this effect is the same on loud sounds as it is on soft sounds. Of course, the actual S/N ratio of a sound would be determined by combining the noise due to the data converters and the noise resulting from fractional phase.

As might be expected, the expressions above show that methods requiring more computation time or larger table size perform better. The performance of any method can be improved by increasing table size, and so the digital-oscillator designer is faced with the common compromise: computation speed versus memory size. Many computer-music systems make available both truncating and interpolating oscillators, so the musician can make the trade-off between signal quality and computation speed based on the application of a particular oscillator.

3.4   Definition of the Waveform

Generally, the musician need not directly specify a numerical value for each location in the wavetable. Ordinarily the computer music program enables a more simple method of entry: either by entering its representation versus time, or by specifying which frequency components it contains. The definition of the waveform versus time can be made by specifying the mathematical equation that relates the amplitude of the desired waveform to its phase. The waveform versus time can also be defined by a piece-wise linear means. Here, the waveform is defined by specifying a number of representative points on the waveform. These points, called *breakpoints*, are the points where the waveform changes slope. When filling the wavetable, the software connects the breakpoints with straight lines. In most programs, breakpoints are specified as a pair of numbers: phase and amplitude at that phase.

The specification of waveforms in terms of amplitude versus time can, however, sometimes lead to unexpected results. If, at the frequency at which it repeats, the waveform has any harmonics above the Nyquist frequency, they will be folded over (aliased), thereby producing unexpected frequencies in the sound. Suppose in a system with a 20-kHz sampling rate, a musician specified a sawtooth waveform (figure 3.4a) and used it in an oscillator programmed to produce a tone at a frequency of 1760 Hz. The sixth harmonic of 1760 Hz would be 10,560 Hz, which is above the Nyquist frequency of 10 kHz. Therefore, the sixth harmonic would fold over to $20,000 - 10,560 = 9440$ Hz. The seventh harmonic, expected at 12,320 Hz, would sound at 7680 Hz, and so on. Figure 3.4b illustrates the intended spectrum of the sawtooth wave and Figure 3.4c shows how unexpected components appear in the spectrum at the output of the D/A converter. A sawtooth waveform has a significant amount of energy in its upper harmonics, and so the resulting spectrum would not sound completely harmonic. Thus, to avoid foldover when specifying waveforms in terms of amplitude versus time, one should define a waveform with little significant energy in the upper harmonics.

A safer way to specify a waveform is in terms of its spectrum. Here, the instrument designer specifies the amplitude, the partial number, and, if desired, the phase of each component. The software then calculates and stores a single cycle of

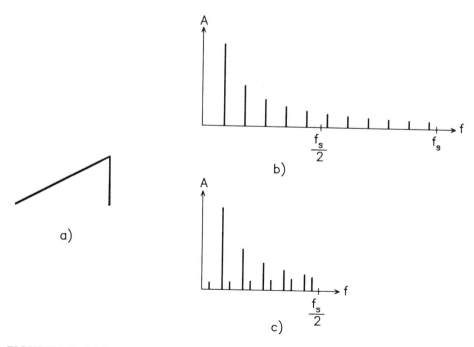

a)

b)

c)

FIGURE 3.4   (a) Sawtooth waveform; (b) its expected spectrum at a 1760 Hz fundamental frequency; and (c) its actual spectrum after conversion at a 20 kHz sampling rate.

the corresponding waveform. Often, the amplitudes of the harmonics are described relative to the amplitude of the fundamental. For instance, one could specify a waveform containing a unit-amplitude fundamental with a third-harmonic amplitude 10 dB below the fundamental and a seventh harmonic 22 dB down. When the waveform is defined in terms of spectral content, the musician easily knows the exact value of the highest harmonic contained in the spectrum. Aliasing of certain waveforms can thus be avoided by limiting the fundamental frequency of the oscillator. For example, on a system with a 40-kHz sampling rate, the fundamental frequency of an oscillator producing 10 harmonics should not exceed 2 kHz.

An oscillator with a fixed frequency samples the stored waveform with a constant sampling increment. Therefore, a periodic waveform is generated, and so the spectrum of the signal contains nothing but exact harmonics. Thus, when describing a waveform in terms of spectral content, using non-integer partial numbers will not result in a signal with an inharmonic spectrum. Suppose an instrument designer, in hopes of obtaining an inharmonic spectrum, specified a fundamental and a partial number of 2.2. When the wavetable is sampled by an oscillator, the resulting signal would be periodic, and therefore have a harmonic spectrum. Instead of generating a component at 2.2 times the fundamental, the energy expected at that frequency would be spread throughout the spectrum as harmonics of the fundamental. Usually this results in a spectrum that is not band-limited, creating the potential for foldover.

3.5   Generating Functions of Time

Chapter 2 demonstrated that the parameters of musical sound are constantly changing. Thus, the inputs to an oscillator almost always vary with time; that is, the amplitude and frequency of an oscillator are controlled by functions of time. An oscillator can be used to generate these control functions, but synthesis systems also include envelope generators and other function generators that, because they are tailored for this specific purpose, can synthesize control functions more directly.

Figure 3.5a shows one of the simplest computer instruments. The output of the envelope generator (figure 3.5b) controls the amplitude of the oscillator, so that the instrument produces a fixed waveform enclosed in the envelope (figure 3.5c).

Simple amplitude envelopes (figure 3.6) have three segments: the attack, which describes how the amplitude rises during the onset of the tone; the sustain, which describes the characteristics of the tone in its steady state; and the decay, which describes how the tone dies away. An envelope generator has at least four input parameters: rise time which is the duration of the attack segment, amplitude which sets the value at the peak of the attack, total duration of the envelope, and decay time. In addition, the shapes of the attacks and decay segments need to be specified. Depending on the type of envelope generator, this can be done in one of two ways. Some envelope generators determine the segment shape by reference to a function stored in a wavetable. In this case, the entire wavetable is scanned exactly once in the time of the segment. Other types of envelope generators have predetermined shapes. For example, several languages implement a unit generator called "linen" which realizes envelopes with strictly linear attacks and decays.

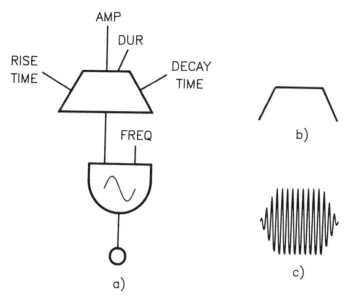

FIGURE 3.5 (a) Simple computer instrument with its amplitude envelope (b) and its output waveform (c).

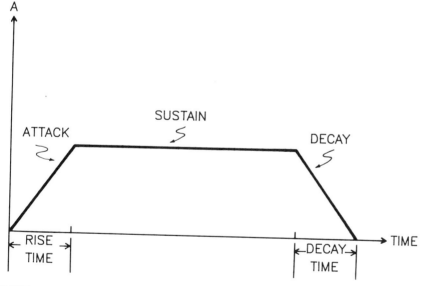

FIGURE 3.6 Simple amplitude envelope.

On many systems, an envelope generator can be used as a signal processor. A signal is applied to the amplitude input of the envelope generator. This results in an output signal that is the input signal encased in an envelope. The instrument of figure 3.7 is identical in function to that of the one in figure 3.5a. Instead of driving the amplitude input of the oscillator with an envelope, a constant (AMP) is applied. This causes the oscillator to produce a waveform with a constant amplitude. Passing

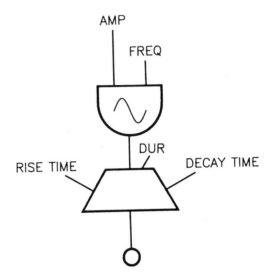

FIGURE 3.7   Another way of imparting an envelope to a signal.

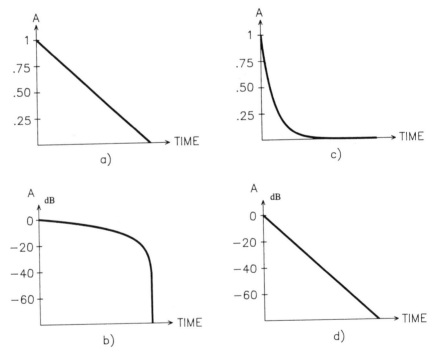

FIGURE 3.8   Decay functions: (a) linear, (b) linear in dB, (c) exponential, and (d) exponential in dB.

this signal through the envelope generator imparts a pattern of amplitude variation onto the waveform.

The shape of the attack and decay portions of the envelope has a great effect on the perceived timbre of a tone. Figure 3.8 depicts the two shapes most commonly encountered in computer music: linear (3.8a) and exponential (3.8c). Because listeners perceive amplitude on a nearly logarithmic scale, a more constant change in loudness will be obtained with an exponential shape than a linear one. Figures 3.8b and 3.8d show how each shape progresses in terms of dB. A sound with a linear decay will appear to linger on after the beginning of the decay, and then suddenly drop off near the end of the tone. The exponential decay reflects a constant change in dB versus time and thus will sound as a smooth diminution of amplitude. Natural vibrations almost always die away exponentially.

A true exponential shape can never reach exactly zero, and so on many systems, the musician must specify the maximum and minimum values of the shape. The ratio of the two is important because it sets how quickly the amplitude changes; that is, the rate of change of the segment in dB/second. If it is desired that the minimum value result in an inaudible signal, it may not be a good strategy to make the value arbitrarily small. Suppose that an exponential attack is to last .1 second and the ratio is chosen as 1:1,000,000 (120 dB). This is a rate of change of 1200 dB/second. Further assume that the system has 15-bit D/A converters, a dynamic range of about 90 dB. Depending on the amplitude of the tone, the envelope will have to rise at least 30 dB before the converter begins to produce a time-varying signal. Because the envelope rises at 120 dB/second, there will be at least a 30 dB ÷ 1200 dB/second = .025 second additional delay in the onset of the tone. Therefore, the ratio chosen should be no greater than the dynamic range of the system, in the case of 15 bits, 16,384:1.

The duration of the attack and decay segments also has a great influence on timbre. In acoustic instruments, the attack is normally somewhat shorter than the decay. A very short attack is characteristic of percussive sounds, whereas longer attacks are found in acoustic instruments, such as the organ, which produce sound by splitting a stream of air across the edge of a surface. Many acoustic instruments have longer attacks on lower pitches. Synthesizing tones with short decays and relatively long attacks produces an effect similar to playing a tape recording backwards. Of course, this may be desirable under some circumstances.

A refinement to the simple envelope generator shown in figure 3.6 is the insertion of a fourth segment between the attack and sustain. An envelope of this type (figure 3.9) is called ADSR, representing its segments—attack, decay, sustain,

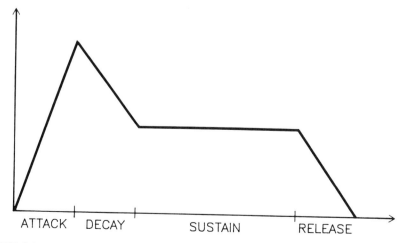

FIGURE 3.9 ADSR envelope.

and release. The ADSR shape is an attempt to imitate the envelopes found in acoustic instruments and is commonly ·used in inexpensive electronic keyboard synthesizers. Here the tone remains in the sustain state until the key is released.

Envelope generators on computer music systems vary in the complexity of the types of envelopes they can realize. In most systems, the available envelope generators permit envelopes with only two or three breakpoints. When the complexity of a desired envelope exceeds the capabilities of the available envelope generators, an oscillator can be used. Figure 3.10 illustrates the realization of an amplitude envelope in this way. The waveform of the envelope-generating oscillator is the desired envelope shape, and its frequency is chosen to be the inverse of the duration of the tone. This way, the envelope will be generated once. Musicians have also used this configuration to realize musical events that are repetitions of a tone, by programming the envelope-generating oscillator to go through several cycles during the duration of the event.

A serious disadvantage of using an oscillator instead of an envelope generator is that the attack and decay times will be altered when the duration is changed. This, unless the shape of the waveform is compensated, will cause quite noticeable differences in timbre over a range of durations.

Envelope generators synthesize functions of time which are best suited for controlling the amplitude of an oscillator. In computer music, other functions are needed to control other parameters of a sound such as the frequency variation of an oscillator. As a result, many systems implement interpolating function generators to provide greater flexibility in realizing functions of time. These are often represented on a flowchart by a rectangle with a mnemonic or picture of the function inside. In using these, the musician specifies the functions of time by listing representative points on the function. For each point a pair of numbers is given: functional value and time elapsed since the previous point. (Some systems use the convention: functional value and time elapsed since the start of the function.) During synthesis the function generator calculates values by interpolating between

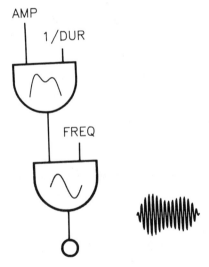

FIGURE 3.10   The use of an oscillator as an envelope generator.

the breakpoints. The interpolation can be either linear or exponential depending on the particular function generator used. For example, one could obtain a smooth glissando by specifying exponential interpolation for a function driving the frequency input of an oscillator. In this case the function values would be given as the frequencies at the end points of the glissando.

3.6 Instrument Definition in MUSIC 4-Type Languages

There are distinct approaches taken within the MUSIC 4 family of sound-synthesis languages (see section 1.3). Despite the sometimes great differences in appearance and syntax of the languages, however, experience in the use of one of them is sufficient preparation for the use of another with comparative ease. All the programs share certain common features. For example, they all use functions stored in computer memory for waveforms and other functions of time, and they include various subroutines for generating the stored functions and wavetables. They all logically separate the score and the orchestra, and all the programs except MUSIC 10 process the score in three separate "passes."

The Princeton-descended languages—MUSIC 4b, MUSIC 4BF, MUSIC 360, MUSIC 7, and MUSIC 11—have a structure that calls for the musician to supply an orchestra of instruments coded in a special language (that varies widely among them) and to provide a score, or note list. The orchestra input for these programs is in the form of statements coded in either a new language or, in the case of MUSIC 4BF, coded in FORTRAN which represent the configuration of unit generators necessary to produce the desired sounds. The score input is in the form of "notes" of data to be "played" by the orchestra program. For example, if an instrument is to include the option of playing tones of different frequencies, then the frequency would be supplied as a "parameter" value on a note statement for the instrument.

The flowchart diagrams in figure 3.11a, b, and c help to illustrate a simple point: A basic instrument design in three different MUSIC 4-type languages is almost the same. In each language the output of the envelope control unit is fed to the amplitude input of the oscillator, and the result of the oscillator is sent to the output of the instrument. In what follows, we will show the actual text that describes the three instruments of the figure in MUSIC 11, MUSIC 5, and MUSIC 4BF, respectively. The examples are intended only to demonstrate the major differences in syntax among the languages.

Coding of instruments in MUSIC 11 language[2] resembles assembly language programming. The first and last statements of the instrument definition, instr 1 and endin, respectively, mark the beginning and end of instrument number 1. The unit generators are linen (linear envelope) and oscil (oscillator). The first argument of linen, p5, indicates that the amplitude of a note played on the instrument is specified as the fifth p-field (p5) of the note statement. The subsequent arguments of the linen—rise time, duration, and decay time—are specified on the note statements as p6, p3, and p8, respectively. MUSIC 11 distinguishes between control rate and sampling rate operations. The result of the linen operation is placed into the storage location designated by the variable k1 which is calculated at the

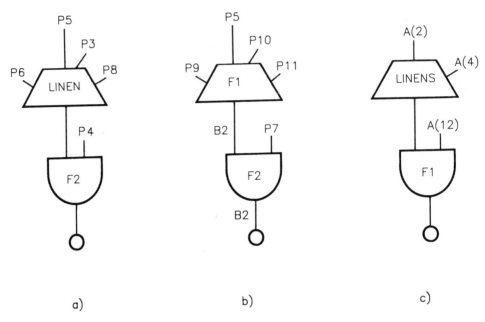

FIGURE 3.11   The simple instrument of figure 3.5 programmed in (a) MUSIC 11, (b) MUSIC 5, and (c) MUSIC 4BF.

```
instr 1
k1 linen p5,p6,p3,p8
a2 oscil k1,p4,2
out a2
endin
```

EXAMPLE 3.1   MUSIC 11 code for the instrument shown in figure 3.11a.

control rate. The position of k1 as the first argument of the oscil unit generator causes the amplitude of the oscil to be controlled by the output of linen. The frequency of the oscil is taken from p4 of the note statement. The third argument, the number of the wavetable used for the waveform of the oscil, indicates that stored wavetable number 2 will be used. The out statement's audio rate argument, a2, causes the result of the oscil operation to be sent to the output of the orchestra.

```
INS 0 4;
ENV P5,F1,B2,P9,P10,P11,P30;
OSC B2,P7,B2,F2,P29;
OUT B2,B1;
END;
```

EXAMPLE 3.2   MUSIC 5 code for the instrument shown in figure 3.11b.

Among Max Mathews' goals in the design of MUSIC 5 were for the language to be as simple to use as possible, for the program to be computationally efficient, and for it to run on any general-purpose computer system with a FORTRAN compiler. The first goal was implemented through user coding of all statements, for both orchestra and score, in the same format: a mnemonic followed by arguments. To enhance execution efficiency, the structure of the execution stage of MUSIC 5 causes each unit generator to contribute a number of successive outputs to a block of output samples. The output block in MUSIC 5 provides the means for interconnecting the unit generators: the output of every unit generator is stored in an array, called an output block, which can then be applied to the input of any subsequent generator.

The INS and END statements serve essentially the same purpose in MUSIC 5 as in MUSIC 11—to delimit the definition of the instrument. In our MUSIC 5 example, we call for instrument number 4 to be defined at time 0. The MUSIC 5 envelope generator, ENV, has seven arguments. The first is the amplitude of the envelope—here supplied by parameter 5 of the note statements for this instrument, as in our MUSIC 11 example. In MUSIC 5 a single wavetable is used to store the shapes of the rise, the steady-state, and the decay. ENV's second argument specifies the wavetable that is to be referenced for these shapes. In our example, function number 1 is used. The third argument designates B2 as the output block for the unit generator. Arguments 4, 5, and 6 are sampling increments for the rise time, steady-state time, and decay time, respectively. The actual values for these will come from p-fields 9, 10, and 11 in each note statement. The final argument of ENV is a temporary location in memory for storing the current position in the wavetable. By convention, it is designated here as the unused parameter number 30.

The first argument of OSC (oscillator), B2, interconnects the two unit generators through the output block by passing the output of ENV to the amplitude input of OSC. The second argument of OSC, its sampling increment, is obtained from P7 of the note statement. The output of the oscillator is sent to output block B2, as indicated by the third argument. The stored wavetable for the oscillator, as shown in argument number 4, is function number F2. The final argument, P29, has a function similar to the final argument of ENV—storage for a pointer to the current location in the wavetable. The OUT statement indicates that the contents of block B2 are to be assigned to output block B1 as the output for the instrument. Chapter 3 of Max V. Mathews' *The Technology of Computer Music*[3] serves as a manual of the MUSIC 5 language.

```
X=LINENS(A(2),A(4))
X=OSCIL(X,A(12),1,A(13))
CALL MONO(X)
RETURN
END
```

EXAMPLE 3.3   MUSIC 4BF code for the instrument shown in figure 3.11c.

Clearly, MUSIC 4BF has a very different appearance from MUSIC 11 and MUSIC 5. A Music 4BF instrument design is written in FORTRAN and links the unit generators as functions and subroutines. The interconnection of unit generators is expressed algebraically, as shown in the example. The use of an array, A, is a means of storing values obtained at initialization time of a note. In the first line A(2) represents the amplitude input to the LINENS (linear envelope unit). A(4) is the first location of a group of array locations containing other initialization-time values such as rise time, duration, and decay time. The input of X to the first argument of OSCIL effects the link between the output of LINENS and the amplitude input of OSCIL. As in the previous examples, the second argument of OSCIL is a frequency input, and the third argument is the number of the stored wavetable. The fourth argument, A(13), is the phase of the oscillator, performing a function similar to the final argument of MUSIC 5's OSC. CALL MONO invokes a subroutine that places the result of the oscillator, X, at the output of the instrument. Chapter 8 of Hubert S. Howe's *Electronic Music Synthesis*[4] contains a detailed description of the MUSIC 4BF program and its use.

3.7   Additive Synthesis

The simple instrument that was shown in figures 3.5 and 3.11 is the first configuration used to synthesize musical sound. It is based on a simplified Helmholtz model of musical sound, which consists of a waveform at a constant frequency enclosed in an envelope. The spectral composition of the waveform is determined from the desired steady-state spectrum of the tone, sometimes taken from a Fourier analysis.

The sound produced by this instrument differs from natural sound in two important respects. First, the amplitudes of all of the spectral components are varied equally by the envelope, so that the amplitudes of the components relative to each other do not change during the course of the tone. Thus, the sound lacks independent temporal evolution of the harmonics, an important characteristic of natural sound. Second, all the spectral components are exact-integer harmonics of the fundamental frequency, not the slightly mistuned partials that often occur in acoustically generated sounds.

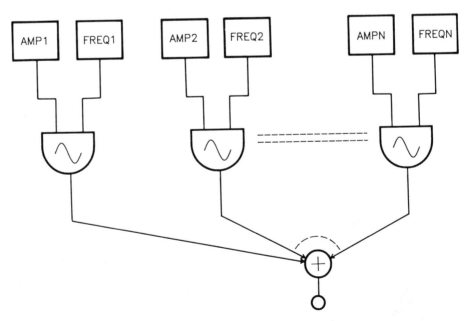

FIGURE 3.12   Basic configuration for additive synthesis. The amplitude and frequency inputs of each oscillator derive from independent function generators. In many cases the function generators take the form of envelope generators or oscillators.

As explained in chapter 2, each spectral component of a sound can be represented by its own independent amplitude and frequency functions. The synthesis of a tone based on this model (figure 3.12) requires a separate sinusoidal oscillator for each partial, with the appropriate amplitude and frequency functions applied to it. The outputs from all the oscillators are added together to obtain the complete sound. Hence, the name additive synthesis is used to designate this technique.

Additive synthesis provides the musician with maximum flexibility in the types of sound that can be synthesized. Given enough oscillators, any set of independent spectral components can be synthesized, and so virtually any sound can be generated.

The amplitude and frequency functions can be obtained from the analysis of real sounds as described in chapter 2. The name "Fourier recomposition" is sometimes used to describe this synthesis from analysis, because it can be thought of as the reconstitution of the time-varying Fourier components of a sound. Additive synthesis has proven capable of realizing tones that are "indistinguishable from real tones by skilled musicians."[5]

Of course, the instrument designer is not restricted to using functions obtained from analyses. When choosing functions, however, it is helpful to have a knowledge of the behavior of functions that describe natural sounds. For example, in many acoustic instruments the higher harmonics attack last and decay first. Knowing this, a musician might choose to synthesize an unusual sound using a set of functions with the opposite characteristic.

New, natural-sounding functions can be generated by interpolating between sets of functions that have been derived by analysis.[6] Musicians can use this technique to transform gradually the sound of one instrument into that of another. The normal way to interpolate between two functions is to take a weighted average between comparable points on each function. For example, to generate a function of time that is 30% of the way between function 1 (F1) and function 2 (F2), the new function is formed as the sum of 70% of F1 and 30% of F2. However, applying this technique to two amplitude functions that peak at different times creates a new function which lacks a single, sharp maximum. Instead, the peak of the function broadens, spread between times of the peaks of the original functions. Upon synthesis, this introduces an additional timbral element that is unrelated to either of the original sounds. To preserve a clear, single maximum and hence, more timbral similarity with the original sounds, the time at which the maximum of the new function occurs is interpolated between the times of the original functions. For example, suppose F1 peaks at .1 seconds and F2 peaks at .15 seconds. The function that is 30% of the way between F1 and F2 would peak at $.7 \times .1 + .3 \times .15 = .115$ seconds. Having established the time of the maximum, the attack portion of the new function is interpolated between the attack portions of the original functions. Similarly, the decay portion is interpolated using the decay portions of the originals.

Additive synthesis produces high-quality sound but requires a comparatively large amount of data to describe a sound, because each of the many oscillators requires two functions. A further complication arises because a given set of functions is normally useful only for limited ranges of pitch and loudness. If a set is determined by analysis for a specific pitch, then it will produce the sound quality of the original source in only a small pitch interval around that point. Any formants present in the spectrum will move directly with fundamental frequency. Thus, much of the timbral similarity between tones of different pitches will be lost. In addition, the functions are highly sensitive to dynamic level, so that a set determined for a *mezzo forte* will produce an unrealistic *pianissimo*. To fully realize the benefits of additive synthesis, it is necessary to have either a large library of function sets or a complex scheme for altering a function set on the basis of pitch and amplitude during performance.

An advantage of additive synthesis is that it provides complete, independent control over the behavior of each spectral component. However, such a large number of controls on the timbre can make it difficult for the musician to achieve a particular sound. A practical disadvantage of additive synthesis is that it requires a large number of unit generators. When synthesizing complex sounds, it is not unusual to employ ten or more oscillators with their associated function generators in the synthesis of a single voice. This differs from the synthesis techniques presented in subsequent chapters, which use fewer unit generators.

3.8   Modulation

Modulation is the alteration of the amplitude, phase, or frequency of an oscillator in accordance with another signal. Modulation has been used for many years in radio communications to transmit information efficiently. Musicians have exploited various modulation techniques in electronic music to create distinctive sounds efficiently.

The oscillator that is being modulated is called the carrier oscillator. When there is no modulating signal, it generates a continuous waveform called the carrier wave. When modulation is applied, the carrier wave is changed in some way. The changes are in sympathy with the modulating signal, so that the output of the carrier oscillator may be thought of as a combination of the two signals. The nature of this combination depends on the modulation technique used and will be examined below.

The spectral components of a modulated signal are classified into two types: carrier components and sidebands. The frequency of a carrier component is determined only by the frequency of the carrier oscillator. The frequency of a sideband is determined by both the carrier frequency and the frequency of the modulation.

3.8A   Amplitude Modulation

There are three main techniques of amplitude modulation: "classical" or "straight" amplitude modulation, ring modulation, and single-sideband modulation. The letters AM are most often used to denote the first type.

Figure 3.13 diagrams an instrument that implements classical amplitude modulation (AM). The carrier oscillator has a constant frequency of f_c and the modulating oscillator a frequency of f_m. For this example, the waveform of each oscillator is a sinusoid. The output from the modulating oscillator is added to a value that expresses the amplitude the carrier oscillator would have, if there were no modulation. The amplitude of the modulating oscillator is expressed as a

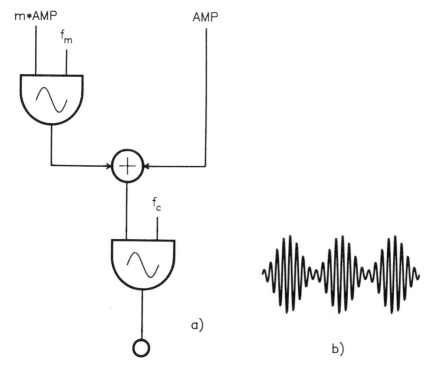

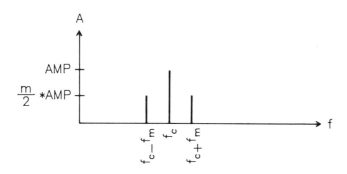

FIGURE 3.13   Simple instrument (a) which implements amplitude modulation and its output waveform (b).

FIGURE 3.14   Spectrum of the AM signal produced by the instrument of figure 3.13.

proportion of the unmodulated amplitude of the carrier oscillator. This proportion is denoted by the variable m, which is called the modulation index. When $m=0$, there is no modulation and the carrier oscillator generates an unmodulated sinusoid. When m is larger than zero, the carrier wave will take an envelope with a sinusoidal variation (figure 3.13b). When $m=1$, the amplitude of the modulating oscillator equals the unmodulated amplitude of the carrier oscillator and 100% modulation is said to take place.

   When both the carrier and modulating waveforms are sinusoids, the spectrum of an AM signal (figure 3.14) contains energy at three frequencies: the carrier frequency (f_c) and two sidebands (f_c+f_m and f_c-f_m). The amplitude of the component at the carrier frequency does not vary with the modulation index. The amplitude of each sideband is a factor of $m/2$ less than the amplitude of the carrier, showing that the modulation process splits the energy between upper and lower sidebands. For example, when $m=1$, the sidebands will have one-half the amplitude of the carrier, and therefore be 6 dB below the level of the carrier.

The frequency of the modulation determines how a listener perceives the AM sound. If f_m is less than about 10 Hz, the ear will track the individual amplitude variations. When f_m is greater than 10 Hz, but small enough that the carrier and both sidebands fall within the same critical band, the tone will sound with a loudness proportional to the average amplitude of the modulating waveform. A value of f_m which exceeds one-half the critical band causes the sidebands to be perceived individually, creating the sensation of additional loudness.

Musicians have used amplitude modulation to create electronic "tremolo" by using a small modulation index and sub-audio modulating frequency. When the modulation index is large (e.g., $m=1$), a markedly pulsating sound will be produced.

3.8B   Ring Modulation

When modulation is applied directly to the amplitude input of a carrier oscillator, without being added to a value representing the amplitude of an unmodulated carrier, the process created is known as ring modulation. Other names for it are balanced modulation and double-sideband (DSB) modulation. Figure 3.15 illustrates the signal flow chart for an instrument where one oscillator ring modulates another. The amplitude of the carrier oscillator is determined only by the modulating signal, so that when there is no modulation, there is no carrier wave

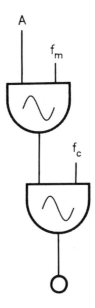

FIGURE 3.15   Simple instrument which implements ring modulation of one oscillator by another.

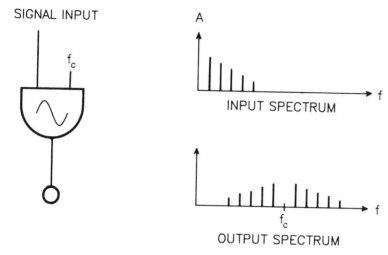

SIGNAL INPUT

A

f_c

INPUT SPECTRUM

f

f_c

OUTPUT SPECTRUM

f

FIGURE 3.16   Alteration of the spectrum of a signal by ring modulation.

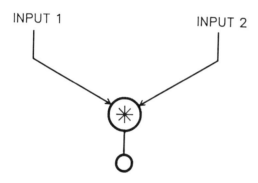

INPUT 1   INPUT 2

FIGURE 3.17   A multiplier as a general purpose ring modulator.

and, in turn, no output from the instrument. This is a notable departure from the configuration used in the AM technique described above.

Although ring modulation operates on the amplitude of the carrier, it is most often used to alter the frequency of a sound. When both the carrier (f_c) and modulating (f_m) signals are sinusoidal, the spectrum of the modulated signal contains only two frequencies: f_c+f_m and f_c-f_m. In other words, there are sidebands but no carrier. Because neither f_c nor f_m appears directly in the spectrum, the frequency of the sound can be quite different. For example, if $f_m=440$ Hz and $f_c=261$ Hz, the resulting spectrum contains energy only at 179 Hz and 701 Hz, frequencies that are not harmonically related to the originals, or to each other. If the amplitude of the modulating signal in figure 3.15 is A, both sidebands have amplitudes of $A/2$.

The frequencies in a sound that is applied directly to the amplitude input of an oscillator (figure 3.16) are changed by ring modulation. Suppose a speech sound with a fundamental frequency of 100 Hz ring modulates a sinusoidal oscillator with a frequency of 1123 Hz. The sound that emerges contains the sum and difference between each harmonic of the speech and 1123 Hz. Thus, the spectral component that was the fundamental of the speech sound is output at both 1023 Hz and 1223

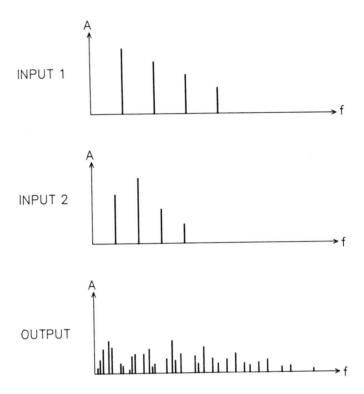

FIGURE 3.18   Ring modulation of two signals to produce a dense spectrum.

Hz, the former second harmonic (originally at 200 Hz) appears at 923 Hz and 1323 Hz, and so on. The formerly harmonic speech now sounds inharmonic and may not be intelligible.

When two signals are combined by multiplication, the result is ring modulation. Thus, the multiplier shown in figure 3.17 is a general-purpose ring modulator. Two signals are often combined this way for the purpose of frequency alteration. Suppose that two sinewaves, with amplitudes A_1 and A_2 and frequencies f_1 and f_2, respectively, are multiplied together. The resulting spectrum will contain the frequencies of f_1-f_2 and f_1+f_2, and the amplitude of each component will be $A_1 \times A_2/2$. Observe that if either signal has an amplitude of zero, there will be no output from the modulator. Composers such as Jean-Claude Risset (see section 3.12) and James Dashow[7] have used this form of ring modulation for the creation of chordal structures.

The multiplication of two complex sounds produces a spectrum containing frequencies that are the sum and difference between the frequencies of each component in the first sound and those of each component in the second. If there are p components in the first sound and q components in the second, as many as $2pq$ components can appear in the output. Thus, multiplication can be used to create dense spectra. For example, if two signals, each with 4 components, are multiplied together (figure 3.18), the resulting sound will have as many as 32 components. There would be fewer components if the two signals were harmonically related. In this case some of the sidebands will have the same frequencies, reducing the overall number of observed spectral components. To avoid aliasing, it

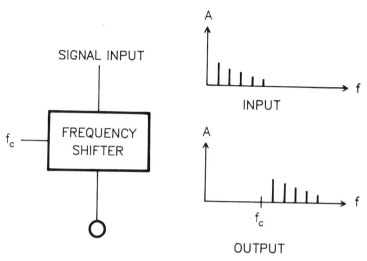

FIGURE 3.19   A frequency shifter, its input, and its output.

should be noted that the highest frequency produced by this process is the sum of
the highest frequency contained in the first sound and the highest in the second.

3.8C   Single-Sideband Modulation

Single-sideband modulation results in frequency shifting. When a sound is passed
through a frequency shifter (figure 3.19), a constant (f_c) is added to the frequency
of each component in the sound. Shifting is not the same as transposition, because
shifting destroys the relationships between the intervals in the sound. Like ring
modulation, shifting is a way to make a harmonic spectrum inharmonic, but unlike
ring modulation, it does not increase the number of components in the sound.

In frequency shifting, the input signal modulates a carrier oscillator located
inside the shifter with a modulation technique known as single-sideband (SSB)
modulation. Whereas ring modulation produces sidebands on both sides of the
carrier, SSB modulation, in theory, produces only upper sidebands (f_c+f_m) or only
lower sidebands (f_c-f_m), as selected by the user. The effect is to add or subtract
every component of the input signal from the frequency of the carrier oscillator
(f_c).

SSB modulators are fairly complicated technically. It is not possible to build or
program one that realizes perfect SSB modulation over a wide range of input
frequencies. The output from actual frequency shifters contains some energy at the
opposite sideband, good shifters suppress the opposite sideband throughout the
audio range to at least 40 dB below the sideband desired.

3.8D   Vibrato Simulation by Frequency Modulation

When a modulating signal is applied to the frequency input of a carrier oscillator,
frequency modulation occurs. Vibrato, a slight wavering of pitch, can be simulated
using the instrument in figure 3.20. The carrier oscillator generates a tone at the
specified amplitude and frequency (f_c), and the vibrato oscillator varies that
frequency, at the vibrato rate, by a maximum amount equal to the vibrato width.

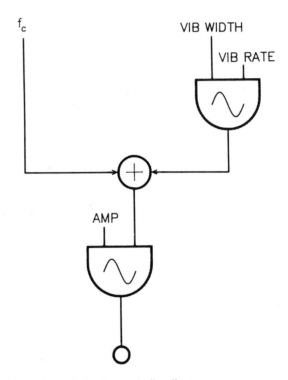

FIGURE 3.20   Simulation of simple, periodic vibrato.

Thus, the instantaneous frequency of the carrier oscillator changes on every sample, varying between f_c plus the vibrato width and f_c minus the vibrato width. Its average frequency is f_c.

In nearly every sound the vibrato width varies with the average frequency. It is usually specified as a proportion of the fundamental frequency of the tone and is ordinarily no more than a few percent of f_c. In order for the frequency modulation to be perceived as vibrato, the vibrato rate must be restricted to frequencies below the audio range. The vibrato found in natural sounds can be quite complex. It often changes during the course of a tone and frequently contains a certain amount of randomness. Chapter 6 will discuss one of the more complicated forms of natural vibrato, that of the singing voice.

When a large vibrato width at an audio rate is used, the aural effect is no longer that of a simple vibrato. In this case, frequency modulation is a powerful synthesis technique capable of producing a wide variety of timbres. Chapter 4 will cover applications of frequency modulation synthesis in detail.

3.9   Noise Generators

An oscillator is designed to produce a periodic waveform with well-defined spectral components. The spectrum is a discrete spectrum; that is, the energy is found at specific frequencies. The opposite of a discrete spectrum is a distributed spectrum, in which energy exists everywhere within a range of frequencies. Most of the noise

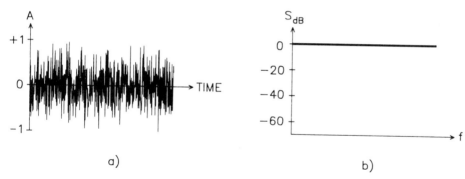

FIGURE 3.21   (a) Segment of the waveform of white noise and (b) the spectrum of ideal white noise.

sounds found in nature have distributed spectra, and thus algorithms designed to generate distributed spectra are called noise generators.

Certain phenomena have the characteristic that their repeated occurrence, even under the same set of conditions, will not always lead to the same result. Members of this class are called random phenomena. Even though the exact outcome cannot be predicted, they exhibit a certain amount of statistical regularity that can be used to describe them and to predict the probability of any given occurrence. The statistical characterization of a random signal is used to determine its frequency content. (Additional explanation of random processes can be found in chapter 8.)

In sound synthesis, randomness is used to generate distributed spectra. In the waveform in figure 3.21a, there appears to be a random distribution of the amplitude of the sample values. This is a picture of a segment of the waveform of white noise. The amplitude of white noise is characterized by a range—the interval within which the maximum and minimum sample values occur. In the figure, the range is −1 to +1. Notice that, unlike a periodic waveform, a repeating pattern of samples cannot be indentified. Thus, signals of this type are referred to as aperiodic. White noise has a uniformly distributed spectrum as shown in figure 3.21b. Between any two frequencies a fixed distance apart, there is a constant amount of noise power. For instance, there is the same amount of noise power in the band between 100 Hz and 200 Hz, as there is between 7900 Hz and 8000 Hz. White noise makes the "hissing" sound often associated with noise generated by electronic means.

The unit generator that produces nearly white noise is often called RAND and has an amplitude input. Its symbol is shown in figure 3.22a. The amplitude input sets the range of the permissible output sample values and hence the amplitude of the noise. If a value AMP is applied to the input, the noise will range between $-AMP$ and $+AMP$.

One would expect an algorithm designed to generate white noise simply to draw a random number on each sample. This makes a good, but not perfect, white-noise source. The spectral distribution of such a generator is shown in figure 3.22b. It deviates slightly from a uniform distribution because of a frequency bias inherent in the process of sample generation. The actual spectral distribution $S(f)$ at frequency f is given by

$$S(f) = \frac{\sin\,[\pi(f/f_s)]}{\pi(f/f_s)}$$

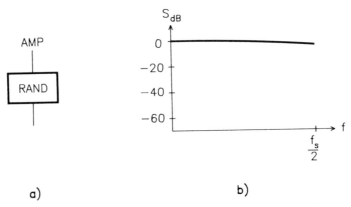

a)   b)

FIGURE 3.22   Digital "white" noise generator (a) and its spectrum (b).

At half the sampling rate, the power is down less than 4 dB from a uniform distribution.

White noise has a very large bandwidth. Sometimes it is desirable to narrow the bandwidth by reducing the amount of high-frequency energy in the noise. A noise source with most of its power at low frequencies will make a rumbling sound. An algorithm that synthesizes this kind of spectrum draws random numbers at a rate less than the sampling rate. The unit generator that accomplishes this is often called RANDH (figure 3.23a) and has two inputs: amplitude and the frequency (f_R) at which random numbers are drawn. (On some systems, the frequency is not specified directly, but by a number proportional to f_R, in the same way that sampling increment is proportional to the frequency of an oscillator.) Choosing random numbers at a rate lower than f_s implies that a random number is held for a few samples, until the next one is to be drawn. For example, if $f_s = 40$ kHz and $f_R = 4$ kHz, the algorithm chooses a random value, outputs it for the next 10 samples, and then chooses another.

When noise is generated by this process, many of the samples are related to each other because their value is the same as the previous sample. This relatedness reduces the noise power in the higher frequencies. The lower the frequency f_R, the smaller the amount of high-frequency energy that will be contained in the noise.

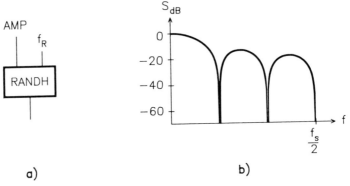

a)   b)

FIGURE 3.23   Digital noise generator (a) in which noise samples are generated at a rate lower than the sampling rate and its spectrum (b).

Thus, f_R can be thought of as a control on the "bandwidth" of the noise. Figure 3.23b illustrates the spectrum when $f_R=f_s/6$. The shape of the spectrum in the general case is given by

$$S(f) = \frac{\sin [\pi(f/f_R)]}{\pi(f/f_R)} \cdot \frac{\sin [\pi(f/f_s)]}{\pi(f/f_s)}$$

A variation on this technique, one that provides noise spectra with even better attenuation of the high frequencies, involves interpolation. As before, random numbers are drawn at a rate (f_R) that is lower than the sampling rate. Instead of holding the value of the last random number until the next one is drawn, the samples in between draws are interpolated linearly between successive random numbers. This can be visualized as connecting successive random numbers with straight lines. The unit generator that performs this algorithm is often called RANDI (figure 3.24a).

Figure 3.24b illustrates the spectrum of such a noise generator when $f_R = f_s/6$. Observe the diminished amount of high-frequency energy. The general shape of the spectrum is given by

$$S(f) = \frac{\{1 - \cos [2\pi(f/f_R)]\}f_R^2}{2\pi f f_s \sin [\pi(f/f_s)]}$$

It is possible to realize noises with other types of spectral distribution such as $1/f$ noise (see section 8.1F), where the spectrum is distributed in inverse proportion to the frequency. Other techniques, such as the one proposed by Siegel, Steiglitz, and Zuckerman,[8] are available for generating random signals with specifiable spectral densities.

How does the computer, which is designed to store and process numbers accurately and reproducibly, obtain seemingly unpredictable random numbers? One way is to sample an external random physical process such as thermal noise, but this requires additional hardware. A less expensive and more commonly used approach is to employ an algorithm called a pseudo-random number generator[9] which produces a sequence of numbers that satisfy most of the criteria for randomness, with the notable exception that the sequence repeats itself. It is possible to make the period of the sequence so long that for most purposes it can be considered random. A pseudo-random number generator actually creates a

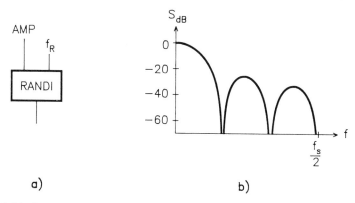

a)   b)

FIGURE 3.24   Interpolating noise generator (a) and its spectrum (b).

discrete harmonic spectrum, but the spectrum is so extraordinarily dense that, for most musical applications, it is indistinguishable from a truly distributed one.

Pseudo-random number generators generally use the most recently generated random number as a basis for calculating the next. As a result, most algorithms give the user the option of specifying a "seed" value. When a seed is specified, the first random number will be calculated on the basis of the seed value. Therefore, starting from the same seed will always yield the same sequence of random numbers. This means that two different computer runs involving the generation of pseudo-random numbers can be made to have exactly the same results.

3.10 Oscillators with Variable Sampling Rates

The method described in section 3.3 for implementing an oscillator uses a fixed sampling rate—a sampling rate that remains unchanged regardless of the frequency of oscillation. Another technique uses a variable sampling rate, so that the sampling frequency varies with the frequency of oscillation. In this method, the sampling increment is set to a fixed integer value (usually one) and the sampling frequency is selected to give the appropriate frequency of oscillation. To obtain the frequency f_0 from a variable-sampling-rate (VSR) oscillator that references a wavetable containing N entries using a sampling increment of one, the sampling frequency must be

$$f_S = N(f_0/SI)$$

In most VSR oscillators, tones in the higher octaves are synthesized by choosing the sampling increment equal to a power of 2. However, the sampling frequency still varies among notes in a given register.

When the sampling rate varies, so does the Nyquist frequency, implying that the low-pass filter on the output of the D/A converter should have a movable cutoff frequency to eliminate components above half the sampling rate. Without the movable filter, low-pitched tones generated by a VSR oscillator have an unmistakable, high-pitched, non-harmonic whine in the background. This can be avoided, however, by using a very large wavetable.

VSR oscillators are usually implemented in specialized, real-time hardware. They have two advantages: (1) there are never any errors due to a fractional sampling increment, and (2) any quantization "noise" is harmonically related to the signal being generated and hence, is noticeable only as a small amount of harmonic distortion. A disadvantage of using VSR systems is that, in most instances, the vocabulary for sound synthesis using variable-sampling-rate systems is restricted to the capabilities of function generators and oscillators: a variable sampling rate makes it more difficult to implement certain algorithms such as those for digital filtering or reverberation.

3.11 Instrument Designs

Each of the chapters of this book in which sound synthesis techniques are discussed includes a number of instrument designs. Because it is anticipated that the readers will be using a variety of musical programming languages, we have used flow charts to express the instrument designs. The instrument designs are offered as a guide to what has been done with a particular sound synthesis technique. The instrument designs are neither exhaustive nor definitive, they are simply offered here as a starting point for the reader to develop a personal vocabulary of designs for computer synthesis.

3.11A   Translating Flow Chart Diagrams into Music Synthesis Code

Translating flow chart diagrams into written instrument definitions is a task that many musicians find initially difficult. Following is a general guide to the process. It is divided into two stages: analysis of the flow chart and coding of the instrument.

There are three steps involved in analyzing a flow chart. The first step is to find the output or outputs from the instrument. This helps to show the basic structure of the instrument. Step two consists in designating the separate branches and subranches of the instrument. By doing this, the musician divides the instrument into its component parts in order to know how to direct the flow of the signal from one unit generator to the next. In step three, the musician finds the sources for all the inputs and the destinations of the outputs of all the branches of the instrument.

When starting to encode the instrument design into the sound synthesis language, it is essential to make certain that the use of all the unit generators in the design is understood as well as the meaning of their inputs and outputs. Consult the manual for the particular sound synthesis language to be sure. Start the encoding with the uppermost unit generator either in the flowchart or in a branch of the flowchart. Write out the unit generator name, label its output (if appropriate in the language used), and fill in its inputs from the initialization values. It is good practice for most sound synthesis languages to list the initialization values in a separate section at the head of the instrument.

Next, follow the same procedure for the subsequent unit generators of the branch or sub-branch until the instrument is coded completely. Keep in mind that inputs of unit generators to which the outputs of other unit generators are connected ordinarily get their values at performance time. Inputs not fed from other unit generators obtain their values at initialization time.

After all the branches of the instrument are encoded, interconnect them by means appropriate to the language used. Finally, direct the results of the instrument into the output(s) by means of an output statement.

Following are some hints for proofreading the code that describes an instrument: (1) check that no unit generators have been omitted; (2) make certain that all unit generators inputs are of the correct form (for example, that an input expecting a frequency in Hz is not given frequency in some other notation); (3) make sure that all unit generators are given the required number of inputs; (4) check to be certain that all stored functions referred to by the unit generator have the right contents.

Common mistakes in instrument coding include sending the output of one unit generator to the wrong input of the next, or sending it to the wrong unit generator entirely. Be meticulous in checking every input of every unit generator and in carefully labeling the branches of the instrument. Ample comments should appear at the head of the instrument to identify its function and characteristics.

After encoding the instrument design, check the code for correct syntax by invoking the orchestra translation program. The translator will make a trial translation of the code into machine language and give error messages if the syntax is faulty. Next, the musician should try out the instrument on a few typical notes in order to hear whether the instrument does what is wanted. It is possible, and indeed common, for a design to be syntactically correct but not to give the desired results. The trial tones will also be helpful in establishing the limits of the instrument's usefulness. Most instruments show great differences in sound depending on such factors as note length, register, and amplitude.

Finally, the instrument must be tested in a musical context to find out whether it is appropriate for the musical articulation desired. At this point such issues as the balance of the instrument with copies of itself in different registers, the balance of the instrument with other instruments in the same and other registers, and masking become important. It is often necessary at this point to recast parts of the instrument to fit the demands of the context in which it will be used.

3.11B Instrument Design Examples

Our first instrument design uses ring modulation to produce a band of noise. Controls on both the center frequency and the width of the band are provided. While more focused noise spectra can be synthesized by filtering white noise (see section 5.8), this method is both efficient and useful for many musical purposes.

As shown in figure 3.25, a noise generator ring modulates a sinusoidal oscillator. This process translates the noise generator's low-frequency noise to a higher frequency region, centering the noise band at the frequency (FREQ) of the oscillator. The amplitude input to the noise generator (AMP) directly controls the amplitude of the noise band. The frequency at which the random noise is generated, f_R, determines the bandwidth of the noise (see section 3.9). If the

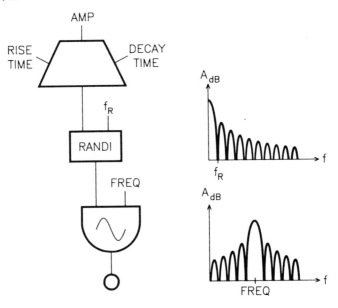

FIGURE 3.25   Generation of noise bands by means of ring modulation.

bandwidth is sufficiently small, the noise will be perceived as pitched. A noise band with a width of 20% of the center frequency will produce a good sensation of pitch. A noise band with a bandwidth of 5% of the center frequency will sound less "noisy" and have a highly focused pitch. A glissando of a noise band can be synthesized by programming the oscillator to glissando. James Tenney realized the glissandoing noise bands of his *Noise Study* in this way.[10]

Figure 3.26 shows another use of a noise band created with random ring modulation. Jean-Claude Risset used this technique to simulate the sound of the snares in a drum instrument.[11] The three oscillators each contribute different components at different amplitudes. The decay of F2 is steeper than that of F1,

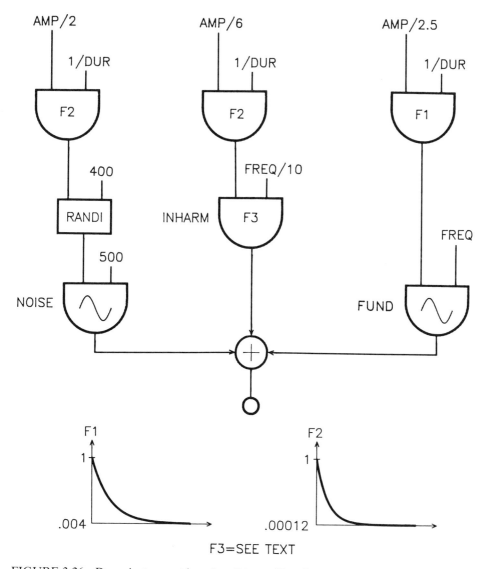

FIGURE 3.26 Drum instrument based on Risset. (*Based on example in Risset's* Introductory Catalogue of Computer Synthesized Sounds. *Reprinted with permission of Jean-Claude Risset.*)

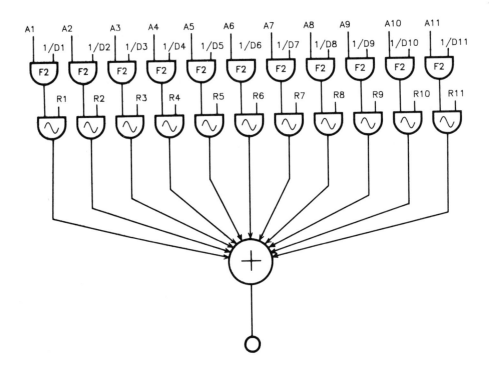

Amplitudes		Durations		Frequencies	
A1	AMP	D1	DUR	R1	FREQ*.56
A2	AMP*.67	D2	DUR*.9	R2	FREQ*.56+1
A3	AMP	D3	DUR*.65	R3	FREQ*.92
A4	AMP*1.8	D4	DUR*.55	R4	FREQ*.92+1.7
A5	AMP*2.67	D5	DUR*.325	R5	FREQ*1.19
A6	AMP*1.67	D6	DUR*.35	R6	FREQ*1.7
A7	AMP*1.46	D7	DUR*.25	R7	FREQ*2.
A8	AMP*1.33	D8	DUR*.2	R8	FREQ*2.74
A9	AMP*1.33	D9	DUR*.15	R9	FREQ*3
A10	AMP	D10	DUR*.1	R10	FREQ*3.76
A11	AMP*1.33	D11	DUR*.075	R11	FREQ*4.07

FIGURE 3.27   Bell instrument based on Risset. (*Based on example in Risset's* Introductory Catalogue of Computer Synthesized Sounds. *Reprinted with permission of Jean-Claude Risset.*)

so that the two oscillators on the left side (labeled NOISE and INHARM), which contain the higher frequency components of the sound, die away sooner than the oscillator on the right (FUND). The latter oscillator samples a stored sine tone producing a tone at the fundamental frequency. The INHARM oscillator samples a stored waveform (F3) consisting of partials 10, 16, 22, and 23 with relative amplitudes 1, 1.5, 2, and 1.5, respectively. When the frequency of the INHARM oscillator is set to 1/10th that of the FUND oscillator, its partials sound at 1, 1.6, 2.2, and 2.3 times the frequency of the fundamental, producing in this way a group of partials that is non-harmonic to the fundamental.

Risset has employed additive synthesis in a number of his works to produce bell-like sounds. A design based on one of the bell sounds of the *Computer Sound Catalog*[12] is shown in figure 3.27. The three principal features that contribute to the bell-like sound are: (1) non-harmonic partials, (2) decay times of the partials roughly inversely proportional to their frequency, and (3) beating of pairs of components, slightly mistuned, on the lowest two partials.

Risset points out that while the partials are inharmonic, they are not tuned arbitrarily. The first five partials of bell tones approximate the following: a fundamental, a minor third, a perfect fifth, a "hum tone" at an octave below the fundamental, and the "nominal" at an octave above the fundamental. The ratios in frequency for this grouping of partials are 1:1.2:1.5:0.5:2. In Risset's design, he extends the series to include higher partials, and tunes the partials to the following ratios— .56:.92:1.19:1.70:2:2.74:3:3.76:4.07.

The waveform of each component is a sinusoid and the envelope (F2) is an exponential decay from 1 to 2^{-10}. The duration used in the *Sound Catalog* is 20 seconds. When implementing the design suggested in the figure, it is advisable to use a method of "turning off" the oscillator pairs after their playing time has elapsed, in order to save computation time.

Another of Risset's designs from the *Computer Sound Catalog* is shown in figure 3.28. It represents a computer instrument that produces an "endless glissando," or Shepard tone. Psychologist Roger Shepard discovered that the apparent register of tones in musical scales could be made ambiguous by carefully controlling the amplitude of the partials of the tones. Shepard produced scales that were perceived as "circular" in pitch—while appearing to move continuously in one direction along the scale, they actually never left the register in which they began. Risset extended this principle to achieve the same effect with glissandoing tones as well.

The design is a highly controlled glissando configuration in which 10 interpolating oscillators track the same amplitude and frequency functions. Each sinusoidal oscillator is controlled by two interpolating oscillators sampling amplitude and frequency functions, respectively. The function F3 which controls the frequency is exponential. This produces a constant change of musical interval per unit time. F3 decays from 1 to 2^{-10}, producing a frequency change of 10 octaves over its duration. Each pair of controlling oscillators has the same initial phase. However, their phase is offset by $\frac{1}{10}$ of a cycle from the phase of a neighboring pair. This corresponds to a phase offset of 51.2 when using a wavetable of 512 locations. Because F3 exponentially decays from 1 to 2^{-10}, the phase offset of $\frac{1}{10}$ cycle results in the 10 oscillators glissandoing downward in parallel octaves. When an oscillator reaches the end of F3, it "wraps around" to the beginning of the function and continues. Ordinarily such a large discontinuity in frequency (a 10 octave jump) would cause a click and destroy the effect of smooth glissandoing. However, during the transition, the amplitude function F2 is at its minimum value, preventing our hearing the click. On the other hand, when a tone passes through the midrange, F2 greatly emphasizes it. The effect of summing the 10 sinusoidal oscillators together is that of a continually glissandoing tone in which no change of register occurs.

Risset has observed that the computer must have sufficient word length to accurately represent the phase in order to prevent noticeable roundoff error. For the acoustical illusion to be effective a sufficient duration must be used. Risset chose 120 seconds for the completion of the entire cycle of ten glissandos. He used the design and other closely related ones in his composition, *Mutations I* (see section 3.12).

A useful class of sounds for certain kinds of musical textures is 'choral tone,"

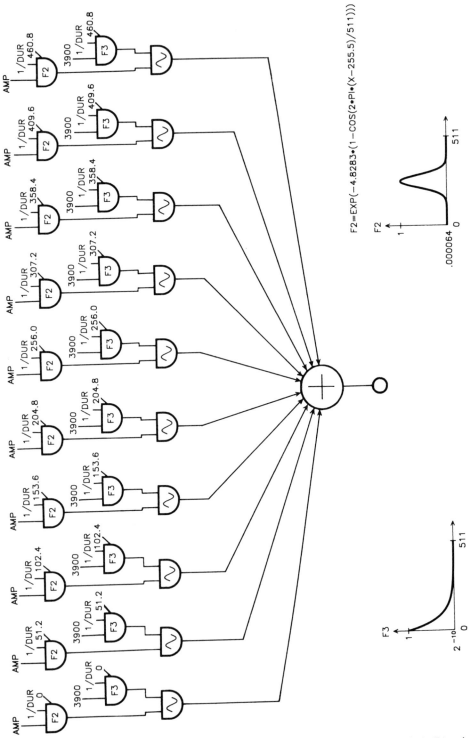

FIGURE 3.28 Design for endless glissando based on Risset. (*Based on example in Risset's* Introductory Catalogue of Computer Synthesized Sounds. *Reprinted with permission of Jean-Claude Risset.*)

which is analogous to the effect in acoustic music of more than one instrument or voice playing a line in unison. A spectral analysis of a group of instruments playing in unison reveals a significant amount of "spreading" in the components of the spectrum; that is, the energy of each component will be more widely distributed about its average frequency than when a single instrument is playing. This is the result of slight mistunings of the instruments and the lack of correlation among their vibratos.

The effect can be approximated by adding another copy of the computer-instrument design at 1 or 2 Hz away from the original and then applying a small (approximately 1%) amount of random frequency deviation to both instruments. The randomness is best implemented with a noise generator that has most of its energy below 20 Hz. Also, because voices do not enter and exit at exactly the same times, a small amount of random deviation in their starting times and durations, as well as in the breakpoints of their envelopes is desirable. A more advanced method that uses delay lines is described in chapter 7.

3.12 Compositional Examples

Jean-Claude Risset has made some of the most elegant applications of fundamental synthesis techniques in the literature of computer music. Since his earliest work in computer music, Risset has shown an ability to find sonically interesting textures that can be realized uniquely by digital synthesis. Risset then builds compositions around these techniques in such a way that the compositional structure and sonic surface are inseparably intertwined.

A good example of a composition in which instrument design and composition-al structure serve to support each other is Risset's *Mutations I*.[13] Regarding the design for the composition, Risset has said, "The title *Mutations* refers to the gradual transformation which occurs throughout the piece, and to the passage from a discontinuous pitch scale, at the beginning, to the pitch continuum in the last part. There is a transition between the scale and the continuum, in particular through a process of harmonic development, which causes the successive harmonics of the notes of a chord to come out. The higher the harmonic order, the finer the pitch step, hence the scale finally dissolves into the continuum."[14]

The opening passage of *Mutations I* contains three elements that illustrate very well Risset's way of integrating instrument design into composition.[15] The passage offers three ways of articulating a group of pitches (figure 3.29). The short notes

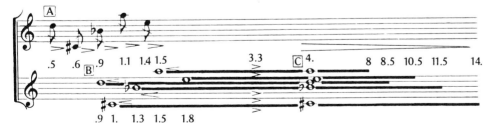

FIGURE 3.29 Three ways of articulating pitches from Risset's *Mutations*. (*Based on example in Risset's* Introductory Catalogue of Computer Synthesized Sounds. *Reprinted with permission of Jean-Claude Risset.*)

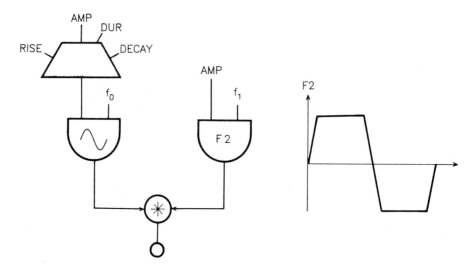

FIGURE 3.30   Ring-modulation instrument from Risset's *Mutations.* (*Based on example in Risset's* Introductory Catalogue of Computer Synthesized Sounds. *Reprinted with permission of Jean-Claude Risset.*)

(A) articulate the tones of a chord (B), which is prolonged with a crescendo–decrescendo envelope. The gonglike sound (C) at 4.0″ echoes the harmony of the chord while fusing the tones into the perception of a unified timbre.

The design of the instrument for this passage brings out interrelations between pitch and timbre. The instrument that plays (A) and (B) is shown in figure 3.30. It uses ring modulation of a sine tone by a square wave specified by amplitude-versus-time approximation. Risset chose f_0 and f_1 to be inharmonic to each other. The instrument has as its predominant frequency the lower sideband of the relation f_1-f_0 (fundamental of the square wave − frequency of the sine wave). The short tones sound somewhat metallic, due to the prominence of non-harmonic partials.

The crescendo–decrescendo chord produces a timbre change as the amplitude of the sidebands, produced by the ring modulation, changes in response to the change in amplitude of the sine tone. The non-harmonic partials emphasized are similar to the ones on the short tones, but because they last longer, the effect is even clearer.

The gonglike tone consists of sine tones at the frequencies of the five preceding fundamentals, all encompassed by the same attack envelope and with different decay rates for the five components. The timbre is unmistakably gonglike, and the pitch quality unmistakably echoes the same harmony as the preceding events.

There is a great resourcefulness in Risset's use of the instruments to realize this passage. A single instrument is used for (A) and (B), with the only difference between them being the sharp attack (.01″) for the short notes and the slow crescendo–decrescendo envelope for (B). The design for (C), with different tunings of partials, is used for gonglike and percussion-like sounds throughout the composition.

Another example of resourcefulness in the use of instrument designs comes in the last part of *Mutations I,* where frequency is presented as a continuum in a variety of ways. The most striking representation is in the "endless glissando," the

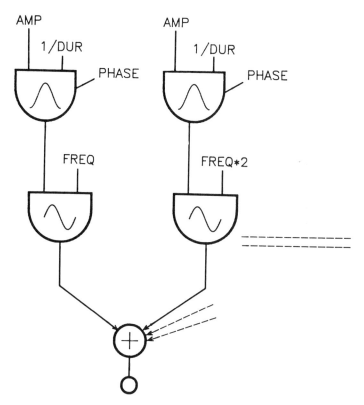

FIGURE 3.31 Design to produce gradual change of octave. The phase of each controlling oscillator is offset from that of the oscillator to its left by an amount equal to the wavetable size divided by the number of branches. (*Based on example in Risset's* Introductory Catalogue of Computer Synthesized Sounds. *Reprinted with permission of Jean-Claude Risset.*)

design for which was described in section 3.11. A variation on that design is used in the last part of *Mutations I*. Here, the glissando is eliminated so that one perceives only the gradual change of emphasis in pitch among the ten octaves (figure 3.31).

Risset's *Inharmonique*[16] for soprano and tape is also based on an acoustic scenario. The composer writes, "In *Inharmonique*, sounds emerge from noise, then the voice emerges from the tape sounds, flourishes, and is eventually sent far away and buried under the tape sounds."[17] The composer continues, "The title *Inharmonique* refers to the systematic use of synthetic tones made up of precisely controlled inharmonic partials. Such tones are composed like chords, and they can either fuse into pitched clangs or be diffracted into fluid textures."

For the noise sounds at the beginning of *Inharmonique*, Risset uses a design for creating bands of noise by ring modulating a sine wave with noise (figure 3.32). The bands of noise change in amplitude, bandwidth, and center frequency throughout each note.[18]

In the instrument design PEAK AMP sets the maximum amplitude for each note. The envelope of each note, multiplied by the peak amplitude throughout the note, causes the amplitude to change in the pattern of F5 or F6. For *Inharmonique*, Risset actually has each note played by a pair of "twin" instruments—one of the

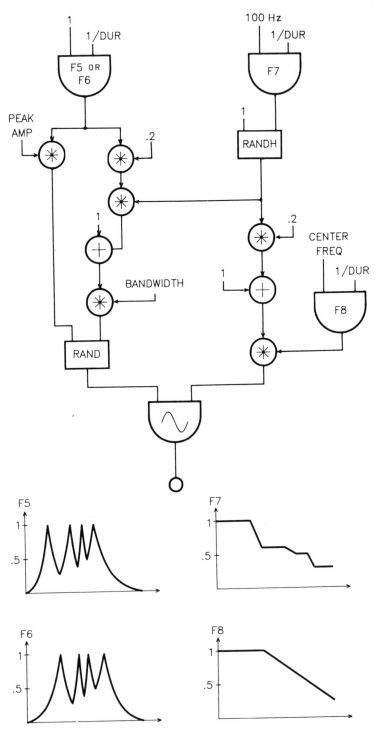

FIGURE 3.32 Instrument from Risset's *Inharmonique*. (*Based on design published in* Inharmonique Analyse de la Bande Magnetique de l'Oeuvre de Jean-Claude Risset *by Denis Lorraine. Published with the permission of Jean-Claude Risset.*)

design shown in the figure using F5 for its envelope, the other identical to it except that its envelope is controlled by the shape of F6. The outputs of the twin instruments are sent to separate channels, and so the effect is an exchange of sound back and forth between the loudspeakers in the course of the note.

The average width of the noise band is determined by the value of the constant BANDWIDTH. The bandwidth changes, however, in response both to the shape of the amplitude envelope and to the output of the RANDH unit generator in the right branch of the instrument. The rate at which the RANDH puts out a new value is 100 Hz at the beginning of each note and decreases through two intermediate rates to 30 Hz for the final sixth of the note. Thus, the envelope is first scaled to the range between 0 and .2 by the first multiplication of the left branch and then to a value between ±.2 by a new random value at the rate of every 100 Hz to 30 Hz. The value 1.0 is then added to make a value in the range .8 to 1.2. The final multiplication in the left branch then results in a bandwidth that fluctuates at random within ±20% of the BANDWIDTH constant.

There is an overall direction to the change of center frequency for each note: The note begins around its initial value and, after 200/512 of its duration, falls linearly to one quarter of its value. The actual value of the center frequency fluctuates at random within ±20% of its value.

While several examples of non-harmonic partials are evident in the "metallic" quality of many of the sounds in *Inharmonique*, there are also passages in which the harmonic series itself is prominent. A tone can be "thickened" by placing next to it identical tones of slightly different frequencies. A good example of this effect can be heard in the section of the work which begins at T=3 minutes. There, the texture is dominated by long, dronelike tones of various durations on A=55, 110, and 220 Hz. Clearly heard above the fundamentals are cascades of tones that are arpeggiating downward through the harmonic series. The effect is caused by the very slow beating of components that are very close in frequency. The spectrum of all the tones is one rich in higher partials that are only slightly less emphasized than the fundamental (figure 3.33).

A single dronelike tone is made by placing nine oscillators with identical waveforms and envelopes very close together in frequency. For example, the nine oscillators of the first tone are tuned to 110, 110.03, 110.06, 110.09, 110.12, 109.97, 109.94, 109.91, and 109.88 Hz. A highly complex pattern of beating is set into motion by the small differences in frequency between not only the nine fun-

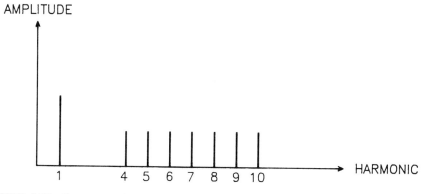

FIGURE 3.33   Spectrum of tones from Risset's *Inharmonique*.

damentals but also all the harmonics of all the tones. The harmonics will beat with each other at different rates; whether they are in phase at a given moment will cause them either to be emphasized or attenuated. This effect is possible only when using accurate, stable oscillators that interpolate between successive output samples.

The cascade effect takes place when the harmonics come into phase successively from the highest harmonic on down to the fundamental. There are many other breath-taking effects in *Inharmonique*, and the reader is directed to a text, in French, by Denis Lorrain for explanation and details of design of both the instruments and the score.[19]

3.13   Other Methods of Instrument Definition

We have chosen to describe synthesis algorithms in terms of unit generators. However, depending on the software available, the specification of algorithms to generate sound can be done at several levels—ranging from step-by-step specification of the algorithm to the modification of an existing model of an acoustical process. For the purposes of discussion, four levels will be defined: direct programs, unit generators, signal-generating models, and extendible models. To permit a musician to work at a higher level, a music-systems programmer preprograms the lower levels.

With direct programs, the musician directly specifies each step of a program to generate sample values. For example, a program might be written to implement a special kind of oscillator. At this level, the musician must be familiar with some non-musical programming language (e.g., FORTRAN). This method of instrument specification gives the musician the flexibility to generate any sequence of sounds. However, to program at this level, certain acoustic, engineering, and programming expertise is necessary. For instance, to use a digital oscillator, the musician would need to know exactly how it works, not just what it does. Working at this level, the overall musical plan can be obscured by the necessary attention to detail. The appendix gives example algorithms, already designed, for various sound generating and processing devices.

The next level of specification, by means of building blocks called unit generators, has been discussed throughout this chapter.

With signal-generating models, the third level of specification, the musician chooses from a set of available synthesis techniques. In this case, the computer is pre-programmed with the appropriate interconnections of unit generators. The musician selects a technique and specifies the parameters necessary to control it. Available sound synthesis techniques often include additive, subtractive, and distortion (nonlinear) synthesis. Additive synthesis, described above, is the summation of several simple tones to form a complex one. In subtractive synthesis (chapter 5), the algorithm begins with a complex tone and diminishes the strength of selected frequencies in order to realize the desired spectrum. Distortion synthesis (chapter 4) encompasses several techniques where a controlled amount of distortion is applied to a simple tone to obtain a more complex one. A widely used member of this class of techniques is frequency modulation, which can be thought of as the distortion of the frequency of a tone. Another technique, waveshaping, is the distortion of the waveform of a tone.

The last level of instrument specification is the extendible acoustic model. This method requires extensive technical research on the part of the music-systems programmers and is relatively undeveloped. The musician is given a model of an acoustic process and allowed to vary the parameters of the model. For example, the software might provide a preprogrammed violin tone and the list of parameters used to generate the tone in terms of some of the physical attributes of the modelled instrument. The musician could then alter the character of the tone by changing such parameters as the volume of the body, the bowing point, the placement of the bridge, and so on. The violin-synthesis algorithm is then altered accordingly producing a change in tone quality. Although a great deal of research has been done to determine acoustic models for the violin,[20] it will require a sophisticated program to implement an extendible synthesis version of one. If such a program were intended to assist violin makers, it would demand an exceptionally accurate model. However, if the musician's purpose were to find sounds that are extensions of the original, far less precision would be required. Alterations to the model should produce modifications in the sound which have the correct qualitative effect, but the quantity of the change could be imprecise. The primary benefit of an extendible model would be to give the musician a means to predict, to some degree, the effect of timbral modification. For instance, an increase in body volume would be expected to lower many of the resonances in the tone.

The extendible model method of timbral specification can be applied to other instruments and to speech. In addition, it has been used for describing processes that modify sounds, such as the specification of reverberation on the basis of the physical characteristics of a room. (See chapter 7.) In the coming years, this method could become a means of providing musicians with a more intuitive approach to computer instrument design than with the direct specification of the parameters of a signal-processing algorithm.

Notes

1. Moore, F. R. "Table Lookup Noise for Sinusoidal Digital Oscillators." *Computer Music Journal*, 1(2), 1977, 26–29.

2. Vercoe, Barry L. *Reference Manual for the MUSIC 11 Sound Synthesis Language*. Cambridge, Mass., Experimental Music Studio, M.I.T., 1979.

3. Mathews, Max. *The Technology of Computer Music*. Cambridge, Mass.: M.I.T. Press, 1969.

4. Howe, Hubert S., Jr. *Electronic Music Synthesis*. New York: Norton, 1975.

5. Risset, Jean-Claude. *Computer Study of Trumpet Tones*. Murray Hill, N.J.: Bell Telephone Laboratories, 1966.

6. Grey, John. "An Exploration of Musical Timbre." Doctoral dissertation, Stanford University, 1975.

7. Dashow, James. "Three Methods for the Digital Synthesis of Chordal Structures with Non-Harmonic Partials." *Interface*, 7, 1978, 69–94.

8. Siegel, L., Steiglitz, K., and Zuckerman, M. "The Design of Markov Chains for Waveform Generation." Proceedings of the Institute of Electrical and Electronics Engineers (EASCON), October, 1975.

9. Knuth, Donald. *The Art of Computer Programming* (Vol. 2) *Seminumerical Algorithms*. Reading, Mass.: Addison-Wesley, 1969, 1–160.

10. Tenney, James. "Noise Study." Decca Records (DL-9103), 1963.

11. Risset, Jean-Claude. *Introductory Catalogue of Computer-Synthesized Sounds*. Murray Hill, N.J.: Bell Telephone Laboratories, 1969.

12. Ibid.

13. Risset, Jean-Claude. "Mutations I." INA-GRM Recording (AM56409), 1979.

14. Schrader, Barry. *Introduction to Electro-Acoustic Music*. Englewood Cliffs, N.J.: Prentice-Hall, 1982, 197.

15. Risset, *Introductory Catalog*.

16. Risset, Jean-Claude. "Inharmonique." INA-GRM Recording (AM56409), 1979.

17. Schrader, *Electro-Acoustic Music*.

18. Lorrain, Denis. "Inharmonique, Analyse de la Bande de l'Oeuvre de Jean-Claude Risset." *Rapports IRCAM*, 26, 1980.

19. Ibid.

20. Hutchins, C. M. "Bowed Instruments and Music Acoustics." In Johan Sundberg (ed.), *Sound Generation in Winds, Strings, and Computers*. Stockholm: Royal Swedish Academy of Music, 1980.

4

SYNTHESIS USING DISTORTION TECHNIQUES

In their efforts to synthesize natural-sounding spectra, musicians have sought means that are more efficient than additive synthesis. Several of the techniques developed have been conveniently grouped into a class called distortion (or non-linear) synthesis. The class includes frequency modulation, non-linear waveshaping, and the explicit use of discrete summation formulae. This chapter will concentrate primarily on the first two techniques, both of which have found extensive application in the digital synthesis of sound. An introduction to discrete summation formulae concludes the chapter.

Whereas additive synthesis uses a separate oscillator for each spectral component, a distortion-synthesis technique uses a small number of oscillators to create spectra with many more components than the number of oscillators. Each distortion-synthesis technique affords the musician single-parameter control over the spectral richness of the sound. Thus, time-evolving spectra can be produced with relative ease.

4.1 FM Synthesis

Audio synthesis by means of frequency modulation (FM), pioneered by John Chowning,[1] is perhaps the single greatest advancement in improving the accessibility of high-quality, computer-synthesized sound. FM may be thought of as the alteration or distortion of the frequency of an oscillator in accordance with the amplitude of a modulating signal. The vibrato instrument described in section 3.8D is an example of an instrument that implements frequency modulation. It uses a sub-audio vibrato rate and a vibrato width of less than a semi-tone, so that the resulting sound has a perceptibly slow variation in its fundamental frequency. However, when the vibrato frequency is in the audio range and the vibrato width is allowed to become much larger, FM can be used to generate a broad range of distinctive timbres that can be easily controlled.

4.1A The Basic Technique of FM

The most basic FM instrument, diagrammed in figure 4.1, consists of two sinusoidal oscillators. A constant, f_c, is added to the output of the modulating oscillator and

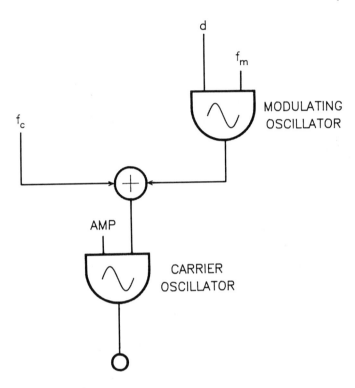

FIGURE 4.1   Basic FM instrument.

the result is applied to the frequency input of the carrier oscillator. If the amplitude of the modulating signal is zero, there is no modulation and the output from the carrier oscillator is simply a sine wave with frequency f_c. When modulation occurs, the signal from the modulating oscillator, a sine wave with frequency f_m, drives the frequency of the carrier oscillator both above and below the carrier frequency (f_c). The change in the frequency of the carrier oscillator is proportional to the amplitude of the signal from the modulating oscillator. When, on a given sample, the output of the modulating oscillator is positive, the frequency of the carrier oscillator is larger than f_c. Conversely, a negative output from the modulating oscillator drives the frequency of the carrier oscillator below f_c.

The peak frequency deviation (or simply, *deviation*) is defined as the maximum amount of change from f_c which the frequency of a carrier oscillator undergoes. The deviation, referred to as d, is set by the value applied to the amplitude input of the modulating oscillator. This value is usually expressed in terms of Hertz or sampling increment. It is not inappropriate for a "frequency" to be applied to an amplitude input: In FM, the digital signal coming out of the modulating oscillator represents a frequency that is to be combined with the carrier frequency.

The maximum instantaneous frequency that the carrier oscillator will assume is f_c+d, and the minimum is f_c-d. If the deviation is large, it is possible for the carrier oscillator to have a negative number applied to its frequency input. In a digital oscillator, this corresponds to a negative sampling increment, and so the oscillator's phase moves backwards. Most, but not all, digital oscillators are capable of doing this. Those that cannot are of limited usefulness for FM synthesis because the maximum deviation cannot exceed the carrier frequency.

4.1B   The Spectrum of Simple FM

In simple FM, both oscillators have sinusoidal waveforms. The frequency-modulation technique can produce such rich spectra that it is seldom necessary to use more complicated waveforms. In fact, when one waveform with a large number of spectral components frequency-modulates another, the resulting spectrum can be so dense that it sounds harsh and undefined.

Because frequency modulation is a well-known technique of radio communication, its spectrum has been well characterized. Figure 4.2 illustrates the spectrum of an FM sound. There are spectral components at the carrier frequency and on either side of it, spaced at a distance equal to the modulating frequency. These sidebands are grouped in pairs according to the harmonic number of f_m. Mathematically stated, the frequencies present in a simple FM spectrum are $f_c \pm k f_m$, where k is an integer which can assume any value greater than or equal to zero. The carrier component is indicated by $k=0$.

The distribution of power among the spectral components depends in part on the amount of frequency deviation, d, produced by the modulating oscillator. When $d=0$, no modulation occurs and therefore all of the signal power resides in the component at the carrier frequency. Increasing the deviation causes the sidebands to acquire more power at the expense of the power in the carrier frequency. The wider the deviation, the more widely distributed is the power among the sidebands and the greater the number of sidebands that have significant amplitudes. Thus, the deviation can act as a control on the bandwidth of the spectrum of an FM signal.

The amplitude of each spectral component is determined by both the deviation and the frequency of modulation. To describe mathematically the amplitude of each spectral component, it is useful to define an *index of modulation, I*, as

$$I = \frac{d}{f_m}$$

The amplitude of each sideband depends on the index of modulation as shown in table 4.1. The amplitude of the carrier (the "zeroth harmonic") is equal to $J_0(I)$. Thus, the absolute value of the amplitude of the kth sideband is given by $J_k(I)$, where J is a Bessel function of the first kind, k is the order of the function, and the argument is the index of modulation. Bessel functions are mathematical functions that can be used to solve several equations, one of which is the FM equation. Their

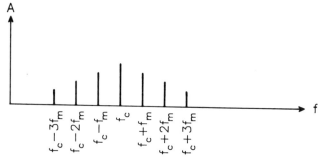

FIGURE 4.2   Spectrum of simple FM exhibiting sidebands through $k=3$.

k	Lower Freq	Amp	Upper Freq	Amp
1	$f_c - f_m$	$-J_1(I)$	$f_c + f_m$	$J_1(I)$
2	$f_c - 2f_m$	$J_2(I)$	$f_c + 2f_m$	$J_2(I)$
3	$f_c - 3f_m$	$-J_3(I)$	$f_c + 3f_m$	$J_3(I)$
4	$f_c - 4f_m$	$J_4(I)$	$f_c + 4f_m$	$J_4(I)$
5	$f_c - 5f_m$	$-J_5(I)$	$f_c + 5f_m$	$J_5(I)$
⋮	⋮	⋮	⋮	⋮

TABLE 4.1 Sidebands of Simple FM

values can be computed by means of an infinite sum, but one of the most convenient methods of evaluation is to refer to the tables of Bessel functions commonly available in handbooks of mathematical functions.[2] Figure 4.3 shows Bessel functions plotted for orders zero through five. When there is no modulation, the index of modulation (I) is zero and the Bessel functions of every order except the zeroth order are zero-valued. Because $J_0(0)=1$, all the signal power resides in the carrier frequency as expected.

The graphs illustrate that in order to obtain significant amplitudes in the high-order sidebands, the value of I must be large. In general, the highest-ordered sideband that has significant amplitude is given by the approximate expression

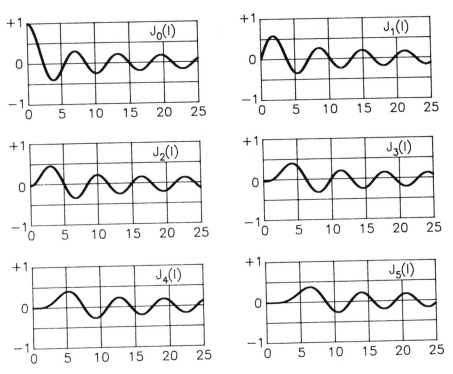

FIGURE 4.3 Bessel functions of orders 0 through 5.

AMPLITUDE

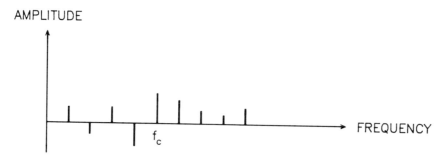

FREQUENCY

f_c

FIGURE 4.4   FM spectrum in which some of the components have negative amplitudes.

$k=I+1$, where I is rounded to the nearest integer. Knowing the carrier and modulating frequencies, this relationship is useful for estimating the index of modulation at which foldover of the highest significant spectral component will occur.

Notice that the Bessel functions shown in figure 4.3 indicate that a sideband can have either a positive or negative amplitude depending on the precise value of I. When the amplitude is positive, the component is said to be "in phase," meaning it has a phase of zero degrees. Conversely, a negative amplitude indicates that the component is "out of phase," and its phase equals 180 degrees. Out-of-phase components are graphically represented by plotting their amplitudes downward as in figure 4.4.

The phase of a spectral component does not have an audible effect unless other spectral components of the same frequency are present. In this case, the amplitude of all these components will either add or subtract from each other, depending on their respective phases.

As shown in figure 4.4 frequency modulation produces components both above and below the carrier frequency. It is quite common for some of the lower sidebands to have negative frequencies. To predict the resultant sound, it is convenient to form a net spectrum by folding the negative frequencies around zero Hertz to their corresponding positions as positive frequencies. The act of folding the component reverses its phase, and so a sideband with a negative frequency is equivalent to a component with the corresponding positive frequency with the opposite phase. If a component, x, is present at the frequency of a folded component, y, then x and y must be combined. In this case the phases of the components are important; if they have the same phase, they are added; if they have different ones, they are subtracted.

As an example, consider the spectrum produced when $f_c=400$ Hz, $f_m=400$ Hz, and $I=3$. Figure 4.5a shows the resulting spectrum with relative phases of the components indicated. Figure 4.5b shows how the phases of the negative-frequency components reverse as they are folded into positive frequencies. For instance, the positive component at -1200 Hz is subtracted from the component at 1200 Hz. Figure 4.5c shows the magnitude of the net spectrum, which corresponds to its audible properties.

Several useful properties can be inferred by examining the ratio of the carrier frequency to the modulating frequency. If

$$\frac{f_c}{f_m} = \frac{N_1}{N_2}$$

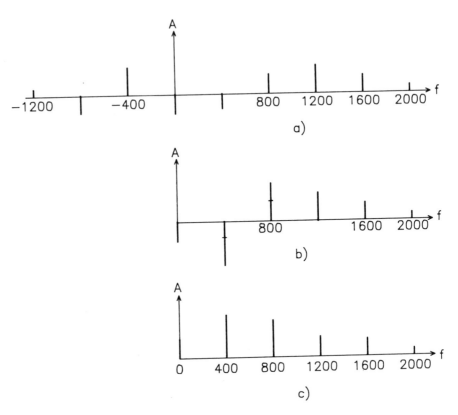

FIGURE 4.5 Method of evaluating the effect of negative frequencies. (a) FM spectrum with negative frequencies; (b) folding negative frequency components around zero Hertz and adding them to existing components; (c) net spectrum displaying just the magnitudes of the components.

where N_1 and N_2 are integers with no common factors, then the fundamental frequency (f_0) of the resulting sound will be

$$f_o = \frac{f_c}{N_1} = \frac{f_m}{N_2}$$

a fundamental equation that applies to other types of distortion synthesis. If $N_2=1$, then the spectrum contains all the harmonics of f_0. If $N_2=M$, where M is an integer greater than one, then every Mth harmonic of f_0 is missing. For example, if $N_2=2$, the spectrum will lack even harmonics. When $N_2=1$ or $N_2=2$, the folded negative-frequency components will coincide with positive components and must be combined. For any other value of N_2, none of the folded negative-frequency components coincides with a positive one. This suggests that spectra produced in the first case will not be as dense as the spectra produced when N_2 is greater than two (assuming the same index of modulation in each case).

If either f_c or f_m is an irrational number, then N_1 and N_2 cannot be defined. An inharmonic spectrum results, such as the one illustrated in figure 4.6a, where $f_c:f_m=1:\sqrt{2}$. When N_1 and N_2 have large integer values, the listener will tend to perceive the tone as inharmonic, because N_1 and N_2 will imply relationships among

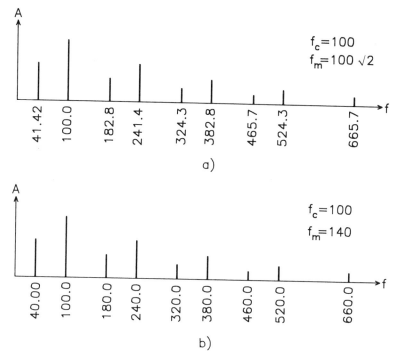

FIGURE 4.6 (a) Inharmonic spectrum produced when $f_c{:}f_m=1{:}\sqrt{2}$. (b) Spectrum produced when $f_c{:}f_m=5{:}7$.

high harmonics with a low fundamental where no "tonal fusion" takes place. For example, sound produced with a ratio of 5:7 (1:1.4), figure 4.6b, is close to that produced when the ratio is $1{:}\sqrt{2}$ (1:1.4142...).

4.1C Obtaining Dynamic Spectra

Because FM has a single index for controlling the spectral richness of a sound, it can be used with relative simplicity to synthesize time-varying, dynamic spectra. The index of modulation controls the spectral content of an FM signal, and so an envelope applied to the index will cause the spectrum to change with time. Figure 4.7 illustrates a simple instrument that produces dynamic spectra. Notice that there are two separate envelopes, one for the spectrum and one for the amplitude. IMAX is the maximum value that the index will assume. To drive the modulating oscillator, IMAX is converted to a deviation by multiplying it by the modulating frequency.

The progression of the spectral components with index can be complicated when the effects of the folded negative sideband are taken into account. After examining the shape of the Bessel functions in figure 4.3, it is not hard to see that the evolution of an FM signal generally has a certain amount of "ripple" in it. That is, as the index increases, the amplitude of any particular component will not increase smoothly, but instead will alternately increase and decrease, sometimes going to zero. The amount of ripple is somewhat proportional to the maximum value of the modulation index. For example, figure 4.8 plots the time-varying

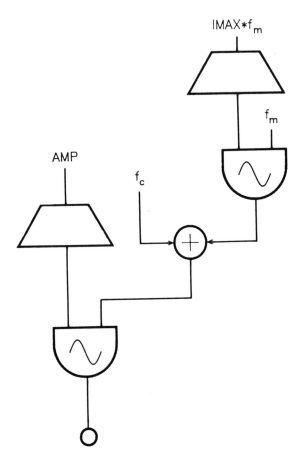

FIGURE 4.7   Simple FM instrument which produces time-varying spectra.

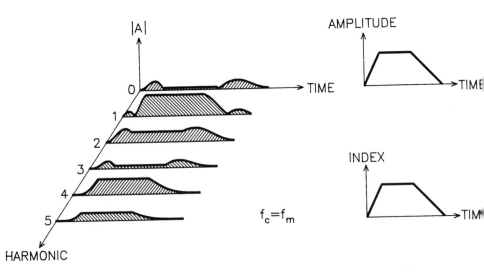

FIGURE 4.8   Dynamic spectrum produced by the instrument of figure 4.7.

spectrum produced by the instrument of figure 4.7 with the parameter values indicated. Observe the ripple in the evolution of the spectrum.

Unlike additive synthesis, frequency modulation allows only certain types of spectral evolutions. Ordinarily, it will not be possible for a musician to match on a point-by-point basis the component amplitudes of a spectrum obtained from an acoustic analysis. However, an effective strategy can be to select the spectral envelope that will realize the desired evolution of the overall richness, the bandwidth, of the spectrum. Because time evolution of the richness of the spectrum is an important element in the perception of timbre, a wide variety of tones can be synthesized by this technique.

4.1D Simple FM Instrument Designs

Figures 4.9 and 4.10 illustrate John Chowning's designs[3] for producing a variety of instrument-like tones with simple FM. On many systems, the functions F1 and F2 could be realized by using envelope generators instead of oscillators. The tone quality produced by the design can be varied by altering any of three factors: the ratio f_c:f_m, the maximum value of the modulation index (IMAX), and the function shapes for the amplitude and for the index of modulation. The amplitude parameter (AMP) should be scaled for all the examples to a value appropriate to the particular system used. The topology of figure 4.9 is used in the first three FM instrument designs that follow.

For bell-like tones, Chowning suggests the following parametric values:

$$DUR = 15 \text{ seconds}$$
$$f_c = 200 \text{ Hertz}$$
$$f_m = 280 \text{ Hertz (i.e., an } f_c : f_m \text{ ratio of 5 : 7)}$$
$$IMAX = 10$$

The function as shown in figure 4.9b is used for both the amplitude envelope and the envelope applied to the index of modulation. The exponential decay of amplitude is characteristic of bell sounds. The shape of the function applied to the index of modulation creates a rich, inharmonic spectrum at the beginning of the tone. During the decay the bandwidth of the spectrum continually diminishes until near the end of the tone, the sound is essentially a sine wave at the carrier frequency. To obtain a bell-like sound, the duration must not be made too short. If the "bell" is not allowed to ring out for at least 2 seconds, listeners will perceive this tone as more of a "clank."

For FM wood-drum like tones, Chowning recommends:

$$DUR = .2 \text{ seconds}$$
$$f_c = 80 \text{ Hz}$$
$$f_m = 55 \text{ Hz}$$
$$IMAX = 25$$

The functions for wood-drum tones are shown in Figure 4.9c. The function used for index of modulation causes an inharmonic spectrum with wide bandwidth during the attack. After a short time, the index drops to zero and the drum tone becomes simply a decaying sine wave at the carrier frequency. The duration is a critical cue for these drum tones and cannot be longer than about .25 seconds without destroying the percussive effect. Raising the carrier frequency in the range of 200 Hz with the same f_c:f_m ratio produces a sound closer to that of a wood block.

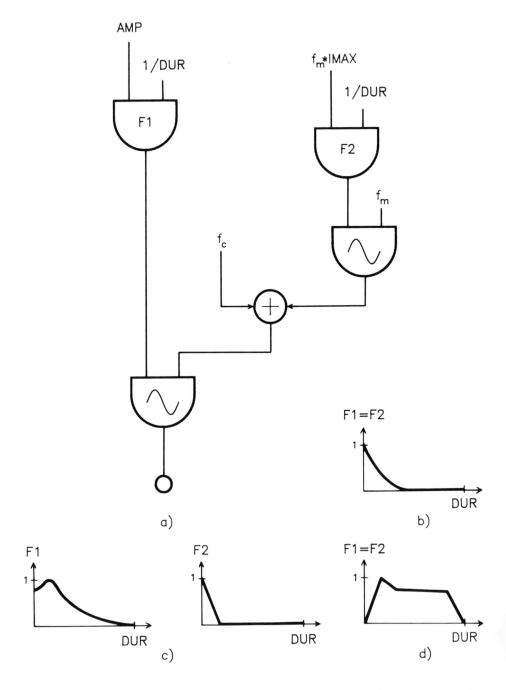

a)

b)

c)

d)

FIGURE 4.9 (a) Basic Chowning FM instrument; (b) function for bell-like timbre; (c) functions for wood-drum sound; and (d) function for brass-like timbre. (*Based on design in "The Synthesis of Complex Audio Spectra by Means of Frequency Modulation" by John Chowning. Published in* Journal of the Audio Engineering Society, *21(7), 1973. Reprinted with permission of the author.*)

FM brasslike tones can be produced with:

$$DUR = .6 \text{ seconds}$$
$$f_c = 440 \text{ Hertz}$$
$$f_m = 440 \text{ Hertz (an } f_c : f_m \text{ ratio of } 1 : 1)$$
$$IMAX = 5$$

The same envelope function (figure 4.9d) is applied to both the amplitude and the index of modulation. Lowering the value of IMAX to 3 yields a more muted brass tone.

Figure 4.10a shows the design for obtaining FM clarinet-like tones. Chowning suggests using the following values:

$$DUR = .5 \text{ seconds}$$
$$f_c = 900$$
$$f_m = 600 \, (f_c : f_m \text{ ratio of } 3 : 2)$$
$$IMIN = 2$$
$$IMAX = 4$$

The shapes of the functions are shown in figure 4.10b. The fundamental frequency produced by this instrument will be $f_c/3$ (300 Hz when using the values above). Notice that because the denominator of the $f_c{:}f_m$ ratio is two, the resulting tone will contain no even harmonics. The use of two modulation indices ensures that the resulting modulation index will never drop below the value of IMIN. Increasing IMAX to 6 produces a more strident attack. A small, constant value may be added to the modulating frequency, causing the folded sidebands to beat with the upper sidebands. This technique can result in a more realistic tone.

4.1E   The Use of Two Carrier Oscillators

An important characteristic of many natural sounds is the presence of fixed formants. Without provision for them, several classes of sounds cannot be satisfactorily synthesized. Even when great care is exercised in choosing the parameters of an FM instrument so that a peak is placed at some desired point in the spectrum, the peak will be valid for only a small range of the values of the index of modulation. Also, the peak in the spectrum is not fixed; it will move with the fundamental frequency of the sound. Passing the signal from any instrument through a band-pass filter (see chapter 5) will yield an accurate, immobile formant, but a more economical and, in many systems, a more practical approach is described below. This method can only approximate fixed formants, but the results are often satisfactory.

The use of two carrier oscillators driven by a single modulating oscillator (figure 4.11) provides a means for formant simulation. The index of modulation of the first carrier oscillator is I1. The modulating signal delivered to the second carrier oscillator is multiplied by a constant (I2/I1) in order to provide a second index of modulation with the same time-variation as the first. The second carrier oscillator produces a spectrum that is centered around the second carrier frequency. Generally, its index of modulation (I2) is relatively small, and so the spectrum has its strongest component at the second carrier frequency. When the two FM signals are added together, the overall spectrum has a peak at the second carrier frequency. The audible effect is to add a formant to the sound. The amplitude of the second carrier oscillator is proportional to (and usually less than)

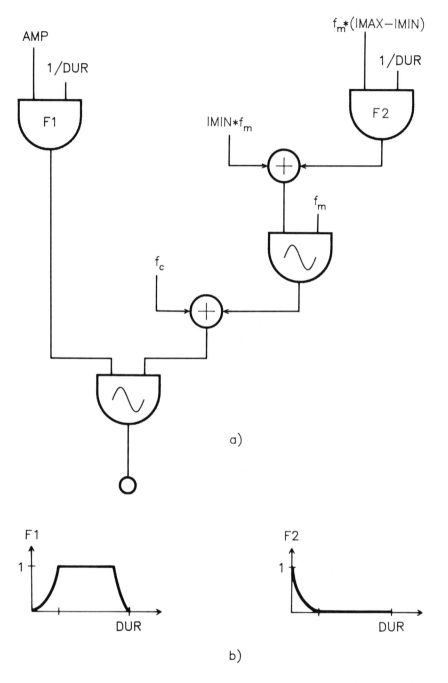

FIGURE 4.10   FM design based on Chowning for clarinet-like timbre. (*Based on design in "The Synthesis of Complex Audio Spectra by Means of Frequency Modulation" by John Chowning. Published in* Journal of the Audio Engineering Society, *21(7), 1973. Reprinted with permission of the author.*)

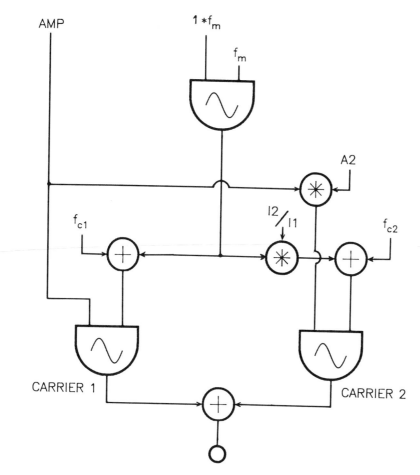

FIGURE 4.11   FM instrument utilizing two carrier oscillators for formant simulation.

the amplitude of the first by the factor A2. The relative strength of the formant can be adjusted by changing this parameter.

The second carrier frequency (f_{c2}) is chosen to be the harmonic of the fundamental frequency (f_0) that is closest to the desired formant frequency (f_f). Mathematically stated,

$$f_{c2} = nf_0 = \text{int} \, [(f_f/f_0) + 0.5] \, f_0$$

That is, n is the ratio, rounded to the nearest integer, of the desired formant frequency to the fundamental frequency. The second carrier frequency remains harmonically related to f_0, and so the value of n changes with f_0 in order to keep the second carrier frequency as close as possible to the desired formant frequency. For example, if the desired formant frequency is 2000 Hz, then for $f_0 = 400$ Hz, the fifth harmonic will be used. As f_0 is increased, f_{c2} will remain the fifth harmonic until f_0 becomes greater than 444.4 Hz, when the fourth harmonic will be closer to 2000 Hz.

4.1F   Double-Carrier FM Instruments

Dexter Morrill has made extensive use of double-carrier FM in his computer synthesis of trumpet tones.[4] The design shown in figure 4.12 is based on one of his algorithms. For convenience, it is divided into a main instrument and a vibrato generator.

In the main instrument, the two carrier oscillators have frequencies at the fundamental frequency and the first formant frequency, respectively. The maximum value of the index of modulation for the first carrier oscillator is IMAX. The peak index of modulation for the second carrier is obtained by scaling the output of the modulating oscillator by the ratio of the second index to the first, IRATIO. The amplitude of the second carrier is 20% that of the first, thus setting the amplitude of the simulated formant at the desired level. The harmonics associated with the formant decay more quickly than the rest of the components of the trumpet tone. On many systems the envelopes will have to be realized with function generators or oscillators because the shapes are too complex for a simple three-segment envelope generator.

The vibrato generator provides an additional frequency modulation of both carrier systems. It imparts a periodic vibrato, a small, random, frequency deviation, and a portamento to each trumpet tone. This part of the instrument ensures a more lifelike tone. The portamento frequency deviation keeps the pitch of the note from sounding too uniform. Its function shape determines the pattern of deviation, and its maximum deviation is set by PORT DEV. The random frequency deviation simulates one of the characteristics of trumpet tones that Risset describes.[5] Vibrato is especially important on longer tones. Some values for the parameters of the instrument adapted from Morrill's example are:

DUR = 1 second	DEC5 = .3 seconds
f_{c1} = 250 Hertz	RANDEV = .007
f_{c2} = 1500 Hertz	f_R = 125 Hertz
f_m = 250 Hertz	VIB WTH = .007
IMAX = 2.66	VIB RATE = 7 Hertz
IRATID = 1.8/2.66	PORT DEV = .03
ATT3 = .03 seconds	ATT1 = .6 seconds
ATT4 = .03 seconds	ATT2 = .06 second
ATT5 = .03 seconds	DEC1 = .2 seconds
DEC3 = .15 seconds	DEC2 = .01 seconds
DEC4 = .01 seconds	

In coding a score for this instrument, Morrill used Leland Smith's SCORE program[6] to obtain, from one note to the next, random deviation of certain values in his parameter lists. This ensured that the succession of notes would not sound mechanical as a result of too great a uniformity of parameter values.

The principle of using more than one carrier frequency to simulate formants is extended in John Chowning's FM design to realize female singing voice on vowels. In this design, Chowning uses two carrier oscillators and one modulating oscillator. The oscillators are all tuned in whole-number multiples of the same frequency.

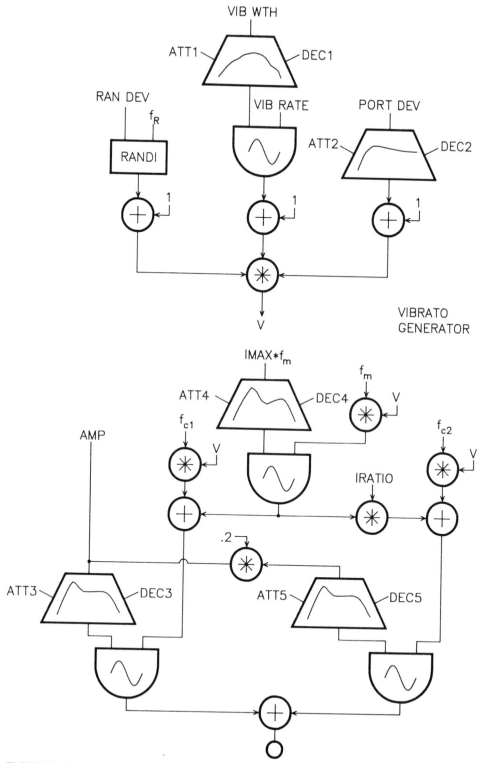

FIGURE 4.12 Double-carrier trumpet instrument based on Morrill. (*Adapted from Morrill's design. Reprinted with the permission of the* Computer Music Journal.)

Chowning has discerned six characteristics of the singing soprano voice which guided his design for synthesis.[7] They are:

1.   There is a weighting of the spectral energy around the low-order harmonics with the fundamental as the strongest harmonic, thus supporting the theory that the lowest formant tracks the pitch period.
2.   There are one or more secondary peaks in the spectrum, depending on the vowel and fundamental pitch, which correspond to resonances on the vocal tract or upper formants.
3.   The formants are not necessarily at constant frequencies independent of the fundamental pitch, but rather follow formant trajectories which may either ascend or descend, depending on the vowel, as a function of the fundamental frequency.[8]
4.   The upper formants decrease in energy more rapidly than does the lowest formant when a tone is sung at a decreasing loudness.
5.   Only the lowest formant is prominent at the amplitude thresholds of the attack and decay portions, while the upper formants only become pronounced as the overall amplitude of the signal approaches the quasi steady state.
6.   There is a small but discernible fluctuation of the pitch period even in the singing condition without vibrato.

Using these principles as a guide, Chowning designed the instrument shown in figure 4.13. The design resembles the trumpet of the previous example in that it uses two carrier oscillators and makes provision for vibrato with a random deviation. The singing-soprano design also includes a slight portamento, but only during the attack portion of the note. The design includes a set of arrays that use the pitch of the note to determine values for the second formant frequency, the amplitude of the second carrier second carrier (A2), and the modulation indices for both carriers. A different set of arrays is used for each vowel. Following is an example of the sorts of values used for the design.

AMP = in the range $0 < \text{AMP} < 1$
PITCH = in the range $G3 < \text{PITCH} < G6$
   f_m = PITCH
   A2 = the relative amplitude of the second carrier, between 0 and 1 in value. See
       figure 4.14.
   A1 = the relative amplitude of the first carrier = 1-A2
   f_{c1} = first carrier frequency = PITCH
   f_{c2} = second carrier frequency = $\text{INT}(f_2/\text{PITCH} + .5)$ where f_2 is the frequency of
       the upper formant, obtained from figure 4.14
   I1 = modulation index for the first carrier. It is computed from the value in figure
       4.14.
   I2 = modulation index for the second carrier. It is computed from the value in figure
       4.14
VIB WITH = $.2\log_2\text{PITCH}$
VIB RATE = between 5 and 6.5 Hertz depending on PITCH

One of the striking features of Chowning's tapes produced with this instrument can be heard in the examples where the two carriers enter one at a time, ten seconds apart. Ten seconds after the entrance of the second carrier, the vibrato with its random deviation is applied equally to the two carriers. Until the application of the vibrato, the two carriers do not fuse into a single aural image of a "voice." Chowning observes that by itself, "the spectral envelope does not make a voice."

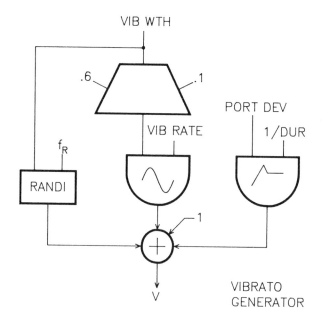

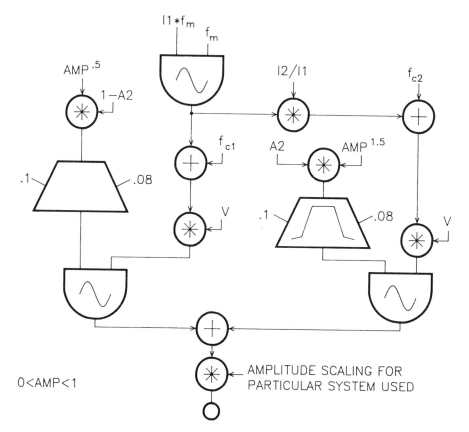

FIGURE 4.13   FM soprano based on Chowning.

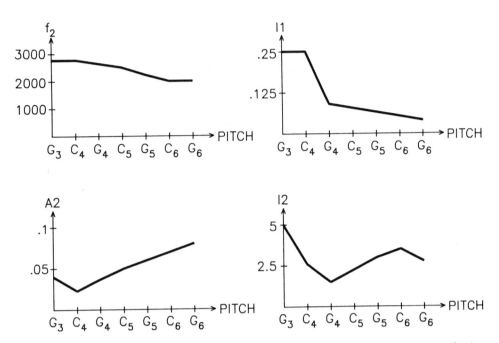

FIGURE 4.14 Parameters used by Chowning for FM soprano. (*From "Computer Synthesis of the Singing Voice" by John Chowning in* Sound Generation in Winds, Strings, Computers, *Publication No. 29 of the Royal Swedish Academy of Music, edited by Johan Sundberg. Reprinted by permission of the editor.*)

4.1G   Complex Modulating Waves

Up to this point, the only FM instruments that have been considered are those in which the waveform of each oscillator is a sine wave. While many interesting timbres can be synthesized this way, certain others require a more complicated modulating waveform. Because the process of frequency modulation produces such rich spectra, a complex modulating wave generally needs to consist of no more than two or three spectral components. Figure 4.15 illustrates an instrument in which the frequency of the carrier oscillator is modulated by a complex wave that is the sum of two sine waves. This instrument could have been realized with a single modulating oscillator whose waveform was the appropriate combination of components, but employing independent oscillators permits variation of the relative amplitudes and frequencies of the modulation components.

The spectrum of this instrument will contain a large number of frequencies. If the carrier frequency is f_c and the modulating frequencies are f_{m1} and f_{m2}, then the resulting spectrum will contain components at the frequencies given by $f_c \pm i f_{m1} \pm k f_{m2}$, where i and k are integers greater than or equal to zero. To indicate when a minus sign is used, the value of i or k will be superscripted with a minus sign. For instance, the sideband with a frequency of $f_c + 2f_{m1} - 3f_{m2}$ will be denoted by the pair: $i=2$, $k=3^-$.

Independent indices of modulation can be defined for each component. I_1 is the index that characterizes the modulation that would be produced if only the first

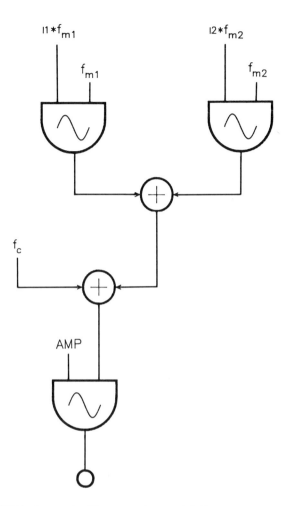

FIGURE 4.15 FM instrument with a complex modulating wave.

modulating oscillator were present; I_2, that of the second. The amplitude of the ith, kth sideband is given by the product of Bessel functions[9].

$$A_{i,k} = J_i(I_1)J_k(I_2)$$

When i or k is odd and the minus sign is taken, the corresponding Bessel function assumes the opposite sign. For example, if $i=2$ and $k=3^-$, the amplitude is $A_{2,3}=-J_2(I_1)J_3(I_2)$. For $i=3^-$, $k=1^-$, the amplitude is $[-J_3(I_1)]\,[-J_1(I_2)]$.

In a harmonic spectrum, the net amplitude of a component at any frequency is the combination of many sidebands. As before, when a sideband has a negative frequency, it is folded around zero Hertz with a change of sign in its amplitude. For example, when $f_c=100$ Hz, $f_{m1}=100$ Hz, and $f_{m2}=300$ Hz, the spectral component present in the sound at 400 Hz is the combination of sidebands given by the pairs: $i=3$, $k=0$; $i=0$, $k=1$; $i=3^-$, $k=2$; and so on. The components at -400 Hz come from $i=2^-$, $k=1^-$; $i=1$, $k=2^-$; $i=5^-$, $k=0$; and so on. The overall amplitude at 400 Hz, $A(400)$, is the sum of the amplitudes of all contributing components.

$$A(400) = J_3(I_1)J_0(I_2) + J_0(I_1)J_1(I_2) - J_3(I_1)J_2(I_2) + \cdots$$
$$+ J_2(I_1)J_1(I_2) - J_1(I_1)J_2(I_2) + J_5(I_1)J_0(I_2) + \cdots$$

The above expression shows only the three lowest order terms for both the positive and negative frequency components. In fact, there are an infinite number of i,k dyads that produce a sideband at ±400 Hz. The actual number that contribute significantly to the overall amplitude is determined by the modulation indices. For given values of I_1 and I_2, one can calculate the maximum values of i and k for which the Bessel functions of that order have significant values. This information predicts the frequency of the highest significant component in the resulting spectrum, and so can be used to avoid aliasing.

Because so many sidebands are produced by this technique, lower indices of modulation can be used to obtain the same amount of spectral richness. This can be advantageous, because the time-evolution of the harmonics is smoother at lower indices.

4.1H   FM Instrument with Complex Modulation

Figure 4.16 shows the flowchart for an instrument based on Bill Schottstaedt's simulation of string-like tones with an FM design.[10] The design entails a single carrier oscillator and three modulating oscillators. It sounds best in the range of a cello when using the following parametric values.

$$f_c = \text{pitch of the note}$$
$$f_{m1} = f_c$$
$$f_{m2} = 3f_c$$
$$f_{m3} = 4f_c$$

$$I1 = 7.5/\log_e f_c$$
$$I2 = 15/\sqrt{f_c}$$
$$I3 = 1.25/\sqrt{f_c}$$

Notice that the indices of modulation vary with the fundamental frequency of the tone. Multiplying the modulation indices by 2 or 3 produces more strident tones, according to the designer.

A vibrato is implemented, similar to the one used in the trumpet design, except that here it is without the undershoot of the pitch of the tone. The chiff or attack noise of the bow is simulated with a noise band centered at 2000 Hz using a bandwidth of 20% of the carrier frequency. The function applied to the noise causes it to cease .2 seconds after the attack of the note.

The increase in spectral richness of the tone during the attack is simulated by adding the envelope F1 to each index of modulation. In his article, Schottstaedt also includes some advice for making other string instrument effects, such as *sul ponticello*, *pizzicato*, and choral effect.

4.1I   Compositional Examples with FM

The compositions by John Chowning represent distillations of extensive research into computer techniques for the synthesis of sound. His expertise in acoustics and psychoacoustics plays a major role in formulating his pieces, as does his interest in expressing physical phenomena mathematically. Yet, artistically, each of his compositions is highly unified—usually around a particular technique or relationship. For example, *Turenas* (1972) demonstrates the travel of sound in a quadraphonic space (see section 7.3B); *Stria* (1976) illustrates the use of computer synthesis of sound to interrelate the small-scale sound design of the composition to its overall formal structure; and *Phonée* (1981) implements the psychoacoustic principle of spectral fusion as a guide to whether its sounds at any given moment seem "electronic" in origin or originating with the human voice.

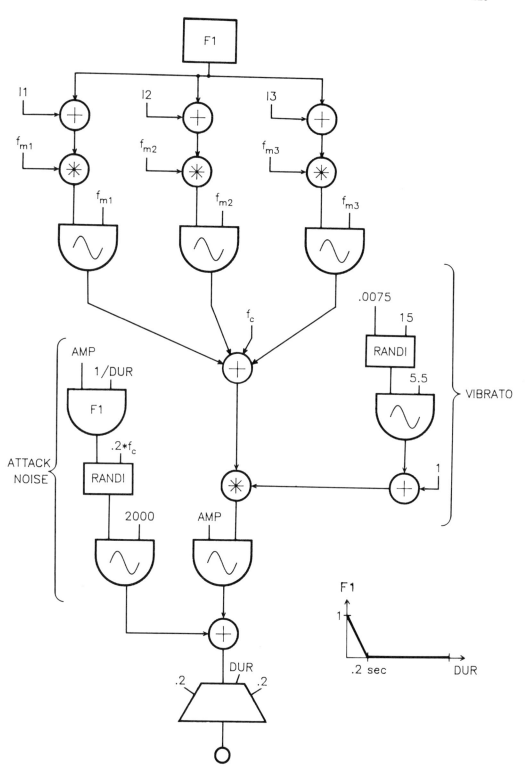

FIGURE 4.16 String-tone simulation utilizing a complex modulating wave based on Schottstaedt.

Several aspects of *Stria* are based on the numerical "golden mean" ratio (1:1.618...) which has been put to various artistic uses throughout the ages. The Greeks thought the golden-mean ratio to embody the most pleasing spatial proportion and used it in architecture to relate the length and width of structures. Bela Bartok used the same ratio in certain of his compositions to relate the durations of movements. Relationships of both time and frequency in *Stria* stem from the projection of the golden-mean ratio. In addition, the climax of the work occurs at the point in time that divides the piece into two sections according to the same ratio. The sounds in *Stria* are predominately long with an almost complete absence of percussiveness. Although there is some change in location of the sound during the course of the 18-minute work, the movement is very gradual.

Chowning devised a unique system of frequencies for *Stria*. The pitch space of the piece is defined as occupying eight pseudo-octaves—an interval of pitch which has the ratio of 1:1.618 instead of the usual 1:2. Each pseudo-octave is divided into nine equal-interval frequency divisions. The eight pseudo-octaves for *Stria* are arranged three above and five below the reference frequency of 1000 Hz.

Figure 4.17 is a sketch of the shape of the eighteen-minute piece, with the pseudo-octave frequency scale at the vertical axis and time indicated on the horizontal axis. The overall shape of the composition represents a mirror image of conventional musical structure, in that the climax occurs at a low point in frequency instead of the more usual high point. Similarly, the conventional relationships between the durations of high and low sounds is reversed. In *Stria*, the longest events are those of highest pitch. They all enter and leave with long rise and decay times. The lower the tone, the faster the rise and decay, and the shorter the tone itself. At the climax of the piece, the lowest tones are also the shortest in the composition.

Each block, one of which is shown in the insert to figure 4.17, is comprised of a number of tones that enter in temporal golden-mean proportions. For instance, in the case of five tones, the center tone enters first and exits last. Each of the five

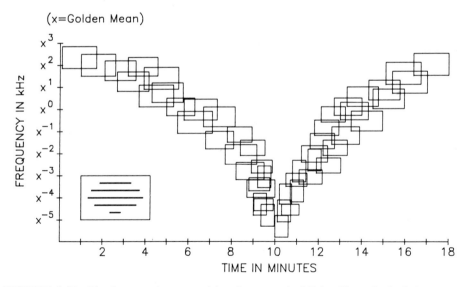

FIGURE 4.17   The large scale compositional structure of John Chowning's *Stria*.

tones of each package is at a frequency represented by one of the nine equal-interval divisions of a pseudo-octave.

The FM instrument design for a single tone reflects the golden-mean ratio as well. One carrier and two modulating oscillators are used. (See section 4.1G) The carrier and modulating frequencies are related in golden-mean proportions, with the second modulating frequency detuned slightly from the first to produce beating, and thus liveliness, in the sound of each tone.

In *Phonée*, Chowning is working with both short, impulsive sounds and long, slowly changing sonorities. *Phonée* posits two extremes of perception as a polarity—bell-like percussion sounds and the timbres of sung vowels. The composition then explores the perceptual gradations between the two extremes. The concern for "timbral interpolation" has occupied the Stanford group for some time, and *Phonée* is, at one level, a compositional application of that facinating phenomenon. There are other perceptual dilemmas to be heard in *Phonée*, as well. For example, there are a number of instances of the effect of vibrato on our perception of spectral fusion. Electronic-sounding timbres turn immediately into the timbres of sung vowels simply by the equal application of properly randomized vibrato to all the spectral components. (The design for implementing this effect is shown in figure 4.13). To produce this effect, Chowning modified the vibrato generator by applying envelopes to the vibrato width and rate so that they are zero at the beginning of the event and increase in value after a time delay of sufficient length for the timbre to be perceived initially as "electronic."

The timbral polarities—bell-like sounds and sung vowels—are realized in different ways. The bell-like sounds are produced by an FM design using an $f_c:f_m$ ratio which is an irrational number, producing a sound containing non-harmonic partials. The vowel timbres are made with a double-carrier design with no inharmonicity of spectral components. The two classes of sounds have other characteristics which differ as well. Bells have a sharp attack with maximal spectral richness in the attack and simplification of the spectrum with time after the attack. Vowel timbres have much more gradual rise and decay shapes and require vibrato for their characteristic quality.

Many of the sounds in *Phonée* fall in the "cracks" between the two polarities. Chowning creates these new sounds by combining salient features of one type of sound with those of the other. Figure 4.18 shows the evolution such a tone. The tone begins with a characteristic bell clang. During the initial decay of the bell tone the highest components decay most rapidly. During the next segment the vibrato is gradually applied individually to each of the remaining components. This causes each component to separate from the percept of a unified bell timbre into an individual "singing voice" on that component. The result is a group of singing voices in the place of the bell tone. Finally, the gradual reduction of the vibrato along with the bell-like decay completes the tone.

The computer instrument for creating these notes is quite complex. It consists of an FM design with as many as six carrier oscillators, tuned inharmonically to each other. To produce the bell-like timbres at the beginnings and ends of tones, the indices of modulation for all but the first oscillator are set to zero, and an inharmonic $f_c:f_m$ ratio is used. Then, in order to create the transformation of each of the bell partials into a singing voice at the same frequency, the indices of modulation are increased. As they increase, random and periodic vibrato are applied to evoke the percept of a singing voice.

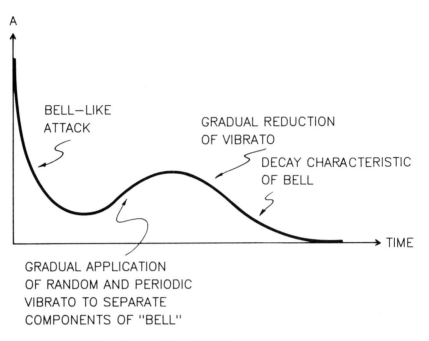

A

BELL–LIKE
ATTACK

GRADUAL REDUCTION
OF VIBRATO

DECAY CHARACTERISTIC
OF BELL

GRADUAL APPLICATION
OF RANDOM AND PERIODIC
VIBRATO TO SEPARATE
COMPONENTS OF "BELL"

TIME

FIGURE 4.18   Evolution of a tone from *Phonée*.

In fact, the overall shape of the composition reflects the structure of one of the characteristic "bell-changing-to-vowel" tones. As the work progresses there is more and more prominence of the singing voice capped by a great profusion of tones sung by a "basso profundissimo." From there to the end, the singing voice plays a less central role.

4.2   Synthesis by Waveshaping

Waveshaping is a second technique of distortion synthesis that realizes spectra which have dynamic evolution of their components. Like FM, it is more computationally efficient than additive synthesis for the realization of complex timbres. Unlike FM, waveshaping provides the capability of generating a band-limited spectrum.

The spectrum produced by a waveshaping instrument changes with the amplitude of the sound. Because this change corresponds to the characteristics of the spectra of acoustic instruments, waveshaping synthesis has proven effective in the production of tones that resemble those of traditional instruments. The synthesis of brass tones has been particularly successful.[11]

4.2A   The Basic Technique of Waveshaping

Waveshaping is the distortion of the amplitude of a sound in order to produce an alteration in its waveform. A simple example of this type of distortion can be heard in the clipping that occurs when an audio amplifier is overdriven. The introduction of carefully controlled distortion to a signal can be used to yield a broad range of

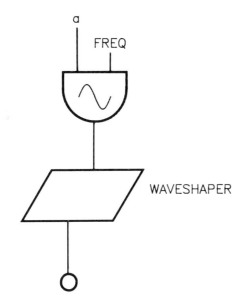

FIGURE 4.19 Basic waveshaping instrument.

musically useful timbres. Like FM synthesis, waveshaping provides for the continuous control of the spectrum by means of an index, making possible dynamic spectra through time-variation of the index.

The signal-flow diagram of a basic waveshaping instrument is shown in figure 4.19. The central element of any such instrument is a *waveshaper* or non-linear processor that alters the shape of the waveform passing through it. In a linear processor, such as an ideal amplifier, a change in the amplitude of the input signal produces a like change in the output signal. For example, doubling the amplitude of the input signal will cause the amplitude of the output to double also. The shape of the waveform is not changed, so that while the amplitude of each spectral component doubles, their strength relative to each other is preserved. In a non-linear processor, the relationship between input and output depends on the amplitude of the input signal and the nature of the non-linearity. Therefore, increasing the amplitude of the input will cause the output waveform to change shape. When the shape of the waveform is modified, its spectrum changes, which generally results in an increase in the number and intensity of the harmonics. Our discussion will concentrate on the use of waveshaping to enrich the spectrum of a simple sound, such as a sine wave.

4.2B Transfer Functions

A waveshaper is characterized by its *transfer function*, which relates the amplitude of the signal at the output to the input. This function can be represented graphically, as in figure 4.20, with the amplitude of the input signal plotted on the horizontal axis and the amplitude of the output signal on the vertical axis. Thus, for a given input value, the output of the waveshaper can be determined by finding the corresponding output value on the graph of the transfer function. By repeating this process for each sample of an input waveform, a graphic description of the output waveform can be constructed, as in the figure.

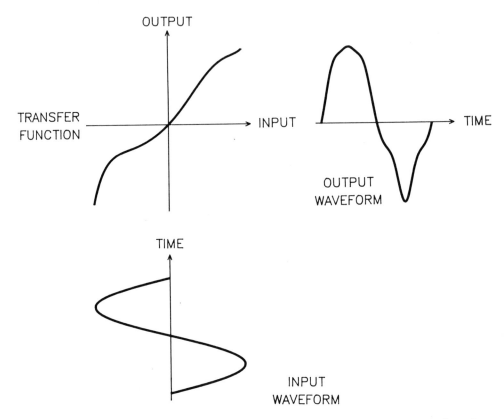

FIGURE 4.20 Waveshaping described by a transfer function. The output waveform is produced by finding the value of the transfer function corresponding to the input waveform.

The shape of the output waveform, and hence its spectrum, changes with the amplitude of the input signal. For the indicated transfer function, figure 4.21 shows the output waveforms and their spectra produced by sinewaves of different amplitudes. Notice that the amount of distortion introduced is strongly dependent on the level of the input signal: The spectrum becomes richer as the input level is increased.

The musician can gain some sense of a transfer function's audible effect from its graphic representation. A processor with a straight-line transfer function (figure 4.22a) will not produce distortion; any deviation from a straight line introduces some form of distortion. The transfer function illustrated in figure 4.22b is linear close to the center of the axes but diverges increasingly from its initial slope. Small signals are thus passed with little alteration of their spectrum, while large ones are substantially distorted. The more extreme the change in slope, the larger the number and intensity of the harmonics added. When the transfer function is symmetric about the center of the graph (figure 4.22b), it is called an odd function and the spectrum of the distortion contains only odd-numbered harmonics. When the transfer function is symmetric about the vertical axis (figure 4.22c), the transfer function is said to be even and thus produces only even harmonics. An even transfer function, therefore, doubles the fundamental frequency of the input signal and hence raises the pitch of the sound by an octave. A transfer function with an

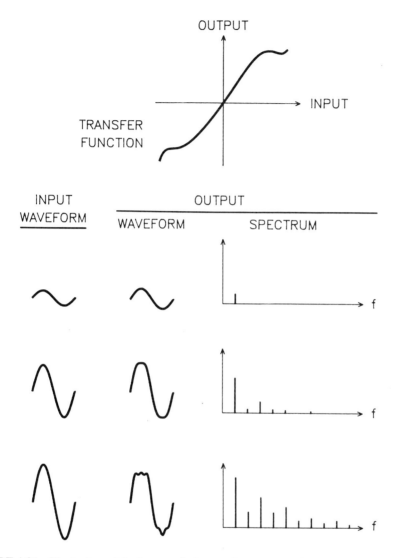

FIGURE 4.21 Illustration of the increase in harmonic content as the amplitude of the input increases.

abrupt jump (figure 4.22d), sharp points (4.22e), or wiggles (4.22f) will produce more harmonics than a smoother function. In fact, a transfer function with a sharp point or an abrupt jump always produces an infinite number of harmonics and thus, aliasing.

The most useful way to describe a transfer function is algebraically. The amplitude of the signal input to the waveshaper is represented by the variable x. The output is then denoted by $F(x)$, where F is the transfer function. This notation indicates that the value of F depends on the value of x. An example of a linear transfer function is $F(x)=.5x$ (figure 4.23a). In this case, any signal applied to the input will be transmitted to the output with its amplitude reduced by one half. A transfer function is non-linear when it has terms that contain x raised to a power other than one or zero, or when it contains other mathematical functions of x, such

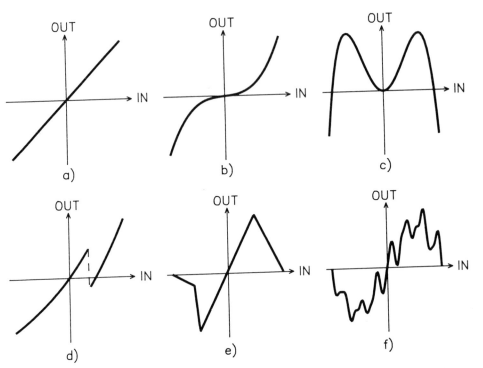

FIGURE 4.22   Six transfer functions: (a) linear, (b) odd, (c) even, (d) with an abrupt jump, (e) with sharp points, and (f) with ripple.

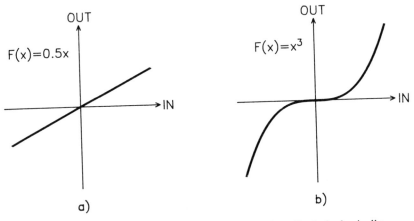

FIGURE 4.23   Examples of transfer functions that are described algebraically.

as the logarithm or tangent. A simple example of a non-linear transfer function is $F(x)=x^3$ (figure 4.23b). In this case, the output will be a distortion of the input because the value of each input sample is cubed as it is passed to the output. Thus, doubling the input causes the output to increase by eight times.

To avoid aliasing in waveshaping synthesis, a transfer function is normally expressed as a polynomial which has the form:

$$F(x) = d_0 + d_1 x + d_2 x^2 + \cdots + d_N x^N$$

The value of each coefficient d_i (d_0, d_1, d_2,...) is chosen by one of the methods given below. The degree or order of the polynomial is N, the value of the largest exponent. When driven with a sine or cosine wave, a waveshaper with a transfer function of order N produces no harmonics above the Nth harmonic. The musician can therefore predict the highest harmonic frequency generated and avoid aliasing either by limiting the frequency of the oscillator that drives the waveshaper, or by tailoring the transfer function accordingly.

4.2C   Calculating an Output Spectrum from a Transfer Function

When the non-linear processor is driven by a sinusoidal waveform, the amplitudes of the various harmonics of the output can be calculated from the transfer polynomial using table 4.2.[12] The table shows the amplitudes of the harmonics produced by a term in the polynomial when the amplitude of the driving sinusoid is one. The symbols along the top of the table, denoted in the form h_j, represent the amplitude of the jth harmonic. Each line in the table has an associated divisor (DIV); the true value of any entry is the listed value divided by the divisor for that line.

As an example, suppose the transfer function $F(x)=x^5$ is driven by a cosine wave with an amplitude of one. That is, the variable x signifies the cosine wave. The table shows that the output will contain the first, third, and fifth harmonics with the following amplitudes:

$$h_1 = \tfrac{1}{16} (10) = 0.625$$
$$h_3 = \tfrac{1}{16} (5) = 0.3125$$
$$h_5 = \tfrac{1}{16} (1) = 0.0625$$

	DIV	h_0	h_1	h_2	h_3	h_4	h_5	h_6	h_7	h_8	h_9	h_{10}	h_{11}
x^0	0.5	1											
x^1	1		1										
x^2	2	2		1									
x^3	4		3		1								
x^4	8	6		4		1							
x^5	16		10		5		1						
x^6	32	20		15		6		1					
x^7	64		35		21		7		1				
x^8	128	70		56		28		8		1			
x^9	256		126		84		36		9		1		
x^{10}	512	252		210		120		45		10		1	
x^{11}	1024		462		330		165		55		11		1

TABLE 4.2   Harmonic Amplitudes Produced by Each Algebraic Term of a Transfer Function

For mathematical convenience the amplitude of the zeroth harmonic is equal to $h_0/2$. Thus, the value in the table is two times larger than the actual amplitude of this particular harmonic. This term has a frequency of zero Hz and therefore serves to offset the output signal by a fixed amount. That is, it is a constant value added to each sample of the signal. Since a constant does not fluctuate, it contributes nothing to the perceived sound. This phenomenon needs to be taken into account, however, since a large offset can cause the sample values to exceed the range of the system without causing the signal to sound louder.

When a polynomial has multiple terms, the output is the sum of the contributions of each term. For instance, if $F(x) = x+x^2+x^3+x^4+x^5$, the spectrum of the output is:

$$h_0/2 = [(\tfrac{1}{2})2 + \tfrac{1}{8}(6)]/2 \quad = 0.875$$
$$h_1 = 1 + \tfrac{1}{4}(3) + \tfrac{1}{16}(10) = 2.375$$
$$h_2 = \tfrac{1}{2}(1) + \tfrac{1}{8}(4) \quad = 1.0$$
$$h_3 = \tfrac{1}{4}(1) + \tfrac{1}{16}(5) \quad = 0.5625$$
$$h_4 = \tfrac{1}{8}(1) \quad = 0.125$$
$$h_5 = \tfrac{1}{16}(1) \quad = 0.0625$$

The reader might recognize the table to be the right side of Pascal's triangle and the entries to be the binomial coefficients. The table can be extended by adding two adjacent numbers on the same line and writing the sum below the space between them. The value of h_0 is twice the value of h_1 from the previous line and the divisor is increased by a factor of two each time. For example, for x^{12}, the divisor would be 2048, $h_0 = 2 \times 462 = 924$, $h_2 = 462 + 330 = 792$, and so on.

As expected, the table shows that a term does not produce harmonics with numbers greater than its exponent. It further indicates that an even power of x will produce only even harmonics and that an odd power generates only odd harmonics. This is another advantage of polynomial representation because it affords the instrument designer independent control of the odd and even harmonics of a sound.

Thus far the analysis has been applied for a sinusoidal input whose amplitude is one. What then, is the general relationship between the amplitude of the input sinusoidal waveform and the amplitude of a given harmonic? Let the input to a waveshaper be a cosine wave with an amplitude of a. The output in polynomial form becomes:

$$F(ax) = d_0 + d_1 ax + d_2 a^2 x^2 + \cdots + d_N a^N x^N$$

where x, as above, symbolizes a cosine wave with an amplitude of 1. The harmonics can still be determined using table 4.2, but with the contribution of each term multiplied by a, raised to the appropriate power. The dependence of the amplitude of any harmonic on the value a is usually indicated by writing the amplitude of the jth harmonic as a function, $h_j(a)$. Using the example of $F(x) = x + x^3 + x^5$ and substituting ax for x, the harmonics at the output will be calculated as:

$$h_1 = a + \tfrac{1}{4}a^3(3) + \tfrac{1}{16}a^5(10)$$
$$h_3 = \tfrac{1}{4}a^3 + \tfrac{1}{16}a^5(5)$$
$$h_5 = \tfrac{1}{16}a^5$$

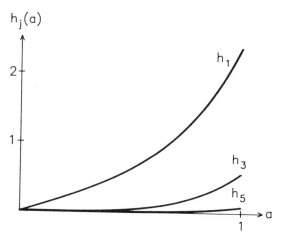

FIGURE 4.24   Harmonic amplitudes versus distortion index for $F(x)=x^5+x^3+x$.

These harmonics' amplitudes are plotted against the value of a in figure 4.24. Notice that the spectrum becomes richer as the value of a increases. Because it exercises so much control over the richness of the spectrum, a is called a *distortion index*. It is analogous to the index of modulation of FM synthesis, in that it is a single parameter that determines the spectral content. For simplicity, the index is often limited to values between zero and one.

When the waveform applied to the waveshaper is non-sinusoidal, the resulting spectrum is more difficult to predict and is often not band-limited. The spectrum of a waveform produced by passing a complex waveform through a non-linear processor cannot be calculated simply as the sum of the distortion applied to the individual spectral components of the input waveform. Instead, a Fourier transform is performed on the output waveform to determine its spectrum. Thus, for reasons of conceptual simplicity and to obtain band-limited spectra, the majority of waveshaping instruments use a sinusoidal oscillator to drive the non-linear processor.

4.2D   Selecting a Transfer Function

The success of an instrument that uses waveshaping synthesis is largely dependent upon the choice of transfer function. There are three approaches to the choice: spectral matching, graphical, and heuristic.

In spectral matching, a transfer function is determined that will make the output of the waveshaper match a desired steady-state spectrum for a particular value of the distortion index. This can be accomplished through the use of *Chebyshev polynomials*, usually denoted as $T_k(x)$, where k is the order of the polynomial. (T signifies that it is a Chebyshev polynomial of the first kind.) These polynomials have the useful property that when the transfer function of a waveshaper is $T_k(x)$ and a cosine wave with an amplitude of one is applied to the input, the output signal contains only the kth harmonic.[13] For example, a transfer function given by the 7th-order Chebyshev polynomial results in an output of a sinusoid at seven times the frequency of the input. (This relationship exists only when the amplitude of the input is one.) Table 4.3 lists the Chebyshev polynomials through the eleventh order. Higher order polynomials can be generated from the relationship:

$$T_{k+1}(x) = 2xT_k(x) - T_{k-1}(x)$$

A spectrum containing many harmonics can be matched by combining the appropriate Chebyshev polynomial for each desired harmonic into a single transfer function. Let h_j represent the amplitude of the jth harmonic in the spectrum to be matched and N be the highest harmonic in that spectrum. The transfer function is then calculated as:

$$F(x) = (h_0/2)T_0(x) + h_1T_1(x) + h_2T_2(x) + \cdots + h_NT_N(x)$$

As an example of spectral matching, suppose that when the distortion index equals one, it is desired that the spectrum contain only the first, second, fourth, and fifth harmonics with amplitudes of 5, 1, 4, and 3, respectively. The transfer function to realize this is:

$$F(x) = 5T_1(x) + 1T_2(x) + 4T_4(x) + 3T_5(x)$$
$$F(x) = 5(x) + 1(2x^2 - 1) + 4(8x^4 - 8x^2 + 1) + 3(16x^5 - 20x^3 + 5x)$$
$$F(x) = 48x^5 + 32x^4 - 60x^3 - 30x^2 + 20x + 3$$

When the distortion index assumes a value other than one, this transfer function generates different spectra. The relationships between the various harmonic amplitudes and the distortion index, a, can be calculated from the transfer function using table 4.2, as before. These amplitudes are plotted three-dimensionally versus index and harmonic number in figure 4.25. Observe that the third and zeroth harmonics are not present when $a=1$, but at other values of the distortion index, they are no longer balanced out. At small values of the distortion index, the spectrum is dominated by the fundamental and the zero frequency term.

Another, more intuitive means of selecting the transfer function is based on the choice of its graphical shape. Some general principles relating the shape of the

$$T_0(x)=1$$
$$T_1(x)=x$$
$$T_2(x)=2x^2-1$$
$$T_3(x)=4x^3-3x$$
$$T_4(x)=8x^4-8x^2+1$$
$$T_5(x)=16x^5-20x^3+5x$$
$$T_6(x)=32x^6-48x^4+18x^2-1$$
$$T_7(x)=64x^7-112x^5+56x^3-7x$$
$$T_8(x)=128x^8-256x^6+160x^4-32x^2+1$$
$$T_9(x)=256x^9-576x^7+432x^5-120x^3+9x$$
$$T_{10}(x)=512x^{10}-1280x^8+1120x^6-400x^4+50x^2-1$$
$$T_{11}(x)=1024x^{11}-2816x^9+2816x^7-1232x^5+220x^3-11x$$

TABLE 4.3 Chebyshev Polynomials through the 11th Order

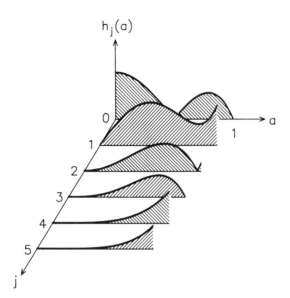

FIGURE 4.25 Harmonic amplitudes versus distortion index for $F(x)=48x^5+32x^4-60x^3-30x^2+20x+3$.

transfer function to the harmonics produced were given above. To avoid aliasing, the selected graphical shape should be approximated by a polynomial, with the order of the approximation set to the highest harmonic number desired. The computer can be programmed to perform this task.

A heuristic selection of the coefficients of the transfer polynomial can sometimes be effective. For best results the instrument designer should choose the signs of the terms carefully. If the signs of all the terms are the same, the function will become increasingly steep with the distortion index, resulting in exceptionally bright timbres. More subdued timbres can be obtained by following the pattern found in the Chebyshev polynomials where the signs of the even- and odd-order terms alternate independently. This will yield a flatter transfer function that produces a less brilliant sound. With experience, the musician can develop an intuitive understanding of the relationship between the coefficients and the sound produced. Interactively altering a set of coefficients originally produced by the combination of Chebyshev polynomials is a good way to begin to develop this skill.

4.2E Considerations for Dynamic Spectra

As FM synthesis, waveshaping facilitates the production of dynamic spectra because the distortion index can be varied with time. Of course, the transfer function of the waveshaper determines the amount and type of spectral controls possible. It would be simplest and probably the most musically useful if the index increased the amplitudes of all the harmonics smoothly. Polynomials that do this without producing extraordinarily brassy sounds are uncommon. If the polynomial is chosen for a less brilliant spectrum, there is often considerable ripple in the evolution of the harmonics with distortion index (unless the spectrum has an unusually small amount of harmonic energy). The higher the order of the transfer function, the harder it will be to obtain smooth spectral evolutions. Also, polynomials that are obtained by matching a spectrum in which the highest harmonics have relatively large amplitudes tend to produce much more spectral ripple than those where the harmonic amplitudes diminish with harmonic number.

If spectral matching is used to determine the transfer function, the smoothness of the spectral evolution can be improved by selecting the signs of the harmonics of the desired spectrum such that the signs of the even and odd harmonics are alternated independently.[14] Thus, the even harmonics would have the pattern, starting with the zeroth, $+, -, +, -, \ldots$. The odd harmonics, starting with the first, would take the same form. When the even and odd harmonics are combined to make a complete spectrum, the overall pattern becomes $+, +, -, -, +, +, -,$ $-, \ldots$. Applying this method to the example of spectral matching given above yields a spectrum to be matched that contains only the first, second, fourth, and fifth harmonics with amplitudes of 5, -1, 4, and 3, respectively. The resulting transfer function is:

$$F(x) = 48x^5 + 32x^4 - 60x^3 - 34x^2 + 20x + 5$$

While the spectrum at the value of the distortion index where the matching takes place is not audibly affected, this method results in a smoother spectral evolution.

As another example, the evolution of the harmonics with index is plotted for two different cases in figure 4.26. Figure 4.26a shows the result when the spectrum, starting with first harmonic, 4, 2, 3, 0, 2, 3, 2 is matched. Figure 4.26b illustrates the evolution when 4, -2, -3, 0, 2, -3, -2 is matched. Observe the vastly different behavior of the first and third harmonics with index.

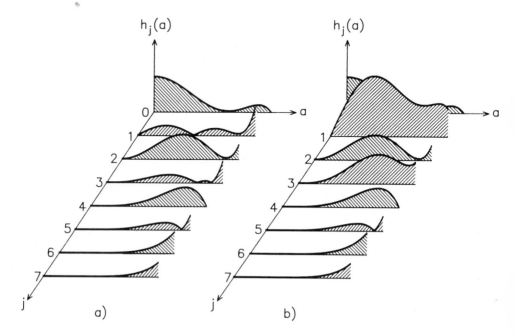

FIGURE 4.26   Harmonic evolution when a spectrum is matched with the amplitudes: (a) 4, 2, 3, 0, 2, 3, 2 and (b) 4, -2, -3, 0, 2, -3, -2.

4.2F   Implementation of a Non-Linear Processor

It is not practical to have the computer calculate the value of the output of the waveshaper by directly evaluating the transfer function for each sample. It is more efficient to calculate values of the transfer function for a number of input amplitudes and to store them in a table prior to performance. (This is similar to storing a waveform in a wavetable that is referenced by a digital oscillator.) In the waveshaper, the output value's location in the table is obtained from the amplitude of the input signal. The instrument designer must assure that the samples entering the waveshaper fall within the range of locations of the table. For example, if a 512 entry table has its locations marked by the integers 0 to 511, then the output of the oscillator driving the waveshaper must be scaled accordingly. Examples of this appear in section 4.2H.

   As demonstrated for the digital oscillator (section 3.3), the use of a finite table size causes small inaccuracies in the output value when the input amplitude falls between entries in the table. In a waveshaper, these inaccuracies are heard as slight increases in the amount of harmonic distortion and therefore are seldom objectionable.

4.2G   Amplitude Scaling

The distortion index also controls the amplitude of the sound, so, as in most musical sounds, changes in spectrum will be accompanied by changes in loudness. This corresponds to the behavior of acoustic instruments, where louder playing ordinarily produces more overtones. Although this general relationship between amplitude and spectrum is correct, it is rare that the desired spectral and amplitude envelopes can both be obtained from a single envelope, particularly when the transfer function provides large amounts of distortion. Excessive loudness variation with spectral content often results, producing excessively bright tones. The amplitude variation with spectral content can be so extreme that the effective dynamic range of the tone of the sound exceeds the limitations of the system. When a secondary amplitude envelope is placed on the output of the waveshaper, the overall envelope of the sound becomes the product of the distortion index and amplitude envelopes. When the interdependence between amplitude and spectrum is tempered, the amplitude envelope can be more easily chosen.

   One method of compensation is to multiply the output of the waveshaper by a *scaling factor* which is a function of the distortion index.[15] If $S(a)$ is the scaling function, then the output is $OUT(ax)=F(ax)S(a)$. Because the scaling function is almost always complicated, it is impractical to calculate its value every time the distortion index is changed. Instead, it is stored as the transfer function of a second non-linear processor which is driven directly by the distortion index, a. Thus, in a waveshaping instrument like the one shown in figure 4.27, the distortion index is applied to both the sinusoidal oscillator and the processor containing the scaling function.

   The scaling is applied to the output signal according to some criterion. The scaling factor can be chosen, in theory, so the sound has the same loudness for

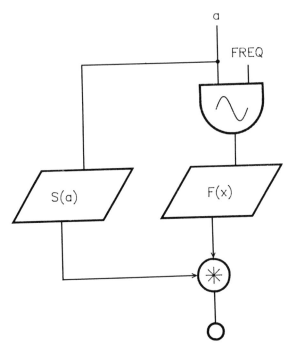

FIGURE 4.27   Implementation of a scaling function by means of a second non-linear
process.

every value of distortion index. However, the perception of loudness also depends
on the frequency and timbre of the sound. A more practical method, therefore, is
to equalize the power in the signal to a constant value. For true power scaling, the
scaling function is chosen as

$$S(a) = \left[(h_0(a)/2)^2 + h_1^2(a) + h_2^2(a) + \cdots h_N^2(a) \right]^{-\frac{1}{2}}$$

The relative strengths of the harmonics still vary with the distortion index just as
they would without scaling, but the amplitude of the entire spectrum is raised or
lowered by the appropriate scaling factor to keep the output power constant.
However, this method does not work when the distortion index equals zero because
the scaling function becomes infinite. The instrument designer may choose to work
around this by setting $S(0)$ to a large, but non-infinite, value.

Peak scaling defines a scaling function where the peak amplitude of the output
waveform is always the same. With a distortion index of a, the input to the
waveshaper assumes values between $-a$ and $+a$. To peak scale the output, it is
divided by the maximum magnitude of the transfer function for that range of
inputs. Thus, the scaling function is

$$S(a) = (\max|F(\alpha)|_{-a \leq \alpha \leq a})^{-1}$$

The audible effect of this kind of scaling varies tremendously with the shape of the
transfer function. When the transfer function is either continuously increasing or
decreasing (i.e., has no peaks or valleys), this scaling method tends to equalize the
power to some extent, although not with the accuracy of true power scaling. When
the transfer function has ripples, an unusual relationship between amplitude and

spectrum results because the scaling function has several plateaus yielding a limited amount of power equalization for some regions of distortion index and considerable power variation in others.

The use and type of a scaling function depends on the choice of transfer function and the type of sound to be synthesized. As FM synthesis, waveshaping with true power scaling allows the amplitude and spectral envelopes to be independent, but at the same time eliminates one of the musical advantages of waveshaping synthesis—the change in spectral content with amplitude. A strategy that is often more effective is to choose a scaling function providing a more restricted variation of loudness with distortion index. For some transfer functions, this can be done with peak scaling, whereas in other cases a modified power scaling function is more effective.

4.2H   Example Waveshaping Instruments

Jean-Claude Risset designed and used in composition a non-linear waveshaping instrument in the late 1960s.[16] The design, shown in figure 4.28, creates clarinet-like tones through non-linear distortion of sine tones into tones with harmonic series containing only the odd-numbered partials.

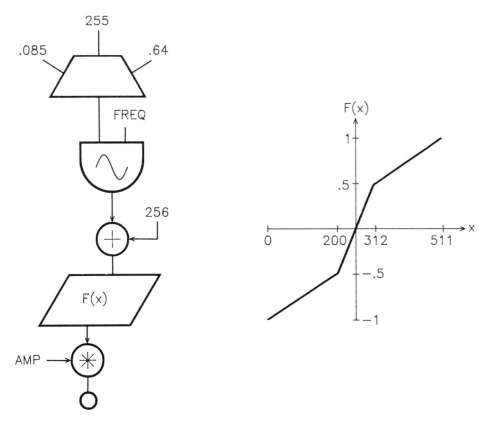

FIGURE 4.28   Waveshaping instrument based on Risset which produces a clarinet-like timbre. (*Based on example in Risset*'s Introductory Catalogue of Computer Synthesized Sounds. *Reprinted with permission of Jean-Claude Risset.*)

The transfer function of the waveshaper is stored in a table with a length of 512 locations. The transfer function is specified graphically in a piece-wise linear manner. The samples from the output of the oscillator fall in the range ±255, which is one-half the table length minus one. To this value is added the constant value of 256. Thus, the values used to reference the waveshaper oscillate in the range from 1 to 511. The entries in the waveshaper table are scaled to the range ±1 and subsequently multiplied by the desired amplitude. As Risset points out, because the transfer function is not band limited, this design, when used at a sampling rate of 20 KHz, will generate objectionable aliasing on tones with fundamental frequencies above about 1500 Hz.

Figure 4.29a shows the design for a non-linear waveshaping instrument that produces simple, "brassy" tones. The design includes a scaling function (F1) to temper the variation of amplitude with spectrum. The linear rise in the distortion index causes distortion in the tone to increase rapidly during the attack. During the steady-state the distortion index has a value of .7, so that the harmonic content is less brilliant. During the decay, the harmonic content of the high frequencies falls off first. The transfer function was obtained by matching the spectrum shown in figure 4.29b.

4.2I   The Use of Ring Modulation with Waveshapers

The technique of waveshaping described above provides strictly harmonic spectra that, in general, become richer with increasing distortion index. This makes it easy to synthesize tones in which the lower harmonics attack first and decay last. However, the basic technique does not readily provide for the synthesis of certain other harmonic evolutions. A simple variation on the basic technique increases the types of sounds that can be synthesized, makes possible inharmonic spectra, and facilitates formant simulation.[17] In this approach the output of a waveshaper is multiplied by a sinusoidal tone as shown in figure 4.30a. This results in ring modulation which produces a spectrum containing a replicated image of the spectrum of the shaped tone both above and below the modulating frequency. The lower image is reversed (figure 4.30b). If the shaped and modulating tones have fundamental frequencies of f_1 and f_2, respectively, the frequencies produced are the sum and difference of f_2 with each harmonic of f_1. That is, $f_2 \pm jf_1$, where $j=0, 1, 2, \ldots, N$ and N is the order of the transfer function of the waveshaper. The corresponding amplitude of each component is $.5(A2)h_j$, where A2 is the amplitude of the modulating wave and h_j is the amplitude of the jth harmonic of the shaped wave.

The result has some similarities to simple FM synthesis. If the ratio of the frequencies is given as

$$\frac{f_1}{f_2} = \frac{N_1}{N_2}$$

where N_1 and N_2 are integers with no common factors, then the fundamental frequency (f_0) of the resulting waveform is

$$f_0 = \frac{f_1}{N_1} = \frac{f_2}{N_2}$$

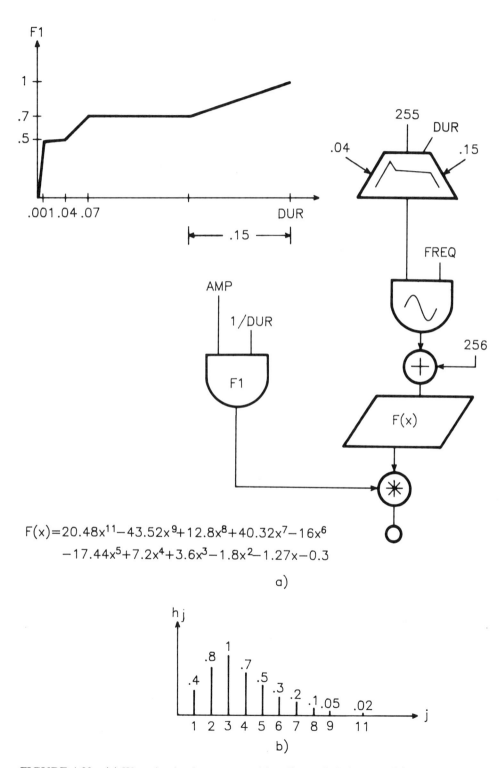

$$F(x)=20.48x^{11}-43.52x^9+12.8x^8+40.32x^7-16x^6$$
$$-17.44x^5+7.2x^4+3.6x^3-1.8x^2-1.27x-0.3$$

a)

b)

FIGURE 4.29   (a) Waveshaping instrument with a "brassy" timbre and (b) spectrum that was matched.

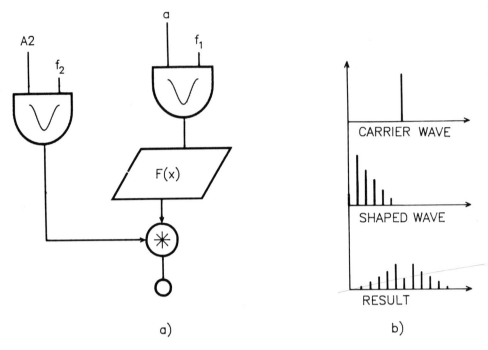

FIGURE 4.30   Use of ring modulation in a waveshaping instrument (a) and its spectrum (b).

When N_1 is even, only odd harmonics are produced. If f_1 or f_2 is an irrational number, then N_1 and N_2 cannot be defined as integers and an inharmonic spectrum results.

   If f_2 is less than f_1 times the order of the transfer function (N), negative frequencies result. These are transformed into positive frequencies by folding them around zero Hertz (see section 4.1B). If there is a component at the corresponding positive frequency, the folded component is added to it to form the net spectrum. The phase of the components must be considered when they are added together. Unlike FM, the folding process does not necessarily reverse the phase of a component. If the modulating waveform and the input to the waveshaper are both cosine waves, the folded components are added in phase. If the modulating wave is a sine wave, the components are out of phase and must be subtracted.

   Placing an envelope on the distortion index realizes a dynamic spectrum. In addition, it is usually necessary to place an amplitude envelope on the modulating oscillator to obtain the desired overall envelope of the sound. If the transfer function has a constant term, the modulating tone is heard even when the distortion index drops to zero. This can be useful in realizing certain timbres.

4.2.J   A Waveshaping Instrument Using Ring Modulation

Figure 4.31 shows a waveshaper that uses the ring modulation technique of section 4.2I to produce a pitched-percussion sound. The instrument has separate envelopes for the distortion index and the amplitude. In addition, the instrument has two sound-producing oscillators tuned inharmonically to each other. The modulating

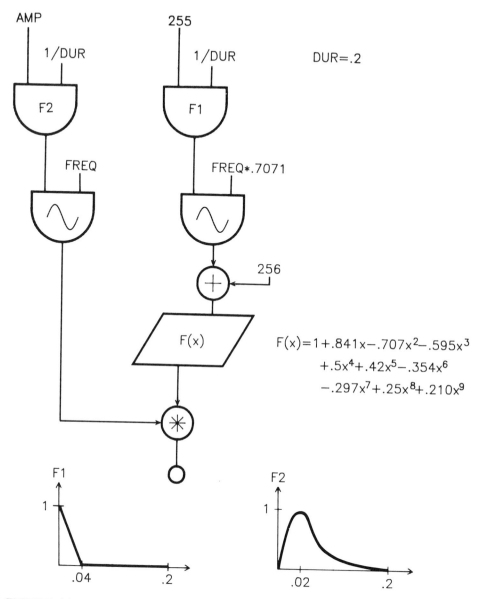

$$F(x)=1+.841x-.707x^2-.595x^3$$
$$+.5x^4+.42x^5-.354x^6$$
$$-.297x^7+.25x^8+.210x^9$$

FIGURE 4.31   Waveshaper that uses ring modulation to produce a drum-like sound.

oscillator is controlled by the amplitude envelope F2, and generates a sine tone of frequency FREQ. As is characteristic of most percussive sounds, F2 has a rapid rise and a much longer, exponential decay. The oscillator driving the waveshaper is controlled by the distortion index and produces a sine tone of frequency .7071 FREQ. The frequencies of the two oscillators are inharmonically related so that multiplying the modulating wave with the shaped wave results in an inharmonic spectrum. During the first part of the tone, the relatively large distortion index causes the shaped wave to occupy a rather wide bandwidth. When the distortion index falls to zero, the constant term in the transfer function allows the pure tone of the modulating oscillator to come through. The duration of the tones should be kept short (<.25 seconds), to retain the characteristic percussive timbre. At lower frequencies the timbre is drumlike, and at higher ones the sensation of pitch becomes much clearer.

4.2K   Use of Multiple Waveshapers

Another extension of the waveshaping technique involves the combination of two waveshaping instruments and a modulating tone[18] as shown in figure 4.32. The outputs of all three elements are multiplied together, resulting in a complex spectrum that is similar in control and characteristics to FM synthesis using a complex modulating wave (see section 4.1G). If the frequencies of the two shaped waveforms and the modulating wave are f_1, f_2, and f_3, respectively, the spectrum of the output contains the frequencies $f_3 \pm j f_1 \pm k f_2$, where $j=0,1,2,\ldots,M$ and $k=0,1,2,\ldots,N$. M and N are the orders of the transfer functions of the first and second waveshapers, respectively. The amplitude of any component is .25 (A3) h_j g_k where A3 is the amplitude of the modulating tone. The amplitudes of the jth and kth harmonics of the two waveshapers are h_j and g_k, respectively. Components with negative frequencies are folded around 0 Hz, as before.

The maximum number of independent frequencies that can be produced is $4 \times M \times N$. Of course, in the case of harmonic spectra, many components overlap or are folded onto each other, reducing the total number of individual frequencies. Because the number of spectral components is proportional to the product $M \times N$, rich spectra can be produced using low-order transfer functions. Low-order transfer functions make it easier to obtain a smooth spectral evolution without causing excessive brilliance.

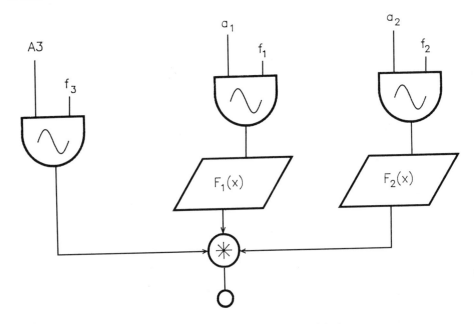

FIGURE 4.32   Use of multiple waveshapers with ring modulation.

4.2L   Use of a High-Pass Filter

Another variation on the basic waveshaping technique involves the use of a high-pass filter in conjunction with a waveshaper. A high-pass filter is an element that allows high frequencies to pass through and attenuates low ones (see chapter 5). This method has been demonstrated by James Beauchamp[19] and has been successful in the synthesis of realistic brass tones. The method is based on a mathematical model of the acoustical processes used to produce a tone on a brass instrument. The parameters of the model are determined from the analysis of actual instrument characteristics.

The spectrum of the sound produced by blowing into an unattached mouthpiece is a non-linear function of its loudness—the harder the player blows, the richer the spectrum of the sound. The body of the natural brass instrument serves not only to resonate the sound from the mouthpiece into a clear pitch, but also acts as a high-pass filter. The computer instrument of figure 4.33 approximates the mouthpiece action with the sine-wave oscillator and the waveshaper. The transfer function is determined by matching a spectrum that is obtained by analysis of actual mouthpiece spectra at different dynamic levels.

The parameters of the high-pass filter are chosen to provide characteristics determined from acoustical measurements on the body of the brass instrument. The high-pass filter emphasizes the higher harmonics, and so the waveshaper does not need to provide as much high-frequency energy. Thus, the transfer function will give a smoother evolution with distortion index, and it will be unlikely that such an instrument will require dynamic amplitude scaling.

Waveshaping with a high-pass filter is generally a useful technique that can be adapted to the synthesis of other types of sound where the parameters are not necessarily determined from analysis. It does, however, require that the digital hardware have a large dynamic range in the numbers that it can represent, because the high-pass filter greatly reduces the peak amplitude of the waveform. The amplitude is reconstituted by the multiplication that is performed on the output of the filter.

In his use of this design to make brasslike tones, Beauchamp chose the transfer function (figure 4.33a) to simulate the non-linear behavior of the spectrum of a cornet mouthpiece played alone.[20] The cutoff frequency of the high-pass filter was fixed at 1800 Hz. The high-pass filter, with a constant setting of its parameters irrespective of the frequency of the instrument, contributes to the most important characteristic of this instrument design—the fact that the instrument maintains the appropriate timbre over its entire range. The particular filter algorithm that Beauchamp uses is a second-order Butterworth filter realized with the bilinear transform (see section 5.12). The filter unit generators found in most sound-synthesis languages will not work for this purpose. Therefore, we included the code for this kind of filter in the appendix.

One of the primary features of this instrument design is that it produces richer spectra at higher dynamic levels. In addition, Beauchamp changes the envelope shape (F1) with the dynamic level of the desired tone. Figures 4.33b, c, and d, respectively, give envelope shapes for three different dynamic levels: pp, mf, and

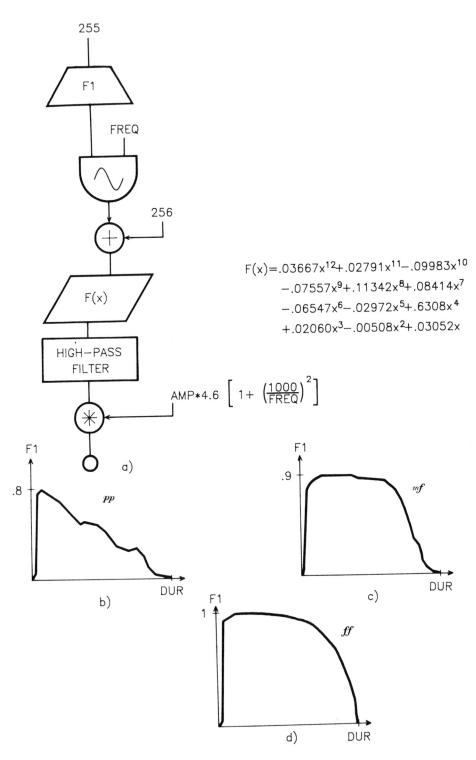

$$F(x) = .03667x^{12} + .02791x^{11} - .09983x^{10}$$
$$- .07557x^9 + .11342x^8 + .08414x^7$$
$$- .06547x^6 - .02972x^5 + .6308x^4$$
$$+ .02060x^3 - .00508x^2 + .03052x$$

$$AMP*4.6 \left[1 + \left(\frac{1000}{FREQ} \right)^2 \right]$$

FIGURE 4.33   (a) Waveshaping instrument based on Beauchamp and the envelopes (b, c, and d) for different dynamic levels. Beauchamp evaluated F(x) over the range of $x = \pm 1.4$ to fill the table. (*Reprinted with the permission of* the Computer Music Journal.)

ff. The louder the tone, the less the amplitude of the tone diminishes during the steady state. These envelope shapes were also derived from the analysis of recordings of cornet mouthpieces.

4.3 Introduction to Discrete Summation Formulae

4.3A Synthesis Using Discrete Summation Formulae

In addition to frequency modulation synthesis and synthesis by waveshaping, the class of techniques known as distortion synthesis includes synthesis by the explicit use of discrete summation formulae. This category encompasses a wide variety of algorithms. Both harmonic and inharmonic spectra in either band-limited or unlimited form can be synthesized by means of various formulae. We will give two examples of harmonic spectra, one band-limited, the other not.

What is a discrete summation formula? The sum of the first N integers can be written as

$$1 + 2 + 3 + \cdots + N = \sum_{j=1}^{N} j \tag{4.1}$$

where j is an arbitrary index, ranging from 1 to N. To evaluate this expression one could simply add the terms individually, but the calculation can be done more simply by taking advantage of the relationship:

$$\sum_{j=1}^{N} j = \frac{N(N + 1)}{2} \tag{4.2}$$

Thus, for example, the sum of the integers 1 through 10 is $(10 \times 11)/2 = 55$. Equation 4.2 is an example of a *discrete summation formula* and the right side of the equation is said to be the "closed form" of the sum. There are many discrete summation formulae and they appear often in digital signal processing. In sound synthesis, a sum of sinusoids can sometimes be represented by a closed form which can be evaluated more simply than the direct addition of sine waves.

As an example, consider the spectrum shown in figure 4.34a which consists of N harmonics, all with equal amplitude. In this example, each of the harmonics is a cosine wave. One way to realize this spectrum is by means of additive synthesis: one oscillator per harmonic, adding the outputs of all the oscillators. The frequency of each oscillator is assigned a value corresponding to a harmonic of the fundamental frequency. Because there are N oscillators, the maximum amplitude that can be produced by their summation is N times greater than the amplitude of an individual oscillator. Thus, setting the amplitude of each oscillator to A/N yields a net output with a maximum amplitude of A. Figure 4.34b shows the flow chart of such an instrument. This instrument can be described mathematically by the summation:

$$f(t) = \frac{A}{N} \sum_{k=1}^{N} \cos{(2\pi k f_0 t)} \tag{4.3}$$

Except for very small values of N, it takes a considerable amount of computation time to calculate the output signal.

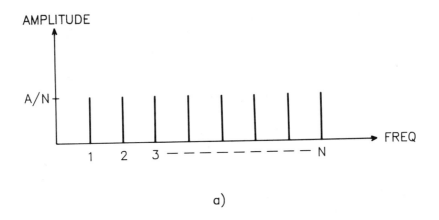

a)

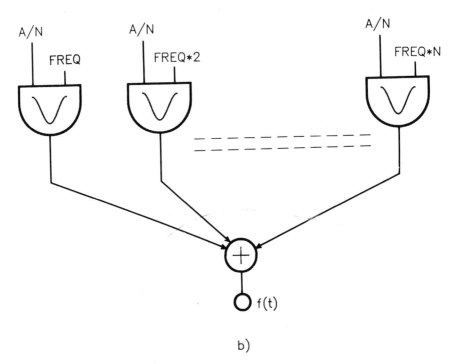

b)

FIGURE 4.34 (a) Spectrum with equal amplitude components. (b) Additive-synthesis instrument to realize it.

Fortunately, equation 4.3 has a closed form[21] which is given by

$$\frac{A}{N} \sum_{k=1}^{N} \cos\left(2\pi k f_0 t\right) = \frac{A}{2N}\left\{\frac{\sin\left[\pi(2N+1)f_0 t\right]}{\sin\left(\pi f_0 t\right)} - 1\right\} \tag{4.4}$$

The right side of the equation can be calculated more easily using the configuration shown in figure 4.35. Regardless of the number of harmonics synthesized, this instrument employs just two oscillators yet realizes the same spectrum as the additive instrument of Figure 4.34b. On many computer music systems, this

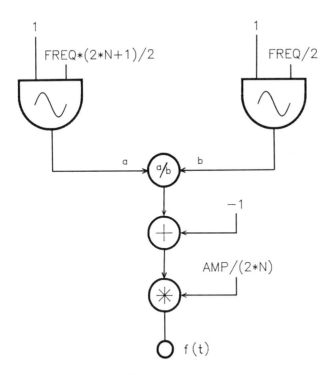

FIGURE 4.35   Implementation of a discrete summation formula (equation 4.4) to generate the spectrum of figure 4.34a.

algorithm forms the heart of a unit generator (often called BUZZ) which synthesizes band-limited pulse waveforms. Section 5.1 includes a more detailed description of this signal in the time domain. This type of pulse generator has found wide use in subtractive synthesis (chapter 5) and speech synthesis (chapter 6).

In programming the instrument of figure 4.35, certain numerical considerations need to be taken into account. The presence of a divide in the algorithm brings up the possibility of division by zero, an operation which causes most programs to terminate abruptly. Thus, the program should check on every sample to see if the output of the right-hand oscillator is zero or very close to zero. If it is, the division operation should be bypassed, and the value of the overall output of the algorithm set directly to the maximum amplitude, in the example, A. This method works satisfactorily for a variety of purposes, but in a few cases it might be necessary to use the following, more accurate technique of handling divisors near zero: in the case of a divisor very near zero, instead of implementing equation 4.4, the algorithm would use the following equation to calculate the output, $f(t)$.

$$f(t) = \frac{A}{2N}\left\{ \frac{(2N+1)\ \cos\ [\pi(2N+1)\ f_0 t]}{\cos\ (\pi f_0 t)} - 1 \right\} \tag{4.5}$$

Combining the oscillator outputs by division can cause numerical roundoff errors (see section 1.5) which can degrade the S/N ratio of the output signal. In order to reduce this effect to a level consistent with other unit generators, many implementations of this algorithm use a wavetable that is twice the size of the usual wave-table for storing the sine wave used by the oscillators.

Figure 4.36A shows another example of a spectrum that lends itself to realization by means of a discrete summation formula. This spectrum can be written mathematically as

$$f(t) = \sum_{k=0}^{\infty} a^k \sin [2\pi(k+1)f_0 t]; \quad a<1 \tag{4.6}$$

Because $a<1$, the amplitudes of the spectral components are decreasing exponentially with harmonic number. For example, when $a=.9$, the amplitudes of successive harmonics, starting with the fundamental, will be given by the sequence:

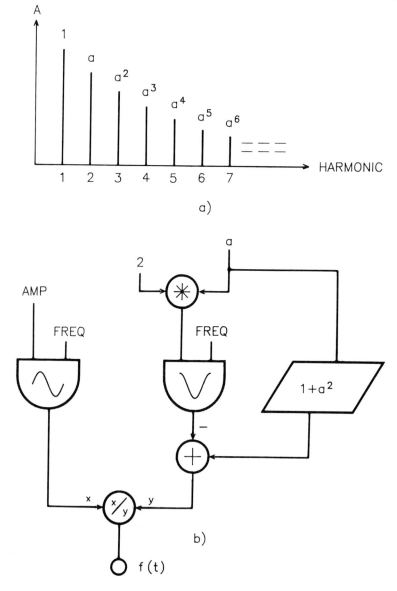

a)

b)

FIGURE 4.36 (a) Spectrum that can be generated by means of the discrete summation formula implemented by (b)

1,.9,.81,.729,... . Unlike the previous example, this spectrum is not band limited. This is noted by the infinity symbol above the summation sign in the equation.

This spectrum can be synthesized most easily by using the relationship[22]:

$$\sum_{k=1}^{\infty} a^k \sin [2\pi(k+1)f_0t] = \frac{\sin (2\pi f_0t)}{1+a^2-2a \cos (2\pi f_0t)} \; ; \; a<1 \qquad (4.7)$$

The instrument (figure 4.36b) that implements the right side of the equation employs two digital oscillators and performs a division on every sample. Happily, for $a<1$, there is no chance of this algorithm dividing by zero. The value of $1+a^2$ is most efficiently evaluated by a non-linear processor as shown in the figure.

This instrument synthesizes dynamic spectra easily because the spectrum can be controlled by the single index, a. Increasing the value of a causes the spectrum of the sound to become richer. As in other types of distortion synthesis, an envelope can be placed on the index to obtain a particular spectral evolution. This discrete summation formula exhibits a smooth evolution of the spectral components as the index is increased. This contrasts with an FM instrument or a waveshaping instrument with a complicated transfer function, where the amplitude of a given spectral component can display a great deal of ripple as the index is increased. Because this instrument produces, in theory, an infinite number of harmonics, the maximum value of a should be chosen such that components falling above the Nyquist frequency have insignificant amplitudes.

As in synthesis by waveshaping, a change in the spectral index results in a change in the loudness of the sound. While this can be a desirable effect, it is often necessary to moderate it by multiplying the amplitude of the sound by a scaling function as described in section 4.2G.

In summary synthesis by means of discrete summation formulae can be used to obtain well-controlled, dynamic spectra. There are many other formulae beyond the ones presented here which can be applied to the synthesis of sound.[23] In fact, mathematical analysis has shown that all distortion synthesis techniques can be described as the implementation of a closed sum. For example, the equation for simple FM, upon which all the instruments in the first part of this chapter are based, is the closed form of a discrete summation formula.

Notes

1. Chowning, John. "The Synthesis of Complex Audio Spectra by Means of Frequency Modulation." *Journal of the Audio Engineering Society*, 21(7), 1973, 526–534. Reprinted in *Computer Music Journal*, 1(2), 1977, 46–54.

2. Jahnke, Eugene, and Fritz Emde. *Tables of Functions with Formulae and Curves* (4th ed.). New York: Dover, 1945.

3. Chowning, "Frequency Modulation."

4. Morrill, Dexter. "Trumpet Algorithms for Computer Composition." *Computer Music Journal*, 1(1), 1977, 46–52.

5. Risset, Jean-Claude. *Computer Study of Trumpet Tones*. Murray Hill, N.J.: Bell Telephone Laboratories, 1966.

6. Smith, Leland. "Score: A Musician's Approach to Computer Music." *Journal of the Audio Engineering Society*, 20(1), 1972, 7–14.

7.   Chowning, John. "Computer Synthesis of the Singing Voice." In Johan Sundberg (ed.), *Sound Generation in Winds, Strings, and Computers*. Stockholm: Royal Swedish Academy of Music (publ. no. 29) 1980, 4–13.

8.   Sundberg, Johan. "Synthesis of Singing." *Swedish Journal of Musicology*, 60(1), 1978, 107–112.

9.   LeBrun, Marc. "A Derivation of the Spectrum of FM with a Complex Modulating Wave." *Computer Music Journal*, 1(4), 1977, 51–52.

10.   Schottstaedt, Bill. "The Simulation of Natural Instrument Tones using Frequency Modulation with a Complex Modulating Wave." *Computer Music Journal*, 1(4), 1977, 46–50.

11.   Beauchamp, J. W. "Analysis and Synthesis of Cornet Tones Using Non-linear Interharmonic Relationships." *Journal of the Audio Engineering Society*, 23(6), 1975, 793–794.

12.   Suen, C. Y. "Derivation of Harmonic Equations in Non-linear Circuits." *Journal of the Audio Engineering Society*, 18(6), 1970, 675–676.

13.   Schaffer, R. A. "Electronic Musical Tone Production by Non-linear Waveshaping." *Journal of the Audio Engineering Society*, 18(2), 1970, 413–417.

14.   LeBrun, Marc. "Digital Waveshaping Synthesis." *Journal of the Audio Engineering Society*, 27(4), 1979, 250–266.

15.   Ibid.

16.   Risset, Jean-Claude. *An Introductory Catalogue of Computer-Synthesized Sounds*. Murray Hill, N.J.: Bell Telephone Laboratories, 1969.

17.   Arfib, D. "Digital Synthesis of Complex Spectra by Means of Multiplication of Non-linear Distorted Sine Waves." Proceedings of the International Computer Music Conference, Northwestern University, 1978, 70–84.

18.   Ibid.

19.   Beauchamp, James. "Brass Tone Synthesis by Spectrum Evolution Matching with Non-linear Functions." *Computer Music Journal*, 3(2), 1979, 35–43.

20.   Ibid.

21.   Winham, Godfrey, and Steiglitz, Kenneth. "Input Generators for Digital Sound Synthesis." *Journal of the Acoustical Society of America*, 47(2), 1970, 665–666.

22.   Moorer, J. A. "The Synthesis of Complex Audio Spectra by Means of Discrete Summation Formulae." Music Department, Stanford University, 1975. (Report no. STAN-M-5.)

23.   Ibid.

5

SUBTRACTIVE SYNTHESIS

Subtractive synthesis creates musical tones out of complex sources by sculpting away selected portions of the spectrum of the source. In subtractive synthesis (figure 5.1), a source with a broad spectrum, such as white noise or a narrow pulse, serves as the raw material out of which a musical tone is formed by filtering.

This chapter considers some useful sources and discusses filtering at length. Musical examples are provided to show the design considerations for computer instruments with noise and periodic sources. Several examples from the musical literature are given. The chapter concludes with a more technical description of the principles of digital filtering, along with a few filter recipes.

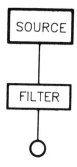

FIGURE 5.1   The basic configuration for subtractive synthesis.

5.1   Sources

Any sound can be used as a source for subtractive synthesis. The subtractive process alters the spectral balance of a sound, and so the technique has the greatest effect when applied to sources with rich spectra. Instruments employing synthesis techniques presented in earlier chapters (e.g., FM synthesis) or external signals (such as sound recorded by a microphone) can be used as sources. However, there are two kinds of signal generators which, because of the inherent spectral richness of their outputs, are commonly used as sources: noise and pulse generators. A noise generator produces a wide-band distributed spectrum (see section 3.9). A pulse generator produces a periodic waveform at a specific frequency with a great deal of energy in the harmonics.

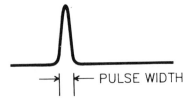

FIGURE 5.2   Generalized waveform of a pulse.

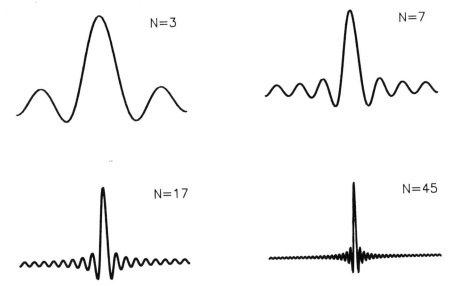

FIGURE 5.3   The waveform of band-limited pulses containing N harmonics.

A *pulse* waveform (figure 5.2) has significant amplitude only during a relatively brief interval of time. The duration of that interval is called the pulse width. When a pulse waveform is repeated periodically, the resulting signal has a rich spectrum. The actual character of the spectrum is determined by the shape of the pulse and by the ratio of the pulse width to the period of the overall waveform. A small ratio (i.e., a narrow pulse) connotes a large proportion of the spectral energy at high frequencies.

Pulses can assume a myriad of shapes—rectangular, triangular, etc.—but very few shapes have band-limited spectra. To avoid aliasing when using a pulse generator in digital synthesis, the musician must select shapes with band-limited spectra. A pulse generator that is commonly used in subtractive synthesis produces a waveform with a shape that depends on the ratio of the fundamental frequency of the pulse to the sampling frequency of the system. This type of pulse is best described in terms of its spectrum. It contains all possible harmonics of the fundamental up to the Nyquist frequency, each harmonic with the same amplitude. The number of harmonics in the spectrum, N, is determined from the fundamental frequency of oscillation (f_0) of the pulse generator and the sampling frequency (f_s) by

$$N = \text{int} \left[f_s/(2f_0) \right]$$

Figure 5.3 shows the waveform for four different values of N. Notice how the pulse

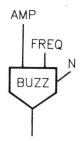

FIGURE 5.4   Flowchart symbol for the band-limited pulse generator known as BUZZ.

gets narrower as N gets larger. To avoid foldover at higher fundamental frequencies, the pulse must contain fewer harmonics, and so the pulse is wider. For example, if $f_s=40\text{KHz}$ and $f_0=440$ Hz, then $N=45$; but for $f_0=1046$ Hz, the signal would contain only 19 harmonics.

Using an oscillator which scans a wavetable to generate this type of pulse spectrum is impractical because N, and hence the shape of the waveform varies with fundamental frequency. Thus, many computer music systems include a unit generator (often called BUZZ) which contains an algorithm for efficiently generating this type of signal. The inputs to this unit generator, shown in figure 5.4, include pulse amplitude, fundamental frequency, and the number of harmonics in the pulse spectrum. Section 4.3A explains the mathematical technique used to generate the pulse waveform.

5.2   Introduction to Filtering

Filters change the characteristics of sounds by rejecting unwanted components in a signal or by otherwise shaping the spectrum. A filter modifies the amplitude and phase of each spectral component of a signal passing through it, but it does not alter the frequency of any signal or any component. This section includes descriptions of low-pass, high-pass, band-pass, and band-reject filters. The effect of filtering on the amplitude of spectral components of input signals is described in detail.

The characteristics of a filter can be described by its *frequency response*, which is determined experimentally by applying a sine wave to the input of the filter and measuring the characteristics of the sine wave that emerges. The frequency response consists of two parts—*amplitude response* and *phase response*. The amplitude response of a filter varies with frequency and is the ratio of the amplitude of the output sine wave to the amplitude of the input sine wave. The phase response describes the amount of phase change a sine wave undergoes as it passes through the filter. The amount of phase change also varies with the frequency of the sine wave.

Filters are usually distinguished by the shape of their amplitude response. Figure 5.5 diagrams the generalized amplitude responses of the low-pass filter and the high-pass filter. A *low-pass* filter (figure 5.5a) permits frequencies below the point called the cutoff frequency (f_c) to pass with little change. However, it significantly reduces the amplitude of spectral components above f_c. Conversely, a *high-pass filter* (figure 5.5b) has a passband above the cutoff frequency where signals are passed and a stopband below f_c where signals are attenuated.

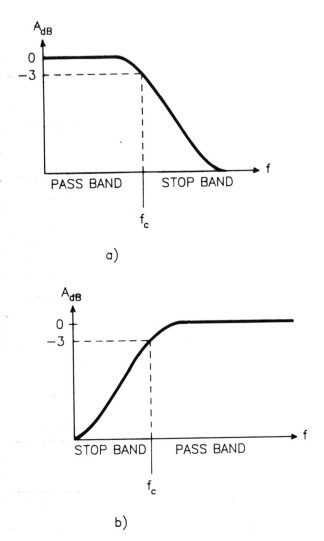

FIGURE 5.5   Amplitude response of a low-pass filter (a) and a high-pass filter (b).

There is always a smooth transition between passband and stopband, and so a rule is necessary for specifying the cutoff frequency: it is most often defined as that frequency at which the power transmitted by the filter drops to one half (−3 dB) of the maximum power transmitted in the passband. This convention is used in this text; it is equivalent to a reduction in the amplitude response by a factor of .707.

A filter that rejects both low and high frequencies with a passband in between them is called a *band-pass* filter. It is characterized either by a *center frequency* (CF or f_0) and a *bandwidth* (BW) or by two cutoff frequencies, an upper (f_u) and a lower (f_l). Figure 5.6 illustrates the generalized shape of the amplitude response of a band-pass filter. The center frequency marks the location of the center of the passband. In digital filters of the type implemented in most computer music programs, the center frequency is the arithmetic mean (average) of the upper and lower cutoff frequencies.

The bandwidth is a measure of the selectivity of the filter and is equal to the difference between upper and lower cutoff frequencies. The response of a

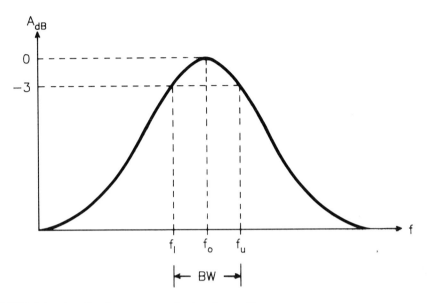

FIGURE 5.6 Amplitude response of a band-pass filter.

band-pass filter is often described by terms such as sharp (narrow) or broad (wide), depending on the actual width. The passband sharpness is often quantified by means of a quality factor (Q). When the cutoff frequencies are defined at the -3 dB points, Q is given by

$$Q = (f_0/BW_{3dB})$$

Therefore, a high Q denotes a narrow bandwidth. Bandwidth may also be described as a percentage of the center frequency. The sharpness of a filter is

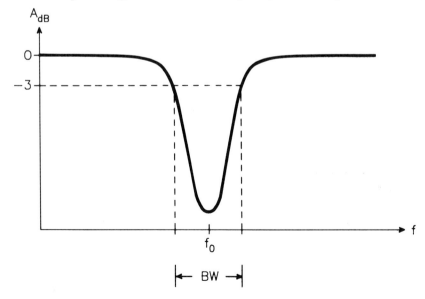

FIGURE 5.7 Amplitude response of a band-reject filter. In certain instances, the bandwidth, BW, is measured between the points at which the amplitude response is 3 dB above the minimum instead of as shown.

chosen according to the application for which it is used. For example, a band-pass filter with a very narrow bandwidth can be used to extract a specific frequency component from a signal.

The fourth basic filter type is the *band-reject* filter. As its name implies, its amplitude response (figure 5.7) is the inverse of a band-pass filter's. It attenuates a single band of frequencies and passes all the others. Like a band-pass filter, it is characterized by a center frequency and a bandwidth; but another important parameter is the amount of attenuation in the center of the stopband.

5.3   A General-Purpose Filter

Most computer music programs include a unit generator (often called RESON) that serves as a general-purpose filter. It is usually a second-order all-pole filter (see section 5.13). The discussion in this section applies to digital filters of that type.

A generalized symbol for a filter element is shown in figure 5.8. This element is a band-pass filter with controlling inputs of center frequency (CF) and bandwidth

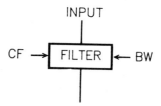

FIGURE 5.8   Flowchart symbol for a filter.

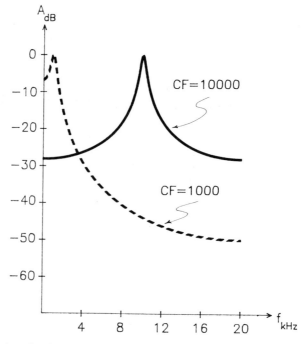

FIGURE 5.9   Amplitude response of two filters with 500 Hz bandwidths, but with different center frequencies. The sampling frequency is 40 kHz.

(BW). Under special conditions it can be used as a low-pass or high-pass filter. For example, a low-pass filter can be made from a band-pass filter by setting its center frequency to zero. Intuitively, one might think that the resulting cutoff frequency would be one-half the bandwidth specified, because the passband centers at 0 Hz. Hence, the upper cutoff frequency of the passband should also be the cutoff frequency of the low-pass filter. However, due to the nature of the approximation made in the implementation of the digital filters found in most computer music programs, the cutoff frequency, f_c, of the resulting low-pass is equal to .707 times the specified bandwidth, not .5. For example, to obtain a low-pass with a cutoff frequency of 500 Hz, specify CF=0 and BW=707 Hz. This approximation will also affect the response of band-pass filters with low center frequencies. As the center frequency of the band-pass filter is brought closer to zero, the passband begins to widen beyond the specified bandwidth. Figure 5.9 illustrates this effect. Observe that the amplitude response is symmetrical when the center frequency is 10,000 Hz and that the left side begins to tilt upwards as the center frequency is decreased.

A high-pass filter can be made from a band-pass filter by setting its center frequency equal to the Nyquist frequency. High-pass digital filters made from the band-pass filters found in most computer music programs suffer from the same approximation problems that affect low-pass filters. To obtain a high-pass filter in this way with a cutoff frequency f_c, specify the bandwidth according to:

$$BW = \sqrt{2}(\tfrac{1}{2}f_s - f_c)$$

For example, a high-pass filter with a cutoff frequency of 15 kHz in a system with a 40 kHz sampling rate is realized by parameters of CF=20 kHz and BW=7071 Hz. As the center frequency of a band-pass filter approaches the Nyquist frequency, the passband warps in the same way described above for filters with low center frequencies.

The other parameter normally associated with filters is midband gain: the ratio of output signal amplitude to input signal amplitude in the center of the passband. The natural, unscaled ratio in a digital filter has a complicated dependence on both center frequency and bandwidth. Thus the amplitude of a signal at the center frequency may be radically changed, causing the filter element to serve also as an amplifier or attenuator. The purpose of a scale factor is to prevent this circumstance by multiplying the filter input by the number that brings the midband gain to 1. Many programs offer the choice of three types of scale factors: one for periodic signals, one for noise signals, and one to leave the filter output unscaled. The filter output is left unscaled when the musician has carefully determined a succession of filter elements to be used in realizing a desired frequency response.

5.4 Stopband Behavior

For simple filters such as those described in sections 5.2 and 5.3, the amount of attenuation in the stopband is smallest near the cutoff frequency and continues to increase away from cutoff. A frequency not found in the passband has usually not been completely removed from the signal; it has been attenuated more than if it had been found in the passband.

The rate at which the attenuation increases is known as the slope of the filter. The slope, or *rolloff*, is usually expressed as attenuation per unit interval, such as 30 dB per octave. In the stopband of a low-pass filter with a 30 dB/octave slope, every time the frequency doubles, the amount of attenuation increases by 30 dB. At four times the cutoff frequency, the attenuation is 30 dB greater than at twice the cutoff frequency; at eight times, the attenuation is 60 dB greater, and so on. A filter used for rejecting unwanted signals must have a steep rolloff. A good example is a low-pass filter used on the input of a analog-to-digital converter to prevent aliasing. Here a steep rolloff enables a wide passband to be used for desired signals. By contrast, a filter used in an instrument design for changing the harmonic content of a source may need a much gentler rolloff to allow a more natural relationship between the harmonics.

The slope of attenuation is determined by the order of the filter. Order is a mathematical measure of the complexity of a filter. In an analog filter, it is proportional to the number of electrical components used. In a digital filter, it is proportional to the number of calculations performed on each sample. (A more detailed explanation of order in a digital filter is given in section 5.11.) In a simple analog low-pass or high-pass filter, the rolloff is 6 dB/octave times the order of the filter. A band-pass filter generally has an even order and the slope both above and below the passband is ordinarily 6 dB/octave times half the order. Thus, the rolloff will be half as steep as that of a low-pass or high-pass filter of the same order. This may be interpreted to mean that half of the filter contributes to the rolloff below the passband and the other half to the rolloff above.

Most digital filters are designed as approximations to analog filters. The rolloff of a digital filter will be similar but not identical to the analog filter being imitated. Due to the nature of digital filters, it is not possible to maintain a constant slope throughout the stopband, and therefore, it is not possible to give a precise relationship between order and rolloff. However, the general character of the relationship still holds—the higher the order, the steeper the slope.

The filter unit generators found in most computer music programs are either first or second-order filters. The filter used to simulate the effect of adjusting the tone control of an amplifier is a first-order filter (often called TONE). Depending on the ratio of cutoff frequency to sampling frequency, it exhibits a 6 dB/octave rolloff over much of its stopband. The resonator unit generator provided (often called RESON or FLT) is a second-order filter. It tends toward a 6 dB/octave slope both above and below the passband.

5.5 Filter Combinations

Filter designers need not be restricted to the four basic filter response shapes described above. It is possible to tailor a filter's amplitude response to an arbitrarily complex contour. This provides the musician with a great deal of flexibility in designing interesting spectra for instruments. One useful and conceptually simple method of obtaining complicated amplitude responses is to use the four basic filter types as building blocks (or elements) that can be combined to form a filter with a desired response.

Filter elements can be combined in *parallel connection*, as shown in figure 5.10a. When two or more elements are connected in parallel, the signal to be filtered is applied simultaneously to the inputs of all the filter elements. The outputs of all elements are added together to form a total output. Essentially, parallel connection adds together the frequency responses of all the elements, with the result that if a frequency is found in the passband of any of the filter elements, it will be passed. Only those frequencies that are not found within the passband of any element will be attenuated. For instance, a band-reject filter can be made by connecting a low-pass and a high-pass filter in parallel. The stopband of the complete filter falls in between the cutoff frequencies of the individual elements. As another example, figure 5.10b shows the amplitude response of a filter with two passbands made by parallel connection of two band-pass filters with different center frequencies.

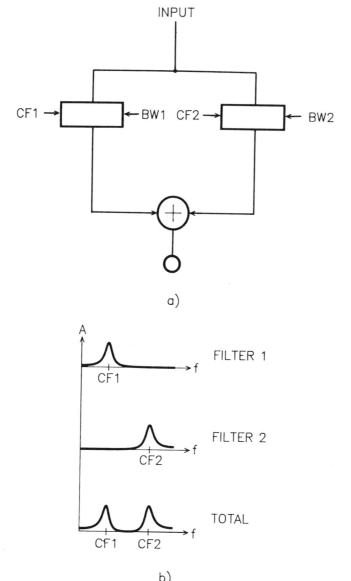

FIGURE 5.10   (a) Parallel connection of filter elements and (b) amplitude response of a filter with two passbands made by parallel connection of two band-pass filters.

The other fundamental method of element combination is *cascade connection* shown in figure 5.11. (This type of connection is called "series" in some places in the literature of computer music.) In a cascade-connected filter, the elements are connected together as links in a chain. The output of the first element feeds the input of the next element, and so forth until the last element, whose output is the output of the entire filter. The amplitude response of the complete filter is calculated by multiplying all the individual responses together. If expressed in dB, the overall amplitude response at a given frequency is the sum of the responses of the individual elements in dB at that frequency.

The order of a filter that is made up of cascade-connected elements is equal to the sum of the orders of all the individual elements, so that the complete filter will have a faster rolloff. For example, consider the cascade connection of the two band-pass filter elements with identical parameters shown in figure 5.12a. The resulting filter will be a band-pass filter with the same center frequency and a

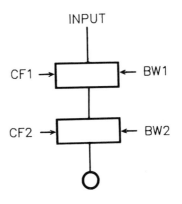

FIGURE 5.11   Cascade connection of filter elements.

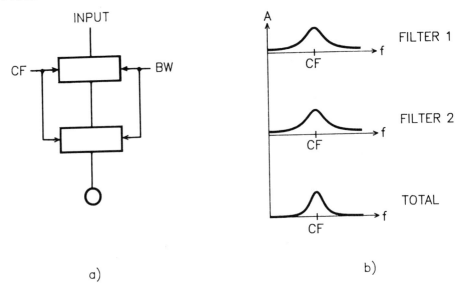

a)

b)

FIGURE 5.12   Cascade connection of identical filters resulting in a narrower filter with faster rolloff.

steeper slope (figure 5.12b). At the frequency at which a single element has an attenuation of 3 dB, the cascade-combination has an overall attenuation of 6 dB. Thus, the 3-dB bandwidth of an individual element becomes the 6-dB bandwidth of the complete filter. The 3-dB bandwidth of the overall filter is equal to the bandwidth at which each individual element contributes 1.5 dB of attenuation. Thus, in this case, cascade connection not only increases the rolloff of the filter, it also decreases the bandwidth. For example, the 1.5-dB bandwidth of a second-order band-pass filter of the type discussed in section 5.3 is about 65% of its 3-dB bandwidth. Suppose two of these filters, each with a center frequency of 1 kHz and a bandwidth of 100 Hz have been connected in cascade. The resultant filter has a center frequency of 1 kHz and a bandwidth of 65 Hz.

Through careful choice of center frequencies and bandwidths, band-pass filter elements can be cascaded to form a filter with steep rolloff but with a passband wider than any of the individual elements (figure 5.13a). This is accomplished by choosing the center frequencies of the elements to be close to each other with overlapping passbands. Figure 5.13b shows that the resultant filter has a wider and flatter passband.

The overall midband gain is less than that of any individual element, but this can be compensated by amplification. The choice of center frequencies and bandwidths for the elements is made most effectively through mathematical analysis, but as this example demonstrates, much can be done intuitively.

Great care must be used when designing a filter using cascade-connected elements with different center frequencies. Note that, unlike parallel connection, the specification of a passband of one element does not guarantee that there will be significant energy passed in that frequency band. If any of the other elements of a cascade connection contribute significant attenuation in that frequency range, the amplitude response there will be quite low. The cascade connection of two

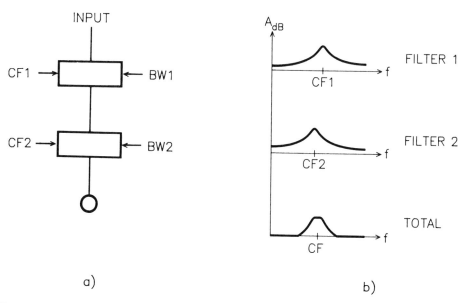

FIGURE 5.13   Cascade connection of two filters with slightly offset center frequencies to obtain a wider, flatter passband with a steeper rolloff.

band-pass filters of different center frequencies is shown in figure 5.14a. The passbands do not overlap, and so the resultant filter will have two peaks in its response curve, but the overall amplitude of the peaks will be small (figure 5.14b). Each passband is tilted because the response of the opposite filter is rolling off. On many systems, a filter of this type can be made useful for subtractive synthesis by multiplying its output by a constant to reconstitute its amplitude. If the samples are represented in floating-point format, as is the case in most of the synthesis programs run on general-purpose computers, boosting the filtered signal will not increase the noise to a detectable level. In systems that use integer format, such as often used in specialized signal-processing hardware, the available range might not be large enough for this method to work without severely degrading the signal-to-noise ratio.

To permit a musician to use cascade connection freely, without the necessity of calculating the overall midband gain of the filter, some computer music programs implement a unit generator that performs a balance function. The user must specify a reference point in the signal flow, as shown in figure 5.15. When this unit generator is used, it modifies the amplitude of the signal entering the balance unit, so that the average power in the signal coming out of the balance unit equals the average power of the signal at the reference point. This is useful when implementing filters made up of several elements because the reference point can be the input to the first element of the filter, and the balance unit can be placed at the output of the filter. Thus, the signal would have the same power coming out as it would have going in. However, this technique is only effective when a substantial amount of the signal power falls in the passband. Obviously, if the input to the filter consists of a single frequency that is outside the passband, the balance function will boost the signal amplitude to compensate for the attenuation introduced by the filter, thus negating the effect of the filter. However, if the signal applied to the filter has many spectral components over a wide range, as is the case with noise or a

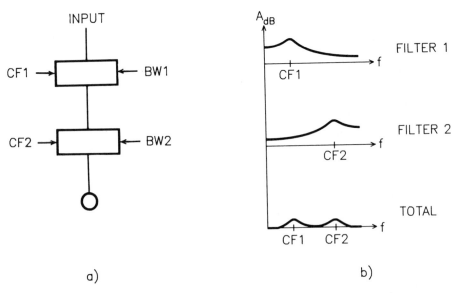

a)   b)

FIGURE 5.14 Cascade connection of filters whose passbands do not overlap.

pulse, the balance function can be quite useful. It allows the musician to modify the spectrum of the signal at will without dramatically altering its power.

To determine the average power of a signal, the balance function rectifies the signal and passes it through a low-pass filter. The process of rectification consists of taking the absolute value of the samples, so that all the negative sample values are changed into positive ones, as shown in figure 5.16. This is a form of non-linear waveshaping (see chapter 4) and has the effect of greatly emphasizing the even

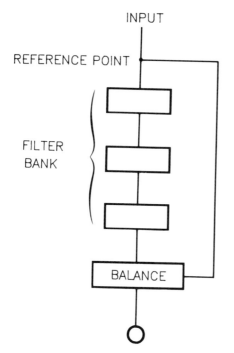

FIGURE 5.15 Use of a balance function to approximately maintain the amplitude of the output at the level of the input.

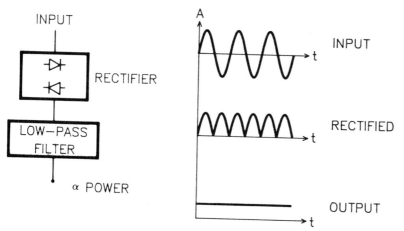

FIGURE 5.16 Method used by balance function to approximate signal power.

harmonic components of the signal, including the zero-frequency (d–c) term. The higher the amplitude of the signal fed into the rectifier, the larger the amplitudes of the even harmonics. The output of the rectifier is then passed through a low-pass filter with a very low cutoff frequency which attenuates all components except for the zero-frequency term. Thus, the output of the balance function is proportional to the signal amplitude; it therefore provides a measure of average signal power. The user may specify the cutoff frequency of the filter, but normally it is sub-audio (usually 10 Hz) if the purpose is to obtain the average power of a signal.

5.6   Adjustable Digital Filters

A digital filter algorithm works by multiplying signals and delayed images of signals by numbers called coefficients. Specifying a set of coefficients to a filter algorithm uniquely determines the characteristics of the digital filter. (See section 5.11.) Most computer music programs contain the algorithms to convert filter characteristics to coefficients, and so users need only specify parameters such as center frequency and bandwidth. However, it takes considerable computer time to calculate filter coefficients from a given frequency response. Thus, if the frequency response of the filter is not going to change during the synthesis process, the coefficients are calculated only once, prior to the beginning of the synthesis. However, the musician is afforded a great deal of flexibility if the frequency response of the filter can be altered during the course of a sound. Therefore, the music programs from the MUSIC 4 family implement two kinds of filter functions. The first type (often called RESON or FLT) has its coefficients calculated only once, prior to the beginning of the actual synthesis process. The second type (often called VRESON) is basically the same filter, but its coefficients are calculated on every sample. The coefficients of the variable filter are calculated with equations that only approximate the desired passband, because the exact calculation takes too much computer time. The approximation used is most accurate for narrow bandwidths. When the bandwidth exceeds 10% of the sampling frequency, the characteristics of the filter actually obtained begin to deviate noticeably. To maximize computational efficiency, the musician uses variable filters only where needed.

When the filter coefficients are calculated on every sample, the need for a reasonable computation time makes impractical the calculation of a scaling factor for midband gain (see section 5.3). As a result, this kind of filter is normally used unscaled. Some computer music programs allow the musician to enter an estimate of the peak amplitude of the output signal. The program uses this guess to scale the gain for an expected peak output of one. However, the success of this technique is completely dependent upon the accuracy of the musician's estimation.

Some programs, such as MUSIC 11, use another method that precisely determines the coefficients, including midband gain, of the adjustable filter without taking an excessive amount of computation time. In this method the computer calculates coefficients at a rate lower than the sampling rate. For example, the new coefficients could be determined on every twentieth sample. The reduced rate at which the filter characteristics can change is not a musical limitation unless the calculation rate falls below about 200 times per second.

A third approach to realizing a variable filter, which has been used in systems with special purpose real-time hardware, entails calculating many sets of coefficients in advance. Each set corresponds to a different filter setting and is stored away in memory. During performance, the characteristics of a filter are changed by calling in the appropriate set. If two filter settings differ only slightly, intermediate settings can sometimes be realized by interpolating the coefficients between them. However, interpolation runs the risk of creating an unstable filter which could add unwanted noise to the sound.

5.7   The Effect of Filtering in the Time-Domain

Every filter, in addition to having a frequency response, has an impulse response. The *impulse response* is a time-domain description of the filter's response to a very short pulse. In addition, it can be used to determine the filter's response to any type of change in the input signal. Sometimes a filter is designed to achieve a specific impulse response (see section 7.1B), but here we will examine the time-domain behavior of filters that were designed to have a particular amplitude resonse.

The preceding discussion of filters was restricted to the frequency-dependent properties of filters. That discussion assumed that the signal applied to the input of the filter had been present long enough for the output of the filter to stabilize. The properties of a filter after it has stabilized constitute its *steady-state* response. But in order to use a filter most effectively, the musician should understand not only its steady-state properties, but also its effect on signals that are changing.

The way in which a filter reacts at the beginning and end of a steady tone is called its *transient response*. At the beginning, the duration of the transient response is the length of time it takes for the filter's output to settle into the steady state; at the end, the duration is the length of time it takes for the output to decay. The transient response depends on the impulse response of the filter and on the envelope of the tone that is applied. The duration of the transient response is

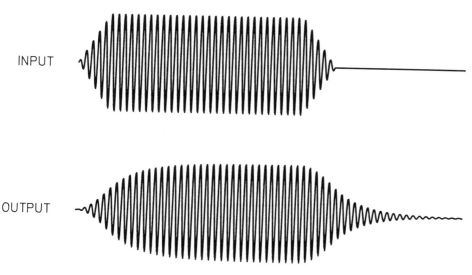

INPUT

OUTPUT

FIGURE 5.17   Alteration of the envelope of a tone by a filter.

inversely proportional to the filter bandwidth. The narrower the bandwidth, the longer it takes for the filter to respond to transients.

For example, when a sinusoidal tone is applied to the input of a filter with a center frequency equal to the frequency of the input signal, the full signal does not appear immediately at the output in most cases. Similarly, once the input tone has ended, the signal at the output of the filter ordinarily does not drop immediately to zero: It takes time for the output to build up to a steady-state value and time for it to die away after the input has ended. Figure 5.17 illustrates the waveforms of both the input and output signals of a filter with a narrow bandwidth. Notice how the filter elongates both the attack and the decay.

Thus, it can be seen that a filter can also modify the envelope of a sound. When using subtractive synthesis, the specification of the envelope of the tone applied to the filter may have to be tempered to allow for the transient response of the filter. This is especially important when large banks of cascade-connected filters are employed since each filter can affect the envelope of the tone.

5.8 Subtractive Instruments that Use Noise Sources

Section 3.11 contains an illustration of an instrument that uses random ring modulation to create a band of noise. The same effect can be achieved by using a digital filter on a noise source. The result will be a more concentrated band of noise, but will require slightly more computer time. Figure 5.18 shows the flow chart for the subtractive-synthesis instrument that produces bands of noise.

With a single filter on a noise source, it is possible to obtain a variety of sound qualities. Differences in center frequency and bandwidth have striking effects. Specifying the bandwidth as a fixed percentage of center frequency provides for the same intervallic width of noise on every filter note, regardless of register. All other factors being equal, the noise bands at various center frequencies will be perceived as belonging to the same class of sounds. A useful general rule for choosing bandwidth is that a bandwidth of around 5% of the center frequency produces a clear pitch at the center frequency and can be used as a melodic, pitched noise instrument. Narrower bands of filtered noise produce even greater pitch focus and sound less "noisy." In the high registers, they sound more like whistles. As the bandwidth becomes a larger percentage of the center frequency, the listener has

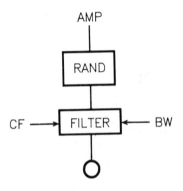

FIGURE 5.18   Instrument that produces "bands of noise."

less and less sensation of pitch until the sound becomes noise, without pitch, in the register of the center frequency. A musician, working within the constraints and patterns of a composition, must find the boundaries that work best in the compositional context.

It is common for a musician to vary either the center frequency or the bandwidth or both, when using filtered noise. Figure 5.19 displays the flow chart for the computer instrument that makes the noise sounds in Charles Dodge's electronic

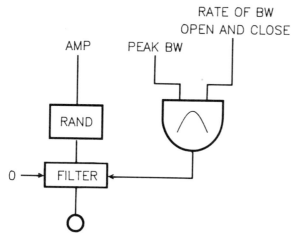

FIGURE 5.19   Noise instrument with variable bandwidth.

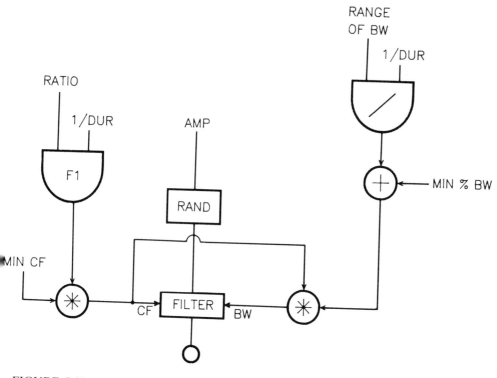

FIGURE 5.20   Instrument for producing glissandoing noise bands.

realization of Samuel Beckett's radio play, *Cascando*.[1] The center frequency of the filter is set to zero, thus converting the filter to a low-pass. The instrument produces sound only when the bandwidth is sufficiently wide to allow noise in the audio range. The cutoff frequency is changed continuously by the controlling oscillator. The amplitude of the oscillator sets the maximum cutoff frequency, and the frequency of the oscillator determines the rate of interruption of the noise. The results fall within a range of sounds described as "rustling," "thumping," and "scurrying."

It is common to apply continuous changes of both bandwidth and center frequency to noise inputs. Figure 5.20 shows an instrument for producing these effects. It uses oscillators to produce a range of time variations in center frequency and bandwidth. The amplitude argument for the left oscillator is fed a ratio of the highest to lowest center frequency and that of the right oscillator the range of bandwidth change. The frequency inputs for the oscillators determine the duration over which the variations are to take place. The waveforms of the oscillators represent the shape of the modulation. A constant is added to the output of each oscillator to ensure that CF and BW maintain minimum values. Consider a case in which the following is desired:

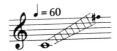

This glissando over an octave and a tritone is in the time span of 4 seconds and has a continuous change in bandwidth from 5% of center frequency at the beginning to 50% of center frequency at the end. The following parameters will be used:

DUR	= 4 sec
MIN CF	= 261.6 Hz
RATIO	= 739.9/261.6 = 2.828
MIN % BW	= .05
RANGE OF BW	= .45

The function F1 is a decaying exponential curve with a ratio of 1:1/RATIO, in this case 1:0.354.

5.9 Subtractive Instruments that Use Periodic Sources

The effect of filtering a periodic source is very different from that of filtering a noise source. Periodic sources are pitched, and so the center frequency and bandwidth settings have no significant effect on pitch perception. Instead, these settings on the filter affect only the timbre. Figure 5.21 shows a simple filter instrument connected to a periodic source. The center frequency and bandwidth are usually set greater than the frequency of the highest pitch to be played by the instrument. The settings are not changed with pitch. This arrangement places a fixed resonance, called a formant, in the spectrum of the sound at the center frequency of the filter. A spectral component that falls near the resonance will be emphasized because it will

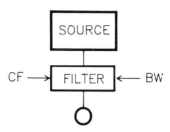

FIGURE 5.21   Filtering a periodic source.

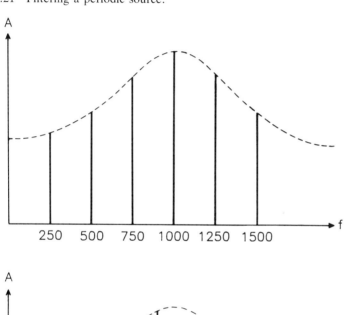

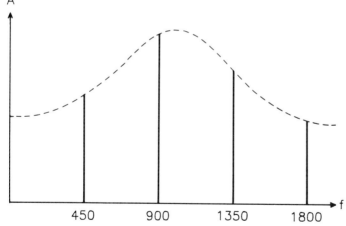

FIGURE 5.22   Two spectra with different fundamental frequencies that display the same formant.

be attenuated less than those farther away from the resonance. The presence of fixed resonances in the spectrum is thought to contribute to our perception of timbral homogeneity. (See section 2.6.) Figure 5.22 shows a formant imparted to the spectra of tones at 250 Hz and 450 Hz by a resonance peak at 1000 Hz. The resonance peak will emphasize the fourth harmonic of the 250-Hz tone, but will emphasize the second harmonic of the 450-Hz tone. The tones will share a timbral similarity because of the common resonance structure.

A subtractive-synthesis technique frequently used in electronic music synthesis, to create musical tones from periodic sources, is called "harmonic enveloping." In this technique, a control signal, such as that from an envelope generator, is applied to the bandwidth input of a filter. This causes the relative strength of the harmonic partials to change with time, affecting both waveform and timbre.

Figure 5.23 shows a design in which the center frequency of the filter is set to zero and the bandwidth is made to change in proportion to the amplitude of the tone. In this instrument, as in many acoustic instruments, the strength of the higher harmonics is in direct proportion to the amplitude of the tone. A tone begins with a nearly pure sinewave. As the loudness increases during the attack, so does the amplitude of the higher harmonics. When the tone dies away, the higher harmonics drop out first. This effect may also be useful in simulating the change in spectral content that often occurs in acoustic instruments when the dynamic level changes.

When using a design such as this, the musician must carefully determine the numerical relationship between amplitude and the cutoff frequency of the filter. One way this can be done is to find the ratio between the highest cutoff frequency and the maximum amplitude. (The exact numerical value for the amplitude will depend on the system used.) The value used for the cutoff frequency is then the product of that ratio and the value of the amplitude input of the oscillator. For example, suppose the amplitude of a note were to rise to a maximum of 20,000 at the peak of the attack and the instrument designer determined that at this value, the cutoff frequency should be 2000 Hz. In this case, the instrument would multiply the amplitude value by the scaling factor .1 before applying it to the cutoff frequency input of the filter. If, as in the figure the low-pass filter takes the form of

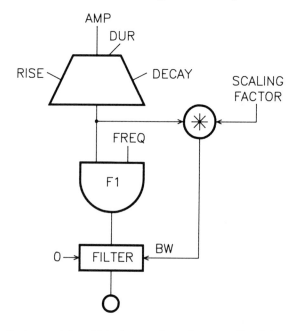

FIGURE 5.23 Instrument in which the spectrum is proportional to amplitude. F1 is a harmonically rich, band-limited waveform.

a band-pass filter with its center frequency set to zero, the actual cutoff frequency will be .707 times the number applied to the bandwidth input of the filter. This should be taken into account in calculating the relationship between amplitude and the cutoff frequency.

With a single filter element, only one resonance peak can be imparted. It is often desirable or even necessary (e.g., for speech synthesis) to impart more than one resonance peak to a signal. Special expertise is required to know how to calculate center frequency and bandwidth for a group of filters used to realize a desired response curve. Although true engineering solutions depend on mathematical analyses, it is often possible, for musical applications, to estimate filter settings that fit a given response curve adequately. The response curve shown in figure 5.24a calls for an amplitude response of a generally low-pass character with five resonance peaks. One way an engineer could synthesize the filter design is by

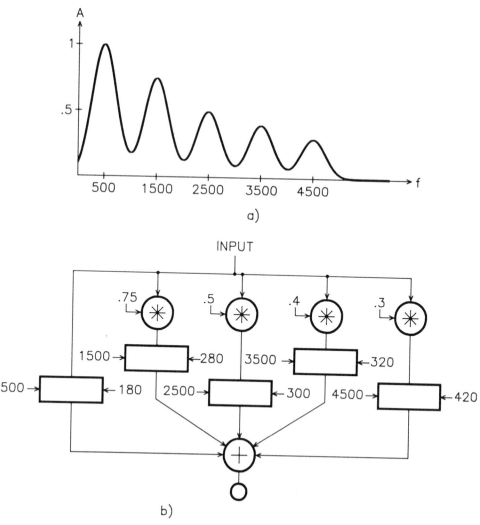

FIGURE 5.24   Rough approximation of the amplitude response, (a) by the parallel connection of five filters as shown in (b).

expressing the response curve as a polynomial and factoring out each second-order filter element. This relatively difficult procedure usually results in a realization using five second-order band-pass filters connected in cascade. However, under certain circumstances, the less mathematical method of parallel-connected filters can be used to roughly approximate the desired response. In the case of the figure, five filters would ordinarily be used because the response exhibits five resonance peaks. The center frequency of each filter would be set to the frequency of one of the resonances. The input to each filter is attenuated by the amount necessary to bring the overall response to the desired shape. In the example, the attenuation multipliers are, from low to high center frequency, 1, .75, .5, .4, and .3. The resulting filter configuration is shown in figure 5.24b. It does not realize the exact amplitude response, but rather represents a fair approximation.

Figure 5.25 contains an example of the use of the balance function in a non-standard way. The three band-pass filters are connected in cascade in the usual way and serve the purpose of imparting resonances to the signal at the center frequencies of 500, 1500, and 3000 Hz. The low-pass filter in the balance function is given a cutoff frequency slightly lower than the fundamental frequency of the signal being filtered. The balance function (section 5.5) estimates the power in the signals at both the input and output of the filter bank by rectification, a form of nonlinear waveshaping. With the relatively high cutoff frequency of its internal filters, the balance function is more responsive to the instantaneous variations in both signals when attempting to make the output signal match the reference signal. The resulting signal contains large amounts of harmonic distortion with more energy in

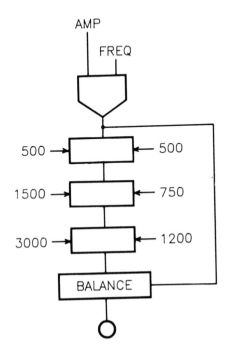

FIGURE 5.25 Non-standard use of the balance function. The cutoff frequency of the low-pass filter inside the balance function is set close to FREQ to produce an unusual ringing in the high harmonics.

the higher harmonics than is usually obtained with other, more direct forms of waveshaping. The sonic texture produced by this filtering method, particularly when reverberated, can be extremely delicate. The sound of this instrument is found in *Earth's Magnetic Field*[2] by Charles Dodge. (See section 7.3B.)

Figure 5.26 shows a method for implementing timbre change with subtractive

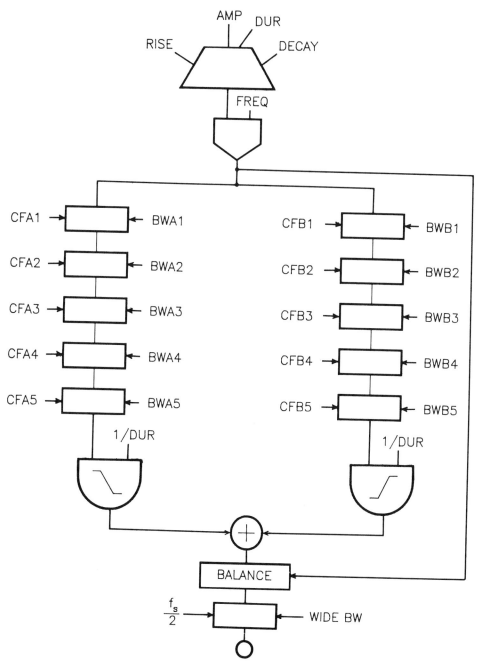

FIGURE 5.26   Instrument to produce "timbre exchange."

synthesis, using banks of filters with fixed center frequencies and bandwidths. Here, the output of each of the two banks of filters, each with its own set of center frequencies and bandwidths, is multiplied by an envelope. The first bank sounds alone for the first third of the note; the two banks exchange amplitude levels during the second third of the note, and the second bank sounds alone for the final third. The design was used for the "lines" in Dodge's *Changes*.[3] (See section 5.10.)

The high-pass filter was included at the end of the instrument design to emphasize the "buzziness" of the source. Most acoustic instruments have an overall low-pass characteristic, but this design was created to produce the opposite effect. To improve computational efficiency, each bank was computed only during the two-thirds of the note in which it sounded.

5.10   Examples of Compositional Application

Changes[4] by Charles Dodge is a work in which there are three textural elements—contrapuntal lines, percussive sounds, and irregularly placed chords. Of *Changes* Paul Griffiths writes, "Every time a chord appears the timbres of the lines are altered: it is as if with each new chord a different color filter were placed in front of the counterpoint."[5] The change in timbre is effected by changing the center frequency settings of the banks of filters through which the pulse is passed. The design of the instrument which plays the lines in *Changes* is shown in figure 5.26.

In *Changes* the center-frequency values were chosen to match the pitch-content of the chords which initiate each timbre-defined section of the piece. The effect of the matching is not heard in pitch, however. It serves simply as a means of creating differentiations of timbre based on the pitch-content of the chords.

The exchange of amplitude between banks of filters was the means for effecting the change of timbre within the note. As *Changes* evolves, there are more and more banks of filters for each note—and thus, more changes of timbre per note. At the end of the work every note of each line is sent through six different banks of filters.

The analogy between color filters and audio filters is made explicit in the composition *Colors* (1981) by A. Wayne Slawson. Slawson has performed research on the relationships between the vowel sounds of speech and musical timbre.[6] From this work, he has developed a theory of sound color postulating relationships in sound color which are analogous to relationships in musical pitch. His purpose is to permit the organization of sound color through musical operations ordinarily employed in the domain of pitch. Slawson postulates a group of rules in order to make a perceptually valid set of relationships in tone color.[7] They establish a basis for the explicit use of sound color relationships in his music.

Rule 1 states, "To hold the color of a sound invariant, hold its spectrum envelope invariant."

This rule implies that two sounds with the same spectral envelope will have the same color even if they result from filtering different sources. Slawson demonstrates this invariance in his composition by imposing the same sequence of filter settings on different sound sources, such as pitched sounds, noise sounds, and frequency-modulated sounds.

Rule 2 states, "To change a color while holding it invariant with respect to one of the dimensions, arrange to move through the color space along contours of equal value associated with that dimension."

The principal dimensions of sound color in Slawson's theory are "acuteness," "openness," "smallness," and "laxness." (The terms for these dimensions are freely borrowed from the literature of acoustic phonetics.) Each dimension characterizes the relation in frequency between the poles of a pair of band-pass filters. For example, acuteness relates the change of the second resonance frequency of the pair to the frequency of the first. Given a fixed frequency for the first resonance, acuteness increases with an increase in the frequency of the second resonance. Openness works in just the opposite way: For a given fixed frequency of the second resonance, openness is increased with a rise in the frequency of the first resonance. The smallness of a sound is increased by raising both resonances together, and laxness increases as both resonances move toward median values. Figure 5.27 shows the two-dimensional space for each of the four dimensions described. The vowels are inserted into the figure as references to some familiar sound colors. The contour lines denoting points of equal value in tone color are drawn onto the four diagrams.

To complete the analogy between pitch and tone color, Slawson includes two more rules that introduce transposition and inversion of sound color into his system.

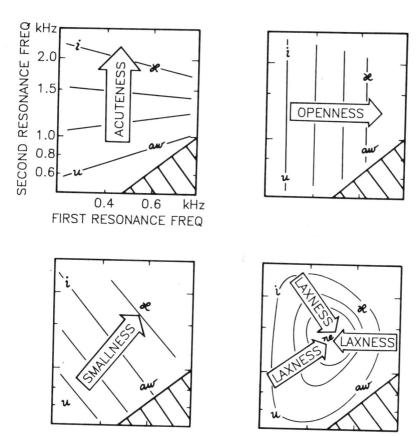

FIGURE 5.27 Equal-value contours of sound color dimensions used by Slawson. The arrows indicate the direction of increasing value for each dimension. (*Reprinted with the permission of A. Wayne Slawson.*)

Rule 3 states, "To transpose a color with respect to a dimension, shift the color in the direction of the dimension (perpendicular to its equal-value contours). When the boundary of the space is reached, 'wrap-around' to the opposite boundary and continue shifting in the same direction." Figure 5.28 shows an example of the transposition of a sequence of colors represented by the vowel sounds nearest in the figure.

For inversion, Slawson complements the values of a particular dimension around the point of maximal laxness. His rule 3b states, "To invert a sound color with respect to a dimension, complement its value on that dimension." Slawson uses the following as an example of the inversion operation in his system. Given the sequence of colors corresponding to the set of vowel sounds u, i, aw, ae, the inversion with respect to acuteness (holding openness constant) would be i, u, ae, aw. The original inverted with respect to smallness would be ae, i, aw, u.

In *Colors*, the most prominent feature of the sonic surface is in the rapid changes of the sound color. Slawson uses a series of nine sound colors that roughly correspond to the vowel sounds: oh, ee, uu, aw, ii, ae, oe, aa, and ne (schwa). Slawson chose this set so that the operations of transposition and inversion with

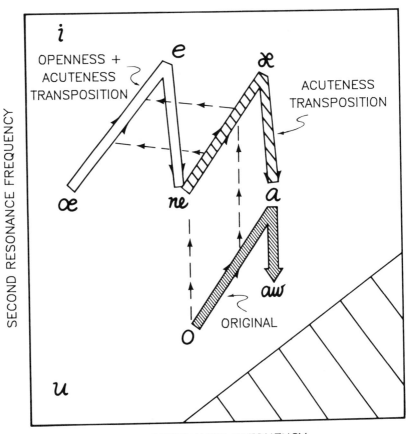

FIGURE 5.28   An example, from Slawson, of the transposition of a sequence of colors. (*Reprinted with the permission of A. Wayne Slawson.*)

respect to acuteness, openness, and smallness would result in reorderings of the set, introducing no new colors and repeating none. The composition deals extensively with the serial property of combinatoriality. The sets used in the piece are chosen to form "color aggregates," a technique based on the model of Milton Babbitt's pitch aggregates.[8] The work is in the form of eleven variations. Throughout the piece, the color series is kept more or less the same, while the sources to the filters are changed considerably. Certain variations involve not only fixed (discrete) sound colors, but also situations in which the sound color changes continuously, as in the dipthongs of speech.

5.11 Digital Filters

A digital filter is a computational algorithm that converts one sequence of numbers (the input signal) into another (the output signal), with the result that the character of the signal so processed is altered in some prescribed manner. Most often, digital filters are designed to obtain a specific alteration that is characterized in terms of the filter's steady-state amplitude response. However, chapter 7 (Reverberation) discusses digital filters that are designed to realize a particular impulse response. Filter design is an advanced art, and a complete treatment of the subject is well beyond the scope of this text. The purposes of this section are to acquaint the musician with general principles of filter algorithms and to present recipes for certain digital filters. FORTRAN code for the algorithms that realize most of these filters can be found in the appendix. For derivations of the recipes, the reader is referred to the extensive literature on digital filtering.[9,10]

The two principal types of digital filter algorithms are *non-recursive* and *recursive*. In both cases the output signal is calculated on every sample as a combination of the current input with previous filter inputs and outputs. A non-recursive filter calculates the present value of the output by combining the present value of the input with past values of the input. In a recursive filter, on the other hand, the present value of the output is a combination of both past values of the output and the present and sometimes past values of the input.

Because the filter uses past input and/or output samples in calculating its output, filter algorithms must have some means of delaying digital signals. The delay is achieved by storing previous values in memory. The number of storage locations necessary is determined by the amount of delay required. For example, an algorithm that determines its output from the present input sample and the previous two output samples would need two storage locations—one for the last output sample value and one for the next to last. After computing the current output sample value, the algorithm moves what had been the previous output value into the location for the next-to-last sample value. The current output sample is then stored as the last sample so that the filter is ready to compute a new output on the next sample. The length of the maximum delay (measured as a number of samples) determines the order of the filter. A high-order filter enables greater complexity or sharpness in its amplitude response, but requires more computation.

Engineers often describe filters in terms of poles and zeros. These terms originate in the mathematical analysis of a filter response. A *pole* places a peak in the amplitude response and a *zero* causes a valley. When a pole or zero is taken alone, its location can be described by the center frequency and bandwidth of the peak or valley that is created in the amplitude response. The height of a peak or the depth of a valley is dependent primarily on the bandwidth. The narrower the bandwidth is, the higher the peak or the deeper the valley. The term "zero" can be misleading. At the center frequency of a zero, the amplitude response of the filter exhibits a minimum, but does not necessarily reach zero.

In a digital filter, zeros are obtained by using algorithms that calculate the output by combining the input with past input samples. Poles are realized by combining the present input sample with past values of the output. Therefore, a non-recursive filter can realize only zeros and, as a result, is sometimes called an all-zero filter. A recursive filter always realizes poles, and when it delays only output samples, it is called an all-pole filter. The discussion that follows will demonstrate how to design filters that achieve poles and zeros specified by their center frequency and bandwidth.

The following notational conventions are used to describe filter algorithms mathematically. The current input to the filter is designated by $x(n)$ and the current output by $y(n)$. Previous input values are denoted by $x(n-m)$ and previous outputs by $y(n-m)$, where m is the number of samples that the value has been delayed. For example, $x(n-1)$ represents the input sample just prior to the current one.

5.12 Non-Recursive Filters

The output from a non-recursive filter is formed by combining the input to the filter with past inputs. Consider a signal-processing algorithm that forms its output sample by taking the average of the current input sample and the previous one. Mathematically, this can be stated as

$$y(n) = 0.5x(n) + 0.5x(n - 1)$$

This first-order filter is an example of a *moving-average filter*. Averaging has the effect of smoothing the waveform, which suggests that this process reduces the amount of high-frequency energy in the signal. To give a general impression of the nature of the amplitude response of this filter, we will apply a digital test signal at a specific frequency to the input and then examine the output for a repeating steady-state pattern. It will be assumed for the purposes of this analysis that all input samples prior to the application of the test signal are zero. When a unit-amplitude, digital signal at 0 Hz given by $\{1,1,1,1,1,...\}$ is applied to the filter, the output is $\{.5,1,1,1,1,...\}$. The first sample (.5) is part of the transient response and shows how the output of the filter builds up to its final value. Beginning with the second sample, the output achieves a steady-state condition that indicates that the filter allows 0 Hz signals to pass without attenuation. At the other frequency extreme, when a unit-amplitude, cosine wave at the Nyquist frequency denoted by $\{1,-1,1,-1,1,-1,...\}$ is applied, the output is $\{.5,0,0,0,0,0,...\}$. In the steady state, the filter completely attenuates components at the Nyquist frequency. The overall amplitude response, $A(f)$, is low-pass in nature (figure 5.29a), with a cutoff frequency at $f_s/4$, and is given by

$$A(f) = \cos\ [\pi f/(2f_s)]$$

There are many variations on the simple moving-average filter described above. One is to increase the number of samples that are averaged. Because the waveform receives additional smoothing, the cutoff frequency is lowered.

Instead of taking the average, the difference between successive input samples can be taken. This can be stated as

$$y(n) = 0.5x(n) - 0.5x(n - 1)$$

The samples are multiplied by 0.5 to scale the amplitude. Using the test signal method above, the reader can verify that in the steady state at 0 Hz, the filter passes no signal, and at the Nyquist frequency, it passes the signal unchanged. Such a filter is high-pass in nature and its amplitude response (figure 5.29b) is given by

$$A(f) = \sin [\pi f/(2f_s)]$$

The cutoff frequency is $f_s/4$.

Consider a filter whose output is the average of the current input and the next-to-last input sample:

$$y(n) = 0.5x(n) + 0.5x(n - 2)$$

Since the input is delayed by two samples, this is a second-order filter. The filter passes both 0 Hz and the Nyquist frequency unchanged. Halfway in between, at $f_s/4$, a cosine wave input signal given by $\{1,0,-1,0,1,0,-1,0,\ldots\}$ produces an output signal of $\{.5,0,0,0,0,0,0,0,\ldots\}$. Therefore, this filter is a band-reject filter that completely blocks signals at $f_s/4$. The overall amplitude response (figure 5.29c) is

$$A(f) = |\cos (\pi f/f_s)|$$

Similarly, it can be shown that

$$y(n) = 0.5x(n) - 0.5x(n - 2)$$

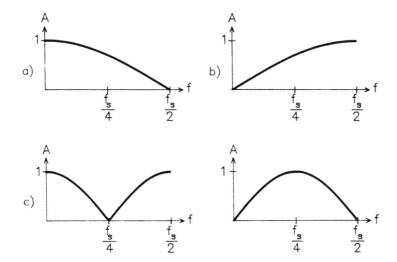

FIGURE 5.29   Amplitude responses of four simple non-recursive filters.

is a band-pass filter with a center frequency of $f_s/4$ and an overall amplitude response (figure 5.29d) of

$$A(f) = \sin (\pi f/f_s)$$

The filters above are non-recursive which, in the general case, take the form

$$y(n) = a_0x(n) + a_1x(n - 1) + a_2x(n - 2) + \cdots + a_Nx(n - N)$$

The number of delays used, N, is also the order of the filter. The values of the coefficients, a_k, control the frequency response of the filter. The impulse response of the filter is the digital signal $\{a_0, a_1, \ldots, a_N, 0, 0, \ldots\}$: a sequence made up of the values of the filter coefficients followed by zeros. In order to realize a desired frequency response, one must calculate the coefficient values for a filter. These calculations are based on the use of an inverse Fourier transform that changes the desired frequency response into an impulse response. Subsequently, the coefficients of the filter are matched to the sample values of the impulse response.

A problem arises because the filters with the best stopband behavior have impulse responses of infinite duration. To realize their behavior perfectly, a non-recursive filter would require an infinite number of delays (N) and coefficients, so that, in general, the actual implementation of a non-recursive filter only approximates the desired response. In practice, N is chosen as a compromise between the accuracy of the approximation and the amount of memory and computation time available for the algorithm. The effect of this foreshortening of the impulse response is to introduce inaccuracies in the frequency response of the filter. These inaccuracies are normally seen in the amplitude response as lower-than-expected attenuation in the stopband.

DESIGN EXAMPLE: Non-recursive approximation of an ideal low-pass filter. Using a non-recursive filter with N delays, an ideal low-pass filter with a cutoff frequency of f_c can be approximated by choosing the coefficients, a_k, according to

$$a_k = \frac{\sin [2\pi(k-\frac{1}{2}N)(f_c/f_s)]}{\pi(k-\frac{1}{2}N)}\left(0.54 + 0.46 \cos \frac{\pi(k-\frac{1}{2}N)}{N}\right)$$

(It can be shown that when $k=N/2$, $a_k = 2f_c/f_s$.)

As an example, figure 5.30 gives the coefficients and amplitude response when $N=10$ and $f_s=40$ kHz for a low-pass filter with $f_c=2$ kHz.

DESIGN EXAMPLE: Second-order all-zero filter. Sometimes it is desirable (e.g., in speech synthesis) to realize a "zero" at a specified center frequency and bandwidth. As explained above, a zero is a region of attenuation, but the amplitude response does not necessarily go all the way to zero at the center frequency. The bandwidth of a zero is measured between the points that have 3 dB less than the maximum value of attenuation. The second-order all-zero filter implemented by the following equation realizes a zero.

$$y(n) = a_0x(n) + a_1x(n - 1) + a_2x(n - 2)$$

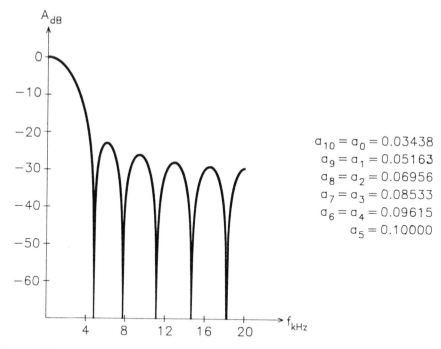

$$a_{10} = a_0 = 0.03438$$
$$a_9 = a_1 = 0.05163$$
$$a_8 = a_2 = 0.06956$$
$$a_7 = a_3 = 0.08533$$
$$a_6 = a_4 = 0.09615$$
$$a_5 = 0.10000$$

FIGURE 5.30 Amplitude response of a 10th-order, non-recursive low-pass filter with a cutoff frequency of 2 kHz.

To obtain a center frequency f_0 with bandwidth BW, the intermediate coefficients c_1 and c_2 are calculated according to:

$$c_2 = e^{-2\pi(BW/f_s)}$$

$$c_1 = [-4c_2/(1 + c_2)] \cos (2\pi f_0/f_s)$$

The next step is to determine a scaling constant, D, which sets the amplitude response in frequency regions removed from the zero. For an unscaled filter, D is set equal to 1. In this case, the response varies primarily with bandwidth and, to a limited extent, with center frequency. When the bandwidth is narrow, the response can be quite large, even greater than 40 dB. Thus the filter also serves as an amplifier. In certain applications, this is desirable, but caution is required because such large amplification can easily generate samples that exceed the maximum range of the system.

A scaling method that makes a filter simpler to use selects D as a combination of the other coefficients, c_1 and c_2, to achieve a certain value of amplitude response at some frequency. Frequently, D is chosen so that the amplitude response is one at 0 Hz, so that low-frequency signals will be passed with little change in amplitude. In this case, D is calculated as:

$$D = 1 - c_1 + c_2$$

The final step is to calculate the actual filter coefficients from the intermediate coefficients and scaling constant.

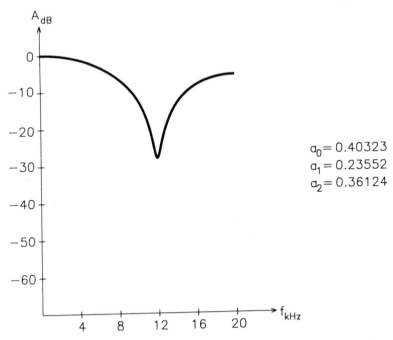

FIGURE 5.31   Amplitude response and coefficients of a second-order, all-zero filter with a center frequency of 12 kHz and a bandwidth of 700 Hz.

$$a_0 = 1/D$$
$$a_1 = c_1/D$$
$$a_2 = c_2/D$$

Figure 5.31 shows the amplitude response and coefficients for a second-order, all-zero band reject filter with an amplitude response of one at 0 Hz, when $f_s=40$ kHz, with $f_0=12$ kHz and BW= 700 Hz.

5.13   Recursive filters

A recursive filter algorithm determines its output by combining past output samples with the current and sometimes past input samples. Consider the simple, first-order recursive filter given by

$$y(n) = ax(n) - by(n - 1)$$

where the output depends on the current input and the value of the last output. The amplitude response of this filter can assume either a low-pass or a high-pass characteristic, depending on the coefficient values. The coefficient b sets the cutoff frequency and the coefficient a is chosen for a specific value of the amplitude response in the passband.

To obtain a low-pass filter with a cut-off frequency of f_c and an amplitude response of one at 0 Hz, the coefficients, a and b, are calculated as follows.

1.   Calculate the intermediate variable C from:

$$C = 2 - \cos{(2\pi f_c/f_s)}$$

2. The coefficients are:

$$b = \sqrt{C^2 - 1} - C$$
$$a = 1 + b$$

As an example, figure 5.32 shows the amplitude response and coefficients for a filter with $f_c = 1$ kHz when $f_s = 40$ kHz.

If a high-pass characteristic with an amplitude response of one at the Nyquist frequency is desired, the coefficients are determined according to:

$$b = C - \sqrt{C^2 - 1}$$
$$a = 1 - b$$

The simple recursive filters above are all-pole filters with a single pole. In the general case, an all-pole filter is given by

$$y(n) = a_0 x_n - b_1 y(n-1) - b_2 y(n-2) - \cdots - b_N y(n-N)$$

The coefficients, b_k, are determined from the characteristics of the desired filter. The number of delays, N, is the order of the filter.

A commonly used filter (section 5.3) is the band-pass filter realized by the second-order all-pole filter given by

$$y(n) = a_0 x(n) - b_1 y(n-1) - b_2 y(n-2)$$

To realize a center frequency f_0 with bandwidth BW, calculate the coefficients b_1 and b_2 according to:

$$b_2 = e^{-2\pi(BW/f_s)}$$
$$b_1 = \frac{-4b_2}{1 + b_2} \cos{\left(2\pi \frac{f_0}{f_s}\right)}$$

The coefficient a_0 is a scaling constant. It controls the ratio of output to input signal amplitude at the center frequency (midband gain). If the choice is $a_0 = 1$, the filter is said to be unscaled and the midband gain varies primarily with bandwidth and, to some degree, with center frequency.

A scaling method that makes a filter simpler to use calculates a_0 from the values of the other coefficients, b_1 and b_2, for a midband gain of one; that is, the amplitude of a signal at the center frequency will be the same coming out as going in. In this case, a_0 is calculated from:

$$a_0 = 1 - b_2 \sqrt{1 - b_1^2/(4b_2)}$$

When the filter is to be used on noise signals with widely distributed spectra, a_0 can be chosen so that as much noise power leaves the filter as enters it. For this case, calculate a_0 as

$$a_0 = \sqrt{[(1 + b_2)^2 - b_1^2]\,[(1 - b_2)/(1 + b_2)]}$$

Figure 5.33 shows the amplitude response and coefficients for a second-order,

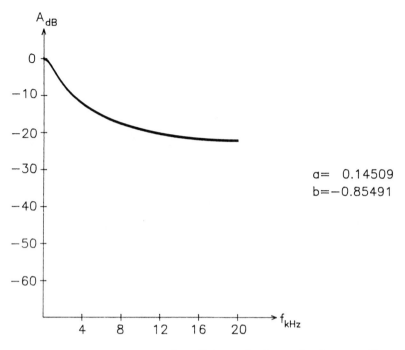

FIGURE 5.32   Amplitude response and coefficients of a first-order, low-pass filter with a cutoff frequency of 1 kHz.

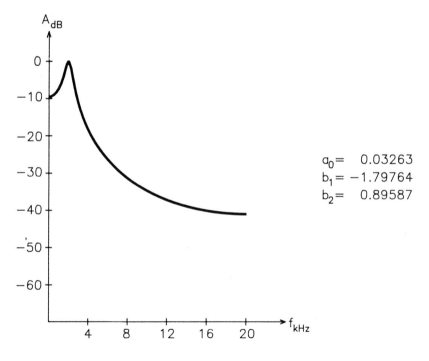

FIGURE 5.33   Amplitude response and coefficients of a second-order, all-pole filter with a center frequency of 2 kHz and a bandwidth of 700 Hz.

all-pole, band-pass filter with a midband gain of one for a periodic signal, when $f_s=40$ kHz, with $f_c=2$ kHz and BW=700 Hz.

The second-order, band-pass filter above is the one that is most frequently found as a unit generator in computer music software under names like RESON or FLT. As described in section 5.3, its amplitude response deforms from a symmetric band-pass shape as the center frequency is brought close to either zero Hertz or the Nyquist frequency.

The most general form of a recursive filter is given by

$$y(n) = a_0x(n) + a_1x(n-1) + \cdots + a_Mx(n-M) - b_1y(n-1)$$
$$- b_2y(n-2) - \cdots - b_Ny(n-N)$$

The filter has both poles (determined by the coefficients b_k) and zeros (determined by the coefficients a_k) and is capable of realizing arbitrarily complex frequency responses. The coefficients are nearly always determined by evaluating formulae that have been derived from mathematical analyses of filter responses. Heuristic selection of coefficients seldom results in a usable filter because it is very easy to make a recursive filter unstable. An unstable filter can oscillate, adding unwanted components to the sound. It may even continue to generate spurious signals after the input signal has decayed to zero.

Analog-filter design has a long history and a well-developed literature. As a result, many procedures for digital-filter design begin with the construction of the mathematical description of the analog filter that has the desired response. The coefficients of the digital filter are then determined by transforming the analog-filter description, using the appropriate mathematical relationships. There are several methods of transformation. Each is tailored to make the digital filter's response match a certain aspect of the analog response. No transformation will result in identical filter characteristics in both analog and digital domains. Thus, the filter designer must choose the type of transform that matches the aspects of performance that are most important in the application.

The *bilinear transform*[11] has been found useful for many audio signal processing applications. When applied to a second-order, analog filter it produces a recursive digital filter implemented with the following equation:

$$y(n) = a_0x(n) + a_1x(n-1) + a_2x(n-2) - b_1y(n-1) - b_2y(n-2)$$

There are many types of analog filter responses, each of which is optimized for certain characteristics. We will apply the bilinear transform to a common one—the *Butterworth response*, which has a maximally flat passband. Several design examples follow to illustrate methods for the calculation of the coefficients of this filter for the four basic filter elements. At the cost of increased computation, a filter of this type gives precision and stopband attenuation that are superior to those of the general-purpose filter in section 5.3.

DESIGN EXAMPLE: Butterworth low-pass filter. The application of the bilinear transform to a second-order, Butterworth low-pass filter results in a digital filter that uses the above equation. For a desired cutoff frequency (f_c) at a sampling rate (f_s), the filter coefficients are calculated as follows:

1.   Calculate the intermediate variable, C, from

$$C = [\tan(\pi f_c/f_s)]^{-1}$$

2. The coefficients are then calculated from

$$a_0 = (1 + \sqrt{2}C + C^2)^{-1}$$
$$a_1 = 2a_0$$
$$a_2 = a_0$$
$$b_1 = 2(1 - C^2)a_0$$
$$b_2 = (1 - \sqrt{2}C + C^2)a_0$$

As an example, for f_s=40 kHz, figure 5.34 shows the coefficient values and amplitude response of a 2 kHz Butterworth low-pass filter.

DESIGN EXAMPLE: Butterworth high-pass filter. A Butterworth high-pass filter with cutoff frequency f_c can be digitally approximated by calculating the coefficients according to

$$C = \tan (\pi f_c/f_s)$$
$$a_0 = (1 + \sqrt{2}C + C^2)^{-1}$$
$$a_1 = -2a_0$$
$$a_2 = a_0$$
$$b_1 = 2(C^2 - 1)a_0$$
$$b_2 = (1 - \sqrt{2}C + C^2)a_0$$

As an example, for f_s=40 kHz, figure 5.35 shows the coefficient values and amplitude response of a 6 kHz, Butterworth high-pass filter.

DESIGN EXAMPLE: Butterworth band-pass filter. A Butterworth band-pass filter with center frequency f_0 and bandwidth BW can be digitally approximated by calculating the coefficients according to

$$C = [\tan (\pi BW/f_s)]^{-1}$$
$$D = 2 \cos (2\pi f_0/f_s)$$
$$a_0 = (1 + C)^{-1}$$
$$a_1 = 0$$
$$a_2 = -a_0$$
$$b_1 = -CDa_0$$
$$b_2 = (C - 1)a_0$$

Due to the nature of the bilinear transform, this band-pass filter cannot be converted into a low-pass by choosing f_0=0 Hz or into a high-pass by choosing f_0=$f_s/2$. The amplitude response of this filter is always zero at both 0 Hz and the Nyquist frequency.

As an example, for f_s=40 kHz, figure 5.36 shows the coefficient values and amplitude response of a Butterworth band-pass filter with f_0=2.5 kHz and BW=500 Hz.

DESIGN EXAMPLE: Butterworth band-reject filter. A Butterworth band-reject filter with center frequency f_0 and bandwidth BW can be digitally approximated by calculating the coefficients according to

$$C = \tan (\pi BW/f_s) \qquad a_2 = a_0$$
$$D = 2 \cos (2\pi f_0/f_s) \qquad b_1 = -Da_0$$
$$a_0 = (1 + C)^{-1} \qquad b_2 = (1 - C)a_0$$
$$a_1 = -Da_0$$

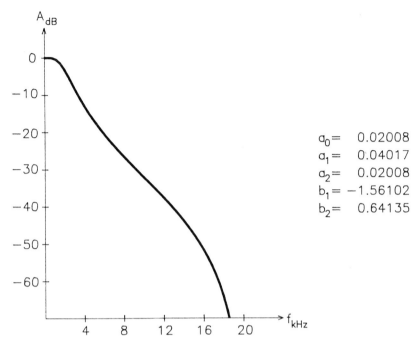

FIGURE 5.34   Amplitude response and coefficients of a Butterworth low-pass filter with a cutoff frequency of 2 kHz.

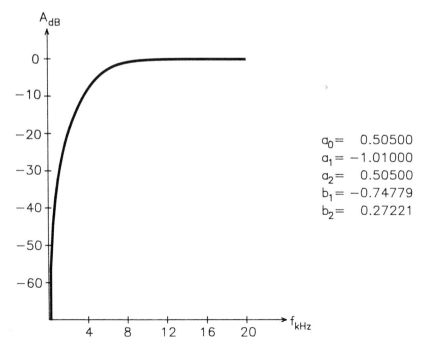

FIGURE 5.35   Amplitude response and coefficients of a Butterworth high-pass filter with a cutoff frequency of 6 kHz.

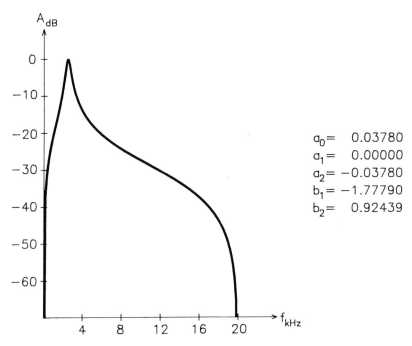

FIGURE 5.36   Amplitude response and coefficients of a Butterworth band-pass filter with a center frequency of 2.5 kHz and a bandwidth of 500 Hertz.

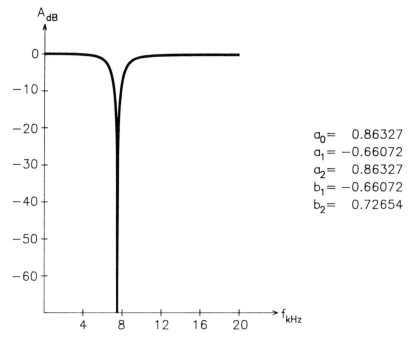

FIGURE 5.37   Amplitude response and coefficients of a Butterworth band-reject filter with a center frequency of 7.5 kHz and a bandwidth of 2 kHz.

As an example, for $f_s=40$ kHz, figure 5.37 shows the coefficient values and amplitude response of a Butterworth band-reject filter with $f_0=7.5$ kHz and BW$=2$ kHz.

A comparison of some properties of non-recursive filters versus recursive filters is given below:

1. A higher-order, non-recursive filter is generally required to obtain the same amount of selectivity in its amplitude response as that of a comparable recursive filter.

2. Errors caused by quantization, computational round-off, and coefficient inaccuracies are usually less significant in non-recursive filters.

3. A non-recursive filter is always stable, whereas recursive filters must be specifically designed to be stable.

Notes

1. Dodge, Charles. "Cascando." Composer's Recordings, Inc. (CRI SD454), 1983.
2. Dodge, Charles. "Earth's Magnetic Field." Nonesuch Records (H71250), 1970.
3. Dodge, Charles. "Changes." Nonesuch Records (H71245), 1970.
4. Ibid.
5. Griffiths, Paul. *A Guide to Electronic Music.* London: Thames and Hudson, 1979, 49.
6. Slawson, A. Wayne. "The Color of Sound: A Theoretical Study in Musical Timbre." *Music Theory Spectrum*, 3, 1981, 123–141.
7. Slawson, A. Wayne. "The Musical Control of Sound Color." *Canadian University Music Review*, 3, 1982, 67–79.
8. Babbitt, Milton. "Some Aspects of Twelve-Tone Composition." *The Score and I.M.A. Magazine*, pp. 53–61, 1955. Reprinted in *Twentieth Century View of Music History*. New York: Scribner's, 1972, 364–371.
9. Oppenheim, A. V., and R. W. Schafer. *Digital Signal Processing.* Englewood Cliffs, N. J.: Prentice-Hall, 1975.
10. Rabiner, L. R., and B. Gold. *Theory and Application of Digital Signal Processing.* Englewood Cliffs, N. J.: Prentice-Hall, 1975.
11. Stanley, William, *Digital Signal Processing.* Reston, Va.: Reston Publishing, 1975.

6

SPEECH SYNTHESIS

The history of computer-synthesized speech begins in the 1950s at Bell Telephone Laboratories, where scientists and engineers were working to replicate the human voice for use in telephone systems. Musicians soon became interested in the possibility of using the synthetic voice as a musical instrument that could surpass the human voice in plasticity and range of capabilities. The element of intelligible language was thus introduced to computer music, bringing with it a broad range of theatrical, intellectual, and poetic possibilities. Even before the synthesis of intelligible speech became feasible with computers, the synthesis of certain speechlike sounds was used to create musical tones with dynamic spectra.

In the last few years, many new types of voice-synthesis systems have been developed which offer great facility of use and accessibility. Adaptations to musical composition and performance have thus proliferated.[1] A musician who wishes to use these new technologies in a sophisticated and imaginative manner, must have an understanding of not only the computer implementation, but also the linguistic, physical, and acoustical mechanisms of speech.

This chapter describes the physical structure of the human vocal tract and the ways that vocal sounds are produced. It outlines the acoustics of phonetics and presents several models for the synthesis of speech on a computer. Methods of realizing music with computer-synthesized speech are also discussed.

6.1 Speech Physiology

Figure 6.1 illustrates the major features of the vocal tract. The speech process begins in the lungs as air is forced up through the trachea, past the glottis (vocal cords), and through the cavity of the pharynx to the mouth (oral cavity). Although vibration of the glottis and the size and shape of the pharynx affect the acoustic characteristics of the voice, it is the tongue which, more than any other element of the vocal tract, creates the articulation of speech. The lips radiate the sound of the voice to the surrounding space and, at the same time, their position determines certain speech sounds. When the velum (soft palate) is lowered, the nostrils contribute to this radiation, creating "nasalized" speech. Each of these articulators—the tongue (tip, middle, and back), the lips, the mandible, the velum, and also the larynx—is controlled separately. Together they are used to produce phonemes, which are the various sounds of speech.[2]

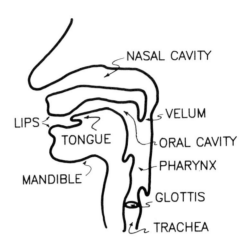

FIGURE 6.1   The principal parts of the human vocal tract.

There are three classes of excitation sources for the voice. "Voiced" sounds are caused by the quasi-periodic vibration of the glottis; "fricative" sounds, by turbulence created by constriction at some point along the vocal tract; and "plosive" sounds, by the sudden release of pressure built up behind a closure in the vocal tract. Fricatives and plosives constitute the class of sounds called "unvoiced" because the sound is produced by noise in the vocal tract, rather than by vibrations of the glottis.

The length and shape of the particular vocal tract determine the resonances in the spectrum of a voice signal. An average vocal tract is about 17 cm in length. When at rest (in the neutral vowel position), it imparts resonances called *formants* that are approximately equally spaced in Hertz: the first formant at about 500 Hz, the second at about 1500, the third at about 2500, the fourth at about 3500, the fifth at 4500, etc. Repositioning of the articulators alters the shape of the vocal tract, thus changing the frequencies of the formants, particularly the lower ones. The frequencies of the lowest two or three formants constitute the cues necessary for phonemic differentiation of vowels.[3] The following interactions give an indication of the relationship between the articulator position and frequencies of the lower formants:[4]

1.   The wider the jaw opening, the higher the frequency of the first formant.

2.   The closer a point of constriction between the tongue and the roof of the mouth is to the front of the vocal tract, the higher the frequency of the second formant.

3.   The greater the degree of backward curving of the tongue tip, the lower the third formant frequency.

4.   Rounding the lips and the lowering of the larynx causes all formant frequencies to be lowered.

Much modern research on the formant structure of speech has its roots in the examination of pictures made by the sound spectrograph, a machine that transforms a voice recording into a graphic representation of its spectral content versus time. For the musician, spectrograms can serve as a good starting point for illustrating the acoustics of speech. *Visible Speech*,[5] originally published as an aide to deaf people learning to speak, is not only an excellent source for these spectrograms, but also provides clear instructions for the inference of phonemes from spectrograms.

6.2   Acoustic Phonetics

There are roughly 41 distinct sounds, or phonemes, in American English. They are usually grouped into four classes: vowels, diphthongs, semivowels, and consonants (table 6.1).

The *vowels* are voiced sounds for which the articulators of the vocal tract assume a fixed position. For example, the /OO/ in "boot" is formed by rounding the lips and raising the back of the tongue. By contrast, the /IY/ in "meet" is the result of a more open position of the lips, with the tip of the tongue placed near the front of the mouth.

Acoustically, the vowels are characterized by their formant frequencies. Peterson and Barney[6] produced the chart in figure 6.2 by plotting the formant frequencies of ten vowels that had each been perceived to be a distinct sound when spoken by a large number of men and children. The figure gives the second formant frequency as a function of the first formant frequency. The encircled areas indicate

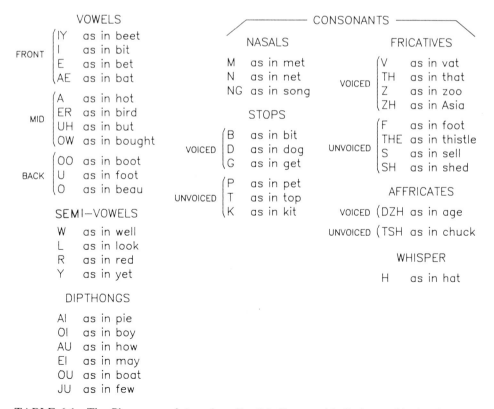

TABLE 6.1   The Phonemes of American English Shown with Orthographic Symbols

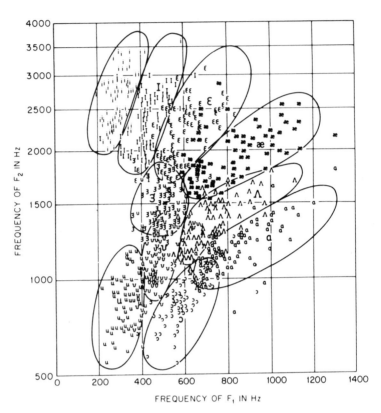

FIGURE 6.2   Plot of second formant frequency versus first formant frequency for the vowels. The data was taken for a wide range of speakers. *From Lawrence R. Rabiner and Ronald W. Schafer,* Digital Processing of Speech Signals, © *1978, p. 43 (after Peterson and Barney). Reprinted by permission of Prentice-Hall, Inc., Englewood Cliffs, N.J., and the Journal of the Acoustical Society of America.*

the broad range of variation within each vowel. Figure 6.3 shows an average of the data for the first three formant frequencies of all American English vowels spoken by males in this study.

A *diphthong* is a succession of two vowel sounds which has a continuous transition from one vowel sound toward the other. The articulation of a diphthong begins at or near the position for one of the vowels and proceeds smoothly to the other. There are six diphthongs in American English: /EI/, /OU/, /AI/, /AU/, /OI/, and /JU/.

Semivowels are transitional, voiced sounds that lack a fixed characterization of resonance structure. Instead, the semivowel appropriates the characteristic resonances of the vowel to or from which it is moving. The semivowels are /L/, /R/, /W/, and /Y/

There are five different classes of consonants: nasals, fricatives, stops, affricates, and the whispered /H/. Each of these is the result of a distinctive arrangement and use of the articulators, but they all include a partial or complete constriction of the vocal tract.

The *nasals*—/M/, /N/, and /NG/—are made by lowering the velum in such a way

FORMANT FREQUENCIES OF VOWELS				
Symbol	Example Word	F_1	F_2	F_3
IY	beet	270	2290	3010
I	bit	390	1990	2550
E	bet	530	1840	2480
AE	bat	660	1720	2410
UH	but	520	1190	2390
A	hot	730	1090	2440
OW	bought	570	840	2410
U	foot	440	1020	2240
OO	boot	300	870	2240
ER	bird	490	1350	1690

FIGURE 6.3   Averaged formant frequencies of ten vowels. *From Rabiner and Schafer (after Peterson and Barney), by permission of Prentice-Hall and the Journal of the Acoustical Society of America.*

that the glottal wave is resonated through the nasal tract as well as through the vocal tract, and is radiated primarily at the nostrils. Nasalization greatly increases the length of the resonance system, and introduces zeros (or antiresonances) into the spectrum of nasalized speech.

The *fricatives* can be either voiced or unvoiced. Unvoiced fricatives are made by passing a steady stream of air through the vocal tract and then constricting it at some point, causing turbulence. The placement of the constriction determines the particular unvoiced fricative. /F/ is created by a contriction near the lips; for /THE/, the constriction is near the teeth. The constriction for /S/ is near the middle of the vocal tract and it is near the back of the mouth for /SH/.

The points of constriction for the voiced fricatives—/V/, /TH/, /Z/, and /ZH/—are the same as for their unvoiced counterparts (/F/, /THE/, /S/, and /SH/, respectively). There are two simultaneous excitation sources for each of the voiced fricatives: the glottis and the turbulence created at the point of constriction.

The *stop consonants* can also be either voiced or unvoiced. They are plosive sounds, produced by the sudden release of pressure built up behind a full constriction of the vocal tract. Again, the location of the constriction determines the characteristics of the particular stop consonant. Both the unvoiced stops—/P/, /T/, and /K/—and the voiced stops—/B/, /D/, and /G/—are distinguished by the placement of the constriction towards the front, middle, and rear of the mouth. To produce voiced stops, the glottis vibrates throughout the build-up and release of the constriction.

The *affricates* /TSH/ and /DZH/ are formed by connecting a stop and a fricative. In forming the unvoiced /TSH/, the /T/ stop is followed by the fricative /SH/, whereas the voiced /DZH/ includes a /D/ stop and a /ZH/ fricative.

The resonances of the *whispered consonant* /H/ assume the positions of the vowel that follows it, since there is no change in articulator position between the two phonemes.

6.3   Computer Analysis of Speech

Successful speech synthesis by computer depends on an accurate analysis of speech. Research in the computer analysis of speech stems from a desire to reduce the amount of data needed to represent a speech signal. In an analysis, the speech wave is broken into segments, called "windows" (see section 2.7) or "frames." For each of these segments, the analysis algorithm determines the attributes of the speech. These characteristics represent the speech sound and can be used later to recreate the analyzed sound. One of the primary functions of the speech analysis is to determine the resonant characteristics of the vocal tract during the segment. Two widely used methods of doing this are *formant tracking* and *linear predictive coding*.

In formant tracking, the analysis transforms the speech signal into a series of short-term spectral descriptions, one for each segment.[7] Each spectrum is then examined in sequence for its principal peaks, or formants, creating a record of the formant frequencies and their levels versus time. The record of change in formant positions with time can then be used to reconstitute the speech signal. Formant tracking works best on a spoken male voice. It is much less accurate on female and children's voices because the relatively high fundamental frequency makes the formants harder to track. In addition, the presence of reverberation on the digital recording of the voice will seriously degrade the accuracy of this technique.

Linear predictive coding (LPC) is a statistical method for predicting future values of the speech waveform on the basis of its past values.[8] The method, which does not involve direct transformation from the time-domain to the frequency-domain, determines the characteristics of a filter that simulates the response of the vocal tract. Just as the vocal tract changes characteristics during the course of speech, the filter response varies from segment to segment. When driven with the proper excitation source, the filter reconstitutes the speech waveform originally analyzed. In LPC analysis, many more descriptors of the speech are derived (typically, 12 to 20) than in formant tracking (6 to 8). LPC analysis is not restricted to spoken male voices, but has been successfully applied to a wide range of sounds. Section 6.11 explains the concept basic to linear prediction.

In addition to the information about the vocal tract, the analysis usually also determines whether the segment of speech is voiced or unvoiced. One analysis technique uses the ratio of high frequency energy of the segment to its low frequency energy as the criterion for making the determination. The ratio is significantly higher during unvoiced speech. Dividing speech into the strict categories of voiced and unvoiced is an imperfect model because a few sounds are members of both. (See below.)

Estimating the fundamental frequency of the voiced segments of speech is often part of the analysis. This can be accomplished by examining either the digitized speech wave directly as a waveform or by transforming it into the frequency domain and examining its spectrum. (However, a simple, discrete Fourier transform does not have sufficient resolution for an accurate determination. More complex techniques must be used.) Creating a pitch detection algorithm that is accurate for all types of speakers is a difficult problem. Many schemes have been developed, each of which has its own limitations and each of which provides optimum performance on a particular type of waveform. At present, there is no single method that is universally successful across a broad range of sounds.[9]

Amplitude is another attribute of speech that is often extracted by an analysis system. The average amplitude of each segment can be found by performing a power averaging of the samples contained in the segment.

6.4 Computer Synthesis of Speech

A flow chart of a general plan for synthesizing speech with a digital computer is shown in figure 6.4. This model has been used by researchers and musicians working with a wide range of computers and natural languages. It is based on the models for analysis given above where the speech waveform has been broken down into segments.

If, at a given moment, the speech is to be voiced, then the excitation source for this model is a variable-frequency pulse generator with a fundamental frequency f_0; if the speech segment is to be unvoiced, a noise generator is used. In either case, the output of the selected source is multiplied by the gain factor (AMP) to obtain the appropriate amplitude. It is then introduced to the resonation system that simulates the response of the vocal tract. The actual form of the resonation system depends on the method of representation: formant tracking or LPC. A resonation system can impart two different kinds of resonances into the spectrum of the speech: poles and zeros (see section 5.11). A pole is a resonance that emphasizes a frequency region. A zero is an antiresonance that attenuates energy in a frequency region. Not all speech-synthesis systems make use of zeros. Zeros are necessary for synthesizing realistic nasal sounds and certain unvoiced fricatives.

For most musical purposes, it is desirable to have a variable-frequency pulse generator with a wide range and fine pitch quantization of the kind described in section 4.3. The pulse generator described there can be used in a frequency range from sub-audio to half the sampling rate with very fine tuning. It generates no frequencies above the Nyquist, thus preventing aliasing. One problem inherent in this pulse generator, however, is that its harmonics are all of equal amplitude. For speech, analysis shows that the glottal excitation source has a rolloff of 12 dB/octave.[10] Thus the pulse generator of section 4.3 is usually followed by a low-pass filter to simulate the glottal function without inappropriate emphasis of the high-frequency region. However, this realization is also imperfect. For instance, the waveform of the pulse generator is a static one that cannot emulate the wideband frequency modulation that accompanies the "start up" of the vocal cords. Many of the future improvements to the quality of synthesized speech will be brought about through the use of more sophisticated excitation sources.

The general model shown in figure 6.4 has certain shortcomings as a synthesis model.[11] For example, for a given segment of speech, the synthesis must be either voiced or unvoiced, but not both. Clearly, certain phonemes such as /TH/, /V/, and /Z/ are combinations of both. This flaw is not serious enough to impair the intelligibility of the speech, but it is noticeable. Ways of circumventing the problem have been devised, but they require a far more complicated synthesis model.[12] Unfortunately, simply mixing the noise source with the pulse generator does not produce the desired effect.

There are two basic methods of performing speech synthesis on a computer: speech synthesis by rule and speech synthesis by analysis. Both methods are based

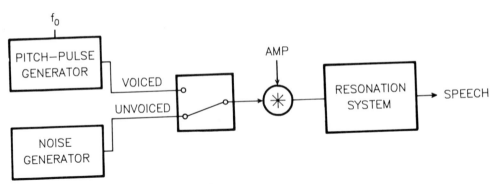

FIGURE 6.4   General plan for synthesizing speech with a digital computer.

on a prior analysis of speech. The difference lies in the way that data is fed to the synthesizer.

Speech synthesis by rule grew out of recorded-voice systems in which the parts of speech were concatenated to make spoken sentences or phrases. The synthesizer uses phonemes derived from research in acoustic phonetics and applies rules for connecting the phonemes into speech. It has been shown[13] that intelligible speech cannot result from simple concatenation of prerecorded phonemes. This is because the acoustic properties of many phonemes of English are altered significantly by the context in which they occur. Some of the factors contributing to change are the position of the phoneme in the word and sentence, its surrounding phonemes, and its stress. To make the adjustments necessary to produce intelligible speech from text, computer programs have been created[14] in which the parameters of prosodics are implemented. These programs apply complex sets of rules for transforming printed English text into the sound of the spoken language. The sound of the speech produced by such systems, although intelligible, is clearly distinguishable from natural speech.

Speech synthesis by analysis sounds more realistic and personal. In speech synthesis by analysis, the synthetic speech is modeled on a recording of a voice speaking the passage to be synthesized. Thus, the speech synthesized from an analysis of a recording contains, from the outset, all of the transitions and timings of the speech. In addition, the resulting synthetic speech has the individual characteristics of the person who recorded the passage.

In making music with analyzed speech data, composers edit the analysis prior to resynthesis. Synthesis by analysis enables the independent alteration of the speed, pitch, amplitude, and resonance structure of the analyzed voice. This method of speech synthesis circumvents the major disadvantage of tape manipulation of the recorded voice—the changes in timbre and intelligibility which accompany changes in tape speed. Editing the analysis also makes it possible to rearrange the order of the elements of the speech, to repeat them, and to form choruses by creating multiple copies of the voice, with different alterations applied to each copy. Section 6.8 describes many of the ways in which an analysis can be edited for musical purposes.

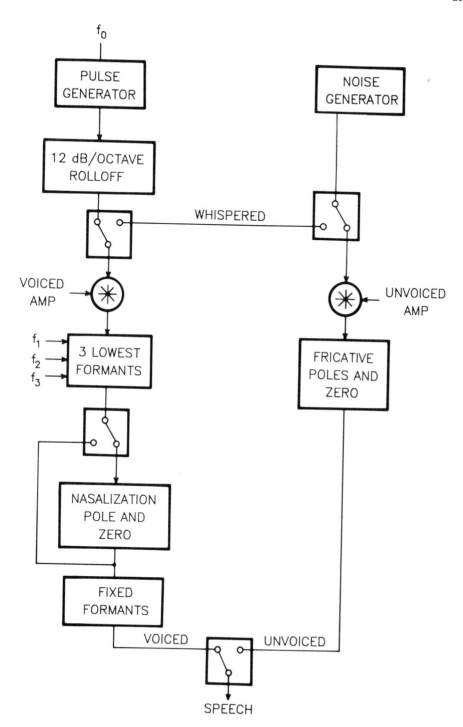

FIGURE 6.5   Speech synthesizer which directly realizes formants.

6.5 Formant Synthesis by Rule

Figure 6.5 shows the implementation of a digital formant speech synthesizer.[15] The synthesizer has two signal paths: one for voiced speech sounds which includes the provision for whispered speech and one for unvoiced fricative and plosive sounds. The left branch includes three variable resonances for simulation of the three lower formants, a variable pole and zero to shape the spectrum of nasalized speech, and fixed resonances for the upper formants. The unvoiced signal path consists of one zero and two poles for simulating the noise spectrum of fricatives and plosives. The user specifies a succession of phonemes giving information such as the following: a code for the particular phoneme, the duration of the phoneme, the frequency of the pulse generator if the phoneme is voiced, and the amplitude. To make intelligible, connected speech, it is necessary to implement the rules for speech transitions. Strategies for accomplishing this difficult task are suggested in several important articles.[16]

A system for direct digital synthesis of speech has been published by Dennis Klatt of M.I.T.[17] His system, for which he publishes FORTRAN code along with a description, uses 26 parameters for the characterization of each phoneme. There are now a number of commercially available synthesizers that interface with microcomputers and implement formant synthesis of speech by rule.

To synthesize a singing voice, a more elaborate model for the vocal tract must be implemented. The configuration of vocal tract and articulators for singing results in a voice quality that is different from that of speech. Sundberg[18] has shown that operatic singers enlarge the pharynx cavity and lower the glottis in the vocal tract as they sing. The resulting acoustical effect is to lower the frequencies of the fourth and fifth formants and to place them closer together in the range of 2500 to 3500 Hz. The bulge in the spectrum so created is known as the "singing formant."

The model for synthesizing vowel sounds in a rich vocal timbre is shown in figure 6.6. In this model, the lowest five formants are individually controlled to simulate the resonances of the singing voice. The higher resonances are included as fixed resonances in the spectrum. There is no provision for nasalization because the nasal tract contributes little to the quality of most sung vowels.

Table 6.2 shows the relative frequencies and amplitudes for the lower five formants on eight vowels sung by a male.[19] (This data was obtained from one singer and thus represents a configuration of resonances unique to a single individual.) In the formant pattern for singing, the first, second, fourth, and fifth formants are lower than in speech, while the third is generally higher. These differences result

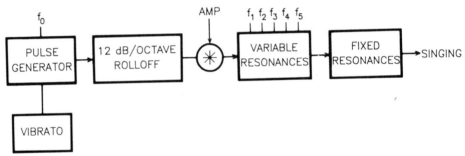

FIGURE 6.6 Formant synthesizer for singing vowels.

Vowel	FIRST FORMANT		SECOND FORMANT		THIRD FORMANT		FOURTH FORMANT		FIFTH FORMANT	
	Freq [Hz]	Amp [dB]	Freq [Hz]	Amp [dB]	Freq [Hz]	Amp [dB]	Freq [Hz]	Amp [dB]	Freq [Hz]	Amp [dB]
A	609	0	1000	−6	2450	−12	2700	−11	3240	−24
E	400	0	1700	−9	2300	−8	2900	−11	3400	−19
IY	238	0	1741	−20	2450	−16	2900	−20	4000	−32
O	325	0	700	−12	2550	−26	2850	−22	3100	−28
OO	360	0	750	−12	2400	−29	2675	−26	2950	−35
U	415	0	1400	−12	2200	−16	2800	−18	3300	−27
ER	300	0	1600	−14	2150	−12	2700	−15	3100	−23
UH	400	0	1050	−12	2200	−19	2650	−20	3100	−29

TABLE 6.2   The Frequencies and Relative Amplitudes of the Formants of Eight Vowels Sung by a Male (*Reprinted by permission of Xavier Rodet*)

Vowel	FIRST FORMANT		SECOND FORMANT		THIRD FORMANT		FOURTH FORMANT		FIFTH FORMANT	
	Freq [Hz]	Amp [dB]	Freq [Hz]	Amp [dB]	Freq [Hz]	Amp [dB]	Freq [Hz]	Amp [dB]	Freq [Hz]	Amp [dB]
A	650	0	1100	−8	2860	−13	3300	−12	4500	−19
E	500	0	1750	−9	2450	−10	3350	−14	5000	−23
IY	330	0	2000	−14	2800	−11	3650	−10	5000	−19
O	400	0	840	−12	2800	−26	3250	−24	4500	−31
OO	280	0	650	−18	2200	−48	3450	−50	4500	−52

TABLE 6.3   The Frequencies and Relative Amplitudes of the Formants of Five Vowels Sung by a Female (*Reprinted by permission of Xavier Rodet*)

from the change in size and shape of the vocal tract when the pharyngeal cavity is widened and the larynx is lowered.

Table 6.3 shows the formants of a single soprano singing five different vowel sounds.[20] The center frequencies and relative amplitudes of these vowels are summarized in the table. In all cases except /OO/, the first formant frequency is higher for the female singing voice than for the male singing voice (table 6.2). A potential source of inaccuracy in the synthesis with the data of the female singing voice is apparent: the fundamental frequency will exceed the frequency of the first formant before reaching even the middle of the soprano vocal range. A fundamental higher than the first formant will cause the voice quality to become muffled and indistinct if left uncorrected. However, Sundberg has observed that female operatic singers have a technique to circumvent this problem. They widen the jaw opening as the fundamental frequency rises. This raises the frequency of the first formant so that it "tracks" the fundamental, and it also shifts the frequencies of the other formants.

Figure 6.7 shows the movement of the first four formants in response to increasing fundamental frequencies.[21] The frequency of the fifth formant is not vowel-dependent, and so it remains fixed at 4.5 kHz in this model.

Synthesis from the five-formant model does not in itself give sufficient audible

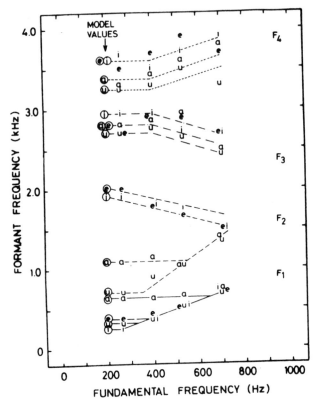

FIGURE 6.7 Formant frequencies for four female sung vowels with change of fundamental. (*Reprinted by permission of Johan Sundberg.*)

cues for the listener to designate the synthesized vocal sound as "singing." To capture the quality of a singing voice more completely, the synthesized sound must incorporate a vibrato of a specific character. The envelope and the onset time of the vibrato are among the cues a listener uses to identify singing. Xavier Rodet and Gerald Bennett emphasize the importance of "aleatoric variations in fundamental frequency."

For a typical male singing voice, the vibrato rate is around 5 to 7 Hz. The width of the vibrato is about ±3% to ±6% of the fundamental frequency. Rodet and Bennett have observed the aleatoric variations in the fundamental frequency of tones sung deliberately without vibrato. To synthesize these subtle changes in pitch, the amount of frequency change was allowed to vary at random in a $1/f$ manner (see section 8.1F) between .5 and 1.5 seconds. The amount of this change was between ±1.1% and ±3.7% for the female and between ±2% and ±5.7% for the male. The values for the periodic and aperiodic fluctuations were added together and interpolated on a sample-to-sample basis, resulting in changes that were always smooth.

A temporal cue that designates vocal sounds as singing can be heard whenever a vocal tone is preceded by a rest. The onset of vibrato in a tone following the rest is typically delayed by about 300 to 600 msec.[22]

Another important characteristic of the singing voice is the transition that occurs when the voice changes frequency. Sundberg[23] states that 75% of the frequency change observed in the voices of trained singers occurs in the first 70 msec. The change is a rapid glissando from one frequency to the next. Sundberg further observes that in a two-note *marcato*-like sequence, the fundamental of a following lower note is approached by descending past it and then coming back up to the correct pitch.

The relationship between amplitude and spectrum must be carefully considered when synthesizing singing voices. Amplitude increases, to a certain extent, with fundamental frequency. The relative amplitude levels of formants 2 through 5 vary in a non-linear way with the amplitude of the fundamental frequency.[24] Failure to provide for this in the synthesis algorithm results in the "volume-control effect" (i.e., a change in amplitude without a concomitant change in the spectrum).

6.6 Synthesis by Analysis of Speech

In all speech synthesis-by-analysis systems, the speech is digitized and analyzed as described in section 6.3. The output from the analysis is in the form of "frames": blocks of data which represent the attributes of the speech for a short period of time. The term frame is analogous to the same term in motion picture technology, where the film is projected at a frame rate great enough to insure the continuity of the visual image. The rate of frames in speech varies, according to system and application, from about 20 to 200 frames per second.

A frame is defined by its amplitude, its duration, and by whether it is voiced or unvoiced. If the frame is voiced, it also includes the fundamental frequency of the source. In addition, all frames include information about the resonances of the vocal tract. The particular method of specification differs from one kind of synthesis model to another. For a formant synthesizer, the resonances are specified as characteristics of band-pass filters. For a linear-predictive-coding synthesizer, the resonances are described by the coefficients for an all-pole filter.

A typical formant-tracking synthesizer is the same as the one that was shown in figure 6.5. Notice that although the analysis system tracks only three formants, the synthesizer generates five. The top two have fixed frequencies at 3.5 and 4.5 kHz, respectively.

Synthesis from formant-tracking, while in many ways outdated in comparison to linear predictive coding, retains certain functional advantages. The principal advantage is the resonance patterns in the voice can be altered without causing the system to become unstable. However, because formant tracking is ordinarily restricted to the spoken male voice, its usefulness is limited.

In linear predictive coding (LPC), the speech is analyzed to find the values of coefficients for an all-pole filter that will reconstitute its waveform. Figure 6.8 shows a diagram of an LPC synthesizer. There is more than one variety of LPC analysis and synthesis: the methods known as covariance[25] and lattice[26] are the two most widely used.

In resynthesis of the voice, the excitation source (periodic pulse or noise) is fed through the all-pole filter to reconstitute the waveform of the speech. A synthesis from an LPC analysis can sound much more realistic than one from formant tracking. Covariance synthesis/analysis preserves even the most subtle individual traits of pronunciation and accent. However, unlike formant tracking, altering the vocal resonances predicted by a covariance LPC analysis is very difficult. In this

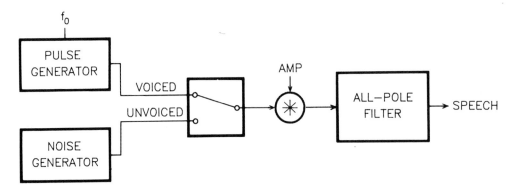

FIGURE 6.8   Digital speech synthesizer using linear predictive coding.

case the coefficients of the all-pole filter bear little obvious relationship to the speech spectrum. Therefore, it is extremely hard to know what changes to make to the coefficients in order to change the resonance structure of the speech. Editing the coefficients usually results in an unstable filter, rather than causing useful changes in the speech spectrum. A technique that has been used successfully to alter the spectrum of LPC-synthesized voice depends on a transformation of all the covariance coefficients as a group, instead of editing only certain ones. It shifts the frequencies of the response of the all-pole filter.[27]

The lattice method produces speech of somewhat lower quality than covariance, but it still sounds better than speech made from formant tracking analyses. The lattice coefficients are more stable than those of covariance, and so a certain amount of editing can be applied to them directly. The lattice coefficients act in a way like vocal tract area-function descriptors. That is, a given coefficient roughly corresponds to a cross-section of the vocal tract at a certain point. Editing certain of the coefficients can cause changes in the speech spectrum that resemble the effect of moving the lips.

LPC synthesis-by-analysis does not restrict the vocal model to the spoken voice, but also can be used with good results for the singing voice, including those of women and children. The LPC synthesis-by-analysis technique works well for the voice because the synthesis system assumes a pulselike vocal source that, like the glottis, is rich in harmonics. The realistic resynthesis of many other types of tones may require different excitation sources or even alternate analysis/synthesis models to be implemented.

6.7   Cross Synthesis

The LPC-synthesis system can be modified to permit the use of a source other than noise or periodic pulse for the excitation of the all-pole filter. The new source may be any recorded (and digitized) or synthesized sound. The only factor that influences the choice of source is the necessity for a relatively broad spectrum in order that the speech be easily understood. However, with this technique, the resonances of the analyzed voice can be used to change the spectrum of the source without necessarily becoming intelligible as speech. This will most often occur when the voiced and unvoiced portions of the analyzed speech do not coincide with the temporal patterns of the new source, or when the new source contains little high-frequency energy. Intelligibility of the new "talking" musical texture can be enhanced by adding noise to the new source during unvoiced frames. An example of that technique can be heard in the "voice of the book" in Charles Dodge's *The Story of Our Lives.*[28]

An example of a technique in which two different voices are "crossed" on synthesis can be heard in Tracy Petersen's *Voices.*[29] Here the excitation source from one voice (with its own voiced/unvoiced pattern and characteristic pitch contour) is fed into the analysis of the other.

6.8 Editing Analyses of Speech

The musician using analyzed speech ordinarily edits the analysis before synthesis. Editing enables the musician to alter certain characteristics of the speech and makes possible a wide range of musical effects. Editor programs for this purpose commonly provide the possibility of selectively modifying the pitch, timing, amplitude, and resonance structure of the analyzed speech. In addition, speech editors often implement operations associated with tape manipulation such as reordering the succession of phonemes and repeating parts of the speech.

Figure 6.9 illustrates the storage of analyzed speech frames in computer memory. The speech is stored in a two-dimensional array where each line represents the parameters of one speech frame with the frames ordered in time. Each column, then, contains the values of a single speech parameter, one frame after the other. The parameter *errn* is a result of linear prediction and is indicative of the voicing of the frame. A large value denotes an unvoiced frame. The threshold between voiced and unvoiced varies somewhat, but is roughly .07 in the system shown here. Other methods of analyzing and storing the voicing informa-

FRAME	PARAMETERS				
	1 Amplitude	2 Frequency	3 Errn	4 Duration	5 to N Resonances
1	90.1	0.0	0.081	0.010	( ) ( ) ( )
2	1345.4	96.0	0.061	0.010	( ) ( ) ( )
3	1984.3	96.0	0.062	0.010	( ) ( ) ( )
4	1918.9	94.2	0.051	0.010	( ) ( ) ( )
5	2583.7	88.3	0.059	0.010	( ) ( ) ( )
6	3143.0	77.1	0.067	0.010	( ) ( ) ( )
7	1587.4	77.3	0.024	0.010	( ) ( ) ( )
8	1091.6	76.4	0.013	0.010	( ) ( ) ( )
⋮	⋮	⋮	⋮	⋮	⋮

FIGURE 6.9 A method of storing analyzed speech data in computer memory. The numerical way in which resonances are represented depends on the analysis algorithm used.

tion are also in use. It is possible, with practice, to read a printout of the frame values of analyzed speech and deduce much the same information as from a "voice print," or sound spectrogram: that is, if the phrase is known in advance, to find the word and syllable boundaries. Graphical presentation of the parameters of amplitude, frequency, and errn yields an even more readable result.

In order to edit the speech analysis, an editing program is devised where a command will change the contents of the array containing the speech frames. Typically, an editing command causes a particular kind of edit to be applied to a certain parameter over a specified range of frames. For example, in order to set the frequency of the voice for a phoneme to 440 Hz, one needs a command that will change the appropriate parameter to the desired frequency for all the frames of the phoneme. Figure 6.10 shows a flow chart for an editing program. First the editing code and data concerning the range of frames, parameter number, and numerical value of edit are decoded. Next, control is transferred to the section of the program where calculations for the given edit command are made. Last, the edit is applied to the particular parameter for the range of frames.

Following is a list of some of the most common alterations found in synthetic speech editing systems:

MOVE: Copy some or all the parameters of a range of frames into another range of frames. This command is often used to create repetitions of phonemes or words.

INTERPOLATE: Interpolate the values of a specified parameter for a range of frames. When applied to the duration parameter, for example, this command can cause the speech to accelerate or decelerate.

TIME: Cause the range of frames to occupy the specified time span. The musician can use this command to impose new rhythms onto the speech without necessarily altering the analyzed pitch contour.

GLISSANDO: Cause the frequencies of a range of frames to change continuously between specified limits with an exponential progression.

CHANGE: Change the contents of a specified parameter in a range of frames to a given numerical value. For example, this command can be used to fix the pitch of the speech for the duration of a phoneme without necessarily altering the natural, spoken rhythm of the speech.

RAISE: Transpose the frequency parameter of a range of frames to another pitch level. This command can be used to change the frequency of the synthetic speech without destroying the natural pitch contour of the analyzed voice.

BOOST: Raise or lower the amplitude parameter of a range of frames by a fixed number of dB. This command also preserves the amplitude contour of the speech on which the analysis is based.

It is practical, even with a limited set of commands, to make music based on editing the analyses of recorded voices. A facility for mixing separately computed voices is most helpful.[30] This can be used, for example, to create polyphony. It can also help in creating a chorus of synthetic voices on the same text by mixing

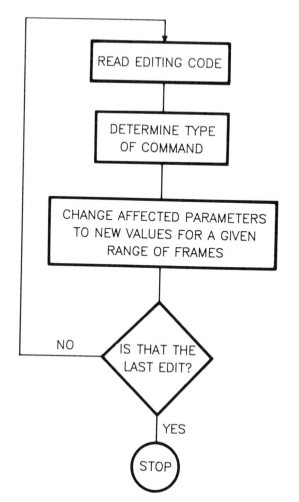

FIGURE 6.10   Flowchart of a speech editing program.

together voices that have been repeatedly synthesized with slight differences in the pitch and timing of the phonemes.

Sometimes, it is important to preserve as many of the characteristics of the original voice as possible. For example, when working with an analysis of a singing voice, it is much more effective to raise or lower the analyzed pitch contour than to change the frequency of a range of frames to the same value. Figure 6.11 shows the original pitch contour of three syllables sung by Enrico Caruso (figure 6.11a) and the effects of two different editings (figure 6.11b and 6.11c). In the first editing (figure 6.11b), the frequency of all frames for the syllable are the same. In the second, (figure 6.11c) the characteristic vibrato and frequency jitter are, while transposed, still preserved. The result in the second case sounds much more realistic.

In the situation where one wishes to make into a pitched line syllables that were originally spoken, it is necessary to change the frequency of the frames to a single value just in order to create the sensation. One way of making the voice sound less "mechanical" is to provide a transition in the pitch of the voice for about 100 msec between the syllables. Figure 6.12 illustrates this technique. Another technique for

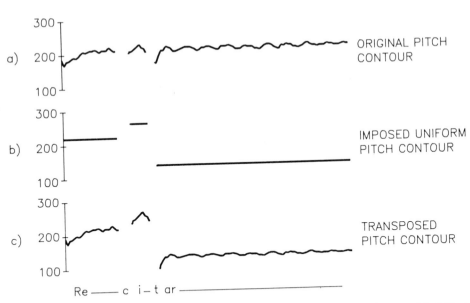

FIGURE 6.11 (a) Analyzed pitch contour of *Recitar* sung by Enrico Caruso. (b) Edited pitch contour with all frames of a syllable set to the same frequency. (c) Edited pitch contour with all frames of a syllable transposed by the same amount, thus preserving the small fluctuations of frequency characteristic of the voice.

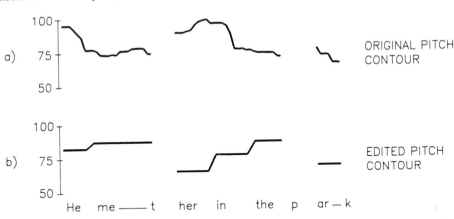

FIGURE 6.12 (a) Analyzed pitch contour of a phrase spoken by a male voice. (b) Edited pitch contour with all frames of a syllable set to insert the same frequency, except for small glissandos inserted between consecutive voiced syllables. The irregular frequency jitter of human speech is retained on synthesis through random fluctuation of the voice around the frequency of the frame.

making the pitched synthetic voice sound more natural is by introducing a small amount of random deviation around the frequency of the voice. A deviation of about ±1.5% to ±3% changing values every 10 msec has been found suitable for this purpose.

Another means of aiding the intelligibility of pitched speech based on a recorded voice is to slow down the voice a small amount. This seems completely natural, since the voice is now articulating both text and music simultaneously. A slowing of from 10% to 50% works very well. One must take care when elongating the time base of the speech that the consonants—the parts of speech by which the text is comprehended—do not become "fuzzy" or slurred. One means to ensure this is to apply the changes in timing of the speech only to the vowel portions of the words.

One note of caution is in order at this point. The full range of editing techniques work well only when the vocal source does not contain the extreme resonances that can be found in some extended vocal techniques such as "reinforced harmonics," and even in female singing in which the first formant tracks the fundamental frequency. Due to the marginal stability of the all-pole filter, in these cases, the result of the synthesis often includes a strong ringing at the analyzed fundamental regardless of the specified pitch.

6.9 Compositional Applications

Charles Dodge was one of the first composers to use synthesized voices in composition. He has composed a series of works in which computer-synthesized voices were used to form the whole fabric of the compositions.[31]

His musical version of Samuel Beckett's radio play, *Cascando*,[32] shows a use of the computer-synthesized voice to articulate text directly and to control the electronic sound of the non-verbal parts of the composition.

In the play of *Cascando*, there are three parts: Opener, Voice, and Music. The Opener is the central character; he controls the other two and relates directly to the audience. He continually asserts and attempts to demonstrate that the Voice and Music are real and not just "in his head." Voice persistently tries to tell a story that will satisfy the Opener, that will be the "right one" so that he may rest, remain silent. Music represents the non-verbal response to the same situation.

In Dodge's musical realization of *Cascando*, the Opener is performed live or represented by a recording of a reading. The part of Voice was realized with speech synthesis by analysis. The part was read into the computer in the musical rhythm and, after computer analysis, resynthesized with an artificial ("composed") pitch line in place of the natural pitch contour of the voice. A raspy vocal timbre was made by infusing the voice with equal parts of noise and pitch during the vowel portions of the speech.

In *Cascando*, every speech by Voice is either accompanied by or followed by a passage by Music. The composer took the position that, despite the Opener's remonstrances, the two parts were in fact "in his head" and therefore integrally connected. For that reason he fashioned Music out of Voice as a representation of the non-verbal side of the Opener. Figure 6.13 shows the computer instrument design for Music. The passage of Voice on which Music was to be based was fed into the instrument. If the Voice were to remain intelligible (i.e., if the passage were a duet for Voice and Music), the incoming voice bypassed a ring modulating oscillator that otherwise would have rendered the Voice unintelligible.

The signal of Voice was then passed to both branches of the instrument: to a bank of comb filters (see section 7.1B) and an amplitude inverter followed by a noise generator and gating mechanism. The amplitude inversion was accomplished by subtracting the voice signal from a constant corresponding to the average peak

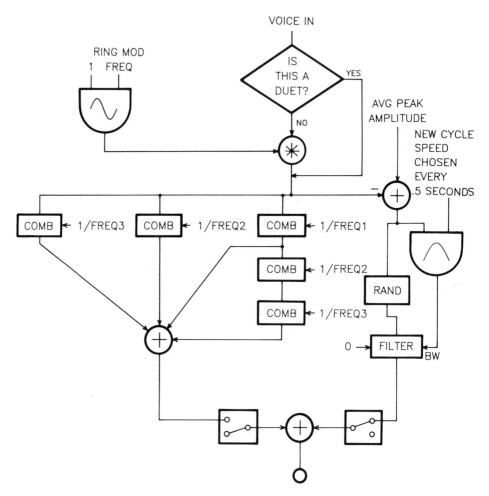

FIGURE 6.13   Computer instrument design for "Music" in Dodge's *Cascando*.

amplitude. When the incoming voice was "on," its signal was comb filtered at three
different frequencies, both in parallel and in series, and fed on to the "non-verbal
syntax" section of the instrument.

When the incoming voice was "off," its absence caused the amplitude inverter
to build up and, as it did so, to drive the noise generator that was then gated
repeatedly to produce "rustling," "thumping," and "scurrying" sounds. The
output of the low-pass filter that acts as the gate was fed to the previously
mentioned "non-verbal syntax" section of the instrument.

The final output of the instrument consists of pitch sound alone, noise sound
alone, or a mixture of the two, depending on parameters set in the score. These
parameters, which control the non-verbal syntax, cause Music for the whole
composition to follow, very slowly, the phonemic succession of the Voice for its
first solo. The preponderance of pitch or noise at a given moment in Music is a
reflection of the phonemic sound (voiced or unvoiced) at the corresponding place in
the first Voice solo. The pitches of the Music partake in the structure as well, in that
the pitch succession for the whole composition is directly related to the succession
of pitches in the first Voice solo.

Paul Lansky's *Six Fantasies on a Poem by Thomas Campion*[33] contains elegant demonstrations of musical uses of linear predictive coding in speech synthesis by analysis. In each of the six movements, Lansky emphasizes a different aspect of a single reading of the poem by actress Hannah MacCay. The composer writes, "my main intention was to explicate the implicit music in a poetry reading so that the reading itself, at the end, is explicitly musical."[34]

The procedure in the first fantasy was to "warp" the pitch contour of the recited poem. Generally, the pitch range of the original was widened and the contours were exaggerated. Then, Lansky mixed together the outputs of three separate syntheses. The pitches all change continuously in parallel intervals while the intervals separating the voices change at different places in the poem.

The second fantasy uses two versions of the synthetic voice with different, sometimes inverted, pitch contours that proceed at different speeds. The voices and phrases end together on the same pitch (usually a vowel), which is then prolonged as a single note. Lansky has pointed out that the coda of this fantasy puts all the prolonged notes together into a paraphrase of a Campion song, "Tune thy music to thy hart." The long tones were made by elongating the desired vowel sound in the way discussed in section 6.8. The particular sound was achieved by applying more than one impulse generator to the voice filter. The generators are tuned very close together, and each has a small random fluctuation of its frequency so that it beats with the other generators. Because the frequency of the beating falls well within the limits of discrimination, the result sounds somewhat smoother than a single randomly fluctuating generator. The reverberation applied to the final result further smooths the output.

Fantasies 3 and 5 make extensive use of reverberation techniques, and so they will be discussed in chapter 7.

In the fourth fantasy, there is no sound other than the multiple versions of the voice that articulates the poem largely in rhythmic unison and in chords that change from one section of the poem to another. The sound is created in a manner similar to that of Fantasy 2, but with the difference that here there is no pitch tracking of the original voice.

The final fantasy displays a pitched background of sustained tones made from vowel timbres that "capture and fix" certain pitches through which the reciting voice passes. This provides a procedure that is analogous to the way in which a comb filter "rings" inputs of certain frequencies. (See section 7.1B) Here the prolonged tone is of the same vowel timbre as the syllable of the text that it prolongs.

In *Six Fantasies on a Poem by Thomas Campion*, Lansky not only elaborates on the uses of linear predictive coding for speech synthesis by analysis, but also demonstrates the signal processing capabilities of certain computer music techniques, such as comb filtering. The combination of the techniques creates a depth of sound quality rarely achieved in computer music synthesis.

6.10   Other Synthesis Methods for Vocal Sounds

Other promising methods of synthesis which have been employed to simulate the voice are FM, FOF, and VOSIM. The use of FM synthesis to simulate the singing voice was discussed in section 4.1F.

The synthesis model of Xavier Rodet,[35] employed in the Rodet and Gerald Bennett study, uses a scheme that creates a spectrum containing resonances without the use of filters. The computer system that implements the scheme is named "Chant." Rodet's method, which he calls FOF (*fonctions d'onde formantique*) synthesis, simulates the speech by triggering multiple oscillators in a harmonic series for short bursts at the beginning of each fundamental pitch period. The user specifies the center frequency, bandwidth, and amplitude of the five formants, as well as the fundamental frequency, amplitude, and other system-specific variables.

In the synthesis methods described earlier in this chapter, a voiced sound is obtained by passing a quasi-periodic, impulsive excitation signal through a filter programmed to emulate the response of the vocal tract. Therefore, the output waveform can be described by the impulse response of the filter. Such a filter can be approximated as a group of second-order filter elements connected in parallel, one for each formant. When filters are connected in parallel, the impulse response of the complete filter is the sum of the impulse responses of the elements. In FOF synthesis, a digital oscillator is substituted for each filter element. Each oscillator is programmed, upon receipt of an impulse, to produce the waveform that is equivalent to the impulse response of the appropriate filter element. Figure 6.14 demonstrates how an impulse train excites each element so that the summation of all the responses results in a speechlike waveform. The π/β input controls the rolloff of the formant.

Rodet has analyzed both the male and female professional singing voices to determine the parameters for a five-element FOF synthesizer and has created a catalog that contains the representation of many phonemes. This method offers the musician the conceptual simplicity of formant synthesis without computing digital-filter algorithms. Two advantages of this system are first, the specified parameters bear a strong correlation to the acoustical attributes of the sound and, second, the parameters must be updated only once per pitch period, making the program relatively efficient, particularly at low frequencies. Both Gerald Bennett and Conrad Cummings[36] have employed Rodet's synthesis technique to produce compositions that make extensive use of synthesis of the singing voice.

VOSIM is a technique that permits the production of rich timbres with direct control over the formant structure of the sound. The technique was developed by Werner Kaegi at the Institute of Sonology at the University of Utrecht as a result of research to determine the minimum data representation for the phonemes of speech.[37] The name is contracted from VOice SIMulation. VOSIM has also successfully simulated the sounds of certain musical instruments using relatively few parameters to describe the sound.

The basic VOSIM waveform (figure 6.15) consists of a series of pulses followed by a time interval during which the signal is zero-valued. Each pulse is a $\sin^2$ pulse; that is, the pulse is the square of a half cycle of a sine wave. The five basic parameters of a VOSIM waveform are: N, the number of pulses per period; T, the duration of each pulse in seconds; M, the amount of delay between pulse groups; A, the amplitude of the first pulse; and b, the amplitude reduction factor between pulses (often specified as a percentage). The amplitude of each pulse after the first is calculated by multiplying the amplitude of the previous pulse by b. For example, if $b=80\%$ and $N=3$, the amplitude of the three pulses would be A, $.8A$, and $.64A$, respectively. The parameters are sometimes obtained by examining one pitch

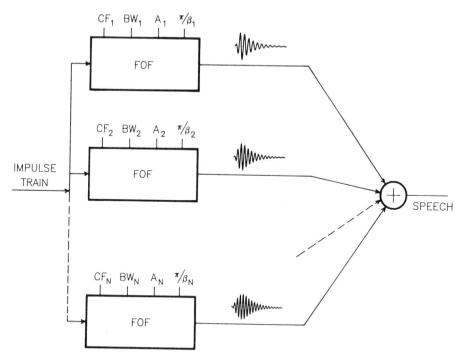

FIGURE 6.14   Basic plan of the FOF speech synthesizer. (*Reprinted with the permission of Xavier Rodet.*)

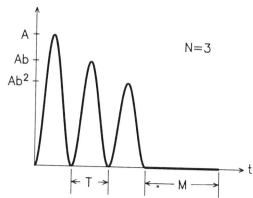

FIGURE 6.15   Basic VOSIM waveform.

period of the waveform to be simulated and selecting the VOSIM parameters that best approximate the observed waveform.

The overall period of the waveform is $NT+M$, so that when it is repeated, the fundamental frequency (f_0) is given by:

$$f_0 = (NT + M)^{-1}$$

The harmonic spectrum that is produced has three peaks. There are strong components at 0 Hz, at f_0, and in the vicinity of the frequency given by $1/T$. This does not mean that the spectrum will actually contain a component at $1/T$, but that any of the harmonics of f_0 which fall near that frequency will be emphasized. Thus $1/T$ can be thought of as a formant frequency. This explains, in part, the success of this technique in the synthesis of natural sounds.

Certain spectral properties can be deduced from the values of N, T, M, and b. Assume for a moment that all the pulses have the same amplitude ($b=100\%$). If $M=kNT$, where k is an integer, then multiples of the $k+1$ harmonic will not be present in the spectrum. For example, when $M=NT$, the spectrum does not contain any even harmonics. Selecting M to be much smaller than NT greatly emphasizes the Nth harmonic of f_0. Double reed instruments, such as the bassoon, have been simulated by choosing $N=2$ and M to be small so that the second harmonic is stronger than the fundamental. Choosing the parameter b less than 100% moderates the peaks and nulls of the spectrum. For instance, when $M=NT$, decreasing the value of b below 100% increases the amplitudes of the even harmonics.

There is always a null in the spectrum at twice the formant frequency ($2/T$). The spectrum of a VOSIM signal is not band-limited, and so aliasing can be a problem for high formant frequencies. When considering aliasing, take into account that above twice the formant frequency the amplitudes of all spectral components are at least 30 dB below that of the fundamental, and above six times the formant frequency they are at least 60 dB down.

Envelopes applied to the amplitude A, the pulse width T, and the delay time M, are used to obtain time-varying spectra as well as smooth transitions between sounds (particularly important in speech synthesis). Changing the value of M changes the pitch of the sound. For example, continuously increasing M causes the sound to glissando downwards. As the pitch is lowered, the perceived amplitude is reduced because the waveform contains less energy. This is due to the longer delay between pulse groups. This effect can be counteracted by applying the appropriate compensating envelope to the amplitude A.

Changing the value of T changes the formant frequency. This is used to achieve time evolution of the harmonics and obtain diphthongs in speech synthesis. This evolution is different from that produced by distortion synthesis techniques such as FM, since it entails formant shifting rather than direct changes in spectral richness. If a uniform pitch is desired while the value of T is being manipulated, a compensating function must be applied to M to keep the sum $NT+M$ constant.

For the synthesis of certain sounds, the value of M is modulated with periodic and aperiodic (noise) signals, a form of frequency modulation. When a noise signal modulates M, the resulting sound has a distributed spectrum with a formant specified by $1/T$. This is used to simulate the fricative sounds of speech, percussion sounds, or the sound of the violin bow striking the string on the attack of a note. Sine wave modulation of M is used for vibrato or wider band FM. The maximum deviation of the FM is limited because the value of M can never be less than zero. The variation of M also changes the power in the VOSIM sound, and so both frequency and amplitude modulation occur simultaneously. The amplitude modulation is significant only for large changes in the ratio NT/M.

Sounds with more than one formant are synthesized by using two or more VOSIM oscillators and adding their outputs. The oscillators can have the same fundamental frequencies with different formant frequencies. This method, with three oscillators, has been used for formant synthesis of speech.

The algorithm to generate the VOSIM waveform is more complex than that of conventional digital oscillators. However, a real-time digital hardware oscillator that is capable of producing VOSIM waveforms complete with modulating signals can be built relatively inexpensively.[38] The inputs to the oscillator typically include pulse width, number of pulses, amplitude, amplitude reduction factor, average delay time, deviation of M, and a choice of sine wave, random, or no modulation. The envelopes on A, T, and M can be implemented either in software or hardware.

6.11   The Concept of Linear Prediction

The technique of linear prediction has been available for many years and has been used in several fields. In recent years, the application of linear prediction to the analysis of speech has proven to be an excellent method for estimating the parameters of speech. The purpose of this section is to acquaint the reader with the basic concept of linear prediction. The reader wishing to approach the formidable mathematics involved is encouraged to begin by examining J. Makhoul's tutorial[39] on the subject.

The following problem is of interest in sampled data systems: Given a digital signal, can the value of any sample be predicted by taking a linear combination of the previous N samples? Linear combination here means that each of the N previous samples is multiplied by its own coefficient and the products are added together. Stating the question mathematically, can a set of coefficients, b_k, be determined such that:

$$y(n) = b_1 y(n-1) + b_2 y(n-2) + \cdots + b_N y(n-N)$$

(The notation used in this equation was introduced in section 5.11 to describe digital filters.) If the answer is yes, then the coefficients and the first N samples of a signal would completely determine the remainder of the signal, because the rest of the samples can be calculated by the equation above.

With a finite N, the predictor coefficients generally cannot be precisely determined. What is normally done is to take a group of samples (one frame) and determine the coefficients that give the best prediction throughout the frame. The relative merit of a set of predictors can be evaluated by taking the difference between the actual sample values of the input waveform and the waveform recreated using the derived predictors. The error, $e(n)$, between the actual value, $y(n)$, and the predicted value, $\bar{y}(n)$, is

$$e(n) = y(n) - \bar{y}(n)$$

Thus for each sample of the speech waveform, a corresponding error value can be calculated. The digital signal, $e(n)$, represents the errors and is called the residual. The smaller its average value, the better is the set of predictors. Schemes for determining predictors work either explicitly or implicitly on the principle of minimizing the residual.

The residual has another use. The original signal $y(n)$ can be exactly regenerated by calculating it according to the following relationship:

$$y(n) = a_0 e(n) + b_1 y(n-1) + b_2 y(n-2) + \cdots + b_N y(n-N)$$

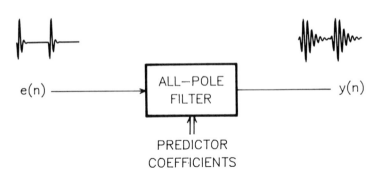

FIGURE 6.16   Use of the predictor coefficients in an all-pole filter to reconstitute the
analyzed speech waveform from the residual.

where a_0 is a scaling factor to give the correct amplitude. (a_0 does not affect the
shape of the waveform, only its amplitude.) The reader will recognize this equation
from section 5.13 as an all-pole, recursive filter with the residual applied to its
input. Figure 6.16 shows this configuration schematically.

Examination of the character of the residual of a speech wave suggests a
further simplification. When the speech is voiced, the residual is essentially a
periodic pulse waveform with the same fundamental frequency as the speech.
When the speech in unvoiced, the residual is similar to white noise. Thus, the LPC
synthesis model that was presented in figure 6.8 is based on this simplification of the
character of the residual. When the non-vocal sounds (e.g., tones of musical
instruments) are analyzed, the residual sometimes has a different character. In this
case, re-synthesis using the excitation sources of the speech synthesizer will
produce sounds that are dissimilar to the original.

The order of the predictor, N, determines the accuracy of the representation.
The accuracy of this method improves as N gets larger, but so does the amount of
computation required. What is the smallest value of N which will maintain
sufficient quality in the speech representation? The answer is directly related to the
highest frequency in the speech, the number of "formant" peaks expected, and the
sampling rate. There is no exact relationship, but in general N is between 10 and 20.
A rule of thumb that has been used by some researchers is to take N as 4 plus the
sampling rate in kHz. Thus, a system with a 15 kHz sampling rate might use $N=19$.

The prediction of the filter coefficients for a frame makes the assumption that
the process of speech production is stationary during the frame; that is, the
excitation and response of the vocal tract do not change during the frame. This is
usually a reasonable assumption, although audible distortion can sometimes result.
This distortion can be minimized by interpolating filter coefficients between frames
during the resynthesis process.

Notes

1.   Cann, Richard. "An Analysis/Synthesis Tutorial" (parts 1, 2, and 3). *Computer Music Journal*, 3(3), 1979, 6–11; 3(4), 1979, 9–13; 4(1), 1980, 36–42.

2.   Rabiner, L. R., and Schafer, R. W. *Digital Processing of Speech Signals*. Englewood Cliffs, N.J.: Prentice-Hall, 1978, 38–106.

3.   Fant, Gunnar. "The Acoustics of Speech." Proceedings of the Third International

Congress on Acoustics, 1959, 188–201. Reprinted in *Speech Synthesis*, edited by James L. Flanagan and Lawrence R. Rabiner, Stroudsburg, Pa.: Dowden, Hutchinson, and Ross, 1973, 77–90.

4. Mattingly, Ignatius. "Synthesis by Rule of General American English." Doctoral dissertation, Yale University, 1968, 133.

5. Potter, R. K., Kopp, A. G., and Green, H. C. *Visible Speech*. New York: Van Nostrand, 1947.

6. Peterson, G. E., and Barney, H. L. "Control Methods Used in a Study of Vowels." *Journal of the Acoustical Society of America*, 24(2), 1952, 175–184.

7. Olive, Joseph. "Automatic Formant Tracking in a Newton-Raphson Technique." *Journal of the Acoustical Society of America*, 50(2), 1971, 661–170.

8. Markel, J. D., and Gray, A. H., Jr. *Linear Prediction of Speech*. New York: Springer-Verlag, 1976.

9. Rabiner and Schafer, 135–158.

10. Fant, Gunnar. "The Acoustics of Speech." Proceedings of the Third International Congress on Acoustics, 1959, 188–201.

11. Rabiner and Schafer, 105.

12. Rabiner, L. R. "Digital Formant Synthesizer for Speech Synthesis Studies." *Journal of the Acoustical Society of America*, 43, 1968, 822–828. (Reprinted in *Speech Synthesis*, edited by James Flanagan and Lawrence Rabiner, Stroudburg, Pa.: Dowden, Hutchinson, and Ross, 1973, 255–261.)

13. Harris, Cyril M. "A Study of the Building Blocks in Speech." *Journal of the Acoustical Society of America*, 25, 1953, 962–969.

14. Rabiner, L. R. "Speech Synthesis by Rule: An Acoustic Domain Approach." *Bell System Technical Journal*, 47, 1968, 17–37.

15. Rabiner, L. R. *Digital Formant Synthesizer*, 823.

16. Rabiner, L. R. *Speech Synthesis by Rule*; Coker, C. H., N. Umeda, and C. P. Browman, "Automatic Synthesis from Ordinary English Text." In James Flanagan and Lawrence Rabiner (eds.), *Speech Synthesis*. Stroudsburg, Pa.: Dowden, Hutchinson, and Ross, 1973, 400–411; Allen, J. "Speech Synthesis from Unrestricted Text." In James Flanagan and Lawrence Rabiner (eds.), *Speech Synthesis*. Stroudsburg, Pa.: Dowden, Hutchinson, and Ross, 1973, 416–428.

17. Klatt, Dennis. "Software for a Cascade/Parallel Formant Synthesizer." *Journal of the Acoustical Sciety of America*, 67(3), 1980, 971–995.

18. Sundberg, Johan. "The Acoustics of the Singing Voice." *Scientific American*, 236(3), 1977, 82–91.

19. Rodet, X., and Bennett, G. "Synthese de la Voix Chantee Par Ordinateur." Conferences des Journees d'Etudes, Festival International du Son, 1980, 73–91.

20. Ibid.

21. Sundberg, Johan. "Synthesis of Singing." *Swedish Journal of Musicology*, 60(1), 1978, 107–112.

22. Ibid.

23. Sundberg, Johan. "Maximum Speed of Pitch Changes in Singers and Untrained Subjects." *Journal of Phonetics*, 7, 1979, 71–79.

24. Bennett, Gerald. "Singing Synthesis in Electronic Music." (Research Aspects on Singing) Stockholm Royal Swedish Academy of Music, 1981. (No. 33)

25. Atal, B. S., and S. L. Hanauer. "Speech Analysis and Synthesis by Linear Prediction of the Speech Wave." *Journal of the Acoustical Society of America*, 50, 1971, 637–655.

26. Makhoul, J. "Stable and Efficient Lattice Methods for Linear Prediction." *Institute of Electrical and Electronics Engineers Transactions on Acousitics, Speech, and Signal Processing*, ASSP-25 (5) 1977, 423–428.

27. Lansky, Paul, and Steiglitz, Kenneth. "Synthesis of Timbral Families by Warped Linear Prediction." *Computer Music Journal*, 5(3), 1981, 45–49.

28. Dodge, Charles. "The Story of Our Lives", CRI Records (CRI SD348), 1975.

29. Peterson, Tracy. "Voices." Tulsa, Okla.: Tulsa Studios, 1975.

30. Lansky, Paul. "MIX, a Program for Digital Signal Processing, Editing and Synthesis." Unpublished paper, Princeton University, 1983.

31. Dodge, Charles, "Speech Songs;" "In Celebration;" "The Story of Our Lives." CRI Records (CRI SD348), 1975.

32. Dodge, Charles. *Cascando*. CRI Records (CRI SD454), 1983.

33. Lansky, Paul. "Six Fantasies on a Poem by Thomas Campion." CRI Records (CRI SD456), 1982.

34. Personal Communication, 1980.

35. Rodet, X. "Time-Domain Formant-Wave-Functions Synthesis." *Actes du NATO-ASI Bonas, July,* 1979.

36. Cummings, Conrad. "Beast Songs." CRI Records (CRI SD487), 1983.

37. Kaegi, Werner, and Stan Tempelaars. "VOSIM—A New Sound Synthesis System." *Journal of Audio Engineering Society, 26*(6), 1978, 418–425.

38. Christiansen, S. "A Microprocessor-Controlled Digital Waveform Generator." *Journal of the Audio Engineering Society, 25,* 1977, 299–309.

39. Makhoul, J. "Linear Prediction, a Tutorial Review." *Proceedings of Institute of Electrical and Electronics Engineers, 63,* 1975, 561–580.

7

REVERBERATION, AUDITORY LOCALIZATION, AND OTHER SOUND-PROCESSING TECHNIQUES

A computer-music technique that has been widely used to enhance both electronically recorded and synthesized music is reverberation. The interest in this technique reflects a fascination on the part of post-World War II composers with the placement of sound sources in an acoustical environment. The development of electronics for multi-channel sound has made the location of the sound source available as an element in electronic music composition. Another musical resource made possible by electronic technology is *musique concrète*—music based on the splicing, mixing, and modification of recorded sounds. The compositional examples at the end of the chapter show how these different topics support and inform each other. Together they form a unified field of sound-processing techniques.

7.1 Reverberation

7.1A Natural Reverberation

Natural reverberation is produced by the reflections of sounds off surfaces. They disperse the sound, enriching it by overlapping the sound with its reflections. This process colors the sound to some extent, imparting a change in timbre. The importance of reverberation is familiar to musicians who have played the same piece in two halls. The effect of the different reverberant characteristics of the two spaces may influence the performance in a variety of ways. For example, the tempo selected to articulate the music may have to be adjusted; the dynamics of certain instruments may have to be changed; and even the seating of the players may have to be rearranged in order to communicate the desired sound.

The amount and quality of reverberation that occurs in a natural environment is influenced by certain factors: the volume and dimensions of the space; and the type, shape, and number of surfaces that the sound encounters. Consider a hypothetical room with no furnishings and perfectly flat, solid walls (figure 7.1). Acoustical energy emanating from the source (*S*) will travel at the speed of sound (ca. 345 m/sec), in all directions. Only a small portion of the sound reaches the listener (*L*) directly. The listener also receives many delayed images of the sound, reflected from the walls, ceiling, and floor of the room. Thus, the reflections lengthen the time that the listener perceives a sound. The amplitude of any sound is reduced by an amount that is inversely proportional to the distance it travels; therefore the reflected sounds not only arrive later, but they also have lower amplitudes than the direct sound. This means that the reverberated sound will have a decaying envelope.

The characterization of the complex process of reverberation in a real room is particularly difficult because the quality of reverberation cannot be quantified objectively. Four of the physical measurements that have been correlated with the perceived character of reverberation are the reverberation time, the frequency dependence of the reverberation time, the time delay between the arrival of the direct sound and the first reflected sound, and the rate of build up of the echo density.

The *reverberation time* indicates the amount of time required for a sound to die away to 1/1000 (-60 dB) of its amplitude after its source is shut off. The choice of 60 dB represents a convenience inherited from early researchers of room acoustics. The reverberation time is not a direct measurement of how long a listener will hear a sound after its source ceases. This time is only proportional to the reverberation time. It depends on other factors as well, such as the amplitude of the sound and the presence of other sounds. If the reverberation time is long enough, sound will overlap extensively with its reflections and build up a dense texture. These overlappings have been traditionally used to emphasize the interval relationships between successive tones. Such environments have been used compositionally by a

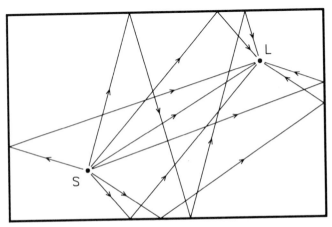

FIGURE 7.1   A few of the paths of sound travel in an ideal room.

number of contemporary composers including Stuart Dempster[1] to build multi-voice textures out of the sound of a single instrument. On the other hand, an unusually short reverberation time will minimize or even eliminate slight overlappings of musical tones. Mario Davidovsky has achieved highly pointillistic textures by using non-reverberant sounds in his electronic compositions.

In his early, pioneering studies of room acoustics, W. C. Sabine[2] concluded that the reverberation time depends on the volume of the room and the nature of its reflective surfaces. Rooms with large volumes tend to have long reverberation times. With a constant volume, an increase in either the surface area available for reflection or the absorptivity of the surfaces decreases the reverberation time.

All materials absorb acoustic energy to some extent, and so when a sound wave reflects off a surface, some of its energy is lost. Hard, solid, non-porous surfaces such as finished cement reflect very efficiently, whereas soft ones such as curtains and porous ones such as plaster absorb a substantial amount of the acoustic energy.

The roughness of the surfaces also has an effect on the nature of the reverberation. When a sound wave strikes a surface that is not perfectly flat, part of the sound is reflected in the expected direction (figure 7.1) and part is dispersed in other directions. The rougher the surface, the greater the proportion of energy that is dispersed. In a concert situation, there are additional surfaces for dispersion, absorption, and reflection, including furniture, carpets, people, and clothing.

The reverberation time is not uniform throughout the range of audible frequencies. Acousticians are not in complete agreement on the specific relationships that should exist between the reverberation times of the various frequency bands to produce "good" sound in a concert hall. However, it is agreed that the influence of reverberation on the spectrum of the sound in a well-designed concert hall favors the lower frequencies in the spectrum. These frequencies will fade more slowly than will the high frequencies. With a few exceptions, absorptive materials reflect low-frequency sounds better than high ones. For example, a heavy carpet can reflect 10 dB less signal at 4000 Hz than at 125 Hz. However, efficient reflectors such as marble reflect sounds of all frequencies with nearly equal efficiency. With small, solid objects, the efficiency and direction of reflection are both dependent on frequency. This causes frequency-dependent dispersion and, hence, a major alteration of the waveform of a sound.

The absorption of sound energy by water vapor in the air also contributes a frequency bias to the reverberation. The attenuation is more pronounced on high-frequency sounds and depends primarily on the humidity. The farther a sound travels through air with any humidity at all, the greater the relative attenuation of its high-frequency components. Thus, the spectrum of the sound towards the end of the reverberation has less high-frequency energy. Surprisingly, the maximum attenuation occurs when the humidity is around 15%.[3]

Another physical quantity that has been correlated with the perceived acoustic quality of a room is the amount of time that elapses between receiving a direct sound and its first reflection. A long delay (>50 msec) can result in distinct echoes, whereas a very short delay (<5 msec) can contribute to a listener's perception that the space is small. A delay in the 10- to 20-msec range is found in most good halls.

After the initial reflection, the rate at which the echoes reach the listener begins to increase rapidly. A listener can distinguish differences in echo density up to a density of one echo/msec.[4] The amount of time required to reach this threshold

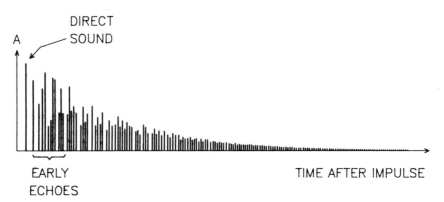

FIGURE 7.2   Simulated impulse response of a hall. The actual number of echoes has been reduced for clarity.

influences the character of the reverberation; in a good situation, it is typically around 100 msec. This time is roughly proportional to the square root of the volume of the room, so that small spaces are characterized by a rapid build up of echo density.

One method for measuring the acoustics of a hall involves placing a spark gap on the stage and an omnidirectional microphone in the audience. Firing the gap produces a short acoustical impulse in a nearly omnidirectional pattern. A record is kept of the sound pressure waves received by the microphone. This record, when corrected for the spectrum of the spark, indicates the impulse response of the room. A simulated impulse response is shown in figure 7.2. It tends to be ragged at first, during the early echoes, but the rest of the waveform is reminiscent of noise with exponential decay. The density of the waveform is the result of the multitude of reflected waves received and the many diverse paths they travel.

An irregular amount of time between peaks is a desirable characteristic for the impulse response of a concert hall, because it indicates a relative lack of frequency bias. If there is a nearly uniform time between peaks, the reverberation in the hall will add a frequency of its own to the sound, resulting in a "metallic-sounding" decay.

7.1B   Digitally Produced Reverberation

In recent years, there has been extensive research into electronic techniques for simulating natural reverberation. The enormous number and great variety of reflective and dispersive surfaces found in a natural environment make creating an exact acoustic model of its reverberation completely impractical. However, using the techniques presented below, reverberation with a natural sound has been simulated efficiently. An electronic reverberator can be thought of as a filter that has been designed to have an impulse response emulating the impulse response of the space to be simulated.

The use of digital electronics to simulate reverberant environments permits a great deal of control over all the parameters determining the character of the reverberation. The characteristics of a digital reverberator can be altered on a short-term basis, thus permitting reverberation to be used as a compositional element.

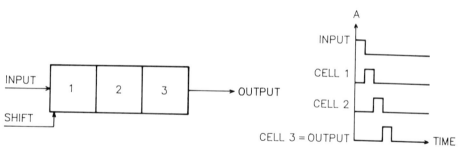

FIGURE 7.3   The operation of a shift register to realize delay.

To simulate the travel time of the indirect sound, a reverberator must have some method of delaying the signal that goes into it. There are two principal techniques for implementing delay digitally: shift registers and circular queues. A *shift register* consists of many memory cells in sequence, each of which can store one sample of a signal. Figure 7.3 shows a shift register used as a simple delay line; that is, a device to delay a signal. For the purposes of this example, the shift register is only three cells long. The figure shows how an impulse propogates from the input to the output. The shift register receives a shift signal at the sampling rate, and so at each sample time, the values stored in the memory cells are shifted one cell closer to the output. At the same time, the first cell is filled with the sample that is present at the input, and the sample value stored in the last cell is taken as the output. Thus, it takes three sampling periods for the impulse to emerge from the delay line, and so the actual amount of delay in seconds is three divided by the sampling frequency. For the example, at a sampling rate of 40 kHz, the amount of delay represented is $3/40,000 = .075$ msec.

In general, a shift register of length m cells provides a delay of m/f_s, where f_s stands for the sampling rate. A large number of cells are required for significant time delays at audio sampling rates. It is difficult for a general-purpose computer to handle data in this fashion, and so shift registers are normally implemented by special-purpose hardware.

On a general-purpose computer, *circular queues* provide the most efficient means for realizing a digital delay line. The queue takes the form of a group of sequential memory cells in which samples are stored (figure 7.4). The computer keeps a pointer that marks the memory cell containing the oldest sample. At every sampling period, the computer uses the oldest value as the output from the queue and then replaces the oldest value with a new one taken from the input. Finally, the pointer is incremented so that it marks what is now the oldest sample in the queue. Figure 7.4b illustrates this action. On every sample the algorithm moves the pointer one cell down the queue, outputs the oldest value, and replaces it with the current input sample. When the pointer reaches the end of the memory block, it is wrapped around to the first cell. Thus, the queue can be thought of as circular. This method for realizing delay makes efficient use of the computer, because once a sample value is placed in a memory cell, it does not move until it is replaced. As in a shift register, the amount of delay produced is directly proportional to the number of cells in the queue. The reverberator algorithms given in the appendix use circular queues.

Sometimes, the scheme used for reverberation requires several different amounts of delay of the same signal. A delay line whose total length is set to the

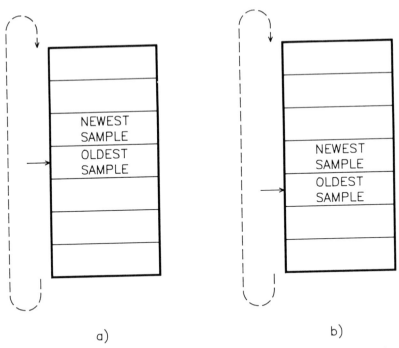

FIGURE 7.4   Circular queue both before (a) and after (b) a sampling interval.

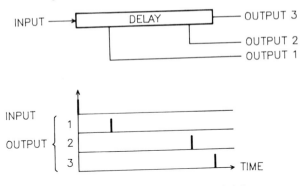

FIGURE 7.5   Tapped delay line giving several values of delay.

longest required delay can be "tapped" to obtain the appropriate shorter delays. Figure 7.5 illustrates the use of a tapped delay line to obtain three different values of delay. The tap points can be varied in software to dynamically change the amounts of the various delays.

The process known as *convolution* uses a heavily tapped delay line to produce reverberation that bears an extremely close resemblance to that of the real hall.[5] The sound to be reverberated is fed into a delay line whose total length is the same as the actual reverberation time for that hall. The delay line is tapped at every sample and the value from each tap is multiplied by the value of the hall's impulse response for that time. All the products are then added together to form the reverberated output signal.

The difficulty with convolution is that it requires an extremely lengthy computation for each sample and one memory cell for every sample period of delay. For example, if the reverberation time is 1.5 seconds and the sampling rate is 32 kHz, then 48,000 multiplications will have to be performed on every sample and the scheme will require enough memory storage to accomodate 48,000 sample values. Even with high-speed techniques for numerical convolution and the use of large, fast computers this method has proved far too slow to be practical.

The recirculation technique of M. R. Schroeder[6] uses a group of recirculating delay elements, and so enables long reverberation times to be obtained using relatively few calculations and short, untapped delay lines. The elements of a Schroeder reverberator are called unit reverberators and consist of two types—comb filters and all-pass networks. A complete digital reverberator is built by interconnecting several unit reverberators. The overall characteristics of the reverberator are determined by the parameters of the individual unit reverberators.

In a *comb filter*, the input signal enters a delay line. When it reaches the output, it is fed back to the input after being multiplied by an amplitude factor g. The time that it takes to circulate once through the delay line is termed the loop time, τ. Consider a comb filter such as the one in figure 7.6, whose loop time is 50 msec. When a unit impulse (a single sample with an amplitude of one preceded and succeeded by samples of zero amplitude) is applied to its input, the impulse begins to propogate in the delay line. The output of the filter is zero until, after 50 msec, the impulse emerges from the delay line. At this time the output of the comb filter is the impulse with amplitude one. Meanwhile, the impulse is multiplied by the factor g and sent back into the delay line. 50 msec later the impulse reemerges from the delay line with an amplitude of g. Once again, the impulse is multiplied by g (yielding an amplitude of g^2) and fed back into the input. The process continues; a pulse is output every 50 msec and each pulse has an amplitude that is a factor of g times that of the preceding pulse. The value of g must be less than one for the filter to be stable. Otherwise the impulse response will continually grow until it exceeds the dynamic range of the system.

The impulse response of a comb filter (figure 7.6b), then, is a train of pulses, spaced equally in time at an interval of the loop time. It therefore will sound at the frequency which is the inverse of the loop time. This frequency, f_0, is sometimes called the natural frequency of the filter and is stated mathematically as $f_0 = 1/\tau$. The response decays exponentially as determined by the values chosen for the loop time and g. Values of g nearest one yield the longest decay times. The decay time is ordinarily specified at the -60 dB point of the decay i.e., as the reverberation time.

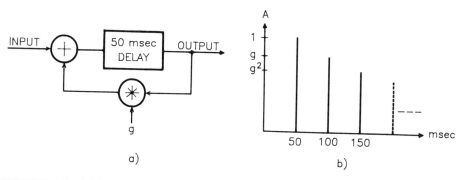

FIGURE 7.6   (a) The internal configuration of a comb filter and (b) its impulse response.

To obtain a desired reverberation time (T) for the unit, g can be calculated, given the loop time (τ), from the relationship:

$$g = 0.001^{(\tau/T)}$$

The loop time for a single unit reverberator is generally chosen in relation to the characteristics of the overall reverberator and will therefore be discussed below.

The comb filter is so named because its steady-state amplitude response (figure 7.7) is thought to resemble the teeth of a comb. The spacing between the maxima of the "teeth" of the comb is equal to the natural frequency. The depth of the minima and height of the maxima are set by the choice of g, where values closer to one yield more extreme maxima and minima.

In addition to its application as a component of a Schroeder reverberator, a comb filter can be used alone for the modification of sound. Thus, many systems make the comb filter available as a unit generator (figure 7.8) with two control parameters: the loop time and the reverberation time. In most implementations the loop time is set before synthesis begins and cannot be changed during the actual calculation of sample values. However, the reverberation time can usually be changed on every sample, if desired.

Passing a sound through a comb filter imparts certain reverberant characteristics to the sound. In addition, the incoming sound causes the filter to ring at its natural frequency, f_0, thus adding an additional component to the sound at that frequency. The ringing exhibits an amplitude envelope similar to that found in most bell-like sounds—a fast attack and a longer, exponential decay. Because the ringing

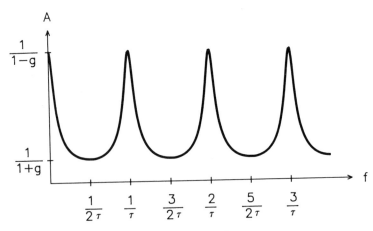

FIGURE 7.7   The amplitude response of a comb filter.

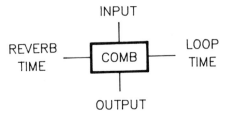

FIGURE 7.8   Flowchart symbol for a comb filter.

decays exponentially and has an amplitude that is directly related to the amplitude of the incoming sound, the output of the filter shows many characteristics of natural sound. Section 7.3B describes the compositional usage made of comb filters in Charles Dodge's *Earth's Magnetic Field* and Paul Lansky's *Six Fantasies on a Poem by Thomas Campion*.

An *all-pass network*, in contrast to a comb filter, passes equally signals of all frequencies in the steady-state (i.e., it has a flat amplitude response with no attenuation). On a steady-state basis, therefore, the relative amplitudes of the spectral components of a sound will not be altered. This does not mean, however, that an all-pass network is transparent to signals. On the contrary, an all-pass network has substantial effect on the phase of individual signal components. More audibly evident is the effect of its transient response, which can impart color to the sound during a sharp attack or after a sharp decay.

An all-pass network is similar to a comb filter but more complex in its implementation. Figure 7.9a illustrates the way in which the signal recirculates

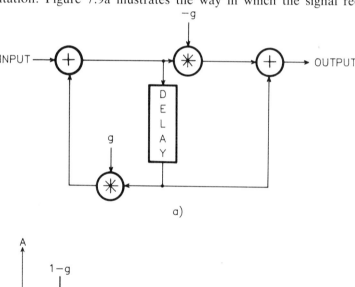

a)

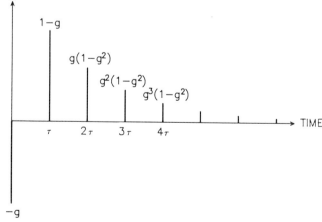

b)

FIGURE 7.9 (a) The internal configuration of an all-pass network and (b) its impulse response.

through the delay line whose length is once again called the loop time (τ). A factor g specifies the decay time of the impulse response and has the same relationship to the reverberation time and the loop time as in a comb filter. As before, g must be less than one for stability.

The impulse response of the network (figure 7.9b), like that of a comb filter, is a pulse train with an exponential envelope. Notice that, unlike a comb filter, there is no delay between the application of the sound at the input and the appearance of sound at the output. The uniform spacing between pulses indicates that when a short impulsive signal is applied, the network will "ring." Figure 7.10 illustrates the reaction of an all-pass network to a tone with an abrupt decay. A sinusoidal tone has been applied to the network long enough to achieve a steady-state condition. When the tone ends, the decaying output waveform has a period equal to the loop time of the network. A frequency ($1/\tau$) is thus produced that is completely unrelated to the frequency of the original input. Fortunately, most sounds have less abrupt decays, so that the effect of the transient response of the network is considerably less noticeable. However, it should be borne in mind that an all-pass filter is not totally "colorless."

Realistic reverberation can be digitally simulated through the interconnection of multiple comb and all-pass networks. When unit reverberators are connected in parallel, their impulse responses add together. When they are placed in cascade, each pulse of the impulse response of one unit triggers the impulse response of the next, producing a much denser response. The total number of pulses produced by units in parallel is the sum of the pulses produced by the individual units. The number of pulses produced by units in cascade is the product of the number of pulses produced by each unit. In either case, pulses that occur at the same time add together, reducing the number of observed pulses.

When comb filters are used in a reverberator, they should be connected in parallel to minimize the spectral disturbances. A frequency that falls in a minimum of one filter might be able to pass through another. All-pass networks, on the other hand, should be connected in cascade since they are, at least in the steady-state,

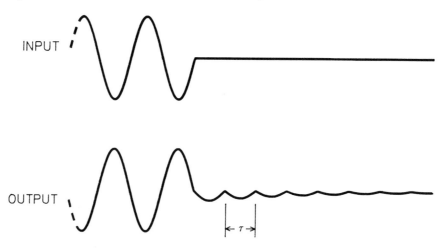

FIGURE 7.10 Demonstration of the transient response of an all-pass network. After the input tone ceases, the network "rings" with a period equal to the loop time of the network.

colorless. In addition, because of their phase response characteristics, connecting unequal all-pass units in parallel can result in a non-uniform amplitude response.

Schroeder proposes two methods of using comb filters (C) and all-pass networks (A) to realize artificial reverberation (figure 7.11). An impulse applied to the reverberator of figure 7.11a initiates a decaying train of pulses from each of the comb filters. The all-pass networks in cascade serve to increase the pulse density. In the configuration of figure 7.11b, each pulse of the impulse response of the first all-pass unit triggers the impulse response of the second, and so on, causing the impulse response to become successively denser. The topology of figure 7.11a is of the type that is implemented in programs such as MUSIC 4BF and MUSIC 360. Other similar configurations are possible so long as the musician follows the rule that comb filters are connected in parallel and all-pass networks are connected in cascade.

The choice of loop times and reverberation times for the interconnected unit reverberators determines the character of the overall unit. Most reverberation design strives for a total impulse response that is fairly dense, that has a reasonably smooth exponential envelope, and for which the time pattern of pulses is random enough to prevent the reverberator from adding an undesired coloration. A good approximation of these characteristics can be obtained by choosing loop times that are relatively prime to each other; that is, where the number of samples stored in the delay lines have no common divisors. To understand how this works, consider the parallel combination of two comb filters, C_1 and C_2. Let the loop time of C_1 equal 40 msec and that of C_2 equal 50 msec. At a sampling rate of 20 kHz, the delay lines required to realize the comb filters must be 800 and 1000 samples long,

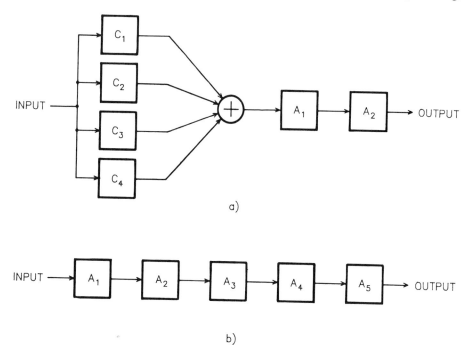

a)

b)

FIGURE 7.11   Two topologies for digital reverberators suggested by Schroeder.

respectively. Because these lengths are both evenly divisible by 200, the impulse response will not have a smooth decay. C_1 will respond with pulses every 40 msec and C_2 will emit them every 50 msec. At 200 msec, 400 msec, etc., the impulses will coincide, producing increased amplitude. A reverberator with this kind of impulse response will tend to produce distinct echoes and have an audible frequency bias. Setting the lengths of the delay lines to the nearest prime number of samples, respectively 799 and 997, produces a markedly better impulse response, while making only minor adjustments in the loop times to 20.05 and 49.85 msec. Now, the first coincidence of pulses does not occur until $799 \times 997 \, / \, 20 \text{ kHz} = 39.98$ seconds. More than two unit reverberators are generally used in an actual reverberator, and they should all have delay lengths that are relatively prime to each other. Delay lengths related in this way provide the densest impulse response for the number of units and tend to distribute the time between pulses more randomly. Also, choosing prime loop times tends to help equalize the amplitude response of parallel combinations of comb filters.

Selection of the actual loop times depends upon the type of environment to be simulated. Recall from the previous section that two of the measurements correlating with the acoustically perceived size of a space are the time delay between the direct sound and its first reflection and the amount of time that it takes for its impulse response to build up to a density of 1 echo/msec. A tiled shower may have the same reverberation time as a concert hall, but there is a definite audible difference between the two. In addition to the differences in the frequency-dependent properties of the reflective surfaces, the substantially smaller volume of the shower and the corresponding closer proximity of the walls to the listener cause not only the first reflections to arrive sooner, but also the echo density to increase more rapidly. Thus, shorter loop times are used to simulate smaller spaces.

For the reverberator of figure 7.11a, comb filter loop times chosen in the vicinity of 50 msec, with the ratio of longest to shortest of about 1.7:1, can provide concert-hall characteristics. In contrast, the tiled shower might be simulated by decreasing the loop times to values in the 10 msec range. The reverberation time of each comb filter is set to the desired time for the overall reverberator. The two all-pass networks must have relatively short loop times or there will be audible repetitions of the signal. If the loop times are too long, the echo density will not reach the 1 echo/msec threshold resulting in an unrealistic sound (e.g., a "puffing" sound when short, impulsive sounds are reverberated). Five or six msec is about the maximum loop time for A_1, and that of A_2 should be even shorter. The reverberation time of the two all-pass networks should be fairly short (less than 100 msec), because their purpose is to increase the density of the overall impulse response, not to lengthen its duration.

As an example, table 7.1 shows a set of parameters that has been used in the reverberator of figure 7.11a to simulate the characteristics of a medium-sized concert hall. The loop times have been chosen to be relatively prime to each other. The reverberation time (RVT) of the overall reverberator is the same as the reverberation time of each of the comb filters. For a concert-hall simulation this value is often in the range of 1.5 to 2 seconds, but the musician can vary this parameter for other purposes.

In the configuration of figure 7.11b, the characteristics of the unit reverberators are chosen in much the same way as in 7.11a. Thus, the loop time of the first 'all-pass network is chosen in relation to the size of the room to be simulated, and

ELEMENT	REVERB TIME	LOOP TIME	
C_1	RVT	29.7	msec
C_2	RVT	37.1	msec
C_3	RVT	41.1	msec
C_4	RVT	43.7	msec
A_1	96.83 msec	5.0	msec
A_2	32.92 msec	1.7	msec

TABLE 7.1   Parameters for a Schroeder Reverberator Simulating a Medium-Sized Concert Hall (RVT indicates the reverberation time for the overall unit)

the remaining loop times and reverberation times are set such that each is shorter than the previous one. The loop time of the final unit must be short enough to ensure adequate echo density.

Figure 7.12 shows the use of a reverberator to impart a sense of spaciousness to the sound of a computer instrument. Ordinarily, the single control parameter for the reverberation is the reverberation time (RVT). As previously stated, reverberation time is defined as the time it takes for a sound at the input to the reverberator to die away at the output to 1/1000th (-60 dB) of its amplitude. It is often useful when specifying reverberation time to specify a greater reverberation time than one imagines the sound to need. This will compensate for the fact that much of the reverberated signal will often be masked by the other tones present in the texture, as well as by any noise in the system. Another factor to consider when using reverberation is the amount of the signal to be reverberated. To give better definition and presence, some part of the signal is usually sent directly to the output, bypassing the reverberator. The ratio of reverberated to unreverberated output is involved in simulating the distance of the source of the sound from the listener. (See section 7.2C.)

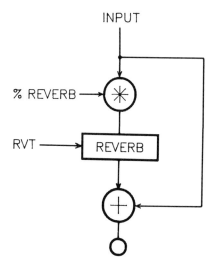

FIGURE 7.12   Use of a reverberator. The proportion of reverberated to direct sound is set by the parameter, %REVERB.

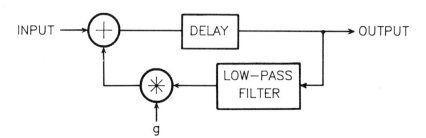

FIGURE 7.13 Inclusion of a low-pass filter in the recirculation loop of a comb filter to shorten the reverberation time of the higher frequencies.

7.1C Variations of Schroeder Reverberators

Up to this point, the discussion has been restricted to methods for the production of colorless reverberation. As mentioned earlier, however, a real concert hall does in fact shade the color of the sound, because lower frequencies tend to have longer reverberation times. To simulate this, a unit reverberator may have a low-pass filter placed in its feedback path so that the recirculating sound loses some its high-frequency energy on every trip through the loop. This is simpler to do in a comb filter (figure 7.13) than in an all-pass network, which requires two low-pass filters (one of which is not unconditionally stable). The characteristics of the low-pass filter are chosen to simulate the difference in reverberation times at different frequencies. These differences may be taken from measured concert-hall data or may be approximated. The use of this configuration has the added benefit of "smearing out" the impulse response, particularly towards the end, so that it is less likely to sound metallic.

Schroeder reverberators have been used in computer music since the mid-1960s, but one problem with them is their lack of early echoes.[7] When the loop times are chosen to achieve the rate of increase in echo density corresponding to a good-sized space, the first indirect sound will arrive noticeably later than it normally would in a real hall. Reducing loop times could help alleviate this problem, but would also cause the echo density to increase too quickly, creating the impression of a smaller space. To simulate early echoes, Schroeder has suggested[8]

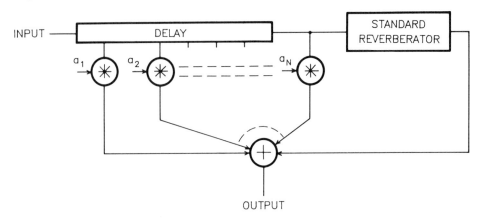

FIGURE 7.14 Method of early echo simulation based on Schroeder.

inserting a tapped delay line in front of his standard reverberator (figure 7.14). The values of the delays and the multiplier coefficients $(a_1, a_2, \ldots, a_n)$ can be obtained by examining the impulse responses of actual halls or by calculating the arrival time and amplitude of the first few echoes from the geometry of a particular room. Normally, the first 80 msec or less of the response is realized in the delay line. The values of the coefficients tend to get smaller for taps further removed from the input. This technique can substantially increase the amount of calculation performed in the reverberator algorithm.

7.1D   Sound Modification Techniques Using Variable Delay Lines

Certain effects can be imposed on sounds by using delay lines whose delay time can be varied on a sample-to-sample basis. Two of the most common uses of this technique are for flanging (phasing) and for producing a chorus effect.

Flanging creates a "swishing," or rapidly varying high frequency sound by adding a signal to an image of itself that is delayed by a short, variable amount of time (figure 7.15a). A typical use of this configuration is to apply a function of time to the delay input that sweeps the amount of delay (τ) from a few milliseconds to zero. This produces the characteristic flanging sound. The DEPTH parameter controls the proportion of the delayed signal in the output, determining the prominence of the effect. Many implementations enable dynamic flanging where the flanging action is proportional to the peak of the envelope passing through the flanger.

A flanger has a frequency response like that shown in figure 7.15b. At any particular value of delay, the minima appear at frequencies that are odd harmonics of the inverse of twice the delay time.[9] Thus flangers produce their effect by dynamically changing the spectrum of the tone being processed. The amount of attenuation at the minima is set by the value of DEPTH which has a range from zero to one. A value of one corresponds to maximum attenuation.

Another musical use of variable delay lines is to produce a chorus effect which changes the sound of a single instrument into that of a group of instruments playing in unison. (See section 3.10.) The technique entails the use of several variable delay lines connected in parallel (figure 7.16). The amount of delay of each line typically ranges from between 10 and 50 msec. The instantaneous value of each delay is set by a random noise generator whose spectral energy is concentrated below 20 Hz.

The prominence of the effect, related to the physical and numerical size of the

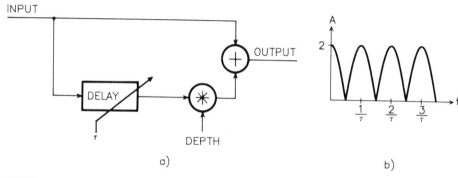

FIGURE 7.15   (a) Internal configuration of a flanger. (b) Frequency response at a fixed amount of delay and DEPTH=1.

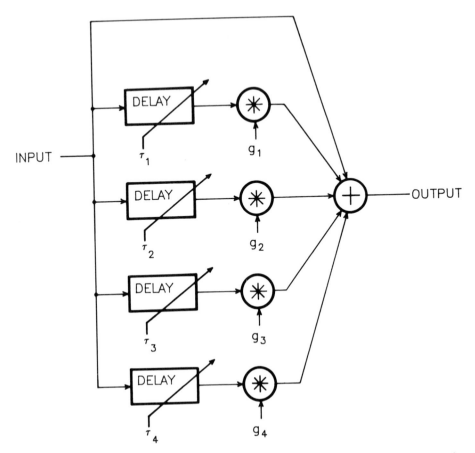

FIGURE 7.16 Method of realizing a "chorus effect" with variable delay lines. (*Based on a design in B. Blesser and J. Kates, "Digital Processing in Audio Signals," in* Applications of Digital Signal Processing, *ed. Alan V. Oppenheim, © 1978, p. 78. Reprinted by permission of Prentice-Hall, Inc., Englewood Cliffs, N.J.*)

perceived ensemble, is controlled by the independent amplitude controls, g, on each channel.

7.1E Synthesis Technique Using a Delay Line

Aside from their widespread use in sound processing, delay lines have also been employed in the synthesis of certain sounds. A particularly successful example is the simulation of plucked-string sounds by means of an algorithm developed by Kevin Karplus and Alex Strong.[10] Figure 7.17a illustrates the flowchart of the basic Karplus-Strong algorithm involving a noise source, a delay line, and a low-pass filter. Initially the delay line is filled with a burst of noise; that is, the noise generator is connected to the input of the delay line until every cell contains a sample of noise. This action places a waveform in the delay line with a broad spectral content. When the delay line is full, the noise generator is disconnected and the output of the delay line is fed through a low-pass filter back into the delay line input. To understand the

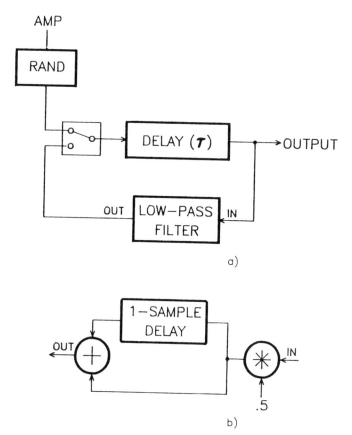

FIGURE 7.17   (a) The basic configuration of the Karplus–Strong algorithm. (b) The flow chart of the averaging filter which serves as a low-passfilter.

acoustical effect of this configuration, suppose for a moment that the cutoff frequency of the low-pass filter is well above the audio range. In this case, the waveform would continuously recirculate through the delay line. The signal observed at the output of the instrument would be a periodic waveform and, therefore, sound with a clear pitch even though a noise generator produced the original waveform.

In practice, the low-pass filter is given a cutoff frequency well below the Nyquist frequency, and so every time the waveform passes around the loop, it loses some of its spectral energy imparting an exponential decay to the waveform. The decay time of the overall tone is inversely proportional to the fundamental frequency of the tone. Therefore, tones sounded at lower pitches exhibit longer decays. Because the filter has a low-pass shape, the higher harmonics lose more energy on each pass than the lower ones. Thus, in the dynamic spectrum produced, the higher harmonics decay more rapidly—a salient characteristic of plucked-string tones.

The low-pass filter most commonly used in this algorithm is the two-point, moving-average filter shown in figure 7.17b (see also section 5.12). This filter determines its output by taking the average of the sample value currently emerging from the delay line and the value of the previous output of the delay line. With this filter in place, the fundamental frequency (f_0) of the generated tone is given by

$$f_0 = \frac{f_s}{N + \frac{1}{2}}$$

where N is the number of samples stored in the delay line. N can be computed from the delay time τ by $N=\tau f_s$. However, the calculated value of N for a particular fundamental frequency will usually have a fractional part which is either rounded or truncated to the nearest integer resulting in a tuning error which can be quite objectionable for high fundamental frequencies (i.e., for small values of N). Thus, accurate tuning can be difficult for registers with frequencies in excess of only a few percent of the sampling rate.

The amplitude of this instrument can be scaled by adjusting the amplitude of the noise generator. However, if this instrument is to be used at different dynamic levels in the same piece, this scaling method will produce the "volume-control" effect. In acoustic instruments, plucking a string more forcefully not only produces a louder sound, but also a richer spectrum. To simulate this effect, the noise generator can be coupled through a separate low-pass filter during the filling of the delay line. The cutoff frequency would be made proportional to the desired amplitude so that softer sounds would have less initial spectral bandwidth.

Because of its computational efficiency and natural-sounding tones, the Karplus-Strong algorithm has been implemented successfully on a variety of systems including microcomputers. A number of extensions of the basic technique are possible including lengthening and shortening decay times, tuning accuracy enhancement, and simulation of sympathetic strings, among others.[11] David Jaffe has used the Karplus-Strong algorithm for synthesis in two of his works: *May All Your Children Be Acrobats* (1981) and *Silicon Valley Breakdown* (1982).

7.2 Auditory Localization

Auditory localization is the human perception of the placement of a sound source. In listening to music in a concert hall, a listener receives cues for sound location from the placement of the actual sound sources in the hall. By using at least one microphone per channel and placing them at different locations in the hall, a great deal of the localization information is preserved in a multi-channel recording. In electronic music, the sound may be perceived as static and one-dimensional unless the illusion of source locality is included in the synthesis. With an understanding of the perception of sound-source location, the placement of the apparent source of sound can also be used as a compositional element in electronic music.

7.2A Localization Cues from Real Sources

To perceive location accurately, the listener seeks clear cues that define the direction and distance of the sound source. The direction is expressed as a three-dimensional angle, so that the description is not limited to sounds on the same horizontal plane as the listener. In determining the direction of a sound source, the audible cues that a listener uses are based upon differences in time and intensity received stereophonically.

Any delay that a listener perceives between the time that a sound reaches one ear and the time that it reaches the other is called the *interaural time difference* (ITD). The listener can use ITD cues to determine the angular direction, measured in degrees, of a sound source.[12] If the sound source is centered behind or in front of the listener, the ITD is zero. As the angle is changed by more than about one degree (that is, as the ITD exceeds about 20 microseconds), a difference in direction can be perceived. Resolution by ITD cues becomes less precise as the sound source moves toward a position that is lateral to the listener.

The *interaural intensity differences* (IID) provide another cue for determining direction. When the sound source is not centered, the listener's head partially screens the ear opposite to the source, casting a "shadow" that diminishes the sound received by that ear, particularly at higher frequencies. In addition, the external ear performs filtering at frequencies above 5 kHz. The amplitude response varies with the direction from which the sound reaches the listener.[13] This filtering helps the listener determine whether a sound comes from above, below, in front, or behind.

The usefulness of the cues depends on the frequency content of the sound. Both ITD and IID cues are ineffective when the spectral energy of the sound resides below about 270 Hz; hence, the direction of such sounds cannot be determined. ITD cues are most effective in the frequency range of 270 to 500 Hz, but are completely inoperative above 1400 Hz. On the other hand, a spectral component below 500 Hz produces no significant IID cues. The amount of intensity difference increases with frequency so that above 1400 Hz IID cues predominate. At 6 kHz the difference can be as much as 20 dB for a lateral sound. In the intermediate region between 500 and 1400 Hz, the cues combine in a complicated manner that depends on the nature of the sound.[14] The two types of cues received from a real source ordinarily correlate well. This is often not the case for sounds produced by electronic sound systems. (See section 7.2B.)

As discussed in relation to reverberation, any sound reaching a listener is comprised of both direct and reflected sound. The relative intensities of the direct and reflected sounds is the primary cue used to estimate the distance at which the sound source is located.

When the sound source is close to the listener, the ratio of direct to reverberant energy is high. As the distance between them becomes greater, the amount of direct energy decreases more rapidly than the reflected energy, so the ratio becomes smaller. At very large distances, little of the sound is received directly. An additional cue at large distances is the loss of lower energy components of the sound. In most cases, this results in the absence of high-frequency components in the sound.

Because reverberation is the basis for determining distance, impulsive sounds are most easily located. Long tones are most difficult because listeners estimate distance almost entirely during the attack portion of sounds.[15]

7.2B Simulation of Directional Cues

To convince an audience of an imagined location, the appropriate directional and distance cues must be provided. This can be done either by placing a large number of loudspeakers around the room, or by using a few speakers and creating the illusion of direction and distance by careful allocation of the signal among them.

The listener to a multi-channel electronic sound system generally receives conflicting interaural (IID and ITD) directional cues. To best understand how the listener resolves these conflicts, it is necessary to consider separately the simulation of these cues in a laboratory situation.

Simulated ITD cues can be accurate only under extremely restricted conditions. Either a single listener must be placed in an accurately chosen position (the distance from the speakers known within 10 cm with the head fixed so that it cannot rotate more than 10° off center) or the listener must wear headphones. This is a consequence of the *precedence effect*: A listener receiving the same sound from multiple sources locates it at the closest source, not at a point between them, unless the separation in time is less than about a millisecond. For example, consider the configuration in figure 7.18 where the listener is equidistant from two loudspeakers, *L* and *R*, which are fed identical signals. In this case, the listener receives equal signals at each ear and believes that the source is centered at position *I1*. Suppose that loudspeaker *R* is moved a few centimeters farther to the right. This is equivalent to leaving loudspeaker *R* in its original position and slightly delaying the signal applied to it. The sound will now reach the left ear before the right one, so that the imagined source location shifts toward the left to position *I2*. If loudspeaker *R* is more than about 35 cm farther from the listener than loudspeaker *L*, the sound travelling from *L* will reach both ears before any sound from *R* arrives. Thus the listener receives the same initial cues that would be provided by a single source located at *L*. The sound from loudspeaker *R* serves merely to reinforce the original sound and does not alter the listener's first impression that the sound emanates solely from *L*.

The sound that reaches an ear from the opposite loudspeaker is called cross-talk. It effectively limits the placement of auditory images to the area between the speakers. It is possible with special filters to compensate for the effect of the cross-talk[16] and create images outside the loudspeakers. However, the filter's response must be calculated on the basis of some exact physical relationship between the listener and the speakers, and so this method is used only in laboratories and by audiophiles who are willing to position themselves with great accuracy. Finally, with or without filters, if loudspeaker *R* is moved a long distance away so that its sound arrives more than 35 to 50 msec after the sound from *L*, an echo will be heard.

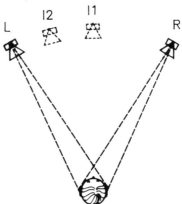

FIGURE 7.18   Listener positioned equidistant from two loudspeakers.

The direction of a sound source may also be simulated by providing the listener with cues of interaural intensity difference (IID). Return to figure 7.18. The two sound sources, L and R, are emitting exactly the same sound with equal amplitude. Again the listener is situated equidistant from the loudspeakers (ITD=0), and so the resulting image is centrally located at $I1$. When the amplitude of the left signal is increased, the image is displaced toward L at an angle that is determined by the ratio of the intensities of the signals delivered to the two loudspeakers. Specific examples of signal allocation formulae will be given in section 7.2F. The IID do not change greatly as the listener moves off center. However, if the sound emitted by the two speakers is identical, the precedence effect can intervene and assign the location to the nearest speaker depending on the spectral composition of the sound.

As stated above, IID cues are most effective for sounds at higher frequencies. In fact, above 1400 Hz the listener relies entirely on IID cues, and so the precedence effect will not be a factor. As a result, systems using only IID cues to localize the sound are most successful on signals with high frequencies or wide bandwidths.

Under certain conditions, it is possible to defeat the precedence effect by splitting the signals among the speakers on the basis of their frequency components. In this technique the sound emitted by the loudspeakers is not identical and therefore, the precedence effect can be avoided. For example, in a technique suggested by Gardner[17] for a two-channel system, the signal applied to one speaker is passed through a low-pass filter while the other speaker receives a version which has been high-passed. The image broadens to fill the area between the speakers. That is, the percept of point source no longer exists. However, the filters must not roll off too steeply or the listener will perceive the frequency differences between the speakers and hence, two sources. Another approach to evading the precedence effect uses a bank of band-pass filters with the inputs connected in parallel. Each filter has a bandwidth of one-third of an octave and together they span the entire audio range. The output of every other filter is added into a given channel; that is, the first, third, fifth, and so on filters would drive the left speaker, and the second, fourth, sixth, and so on would drive the right speaker. When the sound source has a reasonably broad bandwidth, this technique avoids the precedence effect at the cost of a certain amount of image broadening.

7.2C Simulation of Distance Cues

To simulate distance cues, reverberated sound is added to the direct sound. The distance between the listener and the desired image determines the ratio of these signals. Thus, as the distance increases, so does the ratio of reverberated to direct sound. At the same time, the overall amplitude of the sound decreases, with the direct sound dropping faster than the reverberated.

It is useful to separate the reverberation into two components—global and local.[18] Global reverberation returns equally from all directions around the listener. Local reverberation comes from the same direction as the direct signal and derives from reflectors relatively nearby the source. When the sound is located close to the listener, most of the reverberation is global. This models an imaginary environment in which the listener is located in the center of a space with equal reflection in all directions. If the sound source is distant, most of the reverberation is local and comes from the same direction as the source because, in the imaginary environment, the source is closer to reflectors in that direction.

Because the reverberant characteristics vary from one environment to another, there is no absolute ratio of direct to reverberated sound which corresponds to a specific distance. Depending on the characteristics of the space to be simulated (such as its liveliness), the musician selects, at some reference distance the ratio of reverberated to direct sound.

The actual space for performance of the electronic composition must be considered when calculating distance cues, because a room adds reverberation of its own. If the room is anechoic, the apparent source location may be placed anywhere within the room. As the reverberant qualities of a room increase, it becomes less feasible to simulate sources near the center of the listening space, because the percentage of reverberated sound cannot be brought below the level provided by the room. If computer music is to be performed in a room with long, natural reverberation, such as a concert hall, it might be difficult to move the apparent source within the perimeter established by the loudspeaker placement. The location can be moved beyond the loudspeakers by adding artificial reverberation, but it is hard to move it convincingly inside the perimeter because the reverberation of the room cannot be subtracted from what the listener hears.

Any room has so many different kinds of reflectors that the reverberation arriving at the listener is different from each direction. In fact, tests have shown that a low interaural coherence—a measurement that indicates little similarity between the reverberation received by each of the two ears—results in a more pleasing sound and a greater feeling of "immersion."[19] If the loudspeakers emit signals containing identical reverberation, the interaural coherence will be high, so that the sound will seem artificial to the listener. Therefore, each channel should have its own reverberator with slightly different parameters.

7.2D Creating a Listening Space

To simulate localization cues for a sound located at an imaginary point, the loudspeakers must be placed in such a way as to create a listening space within which the cues of localization can be delivered to one or more listeners. Distribution of the signals applied to each channel is calculated on the basis of some physical relationship among the loudspeakers and the listeners. The region in which listeners receive the cues necessary to perceive the illusory location may be thought of as the focal area of the configuration.

The musician must choose the dimensionality of localization and the number and position of the loudspeakers to realize a focal area large enough for the intended audience. The relatively expensive hardware to implement each channel compels the musician to minimize their number. Unless special filters are used with a specially positioned listener, two sources can localize the sound in only a portion of a two-dimensional space. A typical use of this configuration is to move the sound laterally in front of the listener at a fixed distance, essentially a one-dimensional situation. Theoretically, a listener situated in the center of a triangle formed by three loudspeakers could be presented with the cues of a source located anywhere in a two-dimensional plane. However, a system of this nature produces cues that are valid only in an extremely small area. A more practical minimum configuration for creating a full two-dimensional plane uses four loudspeakers that mark the corners of a rectangle in which the listeners are centered. Similarly, four speakers forming a tetrahedron can minimally realize a three-dimensional listening space, but more are required for a listening area of any reasonable size. A configuration with eight speakers marking the corners of a rectangular prism is practical.

Music performed on any of these configurations is subject to certain limitations if the precedence effect is to be avoided. A system can be made valid for all types of sound and with a large focal area by surrounding the listeners with a substantial number of speakers. In this way, the direction of the source can be simulated more accurately in a larger area because actual sources are available in a large number of directions. The actual number of speakers used depends upon the angular resolution desired. Sixteen speakers placed in a circle gives a resolution of 22.5 degrees, which allows a reasonable amount of location capability. More can be added with the corresponding increase in resolution.

Such large numbers of high-quality speakers can be extremely expensive. It is possible to alleviate this problem by splitting the sound on the basis of frequency, because loudspeakers that are obligated to produce only mid- and high-frequency sound can be much smaller and hence less expensive than those that must produce low-frequency sound, as well. The less-directional low-frequency sound can be supplied by a single high-quality loudspeaker, while the mid- and high-frequency sounds are distributed to a number of smaller loudspeakers located on the periphery of the listening space. Because a listener assigns the location of a sound in most cases on the basis of mid- and high-frequency information, this arrangement makes more feasible the simulation of sound source location through IID cues. A cross-over frequency of 200 Hz has proven effective for systems of this kind.[20] This type of system is used in the Sal-Mar Construction, a musical instrument for live performance described in section 9.5.

7.2E   Motion of Sound Sources

The preceding discussion has been concerned with the creation of an illusory location for a stationary source. When the source location is moved about rapidly, another acoustical phenomemon comes into play. The *Doppler effect* describes the change in pitch that results when the source and the listener are moving relative to each other. When a sound source and a listener are moving closer together, the wavefronts of the sound will reach the listener more frequently, causing the perceived pitch to be raised from its stationary value. Conversely, if the source and the listener are moving apart, the pitch will appear lower.

The simulation of a "natural" situation that includes a Doppler shift of frequency can be problematic, because it alters pitch succession, which is often employed as one of the principal means of affecting musical continuity. The most successful applications of Doppler shift in music are those in which the shift of frequency is an integral part of the musical continuity and not simply a "special effect" that can be expected to wear off rather quickly. John Chowning's *Turenas* is a good example of the incorporation of Doppler shift into a musical structure. (See section 7.3B.)

If the listener is stationary, the Doppler shift may be stated mathematically as:

$$f' = f[c/(c - v)]$$

where f is the stationary frequency, f' is the perceived frequency, c is the speed of sound (ca. 345 m/sec), and v is the speed of the source relative to the listener. If the source and the listener are moving closer together, v is positive. Notice that the Doppler effect shifts all the frequencies in the sound by the same interval, preserving the harmonic relationships in the sound. For example, a sound moving at 19.4 m/sec toward the listener is raised by one half step (5.946%). The Doppler shift is not the same as frequency shifting, which adds a constant to all frequency components and consequently destroys the original harmonic structure. (See section 3.8.)

The Doppler shift derives from the relative speed of the listener and the source; that is, the change in distance between them per unit time. Thus, a sound moving in a circle centered on the listener will not change in frequency. A source that is moving directly toward or directly away from the listener will exhibit the maximum shift for its speed. When the source moves obliquely, it is more difficult to calculate the speed of the source relative to the listener. Calculus can be used to transform a given source trajectory into an expression for relative velocity. More often, the computer is enlisted to do the calculation by breaking down the desired trajectory into short segments. The distance between the source and the listener is calculated at the beginning and end of each segment. The change in distance (Δd) over the length of the segment is divided by the time (Δt) that is takes to traverse that segment. The quotient ($\Delta d/\Delta t$) is the average velocity and is used in the equation above to calculate the Doppler shift that occurs during the traversal of that segment. The calculation of distance requires that the computer be given the actual physical dimensions of the listening space: the distance from the listener to the loudspeakers.

The Doppler effect can be used as a compositional element, dramatizing sounds that move past the listener. For example, consider the motion of a source in a straight line as shown in figure 7.19. When the source passes by the listener, the direction of the velocity changes from advancing to receding. This causes a marked

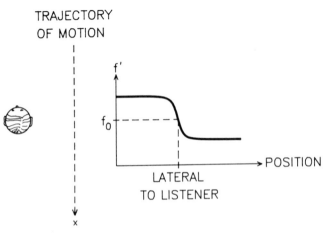

FIGURE 7.19   Doppler shift exhibited by a sound moving past a listener.

pitch change because the pitch goes from being maximally raised to maximally lowered in a short amount of time. The closer the source comes to the listener, the more quickly the change takes place.

7.2F   Designs for Sound Localization

Figure 7.20 shows a design for locating the apparent source of a sound at any point on the line between two loudspeakers. This instrument simulates IID cues only, and so it works best on sounds with significant high-frequency energy. The incoming signal is applied equally to each branch of the design. It is attenuated by the appropriate amount in each channel to "locate" the sound between them. The location is specified by the parameter x, which has a value between 0 and 1. When x is zero, all the sound emanates from the right loudspeaker.

In placing the apparent sound source between the loudspeakers, the power in the signal is allocated according to value of x. That is, the power in the left speaker is given by x and the power in the right speaker is given by $1-x$. The design apportions the power by operating on the amplitude of each signal, and so the square root of each control function is taken before multiplying it by the amplitude

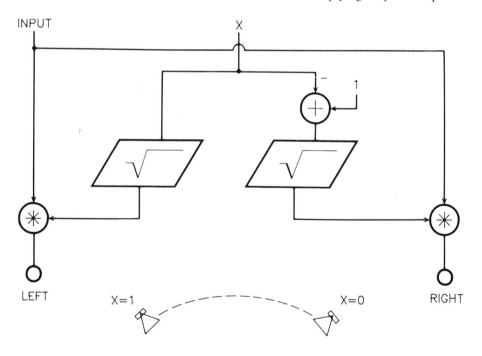

FIGURE 7.20   A stereo method of simulating localization cues.

of a channel. To improve computational efficiency, the square root function is stored in a lookup table. In practice, the value x would be scaled to reflect the dimensions of the table.

By applying the appropriate function of time to x, the position of the incoming signal can be made to appear to move. If the change of x is linear, the sound will appear to move at a constant rate. A non-linear change of x will cause the image of the source to accelerate and/or decelerate.

Figure 7.21 shows a quadraphonic listening space formed by four loudspeakers marking the corners of a square. Through proper allocation of sound among the four loudspeakers, the illusion of source location can be created in the plane containing the listener and the loudspeakers. For computational convenience the angular direction is measured on a scale from 0–512 (as shown in the figure). The conventional measure, degrees, is also shown.

The space is divided into four quadrants. To locate the sound in a particular quadrant, the two loudspeakers marking the boundaries of the quadrant contribute. The allocation of the sound to the loudspeakers depends on the angle (θ) between the intended location (I) and the line bisecting the quadrant. Thus, in any quadrant, the range of θ is ±45 degrees.

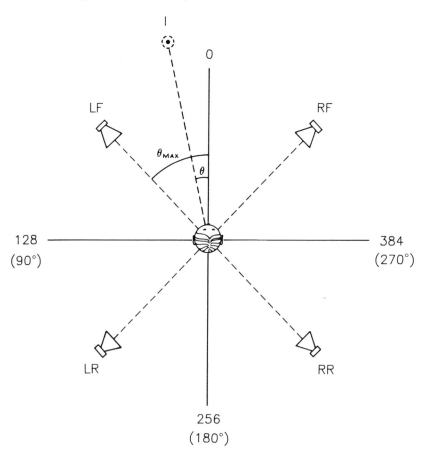

FIGURE 7.21   Geometry of a quadraphonic listening space.

If a sound is located in the quadrant in front of the listener, the amplitudes of the signals at the loudspeakers (S_{LF} and S_{RF}) will be apportioned by:

$$S_{LF} \propto \left[\frac{1}{2}\left(1 + \frac{\tan \theta}{\tan \theta_{max}} \right) \right]$$

$$S_{RF} \propto \left[\frac{1}{2}\left(1 - \frac{\tan \theta}{\tan \theta_{max}} \right) \right]$$

(The symbol, α, designates proportionality.)

In this case, θ_{MAX} is 45 degrees so that $\tan \theta_{MAX}=1$. To save computation time, these angular allocation functions are often stored in lookup tables that are 512 places in length. The 512 positions correspond to the full 360 degree angle that encircles the listener in figure 7.21.

The most important cue a listener uses to judge the distance (D) of a sound source is the ratio of the amplitudes of the reverberated to the unreverberated part of the sound. Figure 7.22 shows a signal-allocation design for placing sounds at desired locations in a quadraphonic space. The design, based on the model of John Chowning,[21] employs reverberators to simulate the effect of distance cues in sound localization. The energy of the direct sound is attenuated by $1/D$, whereas the reverberant energy is attenuated as $1/\sqrt{D}$. Therefore, the reverberant energy decreases less than the direct sound as the distance increases. Sounds that are close to the listener have a higher proportion of direct energy. For reasons of convenience, $D=1$ ordinarily represents the distance between loudspeakers and the listener.

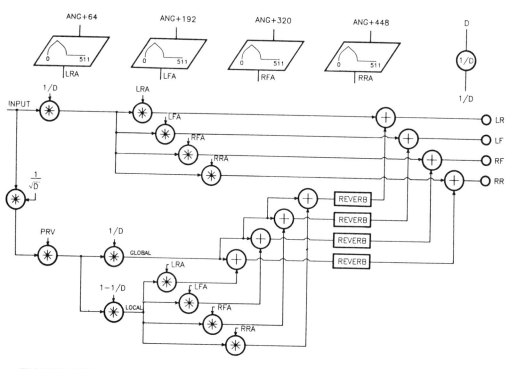

FIGURE 7.22 Quadraphonic "mover" instrument. The loudspeakers are arranged as in figure 7.21. (*Published with the permission of John Chowning.*)

The reverberated energy is divided between local and global reverberation. Because the proportion of local reverberation becomes more significant than global reverberation at large distances, the allocation of the two depends on distance as:

$$\text{GLOBAL} \propto \frac{1}{D}$$

$$\text{LOCAL} \propto 1 - \frac{1}{D}$$

Four different reverberators with slightly different parameters should be used. This simulates a situation in which the reverberant characteristics differ in the four directions out from the listening space.

The instrument shown in figure 7.22 has three controlling parameters: the distance (D), the angular direction (ANG) which is expressed as a value between 0 and 512, and the percentage of reverberation (PRV). The latter parameter sets the amount of reverberation present when the sound is located at the same distance as the loudspeaker. It is chosen on the basis of the desired characteristics of the space to be simulated.

By changing the angular direction and distance as functions of time, the apparent sound location may be changed. Arbitrary paths of sound travel can be programmed by designing a combination of the distance and angular functions. For example, the function F1 shown in figure 7.23 applied to both the distance and angular direction will cause a spiral-shaped path of sound travel. AMAX represents the final angle for the sound, and DMAX the maximum distance.

John Chowning's implementation of a sound localization and movement program utilized computer graphics, so that he could display the sound travel path

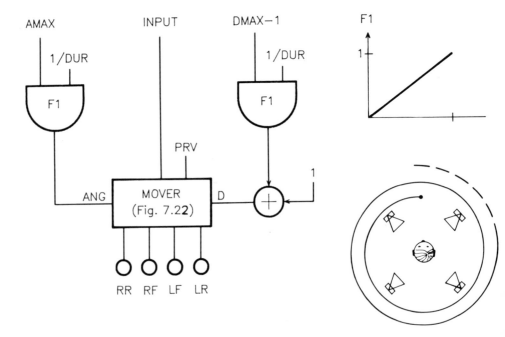

FIGURE 7.23   Realizing spiral motion.

on the screen of a graphics terminal. Chowning included Doppler shift as an indication of sound-travel velocity.

7.3 Other Sound-Processing Techniques

7.3A *Musique Concrète* with the Computer

Musique concrète is the term used by its inventor, the French composer Pierre Schaeffer, to distinguish the new genre from traditional, "abstract" music. Musique concrète is made from recordings of sounds from the "real world." The recordings are subjected to various manipulations in order to adapt them for inclusion into musical textures. The early works of musique concrète were made from sound sources far removed from traditional music. For example, Schaeffer composed his first work using recordings of the sounds associated with trains, and one of the compositions by Schaeffer's colleague, Pierre Henry, is *Variations on a Door and a Sigh*.[22]

The early experiments in musique concrète were made on phonograph records, but the new genre turned to the medium of the tape recorder in the early 1950s. A number of standard tape-manipulation techniques developed and became part of the repertoire of techniques for composing musique concrète—or, as it was called in the United States, tape music.

The principal techniques for making musique concrète with analog tape are: cutting and splicing, tape loops, change of tape speed, change of direction of tape, tape delay, and combinations of the above. The combinations can be either successions of sounds—"montages"—or simultaneous combinations—"mixages."

Cutting and splicing serves as a means for reordering the sounds on tape. It can also serve to extract fragments from a larger context. The Japanese composer Joji Yuasa once made a piece of tape music out of the non-verbal "uhs" and "ahs" uttered in interviews by public figures in response to difficult questions. The traditional tools for cutting and splicing are the razor blade and the splicing block.

A tape loop is made by splicing together the two ends of a tape recording so that the recorded passage will repeat continuously during playback. A tape loop can be made out of a single sound, such as a gong tone; or cutting and splicing can order a diverse group of sounds into a loop. A common use for a tape loop is as a sonic background in front of which events are heard. Steve Reich and Charles Amirkhanian have made entire compositions out of tape loops repeating limited groups of sounds—often fragments of speech.

Change of tape speed is a technique for transposing recorded sound to other frequency levels. Standard tape recorders include provision for at least two speeds and thus enable transposition of a recording by an octave. Most tape music studios, and some tape recorders, include devices for varying the speed of the tape continuously over a wider range. Change of speed is a common way of preventing a tape loop from becoming boring and of creating a variety of pitched material out of a single sound source. American composer Vladimir Ussachevsky has used speed change of tape loops extensively, often on sounds of percussion instruments such as cymbals and piano.

Change of direction of tape provides a further means of varying the recorded sound. Playing a sound backwards reverses its characteristic envelope and spectral evolution. Reversed piano tones, for example, entail a slow crescendo in which the spectrum gets increasingly rich. Reversed recordings of piano and cymbal sounds are often used to crescendo into other sonic events.

Tape delay, also known as tape-recorder feedback, entails the playback and recording of a sound on one machine simultaneously. It adds a reverberation-like effect to the sound.

All of the techniques of tape music can be implemented on a digital computer that is equipped with A/D and D/A converters and sufficient peripheral storage to contain the recorded sounds. (Disk storage is preferable to digital tape for this purpose because the "random access" of disk greatly facilitates the manipulation of the sound.) In fact, the implementation of musique concrète on computers has revived interest in this genre and has also contributed to an advancement in accuracy and ease with which recorded material can be manipulated. Luciano Berio's *Thema* (1958) was made by extensive cutting, splicing, and mixing of fragments of a reading and vocal rendition of part of James Joyce's *Ulysses*. In 1981 Berio commented, "It's surprising now to think that I spent several months of my life cutting tape while today I could achieve many of the same results in much less time by using a computer."[23]

Programs for sound editing enable the manipulation of sound on a computer. The musician working with the computer does not actually handle the medium on which the sound is recorded, and so visual cues and numerical tabulation of sample numbers are used to find the appropriate splice points in the sound. Sound editing with a computer is greatly simplified when the musician can view a graphical representation of the sound versus time on a CRT. Most editing programs using graphics display the sound on several time scales simultaneously. On the most magnified scale the actual waveform of the sound appears. In a more concentrated representation, the pattern of amplitudes of a longer segment is shown in a plot of the same length. This results in a display that emphasizes the envelope of the sound. Thus, the musician can view the sound at various levels—from microscopic to macroscopic. Figure 7.24 shows the display on the CRT for such a system.

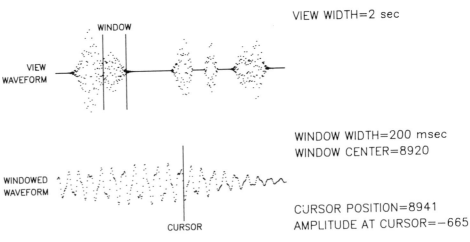

FIGURE 7.24 Display from a sound editing system where the waveform is shown on two separate time axes. The lower waveform is from the "window" in the upper one. (*Based on Lloyd H. Nakatani's Editor. Published with permission of Bell Telephone Laboratories.*)

Digital sound editing systems use computers that are equipped with on-line D/A converters. The musician then can hear designated segments of a sound and check the splice points for accuracy by ear.

Cutting and splicing is done on the computer by specifying the segments to be taken out of the succession of samples and joined together. Most editing programs have provision for repeating segments and putting silence, when desired, between segments. Anyone who has actually spliced tape knows that not all sounds can be joined together smoothly. This is due, usually, to a discontinuity between the waveforms of the two sounds at the splice point. The result of joining them is often an audible click. The sound editing system created by Loren Rush and others at Stanford University's CCRMA implements a means for smoothly joining any two sounds. The technique applies a cosinusoidal attenuation function to the beginnings and ends of the sounds for a specified duration around the point at which they are abutted. Figure 7.25 shows the way in which the sounds are overlapped. DUR is the duration of the splice and F1 and F2 are quarter cycles of a cosine wave and a sine wave, respectively. As a result, the two sounds are both attenuated by 3 dB at the mid-point of the splice.

The joining function illustrates another feature of the manipulation of taped sounds by means of the computer: the imposition of a new envelope on the record-ed sound. This technique has been described in conjunction with the computer implementation of tape loops by composer Stanley Haynes.[24] In the Haynes

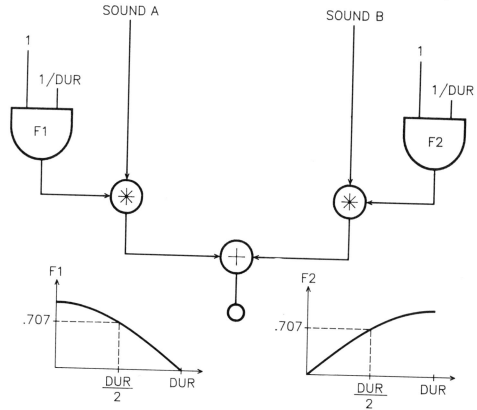

FIGURE 7.25   A method of cleanly splicing two sounds.

example shown in figure 7.26, a 2.5 second segment of a decaying gong tone is "cut out" from the middle of the tone. It is then rectified (all samples are made positive in value) and the average value is calculated yielding a function proportional to the decaying envelope of the sound. From this, an inverse, compensatory function is generated which has the shape opposite in slope to the decay of the gong tone. When the gong tone is multiplied by this function, the result is a more-or-less steady-state tone with no decay. However, at this point, if the beginning is appended to the end of the sound to make a continuous loop, the point of the splice will be obvious to the ear. The method which Haynes suggests for making a seamless sound from the extracted segment is to create two copies of the sound, start playing the second at the mid-point of the first, and continue to overlap the two. The whole sound can be made to appear seamless by applying a bell-shaped envelope to each repetition of each copy of the sound. The result should sound like a smooth tone with a gonglike timbre.

Change of direction of a recorded sound can be made very simply by reading in reverse order the file in which the samples are stored. Tape delay, which is a common technique in the tape studio for producing reverberation-like effects can be made in the computer using delay lines such as those described in section 7.1D.

The effect of a change in tape speed can be achieved on the computer by changing the rate at which a digitally recorded file is converted to analog form. For example, all the frequencies of a sound that was converted to digital form at a sampling rate of 40 kHz will be lowered one octave when converted back to analog form at a rate of 20 kHz. Of course, this technique works well only on systems equipped with a low-pass filter with a variable cutoff frequency that tracks the

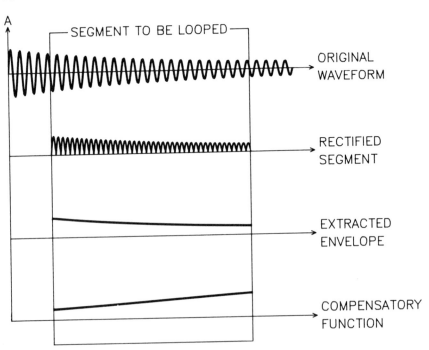

FIGURE 7.26 Method used by Stanley Haynes to obtain a continuous bell-like timbre. (*Printed with permission of the* Computer Music Journal.)

sampling rate because the filter is needed to smooth the output and suppress any components above the Nyquist frequency.

More general, purely digital methods for changing the speed of digitally recorded sounds are available on the computer. *Decimation* raises the frequency of a sound by eliminating samples from the sound before digital-to-analog conversion. *Interpolation* lowers the frequency by inserting new samples between the original ones.

One can raise the frequency of a sound one octave by eliminating every other of its samples. However, aliasing can result especially in situations where the original sound has significant energy in the upper portion of its spectrum. For example, at a sampling rate of 25 kHz, if the original sound has a fundamental frequency of 1 kHz, the sound can contain up to twelve harmonics without aliasing. If before eliminating every other sample, the 1-kHz tone is filtered to contain a maximum of six harmonics, every other sample can be eliminated to create a 2-kHz tone with no aliasing. This is most easily accomplished using a special digital filter called a decimating low-pass filter which not only eliminates the requisite number of samples, but also properly filters the sound.[25]

One might think, intuitively, that the interpolation of sample values between pairs of original samples to lower a sound an octave would create no problems with aliasing. Unfortunately, this is not the case. Simple linear interpolation creates aliased components that can be especially prominent on bright sounds. Some interpolation schemes take into account several samples on either side of the new sample when calculating its value. These methods of higher-order interpolation have been shown to be improvements, but are still audibly imperfect. The best approach uses an interpolating low-pass filter[26] that not only interpolates but also alters the frequency content to minimize aliasing.

For speed changes other than integers, interpolating and decimating low-pass filters can be combined into a single filter algorithm. Figure 7.27 shows a block diagram of such a system. The first block, the interpolator, fills in $m-1$ samples between every pair of samples in the original. The third block, the decimator, eliminates $n-1$ samples between every pair of the interpolated samples. The low-pass filter, inserted between the interpolator and the decimator has a cutoff frequency that depends on the choice of m and n. The filter smooths the interpolated waveform to eliminate any aliasing that would result from the interpolation or decimation process. The frequency of the signal coming out of the system, f_{out}, is given by the relationship:

$$f_{out} = f_{in}(n/m)$$

where f_{in} is the input frequency. Thus, the choice of the integers, m and n, determines the change in frequency. For example, to lower the frequency of a sound by a perfect fourth (a change in frequency by the factor ¾), one would set

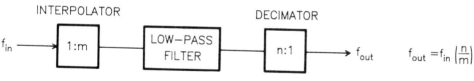

$$f_{out} = f_{in}\left(\frac{n}{m}\right)$$

FIGURE 7.27 Block diagram of an interpolation/decimation algorithm that enables a sound to be transposed.

$m=4$ and $n=3$. Because the interpolation process creates many additional samples, additional memory in the filter algorithms is required to accomodate them. The actual amount depends on the accuracy desired.[27]

In addition to all the standard techniques of tape manipulation that can be implemented on the computer, recorded sounds can be subjected to the full range of techniques used in the computer for modifying synthesized sounds. These techniques include ring modulation, amplitude modulation, enveloping, filtering, and reverberation techniques. The sounds, after transformation, can be further processed for localization and/or further mixed with other synthetic and recorded sounds.

One of the most powerful tools of all for use with recorded sound is synthesis that is based on analysis. By this method, tones synthesized in the computer can be modeled on sound that has been recorded and stored in the computer. Analysis-based synthesis enables a full range of related effects, from the most natural-sounding to the least. Almost all of the work in the synthesis of speech (see chapter 6) has been based on computer analysis, as has most of the work in the synthesis of the singing voice. Some of the compositional examples in this chapter employ synthesis by analysis on recorded sounds other than vocal sounds.

7.3B   Examples of Compositional Uses

John Chowning's composition *Turenas* (1972) demonstrates two important and original techniques: computer simulation of instrument-like tones with FM synthesis and sound travel in a quadraphonic space. The compositional concern in *Turenas* with "naturalness" is expressed in the title which is an anagram of "Natures." *Turenas*, a ten-minute work in three parts, invites the listener to experience a new and very special world of sound.

The most dramatic element of the first and third parts of the work is the travel of the sounds. For the traveling sounds, Chowning designed a computer orchestra of predominately percussive sounds. In doing so, he took advantage of our ability to perceive most easily the location of short, impulsive sounds. Even the more sustained sounds, for example, the electronic "insects" or "bats," have an impulsive aspect such as buzzing or clicking.

For the sound movement in *Turenas*, Chowning wrote a "front-end" for the Stanford MUSIC 10 language which enabled him to display graphically the path of travel for a sound around the listening space. He wrote software that caused calculated patterns to be displayed on a CRT screen. From the sound travel pattern and information regarding the distance between the loudspeakers and speed of sound travel, Chowning's programs generated the control statements necessary to create the desired paths of travel. Figure 7.28 shows an example of a sound travel path heard near the beginning of Turenas together with the controls for the MUSIC 10 orchestra.

The middle part of *Turenas*, while not as active from the standpoint of sound travel, contains some very realistic brass, string, and wind instrument tones made with FM synthesis. This part of the work employs reverberation to create a sense of spaciousness.

Charles Dodge's *Earth's Magnetic Field*[28] makes extensive use of reverberation and location techniques. Both were employed as ways of enhancing a rather simple

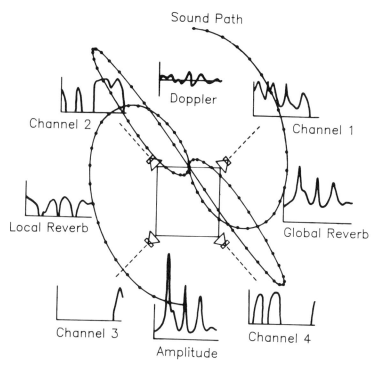

FIGURE 7.28 Sound travel path heard near the beginning of Chowning's *Turenas*. (*Reprinted with the permission of John Chowning.*)

timbre created by subtractive synthesis. There are two principal features of the computer application in *Earth's Magnetic Field*: temporal and timbral. The composition is a musical setting of the succession of values that are produced by an index of the effect of the sun's radiation on the magnetic field that surrounds the earth. Each value of the index represents an average of the readings for a three-hour period, at twelve monitoring stations throughout the world. Because there are eight 3-hour periods in a 24-hour day, the year's activity is represented by 2,920 readings. The form of the original index resembles music notation and is called a "Bartels' musical diagram" after its inventor, Julius Bartels. In a Bartels' musical diagram a reading can assume one of 28 possible values. For the composition, the 28 values of the index were mapped into four octaves of diatonic 'C.' Meantone temperament was used in playing the notes of the piece.

In the year chosen for the composition, 1961, the data exhibits 21 "sudden commencements": points where sudden increases in the values of the index occur. These break points were chosen as the sectional divisions of the work. The 21 sections delimited by sudden commencements were grouped into five parts:

PART	S. C. SECTION
I	1–3
II	4–6
III	7–10
IV	11–15
V	16–21

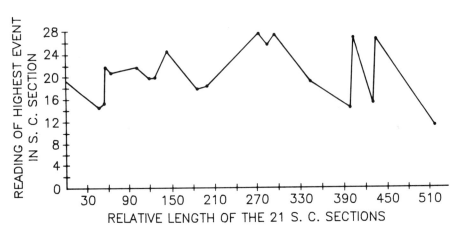

FIGURE 7.29 "Sudden commencement" graph used to control aspects of the composition in Dodge's *Earth's Magnetic Field*.

The graph in figure 7.29 was employed to control several aspects of the composition. It shows the value of the highest reading within a S. C. section versus the length of the section. For example, the changing tempo of the first part of the piece is based on an application of the graphical pattern to speed. Between 30 and 1600 articulations per minute were made with the tempo feature of MUSIC 4BF. The continuous change of tempo is heard in parts I, III, and IV of the work.

A second variety of temporal control is heard in parts II and V. Here a fixed tempo of one beat per second is used. A compositional subroutine was used to group the readings into notes in the following way: a succession of two identical readings was played as a single note lasting for one second. The whole group of intervening readings before the next pair of identical readings was also played in one second. The actual number of different, equally timed tones during the second beat depends on the number of readings that occur between double readings. In the data upon which this piece was constructed, the number of these varies from 2 to 25.

The instrument designs for *Earth's Magnetic Field* use different sorts of filters to create "radiant effects" which reflect in some philosophical sense the nature of the solar radiation itself. The instrument designs also contribute to the gradual transformation that takes place in the sound of the work. The composition begins with tones that focus on the fundamental frequency with simple timbre. These are gradually replaced with diffuse textures with secondary pitches around the fundamental. It is primarily as a result of the instrument designs that the pitches of the individual readings are subsumed into reverberating textures in which certain pitches are favored over others and in which the "aura" sounded around the pitches are equally prominent with, or even more prominent than the notes themselves.

The first part of the work is sounded with the configuration shown in figure 7.30. The sound is plain and straightforward. Its most prominent feature is the continual acceleration and deceleration that outlines the pattern of the sudden-commencement graph.

The second part of the composition employs the fixed tempo of one beat per second. The sound of part II results from feeding the output of the instrument from part I (the "basic instrument") into three reverberation unit generators, with

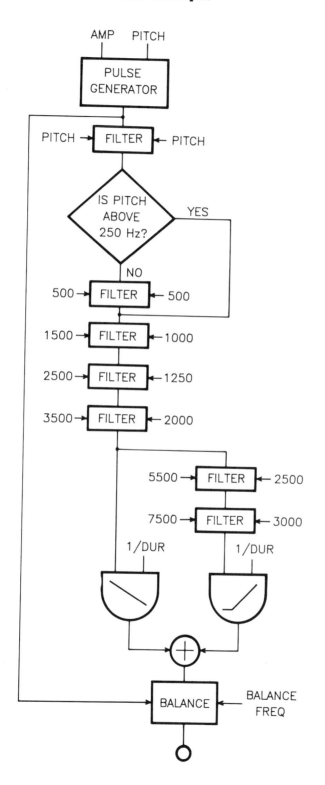

FIGURE 7.30   Basic design for sound of Dodge's *Earth's Magnetic Field.*

reverberation times of 2.5, 5, and 10 seconds. The effect of spaciousness is achieved by positioning the output of each reverberator in a different initial location between the two loudspeakers and moving it slowly between them. The sound in part II is quite bright, due to the reverberation that prolongs the high harmonics created by the non-standard use of a balance unit generator as described in section 5.9.

The third part of the piece again includes continuous fluctuations in tempo. The basic instrument is fed into a single comb filter with a reverberation time of 2.5 seconds and loop time of 30 msec. This causes the loudness of certain tones to be greatly changed. Pitches with periods close to multiples of the loop time of the comb are emphasized, even exaggerated, while tones with frequencies that fall between the peaks of the filter are relatively attenuated. As described above, the comb filter also adds frequencies of its own, due to ringing.

Part IV, using continuous time, feeds the output of the basic instrument into a single all-pass network with the same loop time as the comb filter of the previous section. In this section, not only does the tempo fluctuate in a variation on the pattern of figure 7.29, but so do the amplitude of the tones and their apparent location between the two loudspeakers.

The final part of *Earth's Magnetic Field* uses 6 comb filters and 2 all-pass networks to create "super-reverberated" effects. Once again, the tempo is fixed at one beat per second. There are a great many secondary pitches in this section, caused by the combined effect of several combs and all-passes with different loop times prolonging the harmonics created by the "balance effect."

Roger Reynolds has produced a series of works that "explore the interaction of voice with illusory auditory spaces."[29] Reynolds has taken full advantage of computer techniques for reverberation and localization of sound. He has been especially involved in developing means for controlling the apparent movement of voices in quadraphonic space. Reynold's computer music compositions exhibit a structure in which those aspects of the musical texture created with techniques of reverberation and localization form a central part of the works. His computer compositions all combine live performers and/or recordings of performers with four-channel tape.

In *Voicespace IV: The Palace* (1980), Reynolds contrasts a live singer (who alternates between bass and countertenor registers) with a recording containing computer-processed sound of the singer's voice. The recording for the processed voice consists of a reading of the poem, "The Palace" by Jorge Luis Borges and includes certain 'extended vocal techniques.' The reader, Philip Larsen, a singer highly experienced in experimental vocal music, has an extraordinary voice with a four-octave range. For *The Palace*, Larsen recorded Tibetan Chant drone tones with reinforced harmonics, in addition to various speaking voices. The computer processing of the recorded voice consisted primarily of filtering, exaggerated reverberation, spatial location, and the creation of multiple copies of the processed voice in choruses. Reynolds did not choose geometrically symmetrical paths of sound travel, but rather chose to create paths which, while still recognizable, were irregular. An extremely important feature of this piece is the creation of illusory auditory space. He has designed not just one, but many "host spaces" in which the recorded voice moves on designated paths. The illusory space of The Palace is constantly changing throughout the piece.

The programming system that Reynolds used for The Palace drew from the work of Loren Rush, John Grey, James A. Moorer, Gareth Loy, and others at

CCRMA of Stanford University. One way this system was used was in the production of the 'obsessive' or extremely dense reverberated quality of the processed speaking voice. The reverberation time was 50 seconds—that of an unimaginably large auditory space. The reverberation controls were, effectively, the size of the modeled space, the nature of the reflective surfaces, the proportion of direct to reverberated signal, and the relative weighting of sound in frequency bands of the spectrum.

The sound movement in *The Palace* was made with the program, "QUAD," by Loren Rush. In this program, the user describes the sound path by answering a series of questions. A sound path is drawn with the program and a duration assigned to it. The length of the function describing the sound path and the number of points in the path must be specified in order to precisely define the path. In addition, the distance (in meters) between the loudspeakers must be indicated.

The computer processing of the voice continually "relocated" it by change of reverberation time (and distribution of local and global reverberant energy among the four loudspeakers). Also employed were changes in the nature of the modeled reflective surfaces, and thus, changes of distribution of energy in the frequency bands. At the beginning of the piece, the recorded voice is heard as though in a gigantic space with an intense reverberant quality. It is placed off center to the left front. At the end of the piece, the voice has been relocated, and the reverberation is drier and much less intense. The looping sound near the end of the piece ("the walls, the ramparts," etc.) moves in the complex pattern shown in figure 7.31. Doppler shift, which can be used to simulate the sound of rapidly moving physical bodies in space, was not needed in *The Palace*. For the chorus on the words, "The date which the chisel engraves in the tablet," six replications of each word were clustered in time around the original on a random basis with a Gaussian distribution. (See section 8.1A(5)) Each replication was played back at a slightly different sampling rate and retuned to the original in order to produce a convincing choral effect.

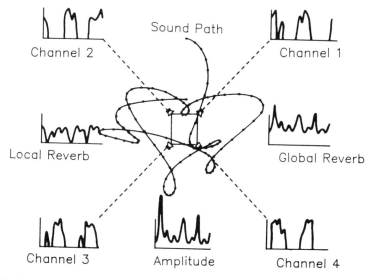

FIGURE 7.31   Sound path and travel functions for Reynolds' *The Palace*. (*Reprinted with the permission of Roger Reynolds.*)

In *Six Fantasies on a Poem by Thomas Campion*, Paul Lansky[30] has used reverberation techniques to create complex, elaborated textures out of simple inputs. (See section 6.9 for aspects of the work that involve voice synthesis.) For *Fantasies* 2, 4, and 6, small amounts of natural-sounding reverberation are applied to enhance the timbre of the voice. The third and fifth *Fantasies* are good examples of the use of comb filters. In the third *Fantasy*, "Her reflection," voiced and unvoiced synthetic speech and recorded voice were fed into large banks of comb filters. Often, as many as eighteen comb filters were used at once. Each was a double comb filter in which the output was fed back into the input. This technique has the effect of sharpening the peaks of the emphasized frequencies and increasing the attenuation of those between. The loop times of the combs were related to each other by one of two methods: equal differences and equal ratios in time.

The result of the process is only occasionally intelligible, and then as highly reverberated speech. More often, only an impression of the voice input is present in the pitched and noisy textures created by the combs.

For the fifth *Fantasy*, banks of comb filters were applied to a whispered reading of the poem, rendering it largely indistinct. Attention is drawn to the percussion sounds made from small portions of the speech. To do this, Lansky designed special filters (like comb filters, but with unity gain factor) to prevent decay of an input signal. He applied a signal to one of the filters, changed the rate at which the signal was sampled, and thus produced foldover, which created the desired musical effect. This is equivalent to creating a wavetable out of digitized sound and then sampling it as an oscillator would using various sampling increments. (See section 3.3.)

In *Nekyia*, composer Gareth Loy has made a composition that is like a non-verbal drama in which the movement of synthetic and concrete material intermingle. The effect is often that of recorded sounds; at other times, it is like that of synthetic variants of recorded sounds. The quadraphonic *Nekyia* extensively employs reverberation and localization of sound as well as techniques of musique concrète. Reverberation and localization are central to the composition, as can be seen in one of Loy's statements about the piece: "One intent with which the piece was shaped included a desire to form images of dense space, where the sound materials could be thought of as sonic actors or dancers, moving in two dimensions."[31] Loy continues, "I wanted the sound-space to surround the listener, to bring the listener into the same plane of motion as the sound-actors." The movement of sound in Nekyia goes beyond its more usual uses. In *Nekyia*, the patterns of circular and spiral movement of sound are used to demarcate the formal structure of the composition.

Concrète sounds play a major role in Nekyia. The vocabulary of sounds captured from the "real world" ranges from the sound of shattering glass, through choruses of crickets, to rolling cymbal sounds. A good example of this can be heard near the end of the work where a "chorus" of rolling cymbal sounds is transposed up by a semitone six successive times. Loy writes, "The method utilized to compose the piece achieves the integration of synthetic and concrete techniques into one control structure." (See section 8.2C for aspects of *Nekyia* involving computer manipulation of musical motives.)

Notes

1. Dempster, Stuart. "Standing Waves—1976." 1750 Arch Records (S-1775), 1979.

2. Sabine, W. C. "Reverberation." In R. B. Lindsay (ed.), *Acoustics: Historical and Philosophical Development*. Stroudsburg, Pa.: Dowden, Hutchinson, and Ross, 1972.

3. Harris, C. M. "Absorbtion of Sound in Air in the Audio Frequency Range." *Journal of the Acoustical Society of America*, 35(11), 1963, 14.

4. Blesser, B., and Kates, J. "Digital Processing in Audio Signals." In A. Oppenheim (ed.), *Applications of Digital Signal Processing*. Englewood Cliffs, N. J.: Prentice-Hall, 1978.

5. Schroeder, M. R. *Music Perception in Concert Halls*. Stockholm: Royal Swedish Academy of Music, 1979 (Publication No. 26)

6. Schroeder, M. R., and B. F. Logan. "Colorless Artificial Reverberation." *Journal of the Audio Engineering Society*, 9(3), 1961, 192. Schroeder, M. R. "Natural Sounding Artificial Reverberation." *Journal of the Audio Engineering Society*, 10(3), 1962, 219–223.

7. Moorer, J. A. "About this Reverberation Business." *Computer Music Journal*, 3(2), 1979, 13–28.

8. Schroeder, M. R. "Digital Simulation of Sound Transmission in Reverberant Spaces" (Part 1). *Journal of the Acoustical Society of America*, 47(2), 1970, 424–431.

9. Bartlett, Bruce. "A Scientific Explanation of Phasing (Flanging)." *Journal of the Audio Engineering Society*, 18(6), 1970, 674–675.

10. Karplus, K., and A. Strong. "Digital Synthesis of Plucked-String and Drum Timbres." *Computer Music Journal*, 7(2), 1983, 43–55.

11. Jaffe, D. A., and J. O. Smith. "Extensions of the Karplus–Strong, Plucked-String Algorithm." *Computer Music Journal*, 7(2), 1983, 56–69.

12. Kuhn, George F. "Model for the Interaural Time Differences in the Azimuthal Plane." *Journal of the Acoustical Society of America*, 62(1), 1977, 157–166.

13. Hebrank, J., and D. Wright. "Spectral Cues Used in the Localization of Sound Sources on the Median Plane." *Journal of the Acoustical Society of America*, 56, 1974, 1829–1834.

14. Gilliom, J. D., and R. D. Sorkin. "Discrimination of Interaural Time and Intensity." *Journal of the Acoustical Society of America*, 52, 1972, 1635–1644.

15. Von Bekesy, G. *Experiments in Hearing*. New York: McGraw-Hill, 1960.

16. Schroeder, M. R. "Computer Models for Concert Hall Acoustics." *American Journal of Physics*, 41(4), 1973, 461–471.

17. Gardner, M. B. "Image Fusion, Broadening, and Displacement in Sound Location." *Journal of the Acoustical Society of America*, 46, 1969, 339–349.

18. Chowning, John. "The Simulation of Moving Sound Sources." *Computer Music Journal*, 1(3), 1977, 48–52. (Reprinted from the *Journal of the Audio Engineering Society*, 19, 1971, 2–6.

19. Schroeder, M. R., *Music Perception in Concert Halls*.

20. Fedorkow, G., Buxton, W., and Smith, K. C. "A Computer-Controlled Sound Distribution System for the Performance of Electroacoustic Music." *Computer Music Journal*, 2(3), 1978, 33–41.

21. Chowning, J., "The Simulation of Moving Sound Sources."

22. Henry, Pierre. "Variations on a Door and a Sigh." Philips (DSY 836-898).

23. Schrader, Barry. *Introduction to Electro-Acoustic Music*. Englewood Cliffs, N.J.: Prentice-Hall, 1982, 181.

24. Haynes, Stanley. "The Musician–Machine Interface in Computer Music." Doctoral dissertation, Southampton University, 1979, 91.

25. Shively, R. R. "On Multistage Finite Impulse Response (FIR) Filters with Decimation." *Institute of Electrical and Electronics Engineers Transactions on Acoustics, Speech, and Signal Processing*, ASSP-23(4), 1975, 353–357.

26. Schafer, R. W., and L. R. Rabiner. "A Digital Signal Processing Approach to Interpolation." *Proceedings of the Institute of Electrical and Electronic Engineers*, 61(6), 1973, 692–702.

27. Moorer, J. A. "Signal Processing Aspects of Computer Music." *Computer Music Journal*, 1(1), 1977, 4–37.

28. Dodge, Charles. "Earth's Magnetic Field." Nonesuch Records (H-71250), 1970.

29. Reynolds, Roger. "The Palace." New York: C. F. Peters, 1980. (Recorded on Vital Records, "Lovely Music," (VR 1801–2), 1982.

30. Lansky, Paul. "Six Fantasies On a Poem by Thomas Campion." New York: CRI Records (CRI SD456), 1982.

31. Loy, Gareth. "Nekyia." Doctoral dissertation, Stanford University, 1979.

8

COMPOSITION WITH COMPUTERS

Composers have been using the computer as an aid to writing music since the mid-1950s. In fact, composition with the computer pre-dates the use of the computer as a medium to synthesize sound. The use of the computer has resulted in a great and healthy diversity of musical styles and ideas.

Although there are a number of different approaches to the matter of composing with a computer, most of the activities fall into two broad categories: aleatoric or "stochastic" music, in which events are generated according to the statistical characterization of a random process, and music where the computer is employed to calculate permutations of a set of predetermined compositional elements. In this chapter, we will examine the techniques of using the computer for both random and deterministic operations. Illustrations of the use of these techniques in actual compositions will be given to help the reader develop a sense of the compositional possibilities of computer-aided composition.

Other approaches to computer-aided composition, not covered here, do exist. For example, some believe that computers provide an ideal medium for testing ideas of music theory[1] in that the computer can be used to construct an instance of music which demonstrates a given theory. The extent to which the computer-generated music coheres can be indicative of the completeness of the theory. For example, notions of hierarchical musical structure such as those of Heinrich Schenker could be tested by inventing a computer-programming system to realize a piece of music. The work in the area of generative grammars in linguistics has been influential on this and other approaches to computer-aided composition.[2]

8.1 Aleatoric Composition with Computers

8.1A Random Processes

There are two general classes of random processes which have been used to generate material for music composition: random processes with independent observations, and processes in which previous results influence the current outcome in some way. When independent observations are taken of a random process, a given result does not depend on any previous results. The values of the results are distributed in a set or range with a pattern characteristic of a particular process. For example, tossing a coin represents a process where the set of possible results has two members (heads and tails), and the distribution pattern gives an equal chance to the two possible outcomes.

One way of expressing the influence of past outcomes of a random process on the current one is through the explicit use of conditional probabilities. In this case, the likelihood of the occurrence of a particular event is based on the results of one or more previous events. The probabilities are often chosen to model something from the "real world," such as a musical style or a natural language. Experiments using conditional probabilities have been made with the goal of modeling English on the basis of the probabilities of occurrence of certain successions of letters.[3] In such a system, for example, if the first selection were the letter "b," there could be a wide variety of choices for the second letter (a, e, i, o, u, y, and so on). Some of the choices would be more likely than others; for instance, there is a greater chance of an "e" following a "b" than a "y." However, if the first choice were "q," then the situation would be very different. In this case, the probability of choosing the letter "u" would be virtually certain.

The correlation of past events with the current one can also be characterized by a spectral description of the process. This can be conceptualized as the spectrum of the signal that would be generated if the random process were used to calculate the samples of a digital signal. These processes have been used to model a wide variety of natural processes such as the profiles of mountain ranges, the "natural unevenness of human-produced vocal and instrumental tones,"[4] and so on. Several composers have determined parameters of musical scores by using a process with a particular spectrum. (See section 8.1H.)

When a random process is used compositionally, it is rare that the raw output from the process is translated into music directly. Certain examples of that approach can be found in the literature, but more often than not the output of the process is tested to examine its suitability for inclusion in the music. The tests can cover a wide range of possibilities, and the output of the same random process can be made into very different kinds of music, depending on the nature of the tests applied.

One should note that the successful composition of music based on random processes resides not so much in the processes themselves as in the conditions under which the randomly generated elements are admitted into the composition. The first half of this chapter examines the outlines of several systems that have been used in the composition of music based on random processes.

8.1B   Probability and Random Processes

The concepts of randomness and probability were introduced in section 3.9 as they related to the generation of noise. This section will expand the discussion of these concepts and present some of the random processes that have been found useful for composition.

The likelihood that a particular event will occur can be expressed as a probability—as the ratio of the number of occurrences of that event to the total number of results of the random process. As an example, let the variable X be assigned to the random process of rolling a six-sided die. X can take on six possible values, which can be written as the set $\{1, 2, 3, 4, 5, 6\}$. If the die is properly balanced, there is an equal chance that any of the numbers will be rolled. Therefore, the probability of rolling a "2," for example, is 1/6. Mathematically, this probability, P, is written as

$$P\{X = 2\} = \tfrac{1}{6}$$

X is known as a *random variable* because its value is not explicitly calculated; instead, it is assigned a value on the basis of a random process. A random variable is normally characterized by the probability of taking on specific values or by the probability that its value will fall within a specified range of values.

Four of the properties of probabilities are:

1.   The numerical value of a probability is always between zero and one. These two values, respectively, indicate the extreme cases in which the event never occurs or the event is certain.

2.   The probability that an event will not occur can be found by subtracting the probability that it will occur from one. In the above example of the die toss, the probability that "2" will not be rolled is:

$$P\{X \neq 2\} = 1 - P\{X = 2\} = \tfrac{5}{6}$$

3.   The probability that any of several events will occur is equal to the sum of the probability of the individual events. For example, the probability of rolling an even number on a die is given by:

$$P\{X = \text{even}\} = P\{X = 2\} + P\{X = 4\} + P\{X = 6\} = \tfrac{1}{2}$$

4.   The sum of the probabilities of all possible events of a process must be equal to one. This mathematically restates the obvious: an event must be found in the set of possible events.

The collection of the probabilities of all possible outcomes of a process is often expressed as a graph, such as that shown in figure 8.1: a plot of the probabilities for the various values that can be assigned to X as the result of rolling a die. In this case, X is known as a *discrete random variable* because the outcomes of the random process can take on only specific values. (That is, there is no chance of rolling, for example, a 3.52.)

Many random phenomena produce results that cannot be categorized into a

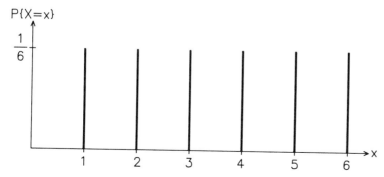

FIGURE 8.1   Probabilities for the result of the random process of rolling a six-sided die.

discrete set of values. For example, the duration of a particular note in an instrumental performance has a certain amount of randomness because each time the piece is performed, the duration of that note will not be precisely the same. It might be possible to ascribe a range to the duration such as from .95 to 1.05 seconds, but there are actually an infinite number of values within the range: .998176..., .998213..., 1.023176..., or any value within the range. The number of possible values is limited only by the precision with which the phenomenon is measured. The results of this kind of process are said to be continuous. Thus, a random variable used to describe this process is known as a *continuous random variable*.

The probabilities of a continuous random phenomenon are normally expressed by a probability density function, $f(x)$. An example of a continuous density function is shown in figure 8.2. This particular function is expressed algebraically as $f(x)=1$ for $0<x<1$, denoting that all outcomes will fall in the range between zero and one. The flatness of the density curve indicates that there is an equal chance of this continuous random variable having a value anywhere in the range. A probability cannot be read directly from the vertical scale of the density graph. Instead, the density function is used to calculate the probability that an outcome will fall within a range of values by finding the area under the density curve in that range; that is, the area bounded on the top by the curve, on the bottom by the horizontal axis, on the left by the lowest number in the range, and on the right by the highest number in the range.

For example, using the density function of figure 8.2, what is the probability that the result will fall between 0 and .2? The area under the curve in this region is a rectangle with a height of 1 and a length of .2. Therefore, the probability is $1 \times .2 = .2$, or a 20% chance. Similarly, the probability is .1 that the result will be between .1 and .2; .01 that it will fall between .19 and .2; .00001 that it will be between .19999 and .2; and so on. Thus, as the region gets smaller, so does the probability. When taken to the limit of an infinitely small range (i.e., a single, exact value), there is a zero probability of drawing that specific number. This may seem strange, but in a continuous process, there is an infinite number of possible outcomes. Because a probability compares the number of ways that an outcome can occur and the number of possible outcomes, there is a zero probability that any specific number will be drawn. Thus, the measurement of probability in the continuous case can only predict the likelihood that a result will fall within a region of possible outcomes.

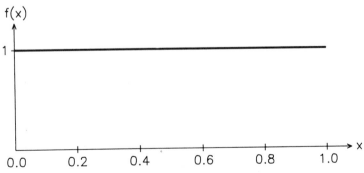

FIGURE 8.2 Probability density function of a continuous random variable that is uniformly distributed.

Both continuous and discrete random variables have been found to be useful in computer music. In the remainder of this section, we will present descriptions of some commonly-used random processes along with algorithms to realize them. Each of the algorithms makes independent observations of a random process; the results generated do not depend on any previous result. There are two principal parameters that characterize any random variable: the range of values that it can assume, and its mean. The mean denotes the mid-point of the probabilities. There is an equal chance that the outcome of a random process will fall above or below the mean.

8.1B(1) The Uniform Distribution

The most commonly-encountered type of random variable has a uniform probability distribution. The discrete random variable assigned to the process of rolling a die, for example, is uniformly distributed because there is an equal chance of obtaining any of the results. Similarly, a continuous random variable is uniformly distributed if there is an equal chance of the result occurring within any two sections of the range which are of equal length. The flat probability density function shown in figure 8.2 above is characteristic of a uniformly-distributed random process. The algorithms for generating random numbers found on most computer systems produce numbers that are very nearly uniformly distributed, but the actual range of values may differ among different implementations. For reasons of mathematical convenience, we will assume that a uniformly-distributed random variable has a range between zero and one. In this case, the mean is .5.

In the algorithms that follow, the random number generating function, RAND, will be used to generate various random variables with other than uniform distributions. RAND, as defined here, generates values in the range of zero to one. The reader is cautioned to make certain that the range of values produced by the random number generator on the system used is the same. If the range of values is different, the output must be scaled appropriately before using it in the algorithms. Otherwise, many of the algorithms will not work as described.

The argument of the RAND function does not affect the value of the function. It is there for reasons of FORTRAN protocol, and we have arbitrarily used "0" for the argument in all cases. On some systems, the argument is used to scale the range of the random numbers or to provide a seed for the random generator. In these cases, the routines below will have to be slightly modified to accomodate the differences.

8.1B(2) The Linear Distribution

Figure 8.3 shows the density function of a linearly distributed, continuous random variable. In the case shown, it is most likely to obtain a low-valued result. The density function is given by:

$$f(x) = \begin{cases} 2(1 - x); \ 0 \leq x \leq 1; \\ 0 \qquad ; \ \text{elsewhere} \end{cases}$$

The algorithm for obtaining this distribution is a simple one: generate two uniformly distributed random numbers, U1 and U2, and then choose the smaller one for the result.

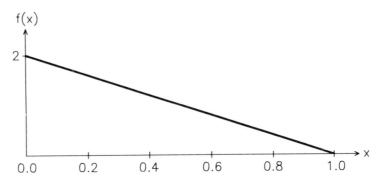

FIGURE 8.3   Probability density function for a linearly distributed random variable.

```
        FUNCTION XLNEAR(KDUMMY)
C    THE ARGUMENT KDUMMY HAS NO MEANING.
        U1=RAND(0)
        U2=RAND(0)
        IF(U2.LT.U1) U1=U2
C    U1 NOW CONTAINS THE SMALLER NUMBER.
        XLNEAR=U1
        RETURN
        END
```

The argument of the RAND function, 0, has no effect on the value of the function. The range of the random variable will be the same as the range of the RAND function, 0 to 1. With this range, the mean of the distribution is .2929. If a discrete random-number generator is used instead of a continuous one, this distribution will also be discrete.

A linear distribution that is the reverse of the one above—that is, where results closest to one are most likely—is obtained when the algorithm chooses the larger of two uniformly distributed random numbers.

8.1B(3)   *The Triangular Distribution*

Figure 8.4 illustrates the probability density of a triangularly distributed random variable, where a middle-valued result is most likely. This distribution can be obtained by generating two uniformly distributed random numbers and taking their average.

```
        FUNCTION TRIANG(KDUMMY)
C    THE ARGUMENT, KDUMMY, HAS NO MEANING.
        U1=RAND(0)
        U2=RAND(0)
        TRIANG=0.5*(U1+U2)
        RETURN
        END
```

The range of the generated random variable is the same as the range of the RAND function, 0 to 1. The mean is the average of the upper and lower limits of the range, in this case .5.

8.1B(4)   *The Exponential Distribution*

An exponentially distributed random variable has a greater probability of assuming values closer to zero. Its density function (figure 8.5) is given by

$$f(x) = \lambda e^{-\lambda x} \; ; \; x > 0$$

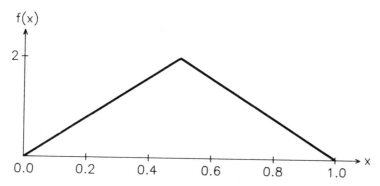

FIGURE 8.4   Probability density function of a triangularly distributed random variable.

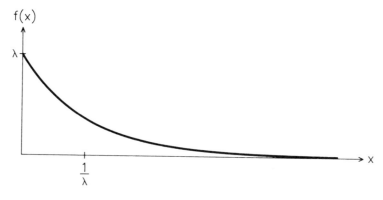

FIGURE 8.5   Probability density function of an exponentially distributed random variable.

It is characterized by a parameter λ which controls the amount of horizontal spread of the function. Choosing a large value for λ greatly increases the probability of generating a small number. The mean of the distribution is $.69315/\lambda$. The random variable takes on only values greater than zero, and there is, theoretically, no upper limit on the size of the number that can be generated. However, the chance of a very large result is quite low. For example, if $\lambda=1$, the mean will be $.69315$ and 99.9% of all results will fall below 6.9078. Looking at it another way, there is only a 1-in-1000 chance of generating a random number greater than $6.9078/\lambda$.

The sizes of many natural phenomemon are distributed exponentially. A good example is the magnitude of earthquakes, where small tremors are much more common than catastrophic shocks.

The algorithm for generating an exponential distribution involves drawing a uniformly-distributed random number with a value between zero and one and taking its natural logarithm.

```
      FUNCTION EXPONE(XLMBDA)
C   XLMBDA IS THE PARAMETER LAMBDA.   IT MUST BE > ZERO.
22    U=RAND(0)/XLMBDA
      IF(U.EQ.0.)GO TO 22
      EXPONE=-ALOG(U)
      RETURN
      END
```

This algorithm checks that the RAND function has not produced a value of exactly zero, in order to prevent an error in the ALOG function. The random number functions found on many systems cannot generate precisely zero, in which case the IF statement could be omitted.

Certain applications require an exponentially distributed random variable that assumes both positive and negative values. The bilateral exponential distribution has this characteristic and a density function (figure 8.6) given by

$$f(x) = \tfrac{1}{2}\lambda e^{-\lambda|x|}$$

(In some places in the literature, this distribution is referred to as the first law of Laplace.) As above, the parameter λ controls the horizontal scale of the density function. Increasing λ causes the distribution to become more compact. The mean of the distribution is zero and its range is unbounded both above and below the mean. 50% of the results fall between $\pm 1/\lambda$.

The following algorithm generates random numbers with a bilateral exponential distribution.

```
      FUNCTION BILEX(XLMBDA)
C  XLMBDA IS THE CONTROLLING PARAMETER LAMBDA.   IT MUST BE >0.
20    U=2.0*RAND(0)
      IF(U.EQ.0..OR.U.EQ.2.)GO TO 20
      IF(U.GT.1.0)GO TO 30
      BILEX=ALOG(U)/XLMBDA
      GO TO 40
30    U=2.0-U
      BILEX=-ALOG(U)/XLMBDA
40    RETURN
      END
```

To prevent errors in the ALOG function, the algorithm includes a check to eliminate cases where the RAND has produced a value of either exactly zero or exactly one. As described above, on many systems these checks can be omitted.

8.1B(5)   *The Gaussian Distribution*

One of the most well-known distributions is the Gaussian or normal distribution. Its density function

$$f(x) = [1/(\sqrt{2\pi}\,\sigma)]\, e^{-(x-\mu)^2/(2\,\sigma^2)}$$

(see figure 8.7) has the shape of a "bell curve" and is characterized by two

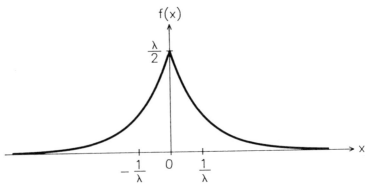

FIGURE 8.6 Probability density function of a random variable which exhibits a bilateral exponential distribution.

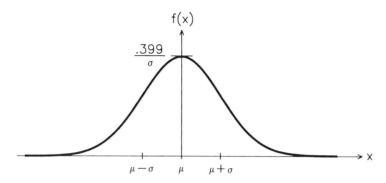

FIGURE 8.7   Gaussian (or normal) probability density function.

parameters, μ and σ. The center of the density function, μ, is the mean value of the random variable. The spread of the density function is measured by a parameter called standard deviation, or σ. 68.26% of all results will occur in the interval with a width of $\pm\sigma$, centered about the mean; the random variable is unbounded, both above and below the mean. 99.74% of all results fall within $\pm3\sigma$.

A Gaussian distribution can be approximated through the summation of uniformly distributed random numbers. The values produced by adding together an infinite quantity of uniformly distributed random numbers are distributed in a Gaussian pattern. In actual practice, a reasonably good approximation can be obtained by adding together a fairly small number. The following algorithm uses 12 and allows the standard deviation and mean to be set independently.

```
      FUNCTION GAUSS(SIGMA,XMU)
C  SIGMA AND XMU ARE THE STANDARD DEVIATION AND MEAN, RESPECTIVELY.
      N=12
C  N IS THE NUMBER OF RANDOM NUMBERS USED IN THE CALCULATION.
      XNOVR2=6.0
C  XNOVR2 IS N/2.
      SCALE=1.0
C  SCALE VARIES WITH N AS:   SCALE=1/(SQRT(N/12))
      SUM=0.0
      DO 20 K=1,N
      SUM=SUM+RAND(0)
20    CONTINUE
      GAUSS=SIGMA*SCALE*(SUM-XNOVR2)+XMU
      RETURN
      END
```

In contrast to a true Gaussian distribution, the random variable generated by this algorithm is bounded. It falls between $\mu\pm6\sigma$. For most purposes this is acceptable because only two results in a billion occurrences of a true Gaussian random process fall outside this range.

8.1B(6)   *The Cauchy Distribution*

The density function (figure 8.8) of a Cauchy-distributed random variable is symmetric, with a mean of zero. The Cauchy density function is given by

$$f(x) = \frac{\alpha}{\pi(\alpha^2 + x^2)}$$

Like a Gaussian density function, it is unbounded both above and below the mean. At its extremes, $f(x)$ approaches zero much more slowly than in the Gaussian case.

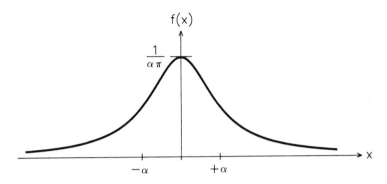

FIGURE 8.8   Probability density function of a Cauchy-distributed random variable.

Thus, values far removed from the mean are more common in a Cauchy process. The density is scaled by the parameter α, with a large α yielding a more widely dispersed curve. Half the results fall within the interval marked by $\pm\alpha$. 99.9% of all results occur between $\pm318.3\alpha$.

   A Cauchy-distributed random variable can be generated by taking the tangent of a properly scaled, uniformly distributed random variable.

```
       FUNCTION CAUCHY(ALPHA)
C   ALPHA IS THE SCALING PARAMETER
       S=3.1415927
C   S=PI
22     U=RAND(0)
       IF(U.EQ.0.5)GO TO 22
       U=U*S
       CAUCHY=ALPHA*TAN(U)
       RETURN
       END
```

To guard against errors in the TAN function, the algorithm eliminates cases where the RAND function has generated a value of exactly .5.

   Certain applications require a Cauchy-distributed random variable that can assume only positive values. For instance, this might be the case when note durations are chosen according to this distribution. The negative half of the density function can be "folded" onto the positive half to obtain a function that is shaped like the right half of figure 8.8, but which has twice the probability density. The random variable produced has a minimum value of zero and no upper bound. Its mean is α. To obtain this case, modify the routine above by setting the constant "S" equal to 1.570796 ($\pi/2$) instead of π. In addition, the IF statement should be changed to check for U=1 instead of U=.5.

8.1B(7)   The Beta Distribution

The density function of a beta-distributed random variable can have several shapes as dictated by its defining parameters a and b. Its density function is given by

$$f(x) = \frac{1}{B(a,b)}\, x^{a-1}\,(1-x)^{b-1}; \quad 0 \le x \le 1$$

where $B(a,b)$ is Euler's beta function.[5] For this discussion, it is sufficient to point out that $B(a,b)$ does not affect the shape of the function. $B(a,b)$ is only a scaling function that gives an area of one under the density curve in the range between zero and one.

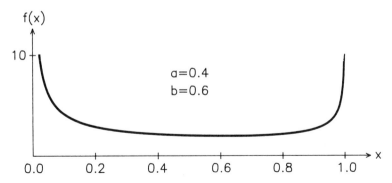

FIGURE 8.9   Probability density function of a Beta-distributed random variable characterized by the paramters shown.

When a and b are both greater than one, the beta density is reminiscent of a
bell-shaped Gaussian density. When $a=b=1$, it degenerates into the special case of
the uniform distribution. Of greatest interest is the case of $a<1$ and $b<1$, which
characterizes a distribution that has the greatest probability near both zero and
one—a shape not found in any of the previously discussed distributions. Figure 8.9
shows the density function for $a=.4$ and $b=.6$. Some of the general relationships
between the parameters and the shape of the density function are:

1. Parameter a controls the probability of values closest to zero; parameter b regulates
those closest to one.
2. The smaller a parameter value is, the greater is the probability at the extreme that it
governs, and the less likelihood there is of a result near .5.
3. When $a=b$, the density is symmetric about .5.
4. When $a{\neq}b$, the density is tilted so that it is more likely to generate results near the
extreme controlled by the smaller parameter.
5. The mean is $a/(a+b)$.

The following algorithm[6] generates a beta-distributed random variable in the
range zero to one.

```
        FUNCTION BETA(A,B)
C   A AND B ARE THE CONTROLLING PARAMETERS.   THEY MUST BE > 0.
        AINV=1./A
        BINV=1./B
15      U1=RAND(0)
        IF(U1.EQ.0.) GO TO 15
16      U2=RAND(0)
        IF(U2.EQ.0.) GO TO 16
20      Y1=U1**AINV
        Y2=U2**BINV
        SUM=Y1+Y2
        IF(SUM.GT.1.0) GO TO 15
        BETA=Y1/SUM
        RETURN
        END
```

For those unfamiliar with FORTRAN, the ** operator is exponentiation. This
algorithm excludes values of the RAND function that are precisely zero. As noted
above, on many systems this check is unnecessary. However, specifying a value for
either a or b that is extremely close to zero creates the potential of an underflow
error during exponentiation.

8.1B(8)   *The Weibull Distribution*

A Weibull-distributed random variable takes on values that are greater than zero with no upper limit. Its probability density can assume several different shapes and is controlled by two parameters, s and t. The density function is given by

$$f(x) = \frac{tx^{t-1}}{s^t} \, e^{-(x/s)^t}; \quad x>0$$

Parameter s serves only to scale the horizontal spread of the probability density, but parameter t has a great influence on the shape of the density. Figure 8.10 illustrates the dependence of the shape of the density function on the value of t. When t is less than one, the density function favors small values. In the special case of $t=1$, the Weibull distribution becomes the exponential distribution. As t increases above one, the density function begins to exhibit a single maximum near the value of s. When $t=3.2$, the density is nearly Gaussian. Large values of t accentuate the sharpness of the peak, thus increasing the chances of generating values close to s. There is a 99.9% probability that an outcome will fall below $6.9^{(1/t)}s$. Thus, it can be seen that choosing a small value for t greatly increases the likelihood of generating a large number.

The following algorithm generates Weibull-distributed random numbers.[7]

```
      FUNCTION WEIBLL(S,T)
C  PARAMETERS S AND T CONTROL THE DISTRIBUTION.  T MUST BE > 0.
20     U=RAND(0)
       IF(U.EQ.0..OR.U.EQ.1.)GO TO 20
       A=1./(1.-U)
       WEIBLL=S*(ALOG(A)**(1./T))
       RETURN
       END
```

This algorithm eliminates values of the RAND function that are exactly zero or exactly one. However, specifying a value for t that is extremely close to zero runs the risk of overflow during the exponentiation operation.

8.1B(9)   *The Poisson Distribution*

A Poisson-distributed, discrete random variable assumes integer values greater than or equal to zero. Its range has no upper bound and the distribution of

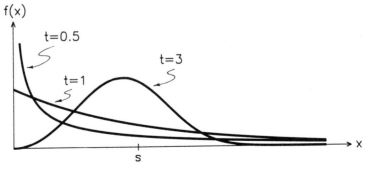

FIGURE 8.10 Weibull probability density function. Notice the great effect that the parameter t has on the shape of the function.

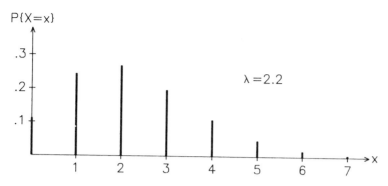

FIGURE 8.11   Probabilities for a Poisson-distributed discrete random variable.

probabilities is controlled by the parameter λ. The probability of drawing the integer j is given by

$$P\{X = j\} = e^{-\lambda}(\lambda^j/j!) \quad x > 0$$

The mean of the distribution is λ. The result with maximum probability occurs at $j=\text{int}(\lambda)$. However, if λ is an integer, the probability that $j=\lambda-1$ will be as great as that of $j=\lambda$. Figure 8.11 shows a Poisson distribution for λ=2.2.

The following algorithm[8] can be used to generate a Poisson-distributed random variable.

```
      FUNCTION KPOISS(XLMBDA)
C   RETURNS A NON-NEGATIVE INTEGER VALUE.
C   XLMBDA IS THE CONTROL PARAMETER LAMBDA.   IT MUST BE > 0.
      N=0
      U=RAND(0)
      V=EXP(-XLMBDA)
90    IF(U.LT.V) GOTO 100
      N=N+1
      U=U*RAND(0)
      GOTO 90
100   KPOISS=N
      RETURN
      END
```

8.1B(10)   *Mapping*

Quite often a particular application requires the transformation of the range of a generated random variable. This practice is called mapping. Let the range of the generated random variable, x, be between a and b. After mapping, the transformed random variable, y, is to fall between c and d. The value of y is calculated from x by using the following relationship:

$$y = \frac{(d - c)}{(b - a)}(x - a) + c$$

If x is continuous, then y will be continuous. Likewise, a discrete x yields a discrete y.

As an example, suppose that a particular application requires a beta-distributed random variable, y, in the range of 1 to 16. The function given above, BETA, produces numbers in the range from 0 to 1. The output of the generator, x, would be scaled according to:

$$y = 15x + 1$$

When a continuous distribution is used to choose parameters that have discrete values, the continuous random variable must be changed into a discrete one. This is accomplished by generating the continuous random variable, mapping it into the appropriate range, and then using the integer function (INT) to obtain discrete results. Because the integer function truncates the fractional part of its argument, the upper limit of the mapped range, d, should be set to one more than the largest integer actually desired. The probabilities of the discrete random variable will have the same shape as the probability density function of the continuous random variable used.

The following algorithm is an example of the use of the RAND function to generate a discrete random variable with uniform probabilities—in this case, the simulation of the rolling of a die.

```
      FUNCTION KDIROL(KDUMMY)
C   RETURNS A RANDOM INTEGER BETWEEN 1 AND 6.
C   THE ARGUMENT, KDUMMY, HAS NO MEANING.
      U=6.*RAND(0)+1.
C   U IS MAPPED SO THAT 1<U<7.
      KDIROL=INT(U)
      RETURN
      END
```

This algorithm assumes that the RAND function does not produce a value of exactly one.

8.1C   Examples of the Use of Random Variables

The most obvious musical use of random processes is to use them to choose some or all of the elements in a musical score. As an example, we will apply the distributions shown in section 8.1B to the selection of pitch. At first, let us simply create 8 different successions of pitches, each one based on a different distribution. In doing so, however, we must make several musical decisions. For example, we must choose the pitch collection into which our randomly generated patterns will be mapped, and the span of musical register over which the mapping will be performed.

For the purposes of the demonstration, let us use twelve equal-tempered divisions of the octave over a three-octave span. Thus, we will work with the 37-tone range of the chromatic scale shown in example 8.1. For a futher restriction, we will limit each example to the first 20 pitches generated by each random process. Example 8.2a–h shows the successions of pitches that result from several of the random processes. The parameter values used to control each process are shown below each example. In each case, the output of the generating algorithm used was mapped into the discrete range 1 to 37, corresponding to the pitches within the 37-tone registral span. In the cases of the Gaussian and Cauchy distributions, the mean of the distribution was set equal to 19 in order to center the distribution within the range. When the random variable was unbounded, as in the case of Cauchy, the boundaries were taken to be the points at which there is a 1/1000 chance of generating a result beyond that limit. These boundaries were used in the mapping equation. The choice of 1/1000 is arbitrary and can be set depending on the dispersion of values desired. In certain situations the mapping algorithm used should include tests to exclude generated values outside the range.

1 2 3 4 5 6 7 8 9 10 11 12 13 14 15 16 17 18 19 20 21 22 23 24 25 26 27 28 29 30 31 32 33 34 35 36 37
Chromatic scale over 3 octaves

EXAMPLE 8.1   Numerical representation of a chromatic scale over three octaves.

a)   Uniform random distribution

b)   Linear distribution

c)   Gaussian distribution

d)   Exponential distribution

e)   Two Poisson distributions   For •, λ =2.2.   For o, λ =18

f)   Cauchy distribution

EXAMPLE 8.2   Pitches chosen by various random processes (*continued on p. 280*).

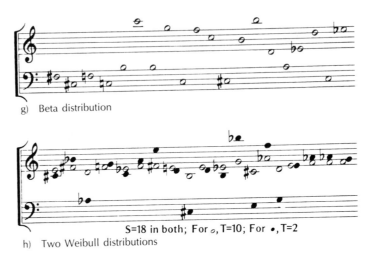

g)   Beta distribution

S=18 in both; For ♢,T=10; For •,T=2

h)   Two Weibull distributions

EXAMPLE 8.2   Pitches chosen by various random processes *(continued).*

Certain observations can be made. The uniform distribution has a more-or-less even distribution of pitches throughout the register. By contrast, the linear distribution places the preponderance of its occurrences in the lower half of the register. The exponential distribution is relegated largely to the lowest octave. Both the Gaussian and Cauchy distributions place pitches toward the midrange. However, in the Cauchy distribution, the dispersion of tones outside the midrange is greater than that of the Gaussian. The majority of the Poisson-distributed pitches are near the value of λ. The Beta distribution emphasizes pitches in the highest and lowest registers. For the Weibull distribution, choosing a large value of t concentrates the pitches in a rather narrow range.

Because the subject at hand is composition (and not, for example, real-time generation of music), we should feel no obligation to present the pitches in the order in which they were generated. The collection of pitches generated can be reordered for other musical purposes. This does not violate the principle by which they were generated, because taking independent observations of a random process prescribes only the distribution of elements and not their order. Example 8.3 shows the same pitch material as example 8.2a, but with the pitches in a new order that results from reversing the order position of the notes within pairs of the original. Example 8.4 shows another use of the same material. The pitches are ordered by taking every other pitch of the original and going through the original ordering twice. Of course, other orderings could easily be made by taking every third pitch of the original, or by any other rule that the composer might wish to impose.

In the previous examples, we chose to restrict our field of choice to pitches derived from twelve semitonal divisions of the octave. The choice of a pitch vocabulary is crucial for determining the kind of music that results from the random selection. Very different results would be obtained by using a completely diatonic collection, a whole-tone collection, a pentatonic collection, or an octatonic collection. Of course, with computer synthesis, there is no need to restrict the vocabulary to equal temperament or, for that matter, to standard divisions of the octave.

EXAMPLE 8.3 A reordering of the notes of example 8.2a by reversing the order of the notes within pairs of the original.

EXAMPLE 8.4 New ordering achieved by taking every other note of the sequence.

Random processes can also be used to structure the rhythm of a passage. One way to do this is to number the succession of attack points as shown in example 8.5, and then to assign an order that depends on the randomly distributed attack times. For convenience we use the same mapping for attack points that we earlier used for pitch—the discrete range 1–37. The 37 attack points are arbitrarily shown in 5 measures of $\frac{2}{4}$ time. Notice that the attack pattern reflects the distribution of the random process used to generate it. For instance, the attacks of the uniform distribution (example 8.6a) show a rather even distribution throughout the range of the thirty-seven attack points. The Gaussian distribution (example 8.6b) clusters its attacks near the middle of the passage. The exponential distribution (example 8.6c) causes the attacks to be clustered at the beginning of the passage, and so on.

Another way to treat random distribution of rhythm is to calculate duration separately from attack time. In example 8.6, each note was given the same duration. Example 8.7 shows what happens when the duration of notes is calculated separately from the attack time. The method used here was one in which the random value in the range 1–37 represents the duration of the tone in sixteenths. Notice that the result, in most cases, is to create a complex musical texture in which the notes overlap. Naturally, the same scheme can be used to affect the dynamics of the tones as well as their orchestration and other attributes, such as timbre and playing style.

The musical possibilities for the use of random distributions in music composition are limitless. The approach requires that the composer assign to the computer

EXAMPLE 8.5 Numerical representation of a succession of attack points.

a)

b)

c)

EXAMPLE 8.6   Attack points chosen by uniform distribution (a), Gaussian distribution (b), and exponential distribution (c).

EXAMPLE 8.7   Exponential distribution of attack point and duration.

most of the specific, note-by-note control over the evolution of the piece. In return, the composer obtains, at the very least, a means by which the music can exhibit patterns and successions that otherwise might not have come to mind. With this method, the composer plans the overall shape of the piece, and the computer fills in the detail using algorithms supplied by the composer. In our later discussions of the music of Lejaren Hiller, Iannis Xenakis, and others, we will show elaborate compositional uses of random-distribution patterns.

In contrast to using a random process to select musical elements directly, random variables are commonly used in a technique known as the "generate and test" method. This technique has been used successfully in a great deal of computer music including the first three movements of the *Illiac Suite* by Hiller and Isaacson.[9] In the generate and test method, as described earlier, a random number is generated, and then subjected to one or another of any number of tests to determine its suitability for the musical situation. For example, when using a range of the 88 tones of the piano keyboard, if the composer desires to have a passage of random music in which all pitches will be members of the diatonic scale of C, the test will exclude all other notes.

8.1D Conditional Probabilities

Thus far, the random processes discussed have made independent observations; that is, the probability of obtaining a particular result is not influenced by any results that have occurred in the past. There is, however, an important class of random variables that exhibit conditional probabilities. In this case, the probability density of the next result depends on one or more past results. Thus, a sequence generated by a process of this type has an amount of relatedness between members of the sequence; that is, the random process prescribes not only the distribution of the members of the sequence, but also their order. There are several algorithmic methods for generating random variables influenced by past events. We will discuss three fundamental techniques: the explicit use of conditional probability tables, random walks, and processes that are specified in terms of their spectra.

A conditional probability is written mathematically in the discrete case as

$$P\{X_n = i | X_{n-1} = j\} = p_{ij}$$

This is interpreted as, the probability that $X=i$, given that the last value of X was j, is p_{ij}. p_{ij} is called a first-order probability because only one previous result is considered. For ease of understanding, the collection of conditional probabilities for a particular process is often presented in the form of a matrix called a *transition table*.

As an example, consider the transition table (Table 8.1). The random process that it describes is the generation of a simple melody composed from four pitches: C, D, E, and G. The columns represent the possible values of the last pitch, and the rows correspond to the possible values of the next pitch.

		LAST PITCH			
		C	D	E	G
	C	0.0	0.3	0.0	0.0
NEXT	D	1.0	0.3	0.3	0.0
PITCH	E	0.0	0.4	0.6	0.5
	G	0.0	0.0	0.1	0.5

TABLE 8.1 A Transition Table for Generating a Simple Melody from Four Pitches.

In this process, if the last pitch was G, for example, there is an equal probability of the next pitch being either E or G. However, there is no chance of selecting either C or D. Similarly, if the last pitch was C, it is certain that the next pitch will be D. The probability of repeating pitch E is .6. When using a transition table such as this, the initial pitch in a sequence can be determined either by some random means or specified directly by the user of the algorithm. From then on, new values are generated using the transition table.

The entries in a transition table can either come from analyses of existing work, or be the result of a compositional design. In the latter case, two rules should be followed: the sum of any column of conditional probabilities must be one, so that the table encompasses all possible results. Secondly, the table designer should avoid choices of probabilities that lead to "dead ends." For instance, if in the example above, the probability that the pitch C follows the pitch C was 1, then once a C was selected, the algorithm would subsequently generate nothing but C's.

The transition table above explicitly expresses the dependence of the current outcome on the previous one. However, the current outcome also depends, to a lesser extent, on earlier values. For example, using the transition table above, what is the probability of generating the sequence DEG if the current pitch is D? The probability of E given D is .4 and the probability of G given E is .1. The probability of both events happening is given by the product of the individual probabilities, and so the probability of DEG is .04, or a 4% chance. How likely is the sequence CDG if the current pitch is C? The sequence CD is certain ($p=1$), but a G never follows a D ($p=0$). Therefore, the sequence CDG is not obtainable using this transition table. Further examination of the table reveals that sequences CCG, CEG, and CGG are also impossible, because only a D can follow a C. Thus, it can be said that if the current pitch is C, there is no chance that the pitch-after-next will be G. From this example it can be seen that even though the transition table includes only first-order probabilities, the current outcome is influenced by results earlier than the previous one. The more distant the result, the less effect it has on the generation of a new value.

The random process above is characterized by the relationship:

$$P_{ijk} = P_{ij}P_{jk}$$

That is, the probability of the sequence *ijk* is the same as the product of the probability that *j* will follow *i* and the probability that *k* will follow *j*. p_{ijk} is known as a second-order probability because it expresses the dependence of the current outcome on the previous two. A process for which the relationship above holds is called a Markov process; it generates a sequence of results known as a Markov chain. A first-order transition table such as the one above is sufficient to describe a Markov process completely because all higher-order probabilities can be calculated by multiplying lower-order probabilities together. In a Markov process, the high-order probabilities tend to be rather small. This indicates that outcomes more than a few removed from the current one have very little influence on the process. There are other methods, in addition to first-order transition tables, which generate Markov chains. A widely used Markov process, the random walk, will be discussed in section 8.1F.

The following subroutine is an example of programming a process described by a first-order transition table. It assumes that the values of the conditional probabilities, p_{ij}, have been previously entered into the transition matrix P(I,J) as part of the main program.

```
      FUNCTION ITT(J)
C   J IS THE NUMERICAL REPRESENTATION OF THE LAST RESULT.
C   THE TRANSITION TABLE HAS BEEN PREVIOUSLY STORED IN ARRAY P.
C   THIS ORDINARILY IS ACCOMPLISHED IN THE MAIN PROGRAM.
      COMMON P(4,4)
      U=RAND(0)
      THRESH=0.
      DO 20 I=1,4
      THRESH=P(I,J)+THRESH
      IF(U.LE.THRESH)GO TO 30
20    CONTINUE
30    ITT=I
      RETURN
      END
```

This algorithm generates one of four possible outcomes represented by the numerical codes 1, 2, 3, and 4, respectively. A process with a different number of outcomes can be accomodated by changing both dimensions of the array P as well as the upper bound of the DO statement from 4 to the desired size.

Many random processes are not Markovian; the higher-order conditional probabilities are not directly related to the first-order ones as above. For instance, the choice of a particular pitch in a traditionally composed musical score is influenced by previous pitches more strongly than in a Markov process. Non-Markov processes are often represented by a transition table of a higher order. If an event is directly influenced by the two previous events, for example, a second-order table would be used. The entries in the matrix would be second-order probabilities of the form: p_{ijk}. The matrix would be three-dimensional and could be visualized as the next event (i) on the first axis, the last event (j) on the second axis, and the second-to-last event (k) on the third axis. A table of any order is theoretically possible depending on how closely linked the random process is with the past. Of course, the complexity of the program to utilize it, the difficulty of conceptualizing it, and the amount of data required to describe it all grow quickly with the order of the table.

8.1E   Uses of Transition Tables

A good example of the results of an elementary statistical analysis of music was made in the 1950s by Harry F. Olson, the inventor of the RCA Sound Synthesizer.[10] In analyzing the successions of melodic tones in eleven songs by the nineteenth-century American composer Stephen Foster, Olson found the relative frequency of scale-step occurrences shown in table 8.2. The scale indicated is that of D major with one chromatic tone, G♯. Olson also tabulated the occurrence of particular rhythmic values in the same group of songs. Table 8.3 correlates the various ways of filling measures in $\frac{4}{4}$ time. Tables 8.2 and 8.3 are known as zeroth-order transition tables because they do not take into account the influence of any previous values. Using these probabilities (but eliminating the possibility of a measure's rest), we generated the melodies in example 8.8. The melodies seem to exhibit little of the musical style on which the transition tables were based.

Table 8.4 tabulates the probabilities for the occurrence of a tone, given the previous tone as analyzed by Olson from the same body of music. Table 8.4 represents a first-order transition table. Example 8.9 shows two different melodic lines made from the transition table. The probability of every note after the first (which we set arbitrarily to D4) was determined from the probabilities in the table.

PITCH	PROBABILITY
B3	.0047
C♯4	.0490
D4	.1578
E4	.0708
F♯4	.1035
G4	.0626
G♯4	.0463
A4	.1824
B4	.1143
C♯5	.0789
D5	.0816
E5	.0481

TABLE 8.2   Relative Probability of Scale-Step Occurrence in 11 Songs of Stephen Foster as Analyzed by Olson (*Published with the permission Dover Publications*)

PATTERN	PROBABILITY
𝅝	.125
𝅗𝅥 𝅗𝅥	.250
♩ ♩ ♩ ♩	.125
𝅗𝅥 ♩ ♩	.125
♩ ♩ 𝅗𝅥	.125
♩ 𝅗𝅥 ♩	.125
𝄾	.125

TABLE 8.3   Relative Probability of Various Rhythmic Patterns in 11 Songs of Stephen Foster (*Printed by permission of Dover Publications*)

EXAMPLE 8.8   Two eight-measure melodies generated with the zeroth-order probabilities of table 8.1 and table 8.2.

Here the examples appear to be somewhat closer to the melodic style of Stephen Foster's songs.

Table 8.5 shows a second-order transition table describing the probability of various three-tone successions. Example 8.10 shows two melodic lines made from

NEXT PITCH

Previous pair		B3	C♯4	D4	E4	F♯4	G4	G♯4	A4	B4	C♯5	D5	E5
B3	D4	0	0	1	0	0	0	0	0	0	0	0	0
C♯4	D4	0	0	.3125	.3750	0	0	0	.3125	0	0	0	0
D4	B3	0	0	1	0	0	0	0	0	0	0	0	0
D4	C♯4	0	0	1	0	0	0	0	0	0	0	0	0
D4	D4	0	.1250	.1250	.5625	.1250	.0625	0	0	0	0	0	0
D4	E4	0	0	.1875	.2500	.5000	0	0	.0625	0	0	0	0
D4	F♯4	0	0	0	.4375	.1875	.1250	0	.2500	0	0	0	0
D4	G4	0	0	0	0	.6875	0	0	0	.3125	0	0	0
D4	A4	0	0	0	0	.2500	0	0	.7500	0	0	0	0
D4	C♯5	0	0	0	0	0	0	0	0	0	0	1	0
D4	D5	0	0	0	0	0	0	0	.1250	.6875	.1875	0	0
E4	C♯4	0	0	1	0	0	0	0	0	0	0	0	0
E4	D4	.0625	0	.0625	.2500	.3125	0	0	.0625	0	.0625	.1875	0
E4	E4	0	.0625	.7500	.0625	.1250	0	0	0	0	0	0	0
E4	F♯4	0	0	.0625	.1875	.3750	.2500	0	.0625	.0625	0	0	0
E4	A4	0	0	0	0	0	0	0	.8125	.1875	0	0	0
E4	D5	0	0	0	0	0	0	0	0	0	1	0	0
F♯4	D4	0	0	0	.7500	.1875	.0625	0	0	0	0	0	0
F♯4	E4	0	.1250	.4375	.1875	.1250	0	0	.0625	0	0	.0625	0
F♯4	F♯4	0	0	.1875	.2500	.3750	.1250	0	.0625	0	0	0	0
F♯4	G4	0	0	0	0	.2500	.1875	0	.3750	.1875	0	0	0
F♯4	A4	0	0	0	0	.1250	0	0	.6250	.1875	0	.0625	0
F♯4	B5	0	0	0	0	0	0	0	1	0	0	0	0
G4	F♯4	0	0	0	.5000	0	.5000	0	0	0	0	0	0
G4	G4	0	0	0	0	0	.5000	0	.5000	0	0	0	0
G4	A4	0	0	.1250	0	0	0	0	.6250	0	0	.2500	0
G4	B4	0	0	0	0	0	0	0	1	0	0	0	0
G♯4	A4	0	0	0	0	0	0	0	0	1	0	0	0
A4	D4	0	0	0	.6875	.3125	0	0	0	0	0	0	0
A4	F♯4	0	0	.3125	.2500	.1875	.0625	0	.1250	.0625	0	0	0
A4	G4	0	0	0	0	1	0	0	0	0	0	0	0
A4	G♯4	0	0	0	0	0	0	0	1	0	0	0	0
A4	A4	0	0	0	0	.2500	.0625	.0625	.3125	.3125	0	0	0
A4	B4	0	0	.0625	0	.0625	0	0	.7500	.0625	0	.0625	0
A4	D5	0	0	0	0	0	0	0	.3750	.3125	.1875	.1250	0
B4	D4	0	0	1	0	0	0	0	0	0	0	0	0
B4	F♯4	0	0	0	.6875	.3125	0	0	0	0	0	0	0
B4	G4	0	0	0	0	0	0	0	0	1	0	0	0
B4	A4	0	0	.0625	0	.5625	.0625	0	.1250	.0625	0	.1250	0
B4	B4	0	0	0	0	.1250	0	0	.7500	0	0	.1250	0
B4	D5	0	0	0	0	0	0	0	.5625	.1250	.3125	0	0
C♯5	B4	0	0	0	0	0	0	0	1	0	0	0	0
C♯5	D5	0	0	0	0	0	0	0	0	.3750	0	0	.6250
D5	A4	0	0	0	0	.8750	0	0	.1250	0	0	0	0
D5	B5	0	0	0	0	0	.0625	0	.3125	.3750	0	.2500	0
D5	C♯5	0	0	0	0	0	0	0	0	.7500	0	.2500	0
D5	D5	0	0	0	0	0	0	0	0	1	0	0	0
D5	E5	0	0	0	0	0	0	0	.3125	0	.6875	0	0
E5	A4	0	0	0	0	0	0	0	1	0	0	0	0
E5	C♯5	0	0	0	0	0	0	0	0	0	0	1	0

PREVIOUS PAIR OF PITCHES

TABLE 8.5 Relative Probability of Occurrence of Three-Tone Sequences in Stephen Foster Songs (*Published by permission of Dover Publications*)

EXAMPLE 8.9 Two melodies generated using the zeroth-order rhythmic probabilities of table 8.3 and the first order transition table (table 8.4) for pitch.

LAST PITCH

	B3	C#4	D4	E4	F#4	G4	G#4	A4	B4	C#5	D5	E5
B3	0	0	.0625	0	0	0	0	0	0	0	0	0
C#4	0	0	.0625	.0625	0	0	0	0	0	0	0	0
D4	1	1	.1250	.3750	.1250	0	0	.0625	.0625	0	0	0
E4	0	0	.3125	.1875	.2500	0	0	0	0	0	0	0
F#4	0	0	.1875	.2500	.3125	.2500	0	.3125	.0625	0	0	0
G4	0	0	.0625	0	.1250	.1875	0	.0625	.0625	0	0	0
G#4	0	0	0	0	0	0	0	.0625	0	0	0	0
A4	0	0	.0625	.0625	.1250	.3750	1	.2500	.5625	0	.2500	.3750
B4	0	0	0	0	.0625	.1875	0	.1875	.1250	.5000	.4375	0
C#5	0	0	.0625	0	0	0	0	0	0	0	.1875	.6250
D5	0	0	.0625	.0625	0	0	0	.0625	.1250	.5000	.0625	0
E5	0	0	0	0	0	0	0	0	0	0	0	0

(NEXT PITCH — row labels at left)

TABLE 8.4 Relative Probability of Occurrence of a Pair of Tones in Stephen Foster Songs. (*Published by permission of Dover Publications*)

EXAMPLE 8.10 Two melodies generated using the second-order probabilities of table 8.4 for pitch choice.

the transition table relating the probabilities of three-tone successions in the music of Stephen Foster. These melodies approach the style more closely than those of the previous examples.

From these musically elementary examples, it should be clear that transition tables afford some possibilities in modeling a randomly generated music on previously composed music. Of course, as previously stated, transition tables can also be the result of compositional thought. The use of transition tables is not favored by all advocates of aleatoric choice of musical elements. Martin Gardner, who favors the generation of music by one-over-f noise, asserts that music based on transition tables, however closely related to the model in the small, is still random in the large.[11]

8.1F   Random Walks and Fractional Noises

A classic example of a Markov process is the controlled random walk. Consider a man on a step-ladder that has three steps. At specified intervals he tosses a coin, and if it comes up heads, he climbs up one step. If it comes up tails, he descends one step. This process is bounded, however, because on the top step the only way to go is down; at the bottom, the only way is up. Thus, there are four possible levels that the man can occupy. Level 1 represents ground level at the bottom of the ladder, and levels 2, 3, and 4 represent the three steps of the ladder in ascending order. Assume that the man is on level 3. The probability that he will next go to level 1, p_{13}, is zero, because he can only move one step at a time. The probability of staying on level 3, p_{33}, is also zero, because he changes levels on every toss. The probability of going to either level 4, p_{43}, or level 2, p_{23}, is .5.

The following algorithm simulates the controlled random walk described above.

```
        FUNCTION IWALK(LAST)
C   THE ARGUMENT, LAST, IS THE PREVIOUS POSITION OF THE WALKER.
        I=1
        U=RAND(0)
        IF(U.LT..5) I=-1
        J=LAST+I
C   THE FOLLOWING TWO STATEMENTS TEST FOR THE UPPER AND LOWER
C   BOUNDARIES, RESPECTIVELY.
        IF(J.GT.4) J=3
        IF(J.LT.1) J=2
        IWALK=J
        RETURN
        END
```

The boundaries of the walk can be changed by altering the test statements above.

The controlled random walk above is described as having reflecting bound-aries, because every time a boundary is reached, the walker is sent in the opposite direction. Another form of random walk uses elastic boundaries; the probability of moving toward a boundary decreases as the walker approaches it. In either case, the presence of the boundaries has the effect of increasing the probability that the walker will be found in a state near the middle. A third type of boundary, the absorbing boundary, causes the walk to cease when the boundary is encountered.

Another variation on a random walk determines by aleatoric means not only the direction but also the distance of the next position from the current one. As an example, consider a random variable whose next value is generated by adding to the current value a Gaussian-distributed random variable with a mean of zero. In this case, called Brownian motion, there is an equal chance of the new value being either above or below the current one. Due to the shape of the Gaussian distribution, small changes in value are more likely than large ones.

Composers such as Tracy Petersen[12] have used controlled random walks on musical parameters such as pitch contour where the boundaries were changed with time.

Random processes characterized by their spectra have been widely applied to the choice of compositional parameters such as pitch. In section 3.9 we described the use of random processes to generate sequences of sample values that, when applied to a D/A converter, produce a "noise sound." The form of the distributed spectrum characteristic of such a signal depends on the process used to generate it. Thus, another way to characterize a random process is by its power spectral density—the variation of the energy in the sequence produced by the process versus frequency. (The spectral characterization applies only to the sequence of values of the random variable used to determine a particular parameter; it says nothing about the acoustical spectra of the actual sounds used in the music. As expected, these spectra will have the characteristics of the instruments that are used to play them.)

White noise has, by definition, a flat spectrum, and so varies with frequency as $1/f^0$. A random walk without boundaries has a spectrum that rolls off as the square of the frequency. Therefore, noise produced by this process is sometimes called $1/f^2$, or Brownian noise. Both white noise and Brownian noise are members of a class of processes called *fractional noises* whose spectrum diminishes as $1/f^\gamma$, where $0 \leq \gamma \leq 2$. A particularly interesting case is $\gamma = 1$, or $1/f$ (one-over-f) noise which has been observed in many naturally occurring phenomena such as noise in electronic devices, annual amounts of rainfall, traffic flow, and economic data, to name just a few.[13] In fact, Clarke and Voss[14] analyzed several examples of music in various styles and found the loudness and pitch of all of them to be distributed as nearly $1/f$.

Values in a sequence generated by $1/f$ noise correlate logarithmically with the past. Thus, for example, the averaged activity of the last 10 values has as much influence on the current value as the last 100, as the last 1000, and so on. This remarkable property means that the process has a relatively long-term memory. In fact, $1/f$ noise has best memory of any noise. White noise has no memory at all; $1/f^2$ noise places such a heavy weight on the previous event that events prior to the previous few have virtually no influence on the current outcome. Other fractional noises such as $1/f^{0.5}$ and $1/f^{1.5}$ have somewhat longer memory, but do not approach the characteristics of $1/f$ noise.

As one might expect, a segment of a sequence generated by white noise has no similarity to any other segment. A segment of $1/f^2$ noise has some similarity to segments nearby, but virtually no similarity to those far removed or to the structure of the overall sequence. However, $1/f$ noise produces patterns said to be "self-similar." Self-similarity is characteristic of much traditional music composition where the local detail mirrors the overall structure of the piece. As a result, some composers have used $1/f$ noise for compositional purposes. Section 8.1H presents a method used by Charles Wuorinen to apply $1/f$ noise to the selection of score parameters.

The following algorithm of R. F. Voss[15] can be used to generate a $1/f$ sequence of integers with 32 possible values, in the range of 0 to 31.

```
      FUNCTION I1OVRF(LAST)
C     THE ARGUMENT, LAST, IS THE PREVIOUS VALUE OF THE SEQUENCE.
      NEW=0
C     THE VARIABLE K EQUALS ONE-HALF THE NUMBER POSSIBLE VALUES.
      K=16
      L=LAST
C     THE VARIABLE PROBIT EQUALS 1/(NUMBER OF POSSIBLE VALUES).
      PROBIT=.03125
20    J=L/K
      IF(J.EQ.1)L=L-K
      U=RAND(0)
      IF(U.LT.PROBIT)J=1-J
      NEW=NEW+J*K
      K=K/2
      PROBIT=PROBIT*2.
      IF(K.GE.1)GO TO 20
      I1OVRF=NEW
      RETURN
      END
```

Statement number 20, J=L/K, relies on the implicit integer data type of FOR-TRAN to truncate the result to an integer. If this program is translated to a language that does not have an integer data type, such as BASIC, the integer function must be used. In this case, the line should read: J=INT(L/K). The algorithm above can be modified to obtain a number of states equal to any integer power of two. This is accomplished by changing the initial values of K and PROBIT according to the relationships shown in the code above. For example, to generate values in the range of 0 to 15 (16 unique values), the initial values of K and PROBIT would be set to 8 and .0625, respectively.

8.1G Examples of the Use of Fractional Noises

Example 8.11 was made by selecting pitches and rhythms at random using white noise. The range of pitches was the two octaves of diatonic C, above middle C. The range of rhythmic values was: $\flat$, $\flat$, $\flat$, $\flat$. Most observers will agree that the passage exhibits little internal relatedness.

Example 8.12 is of brown or $1/f^2$ music. Here, the same ranges of pitch and rhythmic values were used for projecting a melody. The close correlation between adjacent choices results in a music that has been described by Gardner as wandering "up and down like a drunk weaving through an alley."[16]

One-over-f $(1/f)$ noise is generally agreed to produce the most aesthetically pleasing quality of the three types of noise. Example 8.13 shows a melody with the same ranges as the previous examples, and with $1/f$ correlation between successive pitches and rhythms. $1/f$ noise produces what are known as "self-similar" patterns. This appears to be the reason for its greater aesthetic appeal. Its use guarantees that the resulting music will exhibit similar patterns in its large and small dimensions.

EXAMPLE 8.11 "White Noise" music.

EXAMPLE 8.12 "Brown" music generated with $1/f^2$ noise.

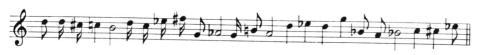

EXAMPLE 8.13 "$1/f$" music.

8.1H Compositional Uses of Randomness

Lejaren Hiller is the first composer to have extensively investigated computer-aided composition. Hiller's computer music tends to fall into two categories: dramatic, often satirical, theatre pieces; and more didactic pieces that demonstrate particular compositional techniques. Examples of the former include *An Avalanche for Pitchman, Prima Donna, Player Piano, Percussionist, and Prerecorded Play-back* (1968) and *HPSCHD* (with John Cage, 1969). Examples of the latter category are *Illiac Suite* (1957), *Computer Cantata* (1963), *Algorithms I* (1968), *Algorithms II* (1972), and *Algorithms III* (in preparation, 1983).

The programs for the *Illiac Suite* were developed by Hiller and Isaacson in the mid-1950s.[17] For this piece, the Illiac computer at the University of Illinois generated the pitches, rhythms, and other characteristics of the music. The computer printed the results in an alphanumeric code that was transcribed by hand into music notation and then scored for string quartet.

Hiller and Isaacson used random processes to generate the music of the *Illiac Suite*. Although the notes were generated at random, the composers wanted some degree of control. Therefore, restrictions were built into the process. A "generate and test" method was applied: each random selection generated was rejected if it failed one of a number of tests of its suitability.

The first three of the four movements of the *Illiac Suite* was produced by the "generate and test" method. These compositional "experiments" were modelled on pre-existing types of music. For example, the melodic and harmonic activity in the first movement were controlled by the rules of cantus firmus and species-counterpoint composition described by Fux in *Gradus ad Parnassum*.[18] In this movement, the "test" questions were designed to determine whether each random-ly generated selection conformed to the rules for melodic succession and harmonic consonance of first-species counterpoint.

The computer program produced random integers in the range 0–15, which represented the tones of two octaves of diatonic "C." Melodic rules were then applied to the randomly generated diatonic pitches to determine their acceptability. Some of the rules of first-species counterpoint used in the first movement were: no melody was allowed to exceed the range of one octave; the melodic line had to begin and end on a member of the tonic triad; melodic leaps of sevenths were forbidden; and under most circumstances, it was prohibited to repeat the highest note of a melodic line. Among the harmonic tests applied to the generated tones were: Only consonant intervals—unison, octave, perfect fifth, major and minor thirds and sixths—were permitted; and the perfect fourth was treated as a dissonance when it created $\frac{6}{4}$ chords. There were additional rules for prohibiting parallel perfect intervals between voices and other rules to govern the motion of voices from one chord to the next.

The second movement begins with the random orderings of 7-tone "white-note music." Successive constraints were applied in the course of the movement until four-part, note-against-note counterpoint was achieved at the end. Movement three includes all twelve tones, as well as greater rhythmic complexity and variety. The pitch and rhythm of this movement were each chosen by means of separate selection processes. The pitch material ranges from random chromatic music to twelve-tone rows. The initial rhythmic scheme for each instrument involves random selection of notes and rests within the measure, followed by random selections for the number of repetitions of the rhythm of each measure.

In the last movement the rules that control the probability of occurrence of an event in each stage of the music are even further removed from the stylistic criteria of traditional composition. Hiller and Isaacson employed Markov chains in the design of these rules. In their 'Markov Chain Music," the composers created "sequences of events in which the choice of each new event can be made dependent on previous events; or, in musical terms, the choice of each new note or interval in a given melodic line can be dependent upon previous notes or intervals in the same melodic line."[19]

In *Computer Cantata* (1963), scored for soprano and a diverse group of instruments plus tape, Hiller worked more extensively with transition tables (this time in collaboration with Robert A. Baker).[20] Figure 8.12 shows an outline of the form of the *Computer Cantata*. The composers used an analysis of random phoneme-succession probabilities in English as a basis for creating the text for the five strophes. Beginning with zeroth-order conditional probabilities in Strophe I and progressing to fourth order in Strophe V, each strophe imposes more constraints upon phoneme succession, as defined by the probabilities of phoneme selection in English. In Strophe V, the constraints are elaborate enough to provide English-sounding words such as "perpus" (purpose) and "sayd" (said).

A plan of progressive similarity was worked out for elements in the music of the strophes as well. The following progression of transition-table order was used for the five strophes: zeroth-, first-, second-, first-, zeroth-order. As a basis for the selection of musical elements, Hiller and Baker analyzed an excerpt from the second movement of Charles Ives' *Three Places in New England* for occurrence of pitches, durations, rests, dynamics, and playing style. The results were used in designing the transition tables. In addition, each of the five strophes contains a "prolog" and/or an "epilog" for which the material was often generated without reference to a stylistic model. For example, figure 8.13a[21] diagrams the patterns of density of attack points (initiations of notes and rests), the density of actual attacks, and dynamics for the Prolog to Strophe I; figure 8.13b diagrams these parameters for the Epilog to Strophe V. The density of attacks is around 2 per second at the beginning of the Prolog; it progresses to around 128 at the end. The Epilog reverses the process; the density is around 16 at its beginning and falls off to around 1 at the end. The figure also shows the inverse relationship between dynamic level and the

I.   Prolog to Strophe **I** (Rhythm Study for Percussion)
      Strophe **I** (Zeroth—order Stochastic Approximation)

II.   Prolog to Strophe **II** (Totally Organized Instrumental Music)
      Strophe **II** (First—order Stochastic Approximation)

III.   Prolog to Strophe **III** (Polytempered Computer Sounds)
      Strophe **III** (Second—order Stochastic Approximation)
      Epilog to Strophe **III** (Polytempered Computer Sounds)

IV.   Strophe **IV** (Third—order Stochastic Approximation)
      Epilog to Strophe **IV** (Totally Organized Instrumental Music)

V.   Strophe **V** (Fourth—order Stochastic Approximation)
      Epilog to Strophe **V** (Rhythm Study for Percussion)

FIGURE 8.12 Outline of the form of Hiller and Baker's *Computer Cantata*. (*Published with the permission of* Perspectives of New Music.)

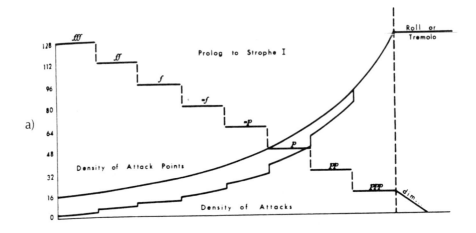

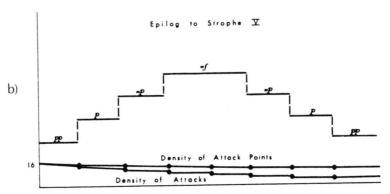

FIGURE 8.13 Patterns of change of attack point density and dynamic level for two sections of "Computer Cantata." (*Reprinted with the permission of* Perspectives of New Music.)

density of attacks in these sections of the piece. This section of the *Computer Cantata* is particularly clear in the way the computer is used to realize a musical intention. Here the composers specified a general shape for the texture and dynamics and left the filling in of the details to the computer.

Other parts of *Computer Cantata* are organized according to serial principles (similar to those found in *Structures* by Pierre Boulez) or other more theoretical considerations (e.g., calculation and control of "harmonic dissonance").

Since writing the *Computer Cantata*, Hiller has continued his developments in computer-aided composition. His composition programs have become increasingly flexible and general. He has incorporated extensive musical quotation as well as procedures such as change ringing, conditional probabilities up to sixth order, and more elaborate rules of melodic writing.[22]

Iannis Xenakis refers to his computer-generated instrumental compositions, *ST/10-1,080262*; *ST/48-1,240162*; *Atrees*, and *Morsima-Amorsima*, as "stochastic music." By this term, Xenakis refers to a "world of sound masses, vast groups of sound-events, clouds, and galaxies governed by new characteristics such as density, degree of order, and rate of change, which required definitions and realizations using probability theory."[23] The Stochastic Music Program (SMP), which Xenakis developed for his computer-aided compositions, relies on probabilistic descriptions of the music. In using SMP, the patterns of distribution of notes take precedence over the selection of the individual notes. Xenakis describes this process by means of an analogy to the way in which clouds or rain are perceived—as a statistical distribution of particles. The shape, density, degree of order, or rate of change among a large number of elements are more apparent than are the characteristics of any single element.

Figure 8.14 shows an overview of the SMP.[24] The following descriptions will help clarify the figure:

"Compute Length of Section"—Here the computer is instructed to choose a section length according to an exponential distribution of values. The composer specifies an average value for the section length. Because the exponential distribution has no upper limit, a maximum value for section length is set. If the generated value exceeds the maximum, another value is chosen.

"Compute Density of Section"—The density, or average number of notes per second of a given section after the first, depends in part on the density of the previous section. The process by which the value is determined is as follows: first, a binary random choice is made to determine whether the density of current section will be greater or smaller than that of the previous one. Next, two random numbers are chosen in the range between zero and the density of the previous section. Then, the absolute value of the difference between the two random numbers is calculated. Finally, the calculated difference is either added or subtracted from the density of the previous section, depending on the results of the first step.

"Define Orchestra for Section"—First, the instruments of the orchestra are divided into timbre classes in which a single instrument can belong to more than one class and each class has more than one member. Then, the composer gives a zeroth-order transition table that is used to determine the timbre classes for a section. The transition table specifies the probabilities for occurrence of each timbre class, and these probabilities are changed by linear interpolation, depending on the density of the section.

"Compute Attack Time of Note"—Time between attacks is chosen by the same method used for the selection of section length. It is a deviation from the average, calculated by taking the average number of notes per second for a section.

"Determine Instrument for Note"—A random number, applied to a timbre-class transition table supplied by the composer, selects the timbre-class for the note. Then, a second random number determines which instrument within the timbre class is chosen.

"Compute Pitch of Note"—If the chosen instrument is pitched, the choice of pitch is limited by the range, designated by the composer, of the instrument. If it is the first note, the choice is random within the range. If the instrument has played before, there is a dependence on the previous choice similar to that described above for determining the density of a section.

"Compute Glissando Speed of Note"—If the timbre class permits glissando, choice of glissando speed is by Gaussian distribution with a mean glissando width of zero. This implies that a slow glissando is more likely to occur than a fast one.

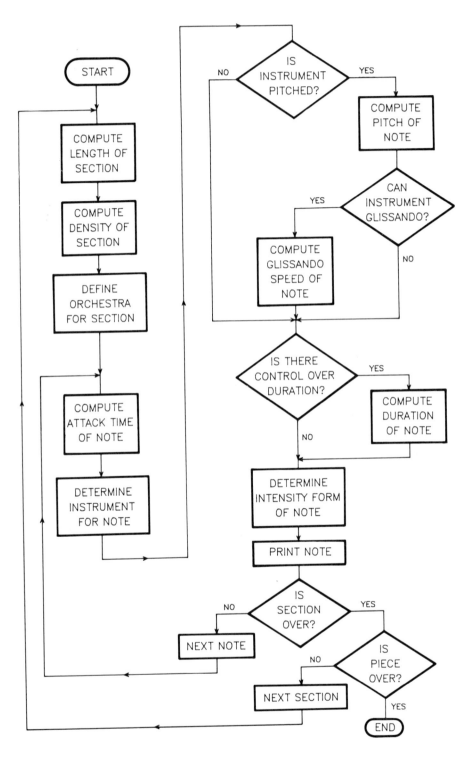

FIGURE 8.14   Overview of the SMP program of I. Xenakis. (*Published with the permission of John Myhill.*)

"Compute Duration"—The duration of a note is determined on the basis of a Gaussian random process that is scaled by a number of factors, such as the frequency of occurrence of an instrument within a timbre class. For example, if an instrument plays few notes, then its notes would generally be longer. Another factor is the maximum length an instrument can play, which is specified by the composer.

"Determine Intensity Form of Note"—Figure 8.15 shows some dynamic shapes available for notes in compositions using SMP. The composer indicates shapes that apply to a particular instrument. The intensity shapes are then chosen at random from within that range.

Upon completion of the calculation of the steps above, the program prints a line describing all the attributes of the note just generated. The program repeats its steps until all notes of all sections have been generated.

More recently, Xenakis, through his Center for Mathematics and Music (CeMaMu) just outside Paris, has been experimenting with the production of computer music through direct digital synthesis of sound.

Before computer composition came to occupy his attention, Gottfried Michael Koenig worked with Karlheintz Stockhausen and Werner Meyer-Eppler in developing the electronic music studio at the West German radio in Cologne. In 1960, he participated in the realization of the tape part for Stockhausen's *Kontakte*. Subsequently, Koenig went to Holland to become the director of the newly formed Institute of Sonology at Utrecht State University. Under his direction, the Institute of Sonology has become a major European center of computer music, focusing on hybrid synthesis and computer-aided composition.[25] The work in computer-aided composition has been oriented around Koenig's interests in serialism and his development of a special system for aleatoric choice of musical parameters.

Koenig has designed two programming systems for computer composition, entitled Project 1 and Project 2.[26] Both systems are intended to produce compositions for acoustic instruments by means of printed output for manual transcription into musical notation.

Project 1 was developed to realize certain of Koenig's own compositional ideas. It resulted in compositions with many common characteristics, but at the same time permitted wide variations among them. Each piece consists of seven 'form sections" in which the distribution of certain compositional variables is calculated by random means. The result of each run of the program depends upon the specific degree of randomness assigned to each of various musical parameters, e.g., timbre, rhythm, pitch-class, octave, register, and dynamics. Koenig used Project 1 to produce a number of instrumental compositions.

Project 2 was designed to be a more general programming system. With it, Koenig produced his composition *Übung für Klavier*. Project 2 gives the user more control over the rules for choosing the values of the various parameters. As an example, consider the selection of durations. The program begins by asking the user "Which Durations?" After supplying the list of allowed durations, the composer specifies the rules by which the computer is to choose among the elements in the list. There are six options:

ALEA: selects randomly.

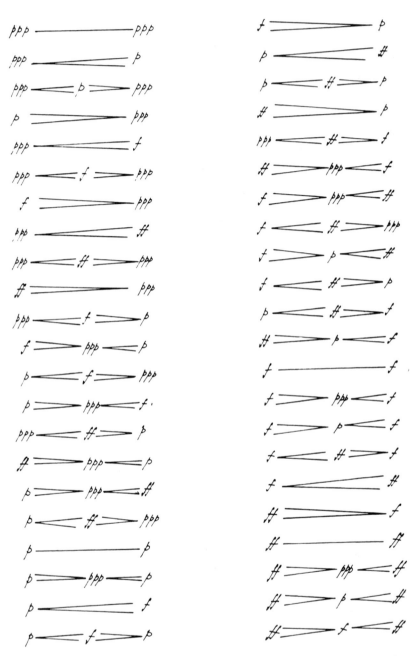

FIGURE 8.15   The 44 intensity forms from four mean intensity values, ppp, p, f, and ff. (*Reprinted by the permission of the Indiana University Press.*)

SERIES: selects randomly but eliminates repetition until each element has been selected once.

RATIO: as in SERIES, repetitions are eliminated, but the check for repetition considers only a specified number of previous elements. The number used depends on the value of the current element.

GROUP: produces repetition of the elements in groups.

SEQUENCE: enables the composer to determine the order of the elements.

TENDENCY: establishes a "window" of a specified size through which sequential elements of a group can be viewed and then chooses randomly among the elements within the window.

The concept of a "window" or "tendency mask" has been influential. It forms an important part of the POD system for computer-aided composition created by Barry Truax.[27] Other composers have used Koenig's programs to produce computer-aided compositions. Otto Laske, for example, has used Project 1 to help create a family of instrumental compositions, the first of which, *Perturbations*, was played at the International Computer Music Conference in 1981.

Charles Wuorinen is an accomplished composer of opera, symphony, string quartets, and a wide variety of chamber music. His electronic composition *Time's Encomium*,[28] realized on the RCA Mark II synthesizer and processed with analog equipment at the Columbia–Princeton Electronic Music Center, won the Pulitzer Prize for Music in 1970.

Wuorinen's religious work, *The Celestial Sphere* (1980) for orchestra and chorus, includes a computer-generated tape interlude in the "pentecostal" movement. Following Christian symbolism relating to the Pentecost, the tape part represents the descent of the dove from heaven to earth. Using the "generate and test" method (section 8.1C), Wuorinen applied rules to the stochastically generated successions of pitches to articulate them in the descending patterns desired for the piece. The particular stochastic process used for generating the pitches was $1/f$ noise.

His compositional method for creating the chords upon which the interlude is based involves the generation of a succession of equal-tempered pitches and the subsequent application of rules to determine the allowed vertical intervals. For example, given a note, x, the next generated note, y, would occur simultaneously with x if the interval separating them were among the several permitted. Otherwise, note y would become the "root" of the next chord. The chords, once generated, are arpeggiated downwards.

Further emphasis on the resulting vertical structures is made by an "echo arpeggiation" of each chord. Figure 8.16 shows an application of the echo arpeggiation to a hypothetical chord. Echo arpeggiation no. 1 simply makes a descending arpeggio of the notes in the chord. Because the chord occupies an interval span of 34 semitones, in echo arpeggiation no. 2 the pitch space between the lowest tone in the range of the piece and the next to the highest pitch of the chord is divided into 34 intervals of equal size. The resulting structure preserves the relative size of adjacent intervals of the first chord, but it now includes tones outside the twelve-tone, equal-tempered system. Successive arpeggiations employing the same method of interval division were used for the third, fourth, and fifth echoes. The structure, thus, is echoed the same number of times as the total number of notes in the chord.

Some other experiments that Wuorinen has made by generating pitch successions with $1/f$ noise bear a closer resemblance to certain of the procedures in his book, *Simple Composition*.[29] For example, again using $1/f$ successions of twelve-tone, equal-tempered pitches, his program generates notes (including pitch-class

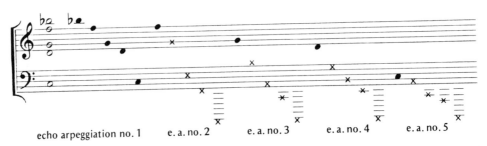

echo arpeggiation no. 1   e. a. no. 2   e. a. no. 3   e. a. no. 4   e. a. no. 5

FIGURE 8.16 "Echo arpeggiations" in Wuorinen's "The Celestial Sphere."

a)

b)

FIGURE 8.17 Generated succession of pitches (a) and Trichordal pitch partition and equal time division rhythmic disposition (b).

repetitions) until an aggregate is formed, i.e., until all 12 pitch classes have each been generated at least once. Then this group of pitches is partitioned into four distinct groups according to membership in the trichords: 0, 1, 2; 3, 4, 5; 6, 7, 8; and 9, 10, 11. The four groups are then articulated at different speeds by dividing a given time span by the number of notes in each group. The partitioning of a hypothetical aggregate and the resulting musical fabric are illustrated in figure 8.17. Naturally, this example shows only one of an infinite number of possibilities.

Charles Wuorinen's explorations into the "generate and test" method using random sequences generated by 1/*f* noise have interrelated serial and stochastic procedures to generate musical passages. His computer-aided composition employs the "effortless arithmetic" available on the computer for the specification of timing and tunings.

Larry Austin is the composer of numerous works of vocal, instrumental, and electronic music. He has been a leading figure in the American musical avant-garde since the early 1960s. Austin has been using computers—both as a compositional aid and a medium for sound synthesis—since the late 1960s. One of the themes that recurs in Austin's output is that of basing some aspects of a piece of music on a natural phenomenon. For example, in his composition *Maroon Bells*, 1976, the melodic lines of a live voice part and a tape "derive from the actual contours" of a mountain range.[30] *Canadian Coastlines*, 1981, was commissioned for broadcast by the Canadian Broadcasting Corporation. It is a piece of stochastic music for which Austin used the computer to generate much of the musical detail. The limits within which the stochastic choices were made were determined by a chart tracing the actual coastlines of a number of bodies of water in and around Canada. The chart used for the composition is shown in figure 8.18.

Canadian Coastlines is comprised of an eight-voice canon, with four parts played live on instruments and voice and four parts prerecorded on tape using a digital synthesizer. The succession of entrances and tempo courses of the eight voices, each given the name of a Canadian city, are shown on the figure. The voice

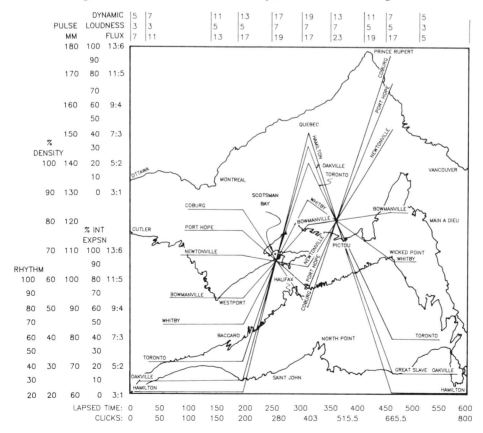

FIGURE 8.18   Chart used by Larry Austin in the composition of *Canadian Coastlines*. (*Published with the permission of Larry Austin.*)

labeled "Hamilton" begins the piece and proceeds at a tempo of ♩=60 until the first 200 seconds have elapsed. The "Coburg" voice enters after 100 seconds rest and plays its canonic voice at ♩=120 so that it catches up to Hamilton at the elapsed time of 200 seconds. The other six voices, by appropriate choice of their tempi between the rates of Hamilton and Coburg, reach the same point in the canon at the same point in time. The composer has chosen tempo relationships throughout the piece to ensure that there are, in the course of the piece, five of the junctures where the voices all come briefly together.

The relationships in tempo can be heard most clearly during the first 200 seconds of the work. Figure 8.19 shows the assignment of instruments to the canonic voices for the version recorded on Folkways FTS 37475. Observe that each line of the canon is assigned a pair of instruments (the human voice is treated as an instrument in the piece) with one instrument playing a "melodic" version of the line and the other a "rhythmic" version. The pair of instruments on a line plays the canon part in unison with the "rhythmic" instrument making many repeated, shorter notes out of the longer notes in the melody.

Other aspects of the music were determined by the stochastic decisions applied to various parameters of the music for every 5 seconds of its 10 minute duration. The algorithms for rhythm, dynamic flux, textural density, and melodic interval expansion make their choices within the limits determined by the four coastlines shown in figure 8.18. Actually, the four coastlines in the figure are made up of seven coastline fragments taken from geographic maps and freely concatenated by the composer to obtain the pattern of change desired for the elements of the music. For example, the uppermost coastline in the figure controls the "dynamic flux"; not the dynamic level as such, but rather the rate of dynamic change at a particular point in the piece. The application of the coastline to the dynamic flux ensures that the piece will begin and end with relatively little dynamic fluctuation. At the high point, however, there will be a great deal of change of dynamic level.

The coastline labeled "Cutler" affects the textual density of a particular canonic line. In other words, it controls the proportion of playing time versus rest for a line. Thus, at the beginning of the piece there will be a 70% probability of a line having a note as opposed to a rest. That probability changes throughout the piece in response to the curvature of the coastline.

The third coastline from the top controls the general intervallic vocabulary for a particular moment of the piece. At the bottom of the "interval expansion" scale

	INSTRUMENT	
VOICE	MELODIC	RHYTHMIC
Hamilton	Viola	Harp
Oakville	Flute	Contrabass
Toronto	Voice	Marimba
Whitby	Euphonium	Marimba
Bowmanville	Synclavier	Synclavier
Newtonville	Synclavier	Synclavier
Port Hope	Synclavier	Synclavier
Coburg	Synclavier	Synclavier

FIGURE 8.19 Assignment of instruments to the canonic voices of *Canadian Coastlines*.

the interval vocabulary is restricted to a predomination of seconds with a few thirds. As the coastline rises to the Northeast, the number of allowed intervals increases from seconds through sevenths and falls back down near the end. The choice for this parameter was based on a variation of $1/f$ noise inspired by Benoit Mandelbrot's concepts.[31] The actual pitches chosen are arrived at indirectly by the succession of intervals. The process shapes the contour of the canon theme by weighting the choice of interval by the direction of the coastline, up or down. The coastline at the bottom of the figure controls the probabilities for rules that affect rhythm.

In addition to the use of the digital synthesizer for some of the sound in *Canadian Coastlines*, Austin took advantage of another aspect of the possibilities of digital synthesis as well. In order to make it possible for the eight canonic lines to be accurately coordinated in live performance, the composer used New England Digital Corporation's Synclavier synthesizer to prepare a separate "click track" for each of the lines. In performance the players wear small, ear-plug style earphones and follow the changing tempi of their parts from the clicks that they hear.

The click tracks make it possible to coordinate a performance of this rather complex work without a conductor. In fact, for the first performance of *Canadian Coastlines*, the musicians coordinated their live performance from broadcast studios in three different Canadian cities—Halifax, Toronto, and Winnepeg. The sound of the full "computer band" was mixed in the CBC studios in Toronto and broadcast throughout Canada from there.

8.2 Deterministic Composition with Computers

8.2A Introduction

Computers are particularly well-suited to aid in the composition of music where, at some level of the composition, there is an amount of repetition or recurrence of musical material. In contrast to the random generation of new musical patterns for compositional use, the computer can be used to manipulate input data that serves as the basic material of the composition. This compositional method is often implemented by first devising a short-hand or code by which the compositional operations and relationships are entered into the computer. The composition is then built through a sequence of commands that invoke programs for the performance of specific permutations and variations on designated parts of the input data. There are two principal types of music to which deterministic techniques are most commonly applied: motivic music and serial music. Canonic textures, which may or may not be either motivic or serial, also lend themselves to this sort of treatment. In this part of chapter 8, we will examine the use of the computer in all these types of music.

8.2B Motivic Music with Computers

A musical motive is the smallest melodic/rhythmic fragment of a musical theme— often only two or three notes—which can be independently varied and manipulated. Willi Apel writes that in the music of Bach and Beethoven, "motives are the

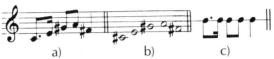

a)   b)   c)

EXAMPLE 8.14   A musical motive (a), its constituent pitch succession (b), and its rhythm (c).

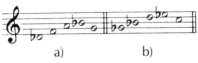

a)   b)

EXAMPLE 8.15   Transpositions of the motivic pitch succession up a half step (a) and up a tritone (b).

very building blocks or germinating cells of the musical composition."[32] One needs only to recall the ♩♩♩ motive of Beethoven's Fifth Symphony to realize how pervasive the motive elements of a musical composition can be.

In this century, motivic variation has been used by a number of composers for the unification of the elements of composition. Certain composers have constructed entire compositions out of single, simple motives.

To ensure sufficient variety in music built on a motive, the motive is typically subjected to an assortment of variation techniques. Some common variations of motives include repetition, transposition, and alteration of melodic contour and rhythmic features.

Example 8.14a shows a melodic/rhythmic motive. Examples 8.14b and c show the separate pitch and rhythmic components of the motive, respectively. Example 8.15 shows the effect of transposition of the pitches of the motive, first by one semitone (8.15a) and then by six semitones (8.15b).

The following subroutine transposes a sequence of pitches by a specified number of semitones. For simplicity, the pitches are represented by numerical codes in the range of 1 to 88, corresponding to the keys on a piano. In this system, for example, middle C is denoted by 40, and the C above that by 52. Many other notation schemes are in use, and the reader may have to adapt the algorithms that follow to the particular system used.

```
      SUBROUTINE TRNPOZ(NPITCH,IN,IOUT,NSTEPS)
C   THIS ROUTINE CAN ACCOMODATE SEQUENCES OF UP TO 20 PITCHES.
C   LONGER SEQUENCES ARE POSSIBLE BY CHANGING THE FOLLOWING DIMENSIONS.
      DIMENSION IN(20),IOUT(20)
      DO 20 N=1,NPITCH
      IOUT(N)=IN(N)+NSTEPS
C   THE FOLLOWING TWO STATEMENTS CHECK FOR PITCHES OUTSIDE THE RANGE
C   OF 1 TO 88 AND SET SUCH PITCHES TO THE APPROPRIATE LIMIT.
      IF(IOUT(N).GT.88) IOUT(N)=88
      IF(IOUT(N).LT.1) IOUT(N)=1
20    CONTINUE
      RETURN
      END
```

The argument NPITCH specifies the number of notes contained in the motive. IN is the first position in the array that holds the list of pitches to be transposed. IOUT is the first position in the array into which the result of the transposition is to be placed. The argument NSTEPS specifies the number of semi-tones encompassed in the transposition. It can be either positive or negative depending on the direction of transposition. The algorithm limits transposed pitches to the range of 1 to 88. For certain applications, the reader may wish to reduce the range.

The following example program illustrates the use of the subroutine. It transposes the motive of example 8.14 up two semi-tones. The array PITCH1 holds the original sequence of pitches as specified by the DATA statement. The transposed list is deposited in the array PITCH2.

```
          INTEGER PITCH1(8),PITCH2(8)
          DATA PITCH1/40,44,48,49,46/
     C  N IS THE NUMBER OF PITCHES IN THE SEQUENCE
          N=5
          NSTEPS=2
          CALL TRNPOZ(N,PITCH1(1),PITCH2(1),NSTEPS)
          STOP
          END
```

Readers wishing to translate FORTRAN code such as this into other programming languages must take note of the way in which arguments are passed to subroutines. Unlike FORTRAN, many languages do not allow an array to be passed simply by specifying the first position in it. In some languages, the arrays of pitches will have to be declared as common, or global arrays, and the routines altered accordingly.

Notice that in transposition, the melodic contour of the original motive is preserved. A common technique for the compositional variation of a motive is that of displacement of its pitches to other octaves. Example 8.16 shows instances of *registral displacement* of the motive in example 8.14a. In example 8.16a the final two pitches are placed one octave below their original. Example 8.16b shows the motive in ascending intervals, and example 8.16c scatters the pitches over a three and a half octave range. Of course, it is common to apply registral displacement to transpositions of motives, as well.

For the following registral displacement subroutine the musician supplies a succession of pitches and displacements. The later is represented by the number of octaves, up or down, which a particular pitch is to move. The subroutine returns the registrally transformed motive.

```
          SUBROUTINE REGDSP(NPITCH,IN,IOUT,REG)
          DIMENSION IN(20),IOUT(20)
          INTEGER REG(20)
          DO 20 N=1,NPITCH
          IOUT(N)=IN(N)+12*REG(N)
          IF(IOUT(N).GT.88) IOUT(N)=88
          IF(IOUT(N).LT.1) IOUT(N)=1
     20   CONTINUE
          RETURN
          END
```

As above, the argument NPITCH specifies the number of pitches in the motive. IN and IOUT designate the first position in the input and output arrays of pitches, respectively. REG marks the first position in the array which holds the registral displacements. There are always as many elements in the array REG as there are in each of the pitch arrays.

a)   b)   c)

EXAMPLE 8.16   Three displacements of the registers of the motivic pitch succession.

As an example, the following program uses the subroutine above to displace the pitches of the motive in example 8.14a (stored in array PITCH1) by the amounts specified in the array REGISTER. The resulting list of pitches is stored in the array PITCH2 and for the indicated data takes the form of example 8.16c.

```
      INTEGER PITCH1(10),PITCH2(10),REGISTER(10)
      DATA PITCH1/40,44,48,49,46/
      DATA REGISTER/-2,-1,0,-1,1/
C   N IS THE NUMBER OF PITCHES IN THE MOTIVE
      N=5
      CALL REGDSP(N,PITCH1(1),PITCH2(1),REGISTER(1))
      STOP
      END
```

Another often encountered operation on the pitches of a motive is that of *inversion*. Example 8.17 shows an inversion of the motive. Notice that the inversion operation is the reversal of the direction of the intervals, exactly in semitones and not simply a changing of the melodic contour of the motive. Naturally, transposition of the inversion is also possible.

The following subroutine inverts the pitches of an input motive.

```
      SUBROUTINE INVERT(NPITCH,IN,IOUT)
      DIMENSION IN(20),IOUT(20)
C   THE FIRST PITCH REMAINS THE SAME
      IOUT(1)=IN(1)
      DO 20 N=2,NPITCH
      IOUT(N)=IOUT(N-1)-(IN(N)-IN(N-1))
      IF(IOUT(N).GT.88) IOUT(N)=88
      IF(IOUT(N).LT.1) IOUT(N)=1
20    CONTINUE
      RETURN
      END
```

The arguments of the subroutine have the same meaning as in the TRANSPOSE subroutine above.

Example 8.18 shows the *retrograde* of the motive. Retrograde is the reversal of the order of the pitches of a motive. The retrograde subroutine produces an exact reversal of the order of the input motive.

```
      SUBROUTINE RETRO(NPITCH,IN,IOUT)
      DIMENSION IN(20),IOUT(20)
      DO 20 N=1,NPITCH
      L=NPITCH-N+1
      IOUT(L)=IN(N)
20    CONTINUE
      RETURN
      END
```

Once again, the same arguments are used. One can also combine the previous routines in order to make an inversion of the retrograde of a motive.

Example 8.19 shows two less-standard operations on motives. In 8.19a the intervals of the motive have been expanded by one semitone so that it contains only

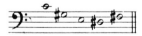

EXAMPLE 8.17   Inversion of the motive's pitch succession.

EXAMPLE 8.18   Retrograde of the motive's pitch succession.

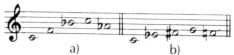

a)   b)

EXAMPLE 8.19   Expansion (a) and contraction (b) of the motive's interval succession.

the perfect fourth, major second, and major third, and no minor seconds or minor thirds. A contraction of the intervals is shown in example 8.19b. Here, all intervals except minor seconds are reduced by a semitone each. The minor second is arbitrarily exempted from contraction in this example to avoid repeating tones.

The following subroutine implements both expansion and contraction. The number of semitones is specified by the argument NSTEPS. A positive value of NSTEPS indicates expansion; a negative one indicates contraction. The algorithm does not permit an interval to be contracted to less than a minor second. Further, if the original motive contains repeated notes, the algorithm retains the repetitions.

```
      SUBROUTINE EXPAND(NPITCH,IN,IOUT,NSTEPS)
      DIMENSION IN(20),IOUT(20)
C  FIRST PITCH REMAINS THE SAME.
      IOUT(1)=IN(1)
      DO 20 N=2,NPITCH
      IF(IN(N).NE.IN(N-1)) GO TO 10
C  IF A NOTE IS REPEATED, DO NOT EXPAND.
      IOUT(N)=IOUT(N-1)
      GO TO 20
C
C  DETERMINE DIRECTION OF INTERVAL; IDRECT=+1 INDICATES ASCENDING.
C                                   IDRECT=-1 INDICATES DESCENDING.
C
C  THE ISIGN FUNCTION RETURNS THE SIGN OF THE SECOND ARGUMENT.
10    IDRECT=ISIGN(1,IN(N)-IN(N-1))
C  COMPUTE NEW INTERVAL AS SUM OF OLD INTERVAL PLUS NSTEPS EXPANSION.
      INTRVL=ABS(IN(N)-IN(N-1))+NSTEPS
C  CHECK FOR INTERVALS LESS THAN MINOR SECOND.
      IF(INTRVL.LT.1) INTRVL=1
      IOUT(N)=IOUT(N-1)+IDRECT*INTRVL
C  THE NEXT TWO STATEMENTS SET PITCH VALUES THAT ARE OUTSIDE THE
C  RANGE 1 TO 88 TO ONE THE RANGE LIMITS.
      IF(IOUT(N).GT.88) IOUT(N)=88
      IF(IOUT(N).LT.1) IOUT(N)=1
20    CONTINUE
      RETURN
      END
```

The arguments IN, IOUT, and NPITCH have the same meaning as above.

There are numerous examples in music literature of operations on the rhythm of motives. Example 8.20 shows three transformations of the motivic rhythm of Example 8.14c. Example 8.20a is an augmentation of the motivic rhythm and 8.20b is a diminution. The operations are shown here in relationship of common music notation. Here, they represent a change in duration in each case by a factor of 2. More complicated relationships, some of which could be very difficult to notate for instrumental performance, can be implemented with ease for computer synthesis.

The third example (8.20c) shows the retrograde of the rhythm of the motive of example 8.14c.

The computer can be programmed to transform rhythmic motives through algorithms similar to those presented above for pitch. It is necessary to represent

a)   b)   c)

EXAMPLE 8.20   Augmentation (a), diminution (b), and retrograde (c) of the motive's rhythm.

the rhythmic values in some kind of numeric code. Naturally, it is assumed that the composer would combine separate operations on the pitch and rhythm of a motive in order to build a composition of this sort.

8.2C   Compositional Uses of Computers with Motivic Music

Computers have proven to be helpful in the composition of music where the clear interrelationships of motivic material are manipulated to form the surface of the composition. Example 8.21 shows the first three phrases of "Cadenza", the fourth of Dexter Morrill's *Studies for Trumpet and Tape* (1975).[33] Here each phrase of the trumpet part has the same shape, ending on a sustained D5. The tape part is similar

EXAMPLE 8.21   The first three phrases of "Cadenza" from Dexter Morrill's *Studies for Trumpet and Tape*. (*Reprinted with the permission of Dexter Morrill.*)

in all three phrases, consisting of a line rising in the bass and followed by the answer of "distant trumpets" in the treble register. The "distant trumpets" consist of computer trumpets playing variations on the opening line of the live instrument. The basic "rising line" was put into the computer and then varied by using the "motive" feature of Leland Smith's SCORE program.[34] The second and third phrases were produced as programmed variations on the first phrase, thus eliminating the necessity to re-enter into the computer all the notes of the subsequent phrases.

Another example of motivic manipulation with the computer in Morrill's composition comes in measures 14, 15, 16 of the same movement (see example 8.22). Here, the computer echoes the trumpet motive in measure 14 and then presents the same motive in rhythmic augmentation and at different transpositions in a descending pattern through measures 15 and 16.

Gareth Loy, whose techniques of musique concrète with computers were discussed in chapter 7, has employed motivic manipulations extensively in his composition *Nekyia*.[35] In addition to the standard motivic techniques of transposition, inversion, retrogression, augmentation, and diminution, Loy employs techniques that can only be realized on the computer. These include "progressive, linear, and non-linear scaling of melodic contours where the scaling itself is subjected to mutation. A simple example would be a gradual pitch expansion or contraction through time of small repeated melodic phrases." One of the motivic techniques that Loy applies to the time dimension of the work is involved in the transformation of a rhythmic motive consisting of "a grace note followed by a sixteenth, followed by a dotted eighth tied to a rest... . This fragment is repeated over and over, each time becoming less and less like the original rhythmic statement of the fragment and more and more like its rhythmic inversion. [This is accomplished by] an interpolation of the duration of the notes in the phrase by millisecond amounts from its rhythmic rectus to its inversion."[36]

EXAMPLE 8.22 Motivic variation in Dexter Morrill's *Studies for Trumpet and Tape.* (*Reprinted with the permission of Dexter Morrill.*)

8.2D Canonic Imitation with Computers

The computer can greatly facilitate the composition of works that include the canonic imitation of one voice by another. The imitation can be applied systematically by computer programs, even when there are subtle differences in speed between the parts of the canon. Example 8.23 shows the opening of *Study No. 36 for Player Piano* by Conlon Nancarrow.[37] The four voices of the strict canon proceed through the melody in the tempo proportions of 17:18:19:20. Thus, all voices have the same number of measures, but all proceed at different tempi. The plan of the piece is for successively faster tempi 85, 90, 95, 100 for the four lines) so that the voices all come to the same place in the canon for a brief moment in the middle of the work. After that point, they diverge but now with the slowest voice trailing the others more and more until it is left to finish the work as it had begun, alone.

EXAMPLE 8.23 The opening of *Study No. 36 for Player Piano* by Conlon Nancarrow. (*Published with permission of Soundings Press.*)

In the Nancarrow example all lines proceed at a fixed, constant tempo. With computer software, it is relatively straight forward to create canonic lines that entail continuous change of tempi, as well. Realization of the lines by means of digital synthesis, as with player pianos, presents no problems that need to be solved by human performers. The limits are simply those of human perception.

One of the most extensive computer-music examples of a canon in which the parts independently accelerate and ritard is Larry Austin's *Canadian Coastlines*, described in section 8.1H.

Another method for producing a computer-music canon in which acceleration and deceleration of the parts occurs is through the use of a score pre-processor such as Score 11.[38] Example 8.24 illustrates the use of Score 11 for this purpose. The two voices of the canonic fragment have exactly the same parameter lists. Their differences lie in the later entrance of the second voice and the "tempo" statements for each voice. The tempo for the first voice accelerates over the first 12 beats from beat=60 to beat=120. It then ritards over the next 12 beats back to the original tempo. The pattern of tempo of the second voice is quite different. The voice enters 6 beats after the first, and then accelerates for 18 beats from beat=60 to beat=120. Example 8.25 shows the music notation for the canonic fragment.

```
i1 0 24;
tempo 12 60 120/ 12 120 60;
p3 rh 8./16/8*2/4*2;
p4 no c4/e/gs/a/fs;
p5 nu 20000;
end;
i2 6 18;
tempo 18 60 120;
p3 rh 8./16/8*2/4*2;
p4 no c4/e/gs/a/fs;
p5 nu 20000;
end;
```

EXAMPLE 8.24   Computer score for a canonic fragment in which the two parts have different patterns of change of tempo.

EXAMPLE 8.25   Music notation for the canonic fragment of example 8.24.

Observe that it would be difficult to create a canon of this sort where the two voices begin with successive entrances and then follow different rates and shapes of acceleration and ritard such that the lines reach their ending points simultaneously. Even though Score 11 supplies a variety of "shapes" from which to choose for the tempo change, it would still be difficult. John Rogers has proposed and implemented a general solution to the problem.[39] Through careful definition of the meanings of acceleration and ritard, Rogers has written software that enables one to map accelerating and ritarding lines into a user-specified span of time. The program then calculates the steepness of the tempo change curve in order to fit the desired span of time. John Melby has employed Rogers' software extensively to create canonic textures in which he varies the acceleration and ritard at different rates within the same time span.

8.2E   Serial Music with Computers

Computer-aided composition has been successfully applied to composition of music based on 12-tone rows. In some ways, 12-tone composition can be viewed as a more systematic approach to motivic composition, because in 12-tone music, all the pitch material is derived from a single ordering of all 12 tones of the chromatic collection. The major difference between them is that a 12-tone row does not imply a registral disposition or a rhythmic pattern. In "classical" 12-tone technique, the operations of transposition, inversion, retrogression, and retrograde inversion are applied to the 12-tone row to produce other orderings of the chromatic collection.[40] Example

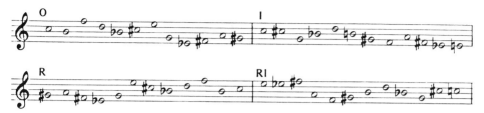

EXAMPLE 8.26   The original (O) twelve-tone row and its inversion (I), its retrograde (R), and its retrograde-inversion (RI).

Original:	0	11	5	2	10	1	4	7	3	6	9	8
Retrograde:	8	9	6	3	7	4	1	10	2	5	11	0
Inversion:	0	1	7	10	2	11	8	5	9	6	3	4
Retrograde–Inversion:	4	3	6	9	5	8	11	2	10	7	1	0

TABLE 8.6   Numerical Representation of Four Forms of a Twelve-Tone Row.

8.26 shows the four basic forms of a 12-tone row. The 12-tone series implies nothing about the musical use in terms of register, and so the notation shows only the pitch-classes without any octave placement.

When making twelve-tone music with the computer, each pitch-class is given a numerical code in the range of 0 through 11. Table 8.5 shows the same twelve-tone row as Example 8.26, this time expressed numerically with 0=C, 1=C♯, etc. This notation enables an operation on a row, or set, to be stated mathematically. Subroutines for the operations of classical twelve-tone music are shown below. The subroutines indicate that transposition is the addition of a constant to the pitch-class number, modulo 12. For example, the transposition of pitch-class 7 by 8 semitones is 3. That is, $7+8=15$; then the remainder of $15 \div 12$ is 3. Inversion is the complementation of the pitch-class number—the result of subtracting the pitch-class number from 12, modulo 12. Retrogression is the reversal of the order of the pitch-classes, and retrograde-inversion is the reversal of order of the pitch-classes along with their complementation, modulo 12.

```
      SUBROUTINE TRNPOZ(NSTEPS,IN,IOUT)
C   TRANSPOSES THE TWELVE-TONE ROW IN ARRAY IN BY NSTEPS.
      DIMENSION IN(12),IOUT(12)
      DO 20 K=1,12
      L=IN(K)+NSTEPS
      IOUT(K)=MOD(L,12)
20    CONTINUE
      RETURN
      END
```

The argument NSTEPS indicates the number of half steps of the transposition. In this subroutine and the ones that follow, the argument IN represents the first position in the array containing the row which is to undergo the operation. Similarly, the argument IOUT denotes the position in the array where the results of the operation are placed.

```
      SUBROUTINE INVERT(IN,IOUT)
C   INVERTS THE TWELVE-TONE ROW CONTAINED IN ARRAY IN.
      DIMENSION IN(12),IOUT(12)
      DO 20 K=1,12
      IOUT(K)=12-IN(K)
      IF(IOUT(K).EQ.12) IOUT(K)=0
20    CONTINUE
      RETURN
      END
```

```
      SUBROUTINE RETRO(IN,IOUT)
C   CALCULATES RETROGRADE OF TWELVE-TONE ROW CONTAINED IN ARRAY IN.
      DIMENSION IN(12),IOUT(12)
      DO 20 K=1,12
      L=13-K
      IOUT(L)=IN(K)
20    CONTINUE
      RETURN
      END
```

The retrograde-inversion operation can be realized by successive application of the RETRO and INVERT subroutines.

As an example, the following program demonstrates the use of the RETRO subroutine. The row to be reversed is stored in the array ROWA which is filled with an example row by the DATA statement. The result of the retrograde operation is deposited in the array ROWB. Notice that the arguments of RETRO denote the first position in each array.

```
C   EXAMPLE CALLING PROGRAM
      INTEGER ROWA(12),ROWB(12)
      DATA ROWA/1,3,5,7,9,11,0,2,4,6,8,10/
      CALL RETRO(ROWA(1),ROWB(1))
      STOP
      END
```

In addition to the classical twelve-tone operations, contemporary composers commonly perform the M5 and M7 operations on the row used. The M5 operation is the reordering of the pitch-classes by multiplying each member of the row by 5, modulo 12. M7 performs a similar permutation through multiplying by 7, modulo 12. The subroutines for M5 and M7, shown below, have the same arguments as the routines above.

```
      SUBROUTINE M7(IN,IOUT)
C   PERFORMS M7 OPERATION ON TWELVE-TONE ROW CONTAINED IN ARRAY IN.
      DIMENSION IN(12),IOUT(12)
      DO 20 K=1,12
      L=IN(K)*7
      IOUT(K)=MOD(L,12)
20    CONTINUE
      RETURN
      END
```

```
      SUBROUTINE M5(IN,IOUT)
C   PERFORMS M5 OPERATION ON TWELVE-TONE ROW CONTAINED IN ARRAY IN.
      DIMENSION IN(12),IOUT(12)
      DO 20 K=1,12
      L=IN(K)*5
      IOUT(K)=MOD(L,12)
20    CONTINUE
      RETURN
      END
```

Composers since the Second World War have applied principles of serialization to additional dimensions of the music. Serial ordering of a number of parameters including rhythm, dynamics, register, timbre, and articulation has been implemented in some cases. In the following dicussion, we will show three different methods that have been employed for serializing rhythm.

The first method, and perhaps the simplest, is to create a series of durations analogous to the series of pitch-classes. Once a durational row is established, it can be subjected to the same permutations as the pitch row. Example 8.27a shows 12 duration classes and their ordering into a series. Example 8.27b shows the inversion, retrograde, and retrograde-inversion of the series. For convenience we use the row shown in example 8.26. Many European composers including Olivier

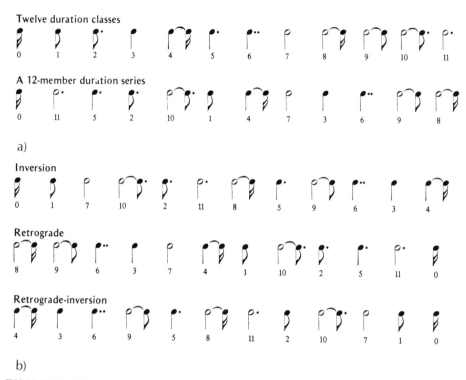

Twelve duration classes

0 1 2 3 4 5 6 7 8 9 10 11

A 12-member duration series

0 11 5 2 10 1 4 7 3 6 9 8

a)

Inversion

0 1 7 10 2 11 8 5 9 6 3 4

Retrograde

8 9 6 3 7 4 1 10 2 5 11 0

Retrograde-inversion

4 3 6 9 5 8 11 2 10 7 1 0

b)

EXAMPLE 8.27 (a) Twelve duration classes and their ordering into a twelve-member duration series. (b) Inversion, retrograde, and retrograde-inversion of duration series shown in figure 8.27a.

Messiaen, Pierre Boulez, and Luigi Nono have employed serialization of rhythm in their works using methods similar to the one demonstrated above.[41] In actual practice there is no restriction against using a different row for each separate musical parameter; nor, for that matter, against using a durational series with, for example, 7 members instead of 12.

For our second method it is common practice to employ the same series for both pitch and rhythm. American composers Milton Babbitt, Charles Wuorinen, and others have used this technique, known as the time-point system.[42] The time-point system equates the modulus of the octave in pitch to the modulus of the measure in time. The implementation of the time-point system, then, is in measures with twelve attack points each, such as 3/4 (12 ♪'s), 4/4 (12^{-3}♪'s), 12/8 (12 ♪'s), and so on.

The "time-pointing" of a twelve-tone row involves the assignment of the pitch-class numbers to the corresponding rhythmic division of the measure. To maintain the correct order of the row, the time points are placed in ascending order within a measure; lower pitch-class numbers are assigned to the proper place in the measure following. Consider the row of example 8.26—0, 11, 5, 2, 10, 1, 4, 7, 3, 6, 9, 8, which translates into the following succession of time points:

0   11   5   2   10 1 4 7   3 6 9   8

The other twelve-tone operations—transposition, retrograde, inversion, and re-

EXAMPLE 8.28 An example from Wuorinen in which the time-point modulus (the measure) varies. (*Reprinted with the permission of Longman, Inc.*)

trograde-inversion—are made simply by "time-pointing" the form of the set derived by that operation or combination of operations.

Wuorinen has pointed out[43] that there can be a wide variety of applications for the time-point system. For example, using the same basic set, there is no requirement for a one-to-one conformance of pitch and time-point set. Thus, the succession of time-point sets may be completely different from the succession of pitch sets. He has also shown how the modulus for the time points may be altered in length for every measure while retaining the basic characteristic of relating all the time points to each other. Example 8.28 shows such a situation. Other examples from his book show situations in which the time-point set determines changes in dynamics instead of changes in pitch.

Serialization of successions of rhythmic proportions has been employed in composition by Henry Weinberg,[44] John Melby, and others. Melby has carried this approach quite thoroughly into computer-aided composition in which the entire surface of the composition is built with compositional subroutines. The rhythmic system that Melby employs begins with the composition of a series of proportions which yields twelve attack points. The series of proportions, not the attack points themselves, are then subjected to transformations by operations. For example, the proportions 1:5, 5:1, 3:2, 2:1, and 1:3 yield the following succession of twelve attack points:

(The ratios mean "one in the time of five beats", "five in the time of one beat", "three in the time of two beats", and so on.) The inversion of the series is 5:1, 1:5, 2:3, 1:2, and 3:1 with musical notation

The retrograde of the series is 1:3, 2:1, 3:2, 5:1, and 1:5, or

Finally the inversion of the retrograde in Melby's system would be: 3:1, 1:2, 2:3, 1:5, and 5:1, or

Unlike the time-point system, there is no provision for permuting the order of the attack points by the operation of transposition. Instead, Melby uses musical tempo as the temporal analogy to transposition in pitch. For example, playing the same passage 3:2 faster would be analogous in Melby's temporal system to transposition in frequency by the interval of the perfect fifth.

Because Melby implements his rhythmic system in compositions where the sound is computed by digital synthesis, he is able to project voices in different tempi simultaneously, thus implementing a polyphony of temporal relationships analogous to the polyphony of simultaneous voices at various transposition levels in pitch. Without the feature of simultaneous different tempi, his music—to continue the analogy—would consist of polyphony of pitch but monophony of tempo.

In addition to rhythm, Melby has applied the principles of serialism to a number of other musical parameters. In the next section, we will examine his use of the computer in the composition of one of his works.

8.2F Compositional Uses of Computers in Serial Music

John Melby creates the surface detail of his music by means of compositional subroutines, thus eliminating much of the hand-calculation and manual input often associated with computer synthesis.

The results of compositional subroutines can be heard in certain passages of Melby's *Forandre: Seven Variations for Digital Computer*.[45] In Variations Two and Six, for example, rapid streams of pitches are played over "cantus firmi." The fast notes are twelve-tone rows for which Melby specified only order of set succession, speed of notes, and register. The computer generated the actual pitches by means of general directions indicated by the composer in a compositional subroutine.

Melby's composition *Chor der Steine* (1979)[46] won first prize in the annual Electro-Acoustic Music Competition in Bouges, France. The work, realized using the MUSIC 360 language, was the result of an elaborate computer-aided system for

P1 — Instrument number.
P2 — Starting time.
P3 — Duration.
P4 — Amplitude.
P5 — Pitch.
P6 — Amplitude factor for output channel A.
P7 — When >0 causes rearticulations of the note.
P8 — If the note is rearticulated, P8 determines, indirectly, the repetition rate.
P9 — Another indirect control on repetition rate.
P10 — When >0 determines the interval of a tremolo or trill on the note.
P11 — A "bookkeeping" value used to determine the duration of certain notes.
P12 — When >0 causes the attack of the note to be accented. The accenting is applied to all notes on downbeats of measures.

TABLE 8.7   Parameters Used in Melby's *Chor de Steine*.

composition. The orchestra for the composition consisted of 15 or more instrument designs that implemented various sound-synthesis techniques, including additive, FM, and subtractive synthesis. Table 8.7 shows a list of the twelve parameters for each note of *Chor der Steine*. An important aspect of Melby's methodology is that all instrument designs for a composition assign the same meaning to the same parameter number. In this way a single group of compositional subroutines can be applied to all note statements of all instruments.

For example, the assignment of instrument number according to various criteria is one way in which Melby partitioned the pitch successions into various groupings. For a given line, Melby assigned one computer instrument if the note was "on the beat" and another if the starting time was off the beat. If the note was on the beat, it would also be "accented"—played at twice the amplitude for the attack portion of the tone.

Compositional subroutines were employed to supply the pitch successions of *Chor der Steine*. First Melby provided an ordering of the twelve tones without respect to register. For this piece the first-order all-combinatorial set[47] used was: 0,3,2,1,4,5,6,7,11,8,10,9. Next, Melby's program called compositional subroutines to manipulate and articulate the twelve tones. The permutation options available in the system were transposition, inversion, retrogression, retrograde-inversion, M5, and M7. Additional compositional subroutines assigned octave placement of the particular pitch-classes. One method created passages in which the 12-tone rows ascended or descended over six or seven octaves. Another method set the octave constant for a line and then changed the octave of certain notes. For example, all the notes on the beat could be set to the same octave number. Once a line or texture of lines was set, all or any part of it could be copied in canon by means of a routine to which the single argument was the duration of the canonic offset.

An option of trill or tremolo was also available through the compositional subroutines. A routine set the width of the trill in semitones and caused the note to trill either to the next note in the row or to the note *n* places hence in the row, where *n* is a variable input to the routine by the composer. The rate of the trill depended on the tempo assigned to the row of which the note was a member.

In *Chor de Steine*, Melby worked extensively with temporal relationships. For this purpose, he used a compositional subroutine developed by John Rogers. (See Section 8.2D.) The function of Rogers' programs is to perform the computations necessary to enable simultaneous different tempi in which changes of tempi occur. There were further subroutines that operated on the durations of the notes. Before acceleration or deceleration had been applied to a line, the notes of that line could be shortened or lengthened.

To summarize, Melby has used the logical and arithmetic powers of the medium to implement serial rhythmic and pitch operations, by programming the computer to execute many of the tasks that formerly had been performed by the composer. The great advantage of such a system for the composer is that the music can then be composed at the level of phrase and section. Melby specifies a background onto which a foreground is overlaid with the aid of computer programs.

Barry Vercoe's *Synapse for Viola and Computer-Synthesized Tape*[48] has a number of interesting features. It is a twelve-tone work in which the combinatorial relationships[49] between viola and tape are carefully controlled. The overall shape of the work involves a progression from relative clarity of texture and rhythmic homophony in the first few measures (example 8.29) through a middle section of great contrapuntal subtlety, to a very diverse and dense polyphony before the climax of the work. There is a return to relative simplicity near the end of the work. Example 8.30 shows the performance score for the point in the work where the texture is at its thickest. Here, where the viola and tape each play six-note groups, the tape part was composed with the aid of a computer program that disposed the six-note groups according to the set form designated by the composer. Vercoe specified only the set form and the general dynamic and envelope characteristics of the music for the passage; the computer supplied the sound on the basis of the composer's general directions.

Vercoe composed *Synapse* during a very short period of intense activity in the fall of 1976. He employed two useful methods when working on the composition. First, he would compose a passage at his desk at home, and then, later that same day, program the computer to play the passage at MIT's Experimental Music Studio. This gave him an immediate aural feedback on his musical ideas.

EXAMPLE 8.29   Opening of Barry Vercoe's *Synapse*. (*Published with the permission of Barry Vercoe.*)

EXAMPLE 8.30   Section from the middle of *Synapse*. (*Published with the permission of Barry Vercoe.*)

Because the first performance was to take place shortly after the completion of the composition, Vercoe took advantage of another feature of computer synthesis of sound for making the task of learning the viola part easier. He prepared a tape for the violist with synthesized accompaniment in one audio channel and computer realization of the viola part in the other. Using this tape, the violist could practice the part either with the accompaniment alone, or with a "correct" performance of his own part with which to play along. This method helped Marcus Thompson learn to play the difficult part in a very short time.

Notes

1. Howe, H. S., Jr., and Kassler, Michael. "Computers and Music." In Stanley Sadie (ed.), The New Grove Dictionary of Music and Musicians. Washington, D.C.: Groves Dictionaries of Music, Inc., 1980, 603–615.
2. Roads, Curtis. Composing Grammars (2nd ed.). San Francisco: Computer Music Association, 1978.
3. Pierce, J. R. Symbols, Signals, and Noise. New York: Harper Row, 1961. (See chapter 3.)
4. McNabb, Michael. "Dreamsong: The Composition." Computer Music Journal, 5(4), 1981, 36–54.
5. Kreysig, Erwin. Advanced Engineering Mathematics (2nd ed.). New York: Wiley, 1967, 714.
6. Knuth, Donald. The Art of Computer Programming (Vol. 2) Semi-Numerical Algorithms (2nd ed.). Reading: Addison-Wesley, 1973, 115.
7. Ruckdeschel, F. R. BASIC Scientific Subroutines (vol. 1). Petersborough, N. H. : Byte McGraw-Hill, 1981, 157.
8. Knuth, 117.
9. Hiller, L., and Isaacson, L. Experimental Music. New York: McGraw-Hill, 1959.
10. Olson, Harry, F. Music, Physics, and Engineering (2nd ed.). New York: Dover, 1967, 430–434.
11. Gardner, Martin. "White and Brown Music, Fractal Curves and 1/f Fluctuations." Scientific American, 238(4), 1978, 16–31.
12. Petersen, Tracy L. "Interactive Digital Composition." Proceedings of the 1978 International Computer Music Conference, Northwestern University, 1978, 167–174.
13. Keshner, Marvin. "1/f Noise." Proceedings of the Institute of Electrical and Electronic Engineers, 70(3), 1982, 212–218.
14. Clarke, J., and R. F. Voss. "1/f Noise in Music: Music from 1/f Noise." Journal of the Acoustical Society of America, 63(1), 1978, 258–263.
15. Gardner, 1978. (See Voss's algorithm.)
16. Ibid.
17. Hiller and Isaacson, 1959.
18. Fux, Johann Joseph. "The Study of Counterpoint," (Alfred Mann, trans. and ed.). New York: Norton, 1975.
19. Hiller and Isaacson, 1959, 132–135.
20. Hiller, Lejaren A., Jr., and Baker, Robert A. "Computer Cantata: A Study in Compositional Method." Perspectives of New Music, 3(1), 1964, 69–90.
21. Ibid.
22. Hiller, Lejaren A. "Composing with Computers: A Progress Report." Computer Music Journal, 5(4), 1981, 7–21.
23. Xenakis, Iannis. Formalized Music. Bloomington: Indiana University Press, 1971, 182.

24. Myhill, John. "Stochastic Music Program." *Proceedings of the Third International Computer Music Conference*, Northwestern University, 1978, 272–317.

25. Roads, Curtis. "An Interview with Gottfried Michael Koenig." *Computer Music Journal*, 2(3), 1978, 11–16.

26. Koenig, Gottfried Michael. "The Use of Computer Programmes in Creating Music." Music and Technology, La Revue Musicale, Paris, 1971, 93–116.

27. Truax, Barry. "The POD System of Interactive Composition Programs." *Computer Music Journal*, 1(3), 1977, 30–39.

28. Wuorinen, Charles. "Time's Encomium." Nonesuch Records (H-71225), 1969.

29. Wuorinen, Charles. *Simple Composition*. New York: Longman, 1979.

30. Austin, Larry. "Hybrid Musics: Four Compositions." Irida Records (022), 1980. (See especially the album notes.)

31. Mandelbrot, Benoit B. *Fractals: Form, Chance, and Dimension*. San Francisco: Freeman, 1977.

32. Apel, Willi. *Harvard Dictionary of Music* (17th printing). Cambridge, Mass.: Harvard University Press, 1966, 462.

33. Morrill, Dexter. "Studies for Trumpet and Computer." Chenago Valley Music Press, 1975. (Recorded on Golden Crest Records, (RE-7068, 1976.)

34. Smith, Leland. "Score: A Musician's Approach to Computer Music." *Journal of the Audio Engineering Society*, 20(1), 1972, 7–14.

35. Loy, Gareth. "Nekyia." Doctoral dissertation, Stanford University, 1979.

36. Ibid.

37. Nancarrow, Conlon. "Study No. 36 for Player Piano, Selected Studies for Player Piano." In Peter Garland (ed.), *Soundings* (Book 4). Berkeley, Calif.: 220–272, 1977.

38. Brinkman, Alexander. "Data Structures for a Music-11 Preprocessor" (Score 11). Proceedings of the International Computer Music Conference, North Texas State University, Denton, Texas, 1981.

39. Rogers, John, and John Rockstroh. "Score Time and Real-Time." *Proceedings of the 1978 International Computer Music Conference*, Northwestern University, 1978, 332–353.

40. Babbitt, Milton. "Some Aspects of Twelve-Tone Composition." *The Score and I.M.A. Magazine*, 1955, 53–61. (Reprinted in *Twentieth Century View of Music History*, New York: Scribner's, 1972, 364–371.

41. Smith-Brindle, Reginald. *Serial Composition*. London: Oxford University Press, 1966, 163–167.

42. Babbitt, Milton. "Twelve-Tone Rhythmic Structure and the Electronic Medium." *Perspectives of New Music*, 1(1), 1962, 49–79. (Reprinted in *Perspectives on Contemporary Music Theory*, Benjamin Boretz and Edward T. Cone, eds., New York: Norton, 1972, 148–179.

43. Wuorinen, 1979, 139–140.

44. Weinberg, Henry. "A Method of Transferring the Pitch Organization of a Twelve-Tone Set through All Layers of a Composition." Doctoral dissertation, Princeton University, 1966.

45. Melby, John. "Forandre: Seven Variations for a Digital Computer." *Proceedings of the American Society of University Composers* (Vol. 7–8), 1973. (Recorded supplement.)

46. Melby, John. "Chor der Steine." Advance Records (FGR-285), 1982.

47. Babbitt, 1962.

48. Vercoe, Barry. "Synapse." Composers Recording Inc. (CRI SD393), 1978.

49. Babbitt, 1962.

9

REAL-TIME PERFORMANCE
OF COMPUTER MUSIC

Most of the work in computer music between 1955 and 1980 was classified as "research" and was done in universities; much of the work in developing real-time performance systems has been done by commercial enterprises.

In this rapidly developing field, any treatment of specific products and commercially available systems must be undertaken by periodical journals that can respond to the rapid changes that are continually taking place. This chapter will present an overview of the field and some insights into the general considerations for design and use of real-time systems. The work of a number of individuals involved in the live performance of computer music is also discussed.

9.1 Modes of Synthesizer Operation

The choice of the modes of operation of a real-time computer system is influenced by compositional and musical references as well as by hardware and software limitations.

In the "electronic organ" mode of real-time computer music, the synthesizer has preset instrument designs in much the same way that an organ is equipped with stops. The instrument is played manually, usually by means of an organ-type keyboard. The number and complexity of the preselected sound designs varies from one system to another, but generally, a wide range of timbres and types of sounds is available. The range on most systems is at least as broad as that found on most electronic organs. The performer can use pre-programmed ("canned") instruments, sounds designed for a specific composition, or a combination of the two.

There are several advantages to the "electronic organ" mode. In addition to the wide range of timbres generally available, some systems allow the performer to interact with the sound of the instrument by "tuning" the timbre with controls on the console. The successful use of these systems generally depends heavily upon the traditional skills of a keyboard performer.

As Stanley Haynes noted in his dissertation, "The most distinctive innovation offered by the computer-controlled digital synthesizer is the possibility of preparing in advance material which may be accurately reproduced in performance but may also be modified using real-time controls."[1]

In the "music minus one" mode, the live performer adds an additional part to a pre-programmed musical texture, usually by means of an organ keyboard. The prerecorded texture consists of all score and sound materials not to be performed live. The instructions and data are prepared in advance and stored on some medium (usually floppy or hard disk). During the performance, the live keyboard part is played simultaneously with the materials as they are retrieved from the disk.

The live computer-music performance system often functions in this mode as a multi-track recording device. The performer can make one pass at a part of a musical texture and then replay that track while recording the next layer, and so on. The individual layers are stored as computer instructions and data, however, and so can be edited easily and directly. The "music minus one" mode has a greater flexibility and facility of performance than the "electronic organ" mode, because only part of the musical score is performed live. Thus, the textures generally can be denser than is otherwise possible with a performer. One of the earliest implementations of this mode was designed for the GROOVE system—a digital/analog hybrid system at the Bell Laboratories.[2] (See section 9.3.)

"Player piano" mode stands at an opposite extreme to the "electronic organ" mode. Here the score and orchestra information are prepared in advance of the performance. The live-performance system runs on its own during the performance. This might in some cases result in a situation little different from playing a tape recorder at the concert. In others, however, it could offer significant differences. For example, by using random processes, the score can differ greatly from one performance to another.

"Conductor" mode, where a pre-established score is "interpreted" during playback, is related to the "player piano" mode. However, in "conductor" mode the performer intervenes to influence the evolution of a performance. The degree of intervention and interaction can range from control of nuance in the sound of a predetermined score to control over random processes that create an entire score. One of the ways "conductor" mode is used is to initiate the performance of predefined subscores at the desired times. (See SSSP system, section 9.3.)

9.2 Peripheral Devices for Manual Control of Live Performance

To communicate with the computer, the musician uses peripheral devices that place restrictions on the possibilities for interaction. In conjunction with the selection of software, the composer can choose the control devices that give the performer the degree of freedom appropriate to the composition. In this section, a number of the peripherals used today in live-performance systems will be discussed.

The piano-style keyboard (*clavier*) is often employed simply to play the computer synthesizer in real time. The type of clavier varies from one system to another. Some claviers act simply as a group of switches to transmit pitch and timing information, whereas others include information about the velocity and/or key pressure as well. Some keyboards determine the velocity of a key by measuring the time it takes for the key to travel from up to down, or the reverse.[3] The most common use of this information is to control the amplitude of the tone. Clearly, this affords the performer a greater degree of freedom in musical interpretation. The velocity can be used in more elaborate ways as well. For example, the Crumar

General Development System (GDS)[4] allows the musician to determine, as a lower bound, the amplitude and timbre that occur when a key is struck slowly and, as an upper bound, the results when a key is struck with maximum speed. The results of a velocity intermediate to the extremes are determined by interpolating between the bounds. This is done by associating one set of envelope shapes with the lower bound and a different set with the upper bound. The envelopes control such features of the sound as amplitude and the index of modulation in an FM configuration or the harmonic-amplitude strength and time-evolution pattern in an additive-synthesis instrument.

In addition to velocity, a few claviers sense the pressure applied to a depressed key. This enables the performer to alter the sound during the steady state of the tone.

When the synthesizer is polyphonic and its "voices" have been programmed with different timbres, the allocation of keys to the voices becomes an issue. One method of allocation is to split the keyboard among the synthesizer voices on the basis of register. Another method, which has been called the "rolling mode," cycles among a number of synthesizer voices with the next voice of the rotation at each key initiation.

The *data terminal*, either CRT or hardcopy, is of limited use in real-time interaction with a computer. It is usually employed for encoding programs or entering scores of precomposed works. In a performance situation, the time it takes to enter anything meaningful into a terminal is so great that it is not normally suitable for the specification of individual musical events in real time. Instead, in a performance situation, a terminal is used at a higher level to control and specify groups of musical events. The Structured Sound Synthesis Project (SSSP) group at the University of Toronto has made extensive use of a CRT terminal with a programmable cursor.[5] They have enhanced the utility of the terminal by using non-standard typing conventions that obviate the necessity of keeping both hands on the keyboard of the terminal. For example, to avoid the need to press "carriage return" after each numerical datum is typed, the SSSP system permits one to type any non-numeric key instead. Some data terminals include "special function " keys that facilitate the interaction with the computer. Unlike other keys on the terminal, their meaning is defined in the software. They can be designated to perform special tasks in live performance. For example, one could use a special function key to transpose a musical passage during performance if the performance program had empowered the key to do that task. In addition, their meaning can be changed during performance by the software (in which case, they are called "soft keys"). The current function of each soft key is written on the screen of the CRT. Soft keys can considerably simplify the control panel of an instrument because a separate control device, such as a switch, does not need to be provided for every function.

A graphics terminal can display data in the form of both line drawings and collections of characters. This enables the performer to comprehend a great deal of information at a glance. The form of the display can vary from graphs of parametric change to musical notation. Their use in live performance is somewhat limited due to the amount of information that must be provided to the terminal by the controlling computer.

A few terminals have hardware which senses the position of a pointer when it is brought close to the screen of the terminal. With such a terminal, a user can input data and select modes of operation simply by pointing manually at objects on the screen.

A *switch* can have two types of action: momentary or "latched." Momentary switches are of the kind ordinarily found on data terminals and are generally used as triggers. Latched switches take the form of special hardware or software and are used to select among possible modes of operation.

Both kinds of switches are implemented with push buttons in such systems as New England Digital Corporation's Synclavier I and II.[6] They allow a wide range of communication from the performer to the synthesizer. For example, a particular button is depressed to call up stored instrument designs from memory; others have different functions, such as signaling that digital recording of key depression is to commence or end.

By contrast, other systems use a few switches, the function of which can be changed dynamically by the software. For example, among its several uses, a switch in the SSSP system can start or stop eight independent scores during performance and tell scores whether or not to recycle when their playing is complete.

In contrast to switches, knobs and sliders provide the most common sort of continuous control. Most knobs and sliders are bounded because their motion is limited by mechanical stops. The extremes of motion produce the defined minimum and maximum bounds. An advantage of a bounded knob or slider is that the user can estimate at a glance the value of the parameter it controls. Its principal disadvantage is that a single device can be assigned to control only a single, independent parameter. Knobs and sliders have been used widely in computer performance to control everything from tempo of lines to aspects of timbre. The overall pattern of all the sliders on some systems has been used as a graphical means of defining the shape of a control function such as an envelope. At IRCAM, a device consisting of 32 linear sliders, known as the "Cockerell Box" (after its builder, David Cockerell), has been employed in real-time, computer-music situations. The sliders were placed side-by-side, so that during performance the pattern of all 32 sliders may be seen at a glance. With that number of sliders, however, the exact position of a particular slider (number 14, for example) can be difficult to discern without counting.[7] When it is necessary to count the sliders to find a specific one, real-time interaction is seriously impaired.

A control method that can be realized only in a computer-based system is that of an unbounded knob or slider.[8] Instead of sensing the position of the controller, the system determines the direction and amount of motion and adds that to the value of the parameter currently assigned to the device. The principal advantage of unbounded knobs and sliders is that a single device may be assigned to control any parameter, and it may be dynamically reassigned as necessary during a performance. The disadvantage is that the value of the parameter cannot be estimated by directly observing the position of the controlling device. This problem is overcome by exhibiting the parameter values on a visual-display device.

A digitizing tablet consists of a flat pad that senses the position of a manually positioned pointer such as a stylus or other marking device. Digitizing tablets are most commonly used in conjunction with the CRT display screen of a terminal. The tablet is used either to point out objects already displayed on the screen or to position an object at a desired place on the screen.[9] The SSSP system uses a digitizing tablet to position the cursor on the CRT terminal so that the musician can point out elements for real-time, interactive manipulation. After the elements for modification have been designated, the positioning of the cursor can be used to produce continuous changes in them. In addition, there are four buttons on the marking device. When the cursor marks an element on the screen, each button is defined to produce a different effect on that element.

Light pens are used in conjuction with CRT terminals in substantially the same way that a marking device is used with a digitizing tablet. The light pen can be used to "draw" on the CRT screen or point out objects displayed there. The Fairlight CMI[10] is an example of a live-performance computer-music instrument that makes extensive use of a light pen.

A joystick is a wand whose position can be sensed in either two or three dimensions. In Max Mathews' Conductor program, a three-dimensional joystick was used to control the relative amplitudes of the individual voices of a polyphonic texture. Raising the wand in the center of the three dimensions caused the overall loudness of the ensemble to increase. Moving the wand near to an X or Y extreme caused only the voice assigned to that position to become louder.

Considerable research has gone into the development of new types of transducers for musical performance with computer-controlled digital synthesizers. An example that takes advantage of traditional performance skills is Max Mathews' "Sequential Drum."[11] The instrument consists of a rectangular surface that has been wired to exhibit four characteristic signals when struck: a trigger pulse, a voltage in proportion to the force of the stroke, and two voltages that indicate the x and y locations of the stroke. The musical implementation of the sequential drum begins by entering into the computer the sequences of pitches to be played. The performer on the drum then controls the rhythm of the sequence (by timing the strokes), the amplitude of the notes (by the strength of the strokes), and their timbre (by the x and y positions of the stroke).

Mathews has demonstrated an implementation of the sequential drum for use with both single line and polyphonic musical textures. In each case, a drum stroke plays the next note (or chord) of the score. One of the marvels of playing a stored score in this way is that while one can impart performance nuance through the drum stroke, one cannot play a "wrong note."

Mathews has proposed another transducer for live computer performance which relies on skills built up from previous performance experience on acoustical instruments: "the sequential piano." "The piano would have only ten keys, one for each finger of the player. Conceptually, the task of the computer can be thought of as moving the right key from the 88 normal piano keys and placing it under the finger of the performer at the right instant so that when he depresses his finger, the right note will be played."[12] Thus, the full range of the piano keyboard would be available to the player with the minimum number of control devices.

9.3 Conductor Programs

Max Mathews' Conductor Program and William Buxton's SSSP system are the two most influential systems in the literature of computer music for enabling the performer to act as a conductor of computer synthesis instruments.

Mathews implemented his Conductor Program on the GROOVE system, which was in use at the Bell Laboratories from 1968 to 1979.[13] His program divides the use of the system into three steps: (1) score input, (2) rehearsal, and (3) performance.[14] The score, a note list consisting of pitches and durations, was entered into the computer one note at a time from a keyboard. In rehearsal mode, the musical parts were played separately (and repeated if necessary) in order to adjust phrasing, accents, dynamics, and other aspects of the performance style. The controls for these involved various input devices including knobs, buttons, and piano-like keys.

In performance mode, real-time control is exercised over the tempo as well as the dynamic level and balance within the ensemble. For dynamic control, one of the conductor's hands controlled a three-dimensional "joystick" (wand), the operation of which was described in section 9.2.

The other hand controlled tempo either by turning a knob or by beating time on a key. Mathews found that passages with continuous fluctuations of tempo were more easily "conducted" by use of a knob. Beating time on a key was found to be more useful for musical passages involving sudden changes of tempo. Both methods of setting the tempo required a determination of the proper response time. If the mechanism responded too quickly to a change in the state of the system, it might exaggerate flaws in the performer's time keeping; if it responded too sluggishly, it would be insensitive to the performer's directions.

Mathews' Conductor Program was a valuable tool for investigating the potential for interaction between musician and machine in the evolution of real-time musical performance. In addition to Mathews, the system was used by performers Paul Zukofsky and Gerard Schwartz to produce conducted computer performances of older music as a means of investigating performance nuance in computer music. The system was also used by composers Emmanuel Ghent, Laurie Spiegel, and others to realize original compositions. (See section 9.5.)

William Buxton and the SSSP group at the University of Toronto's computer-graphics laboratory have a conducting system that is geared less to transcription, rehearsal, and performance of existing music, and more to performing works newly composed for their system.[15] The group uses a fully digital system that includes a microcomputer to control a custom-built digital synthesizer.[16] Several perform-ance-time transducers are attached to the system, including a CRT terminal, a digitizing tablet, and a slider box containing unbounded sliders for continuous control of parameters. When in the studio, the system can be connected to a host minicomputer which enables more sophisticated user interaction for tasks such as the entry and editing of scores.

Use of Buxton's system begins with score input, ordinarily done on the host computer.[17] The meaning of "score" for the SSSP system is somewhat specialized. It refers to any group of previously composed notes (up to a maximum of about 800) that the user collects together in a data file as a "score." Notes within a score can be played with different timbres and can overlap in time (up to a maximum of sixteen simultaneous voices). More than one score can be played at a time. The SSSP conductor[18] initiates the performance of the scores singly or in groups. A score may even be overlapped with itself, as in a canon. Thus, the conductor may obtain any desired temporal relationship among the scores. The conductor has control over any parameter of all scores—the same sort of control as an in-strumental conductor, who might wish to signal a particular group of instruments within an ensemble to play louder without changing the dynamic level of the rest of the ensemble.

For each active score, the conductor has real-time control over seven para-meters of each note of the score. The seven parameters as they appear on the CRT terminal are shown in figure 9.1. The name of the score to which the notes belong is indicated under the column labelled "SCORE." 8VE shows any change of octave from the original level at which the note was entered into the system. TEMPO shows the number of beats per minute for the score. Changing the TEMPO value actually alters the time span separating the starting time of one note from that of the next. ARTIC controls the note durations independently of the starting times. Increasing ARTIC can result in the overlap of successive notes; reducing it results in greater separation between the notes. AMP controls change of specified dynamic level. RICH changes the scaling for the "index of modulation" in the FM instrument design used in the SSSP system. When RICH=0, the oscillator produces a sine wave. CYCLE is a binary switch that, when set to 1, causes a score to cycle repeatedly; when set to 0, to play once. CYCLE=1 indicates a mode of operation commonly found in analog synthesizers: a sequence of notes that recycles continuously. In the SSSP system, the implementation is more flexible than in most analog synthesizers: notes in a score may be played with different timbres, overlapped, or permitted to occur simultaneously. ON/OFF, another binary switch, causes the score to rest immediately when set to 0 and triggers it to play when set to 1.

The conductor has real-time control over the seven parameters of the notes in a maximum of eight simultaneous scores. Individual parameters may be changed from their current values in one of two ways: (1) pointing to them with the cursor from the digitizing tablet and typing the new value, or (2) continuously changing the parameter by sliding the marking device on the tablet. The changes made in this way are continuously updated at the appropriate place on the CRT display.

It is also possible during performance on the SSSP system to affect real-time control over more than a single parameter at a time. For example, scores can be grouped together so that a single gesture triggers all to begin simultaneously. Continuous control of parameter groups can also be realized with special devices for continuous control of the system. Such devices include two unbounded sliders, the movement of the cursor in the x and y directions on the tablet, and four software ramps. The software ramps change parameters at specified rates. A software ramp assigned to control AMP will cause either a crescendo or a decrescendo, depending on the direction of change designated. The operation of the ramps requires no manual intervention by the conductor once they are triggered. One interesting feature of the control system is in its ability to have two members of a group tied together in such a way that a control transducer has the opposite effect for each. For example, if this principle were applied to the amplitude of two scores, the scores would "cross-fade" as the control device was activated.

SCORE	8VE	TEMPO	ARTIC	AMP	RICH	CYCLE	ON/OFF
demo	0	60	60	0	0	1	0

FIGURE 9.1 The CRT screen display of note parameters values for an SSSP score. (*Published with the permission of the* Computer Music Journal.)

The SSSP real-time digital synthesis system has proven to be an effective and reliable musical instrument. A number of different composers have performed on the machine at public concerts. Buxton is continuing to experiment with additional transducers, such as piano-type keyboards and touch-sensitive devices, to improve further the interface between musician and machine.

9.4 Microphone as Transducer

Within the field of real-time computer music synthesis, an area that holds great potential is the use of the sound of a musical instrument or voice as a source for controlling synthesis. In this mode of operation, a microphone converts sound into an electrical signal that is subject to real-time analysis, and the results of the analysis are used to control a synthesizer. The real-time analysis is either performed on the computer or, when too complicated for real-time digital implementation, with analog hardware.

There are three attributes of a musical tone which are commonly extracted for use as control signals: the starting time, determined by a threshold detector; the amplitude envelope, extracted by an envelope follower; and the frequency, discriminated by means of a pitch detector. Of the three processes, pitch detection is by far the most difficult. It is often accomplished with external hardware.

The output of an envelope follower has many applications. For instance, it can be imposed on another sound by means of a multiplier. Envelopes can also be applied to control a parameter of a unit generator such as the cutoff frequency of a filter. Many unusual effects can be derived by performing mathematical operations on the envelope before using it as a control signal. For example, subtracting the envelope from a constant that is larger than the maximum value of the envelope yields a signal that has reverse characteristics of the original. When the original has a high value, the processed envelope will have a low one.

One of the common uses in live performance of a pitch detector is to track the frequency of a live instrument or voice and then to play an oscillator at the tracked frequency or in some ratio with the tracked frequency.

A more elaborate scheme for tracking a live instrument has been suggested by Stanley Haynes.[19] In Haynes' design (figure 9.2), the live signal is digitized and passed through the pitch detector. The pitch information obtained is then used to set the center frequencies and bandwidths of a bank of four band-pass filters. The four filters, respectively, are set to pass (1) the fundamental and second harmonic, (2) the third through seventh harmonics, (3) the eighth through fifteen harmonics, and (4) the sixteenth harmonic and above. The output of each of the four filters is then applied to an envelope-following program that produces a time-varying output in the pattern of energy in its band. These signals can be used as real-time controls for some aspect of the computer synthesis taking place at the same time.

Another use of microphone input to the computer for live musical performance is that of direct computer modification of live musical sound. The more sophisticated digital synthesizers can be programmed to perform the operations of *musique concrète* by modifying the incoming, digitized, musical sound in real time. Many techniques, among them modulation, filtering, and reverberation, lend themselves to real-time implementations. See section 7.3A for a description of the techniques of *musique concrète*.

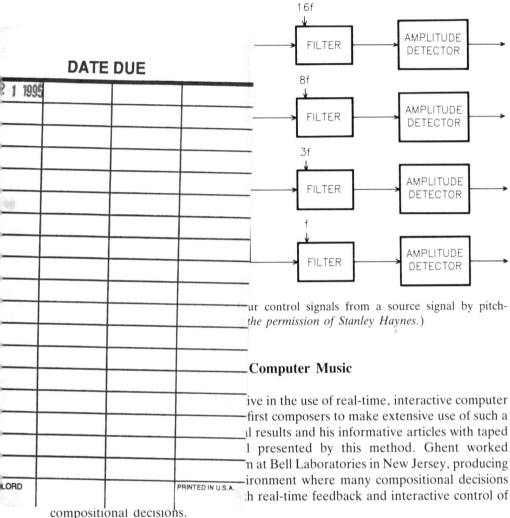

—ur control signals from a source signal by pitch-
the permission of Stanley Haynes.)

Computer Music

ive in the use of real-time, interactive computer
first composers to make extensive use of such a
il results and his informative articles with taped
l presented by this method. Ghent worked
n at Bell Laboratories in New Jersey, producing
ironment where many compositional decisions
h real-time feedback and interactive control of
compositional decisions.

For his *Divertimento for Electronic Violin and Computer Brass* (1974),[20] Ghent's selection of rhythmic and pitch successions began with a table containing 54 pitches. Probabilities of occurrence were assigned to each of these pitches, such that the selection was heavily weighted in favor of a B♭ tonality. Each pitch was assigned, again probabilistically, one of three possible durations. Ghent could then apply one of a number of transformations that would alter the succession of elements in the table. With several real-time devices—a 3-D wand, switches, knobs, and a piano-type keyboard—Ghent could exercise real-time control over the evolution of the composition. He was free to accept or reject versions of the piece and to revise segments as many times as necessary.

The principal transformations used by Ghent were similar to the traditional motivic operations of inversion, retrograde, and retrograde-inversion. He also employed a rotation-like operation he calls "translocation." These operations were applied in real-time to the contents of the 54-location table.

The real-time selection of translocation level, for example, was implemented by means of a clavier. Ghent pressed the key corresponding to the first note of the desired translocation level. Further, the composer could select among original, inverted, and retrograde forms simply by pressing buttons. The rate of note succession was determined by rotating a knob that controlled the rate at which the 54-location table was sampled. After a sequence had been slowed down, other compositional algorithms could be invoked to interpolate new pitches between notes of the original sequence.

Another real-time control was employed to eliminate notes from the sequence. It determined whether selection for omission was made by random means within certain limits or by the omission of every nth note.

In other compositions,[21] Ghent has algorithmically applied various constraints on the compositional choices. For example, in one of his compositions, he restricted the overall registral span to a specified width, within which a random choice is made as to whether a chosen interval is to be played up or down.

Salvatore Martirano has taken the direction of building his own hybrid computer music system for real-time performance.[22] He calls his system the Sal-Mar Construction. This portable system delivers its higher-frequency sounds to a great many (up to 96) small loudspeakers positioned in the performance space above the heads of the audience. The sounds are routed selectively to the loudspeakers in such a way that there can be frequent migration of sounds during a performance. (The less directional low-frequency sounds are played through larger loudspeakers on the stage.)

The music is made interactively with the Sal-Mar Construction. Martirano plays the system in real-time through a binary coding scheme that is implemented with push buttons. During performance he indicates the general range of values of the music's parameters. The machine chooses the events for a particular performance on a controlled random basis within the ranges indicated.

In addition to the audible element, the Sal-Mar Construction itself constitutes a striking visual display. The rather large hybrid system on the stage with its profusion of wires gives the impression of a calculated combination of orderliness and chaos. The loudspeakers suspended above the audiences have small, amber-colored light bulbs that flicker when the loudspeaker is activated. Thus, the lights visually trace the paths of travel of sounds in the music.

Composer Joel Chadabe performs live computer music with a New England Digital synthesizer that permits real-time interaction through joysticks, proximity-sensitive antennae (modified Theremins), pitch sensors, and a microphone; he intentionally omits a clavier.[23] Chadabe uses the control devices to influence the live, stochastic generation of pitch, rhythm, timbre, and texture. For example, in Chadabe's *Solo*, he "conducts" the computer by placing his hands near two proximity-sensitive antennae. Chadabe writes, "As I move my right hand closer to the right antenna, I control speed by increasing the duration of each note. As I move my left hand closer to the left antenna, I control "instrumentation' by passing my hand through 'zones' in which certain 'instruments' are playing. The sounds of the computer-generated 'instruments' were modelled after the sounds of certain instruments, specifically: xylophone, clarinet, and flute. However, after I began to work with them, electronic considerations became primary and the computer sounds came less and less to sound like the acoustic models which at first gave rise to their character. When my left hand is farthest from the left antenna only the xylophone is playing. As I move my hand in towards the antenna, I cause instruments to play in addition to the xylophone: first one clarinet, then two clarinets, then two flutes, and then, closest to the antenna, two clarinets and two flutes together."[24]

Chadabe uses the PLAY II language to create his computer compositions. The composer designed the language with Roger Meyers, who often appears with Chadabe in concert.

The situation of Chadabe and Meyers is fairly typical of a kind of composer/ performer of computer music that is found today with increasing frequency. Often using small, portable hybrid systems, these composer/performers create their computer music live in concerts.

David Behrman has been using live electronics in his music since the 1960s. He uses a hybrid system in which interaction between a live instrumentalist and the computer is established. Behrman's *Solo with Melody Driven Electronics* uses the computer to play certain pitches on pretuned oscillators in response to the pitch played by the live instrument. The pitch on the live instrument is sensed by an analog pitch detector built by Gentle Electric Company.

The personal computer system will undoubtedly play a greatly expanded role in the performance practice of the 1980s and beyond. The great diversity of hardware configurations and musical goals indicate that there will be a profusion of different sorts of personal computer music-system designs in the years to come. Nevertheless, there have emerged a few standardized "digital synthesizers" on which some composers have begun to create works which, presumably, could be realized in performance by others using the same type of machine. In fact, what would be required to reconstitute the piece would be a score in music notation, a floppy disk containing the computer instrument designs and note sequences for the piece, and an audio tape of a previous performance of the piece. The audio tape would show the second performer how to interpret any performance situations that might arise in the piece and which could not easily be expressed in the music notation or stored on floppy disk.

Jon Appleton's *Sashasonjon, In Memorium: Alexander Walden*[25] is an example of the sort of performance practice which goes into realizing a composition on one of the standardized digital synthesizers. Appleton wrote his piece for realization on the Synclavier II, which he himself plays.

Prior to the performance, the composer must preload the note sequences to be used in the composition onto a floppy disk. This is done by playing in "record mode" or by encoding the notes one at a time in a score-input language. Any predefined instrument configurations must be stored onto floppy disk before performance, as well.

At the setup time for a performance of *Sashasonjon*, the composer inserts the floppy disk containing the first stored note sequence into the disk drive, which reads its contents into computer memory. The procedure is repeated with the floppy disk containing the instrument designs for the composition. The digital synthesizer is ready as soon as the appropriate buttons are pressed to establish which of the stored instruments are to be played first. For the opening of the composition, the keyboard is logically divided into two registers, each with a different computer instrument assigned to it. The tuning of a keyboard octave at the beginning of the piece is "stretched" to a frequency ratio of 3:1 (1.6 octaves). It is set by pressing the "tuning" button and turning a knob to the desired value shown in a digital readout.

With this setting, each keyboard semitone sounds an interval of 1.6 semitones. The digital synthesizer's software puts this into effect by retaining the frequency of middle C as 261.6 Hz and "stretching" the octaves in both directions around the midpoint. For the first part of the piece, in which the keyboard is played normally, the music notation shows the notation for which keys to press. However, it is not a direct indication of which frequencies will sound, due to the tuning. Figure 9.3 shows the set-up instructions and opening phrase of *Sashasonjon*.

Figure 9.4 shows a passage from the second section of the piece, where Appleton overlays the first note sequence with a passage played live on the keyboard. While this is being done, Appleton presses the "start" button to begin the digital recording feature of the system. After playing a few more bars, he then presses the "loop" button, causing the music heard since pressing the start button to repeat. The loop continues, while being overlaid by the first note sequence and by live performance on the keyboard, until the stop button is pressed. Then, when the first note sequence comes to its end, the keyboard is retuned to standard equal temperament and another passage of music is played on the keyboard alone.

There are a number of other features of the composition which show Appleton's uses of the Synclavier II. For example, he retunes the keyboard to an octave ratio of 4:1 (16:1 in terms of frequency) at a later point in the piece, causing the keyboard semitone to equal a major third. He makes further use of the loop feature and performs two additional operations on the looping material. First, by pressing the "transpose" button of the digital recording feature, he causes the looping material to change pitch level by the interval indicated by the key pressed

FIGURE 9.3   Opening phrase of Appleton's *SASHASONJON* showing setup instructions. (*Published with the permission of Jon Appleton.*)

FIGURE 9.4   The section of Appleton's *SASHASONJON* where the performer starts "Sequence 1," continues to play at the clavier, and then makes a loop out of the motif. (*Published with the permission of Jon Appleton.*)

above or below middle C. Also, the speed of the looping material is changed continuously by rotating a knob. Just as looping and speed control have their predecessors in classical tape studio technique, so does the next operation used in *Sashasonjon*—"fast rewind." Here, the entire stored note sequence is rapidly played backwards. The program emulates the rewinding of a tape recorder; the sound starts slowly and speeds up as the machine gathers momentum.

Throughout the composition, Appleton changes tone qualities by calling in new groups of computer instruments to play the material from the keyboard, from stored note sequences, and from passages playing in loop mode.

Morton Subotnick, one of the first composers to work extensively with analog synthesizers, has created a composition for acoustic instruments and real-time digital synthesizer. *THE DOUBLE LIFE OF AMPHIBIANS, Part 1—Ascent into Air*[26] was created on commission for IRCAM and uses a live digital synthesizer along with an ensemble of amplified acoustic instruments made up of two cellos, two clarinets, two trombones, two percussion, and two pianos.

Regarding this composition, Subotnick writes,

THE DOUBLE LIFE OF AMPHIBIANS is a metaphor which is used to provide a model for the structure of the work as well as suggesting the nature of the musical materials.... In many respects, working in art with technology is a clear example of this metaphor. We are at an evolutionary point in the development of this extension (transformation?) of our ability to communicate, i.e., the transformation of the content as well as the mode of communicating. This metaphor is expressed at many levels of the work. The following is an outline of some of these ways:

1. Each instrument has a double, placed on opposite sides of the stage.
2. The computer acts as a paralleled instrument, responding to all gestures of the celli while existing in its separate place both timbrally and spatially.
3. The two pianos and percussion form one group together, while the celli and the computer form a second group...but,
4. These two [groups] together create a liquid-like environment for the work...an environment of a timbral and textural medium which is articulated by "waves" of amplitude and spatial changes.
5. The clarinets and trombones create a more "normal" musical reality, utilizing more recognizable musical materials which produce a counterpoint to the music of the celli, pianos, percussion, and computer.
6. In the fifth and final section [part], the elements finally converge to form a synthesis and transformation of all the preceding "doubleness" (ascent).

Throughout there is a gradual evolution of the relationship of "instrumental" to "synthetic" sound so that, by the end, the two become a single homogeneous texture."[27]

The synthesizer for the first performance of Subotnick's piece was the 4C synthesizer designed by Pepino Di Giuno at IRCAM. Curtis Abbott wrote the basic software to control the synthesizer from the computer, and Stanley Haynes acted as Subotnick's assistant for programming the computer[28] to realize the composition. Subsequent performances of the work have employed a digital synthesizer designed and built by Donald Buchla.

Before the performance, the digital synthesizer is loaded with the instrument designs and sequences of notes. The basic instrument design for this piece involves either two or four tone-generating oscillators for each pitch. The waveform for each oscillator has a steady-state spectrum determined by prior analysis of certain acoustic instruments. But in this instrument, there is virtually no time when that waveform is heard in its steady-state. That is because the two (or in some instances, four) oscillators are tuned to simulate the slight beating of the sort heard between two strings on the same note in the upper registers of the piano. Furthermore, every note of the instrument has separate envelopes for the amplitude of each oscillator and a time-variant function that controls the amount of mistuning between the oscillators.

The synthesizer has two principal roles in Subotnick's composition: it acts as a source for synthesized sounds and it acts as an agent for locating in the quadraphonic space its own synthesized sounds as well as those of the trombones, clarinets, and cellos. Figure 9.5 shows the relationships between the digital synthesizer and the acoustic instruments, each of which is played into a microphone. The output of the microphone is mixed with other sounds, amplified, and played through one of the four loudspeakers in the hall. In fact, the amplification of the instruments whose sounds are located by the computer is not noticeable until the sound goes out around the audience. With these movements of sound, the rate and shape of the travel reinforces the musical gestures of the instruments, because the speed and sound path result from the sound of the cellos directly.

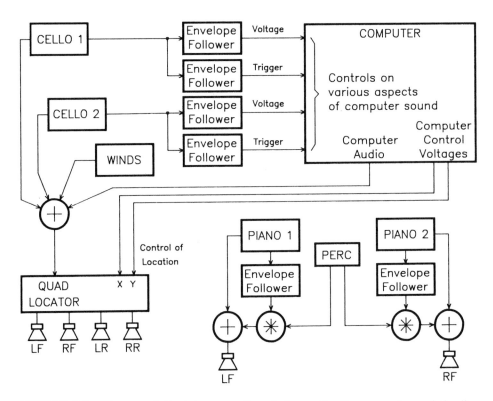

FIGURE 9.5 Diagram of the interconnections between the live computer and the live instruments of Subotnick's *The Double Life of Amphibians, Part 1–Ascent into Air.* (*Published with the permission of Morton Subotnick.*)

As noted above, all aspects of the manner of the performance on the synthesizer are controlled in real-time by the acoustic output of the pair of cellos. Each cello plays through a microphone into three analog envelope followers that act as sources for control voltage, trigger pulses, and threshold-detected pulses. The use of the synthesizer always parallels the two cellos. Thus, the synthesizer is not a soloist in any sense. At most points in the piece, the synthesizer plays under the direct control of the sound of one of the cellos. At its most independent, it plays in response to a trigger pulse from one of the cellos, and then, ordinarily, only for a short time before more control information is received. The effect is for the computer sound to be added to the sound of the acoustic instruments, creating in many places timbres and textures that are subtle combinations of acoustic and electronic sounds.

An example of the control of the synthesizer by the cellos can be seen in part 1 of the work, where cello 1 controls three aspects of the synthesizer's performance. The amplitude of the cello tones directly controls the amplitude of the synthesizer tones. It also affects the rate of sound movement between front and rear loudspeakers, with loud sounds causing slow movement of sound and soft sounds causing rapid movement. The rate of repetition of some tones on the synthesizer is also affected by the dynamics of cello 1, with the same correlation of dynamics to speed as in the previous example. Example 9.1 shows the relationship between cello 1 and the synthesizer at this point in the piece.

Another example of control of the synthesizer by the celli is seen in example 9.2 from part 2 of the work. Here the amplitude of cello 1 controls the amplitude, transposition, and left–right location of the synthesizer's sound.

The use of the two cellos to trigger stored sequences of notes from the synthesizer can be seen in example 9.3 from part 3 of the work. In addition to the trigger pulses, the cellos output control voltages to the channel locators. The amplitude of cello 1 controls the rate of left–right movement of sound and that of cello 2 the front–rear movement.

In part 4, the synthesizer begins to control the location of the instruments whose microphone outputs are linked to it. Example 9.4 shows that the rate and distance of movement are determined by the envelopes of the extremely high and low notes in the cellos.

Throughout part 4, the pitches of the synthesizer are fixed by the amplitude of the cello that is not triggering the note. This is accomplished by means of a sample-and-hold unit that fixes a level in proportion to the amplitude of the cello tone with silence resulting in a very low tone and a loud cello tone causing a high tone in the synthesizer.

In the fifth and final part of the work, the homogeneity mentioned in Subotnick's introductory remarks is effected by amplifying the sound of all the instruments. The ending of the work is a chordal sound that encompasses the entire timbral range of the work. In this section, there is no distinction to be drawn between the sound of the instruments and that of the synthesizer.

EXAMPLE 9.1 The score for the passage near the opening of Subotnick's *Ascent* where the cello 1's tones affect the amplitude of the synthesizer, the rate of movement of sounds between the front and back loudspeakers, and the rate of repetition of certain synthesizer tones. (*Reprinted with permission of the Theodore Presser Company.*)

EXAMPLE 9.2 Score from part 2 of *Ascent* where cello 1 controls the amplitude, transposition, and left–right location of the synthesizer's sound. (*Reprinted with permission of the Theodore Presser Company.*)

EXAMPLE 9.3   Section from part 3 of *Ascent* where the cellos both trigger and control synthesizer sounds. (*Reprinted with permission of the Theodore Presser Company.*)

EXAMPLE 9.4   Section from part 4 of *Ascent* where the cellos control the location of the sound of those instruments whose microphone outputs are linked to them. (*Reprinted with permission of the Theodore Presser Company.*)

Notes

1.   Haynes, Stanley. "The Musician-Machine Interface in Digital Sound Synthesis." Doctoral dissertation, Southampton University, Southampton, England, 1979, 139.

2.   Mathews, Max V., and F. R. Moore, "GROOVE—A Program to Compose, Store, and Edit Functions of Time." *Communications of the ACM*, *13*(12), 1969, 715–721.

3.   Alles, H. G. "Music Synthesis Using Real-Time Digital Techniques." *Proceedings of the Institute of Electrical and Electronic Engineers*, *68*(4), 1980, 436–449.

4.   Manufactured by Music Technology Inc., Garden City Park, N.Y.

5.   Buxton, William, W. Reeves, G. Fedorkow, K. C. Smith, and R. Baecker. "A Microcomputer-Based Conducting System." *Computer Music Journal*, *4*(1), 1980, 8–21.

6.   Manufactured by New England Digital Corporation, White River Junction, Vt.

7.   Haynes, 1979.

8.   Buxton, W. et al., 1980.

9.   Newman, W. M., and R. F. Sproull. *Principles of Interactive Computer Graphics* (2nd ed.). New York: McGraw-Hill, 1979, 147–181.

10.   Manufactured by Fairlight Instruments Pty. Limited, Sydney, Australia.

11.   Mathews, Max V. "The Sequential Drum." *Computer Music Journal*, *4*(4), 1980, 45–60.

12.   Ibid, 49.

13.   Mathews and Moore, 1969.

14.   Mathews, Max V. "The Conductor Program." Abstracts of papers read at the First International Conference of Computer Music, Cambridge, Mass., M.I.T., 1976.

15.   Buxton, et al., 1980.

16.   Buxton, W., E. A. Fogels, G. Fedorkow, and K. C. Smith. "An Introduction to the SSSP Digital Synthesizer." *Computer Music Journal*, *2*(4), 1978, 28–38.

17.   Buxton, W., R. Sniderman, W. Reeves, S. Patel, and R. Baecker. "The Evolution of the SSSP Score Editing Tools." *Computer Music Journal*, *3*(4), 1979, 14–25.

18.   Buxton, W. et al., *A Microprocessor-Based Conducting System*, 1980.

19.   Haynes, 1979.

20.   Ghent, Emmanuel. "Real-Time Interactive Compositional Procedure." Paper delivered at First International Conference on Computer Music, Cambridge, Mass., M.I.T., 1976.

21.   Ghent, Emmanuel. "Interactive Compositional Algorithms." *Proceedings of Second International Computer Music Conference*, La Jolla, Calif., 1977.

22.   Robinson, Michael. Unpublished overview of the SAL-MAR Construction. Urbana, Ill., July, 1978.

23.   Chadabe, Joel. *Program Notes* (to concert by Composer's Forum, Inc. at Paula Cooper Gallery). New York, May 20, 1980.

24.   Ibid.

25.   Appleton, Jon. "Sashasonjon." Unpublished score. Folkways (FTS-37461) New York, 1980.

26.   Subotnick, Morton. *The Double Life of Amphibians*, Part 1—*The Ascent into Air*. Bryn Mawr, Pa.: Theodore Presser, 1982.

27.   Subotnick, 1982. (See *Introduction* to score.)

28.   Abbott, Curtis. "The 4CED Program." *Proceedings of the International Computer Music Conference*, Queens College of the City University of New York, 1980. (Compiled by Hubert S. Howe, director.)

APPENDIX

SYNTHESIS ALGORITHMS

The purpose of this appendix is to present algorithms for many of the unit generators described in this text. The collection of algorithms is not, however, a sound synthesis language. It is included to give more technical detail about the internal workings of the unit generators and to provide a basis on which new algorithms can be developed. The overall structure and the majority of the algorithms are based on the MUSIC 4BF language developed at Princeton University by Godfrey Winham and Hubert S. Howe, Jr. on the model of Max V. Mathews's Music 4. The reader should be aware that the algorithms presented here may not be identical to those at Princeton.

The programming language FORTRAN has been used to express the algorithms primarily because of its widespread availability and the relatively high execution speed of its compiled programs. In FORTRAN, variables beginning with the letters A–H and O–Z are represented as floating-point numbers. Variables beginning with I–N are integers. (See section 1.1.) Throughout the appendix the sample values are represented in floating-point format. This format can represent a large range of numbers and minimizes the likelihood of errors during intermediate calculations due to overflowing (or underflowing) the maximum (or minimum) values. Standard floating-point format has an accuracy of approximately seven decimal digits. This, in most cases, keeps the effect of round-off errors well below audible levels. The algorithms can be converted to integer format but special attention must be paid to the range and accuracy required for each calculation. The filtering algorithms would be particularly difficult to realize in integer format.

The FORTRAN listings below can be adapted to many other languages and even to direct hardware implementation. Anyone attempting to adapt the software to another language, however, should note the way subroutines are passed parameters and store intermediate results in the particular language used. Because this software takes advantage of the ability in FORTRAN to reference arrays that are outside the boundaries of the declared arrays, the adaptor may have to change the size of the arrays to accomodate different languages.

To improve computational efficiency, several of the algorithms refer to wave-tables (see section 3.3). A table size of 512 entries has been defined. The wavetables are held in the array F(512,NF), where NF is the total number of wavetables.

There are many methods of filling a wavetable. We will give two examples: (1) A waveform specified by the number and amplitudes of its harmonics and (2) a transfer function for use in a non-linear processor specified as a polynomial. In each case,

343

the stored function is normalized so that the maximum magnitude found among the entries is one. This assists the programmer in determining the peak amplitude produced by a unit generator. Both subroutines receive their input data by means of the common array, P. The main program would call routines to fill the array with the appropriate values prior to the execution of either of these subroutines.

The subroutine SINFIL adds sinewaves together to form a composite waveform. Each partial is described by three parameters—harmonic number, amplitude, and phase. The phase is scaled so that one cycle of the sinewave has a phase of 512. The descriptors are stored in groups of three consecutive variables beginning in P(4). Thus, for example, information on the first partial would be contained in P(4) through P(6), the second partial would be specified in P(7) through P(9), and so on. A value of zero in the partial number indicates that there are no more partials in the array P.

```
        SUBROUTINE SINFIL(DUMMY)
C
C  FILLS WAVETABLE WITH THE SUM OF SINE WAVES.
C
C  THE ARGUMENT HAS NO MEANING AND IS THERE FOR PROTOCOL.
        COMMON P(32),F(512,1)
C  P(1) STORES THE WAVETABLE NUMBER.
        NF=INT(P(1))
C  ANG IS 2*PI/512.
        ANG=.0122718
        XMX=-1.
        DO 20 K=1,512
        PHS=ANG*FLOAT(K-1)
        SUM=0.
        DO 30 J=4,28,3
        IF(P(J).EQ.0.) GO TO 35
C  PHZ IS THE PHASE OF THE PARITAL IN RADIANS.
        PHZ=ANG*P(J+2)
        SUM=SUM+P(J+1)*SIN(P(J)*PHS+PHZ)
30      CONTINUE
35      XMX=AMAX1(XMX,ABS(SUM))
        F(K,NF)=SUM
20      CONTINUE
C  SCALE THE TABLE FOR A MAXIMUM MAGNITUDE OF ONE.
        DO 40 K=1,512
        F(K,NF)=F(K,NF)/XMX
40      CONTINUE
        RETURN
        END
```

The subroutine POLYF fills a wavetable with a polynomial of the form $F(x)=a_0+a_1x+a_2x^2+a_3x^3+\ldots+a_Nx^N$, where N is the degree of the polynomial. The value of x is scaled so that F(1,NF) corresponds to $x=-1$; F(256,NF) corresponds to $x=0$; and F(511,NF) corresponds to $x=1$. As above, NF denotes the wavetable number and is stored in P(1). The degree of the polynomial is stored in P(4). The values of the coefficients, a_j, are stored in the array P beginning with P(5).

```
        SUBROUTINE POLYF(DUMMY)
C
C  FILLS WAVETABLE WITH A TRANSFER FUNCTION DESCRIBED BY A POLYNOMIAL.
C
C  THE ARGUMENT HAS NO MEANING AND IS THERE FOR PROTOCOL.
        COMMON P(32),F(512,1)
C  THE FUNCTION NUMBER IS STORED IN P(1).
        NF=INT(P(1))
C  P(4) INDICATES THE DEGREE OF THE POLYNOMIAL.
        NDEG=INT(P(4))
        XMX=-1.
        DO 30 K=1,512
        X=FLOAT(K-256)/255.
        X1=1.
        SUM=0.
        DO 20 I=0,NDEG
        SUM=SUM+X1*P(I+5)
```

```
            X1=X*X1
20          CONTINUE
            XMX=AMAX1(XMX,ABS(SUM))
            F(K,NF)=SUM
30          CONTINUE
C   SCALE VALUES FOR A MAXIMUM MAGNITUDE OF ONE.
            DO 40 K=1,512
            F(K,NF)=F(K,NF)/XMX
40          CONTINUE
            RETURN
            END
```

The unit generators take the form of functions and subroutines. At the end of this appendix an example is given of how to link the unit generators together in a program to form an instrument.

The function OSCIL implements a truncating oscillator. It samples a waveform that has been stored previously in the array F(I,NF), where I designates the table entry and NF denotes the wavetable used. This algorithm expects a wavetable that is 512 entries in length. The arguments of the function are as follows:

AMP Determines the amplitude of the digital signal produced by the oscillator. If the values of the entries in the wavetable are scaled between ± 1, the value of OSCIL will fall between $\pm$AMP.

SI The sampling increment. It sets the frequency of oscillation as described below and in section 3.3.

NF Designates the wavetable to be used.

PHS The current phase of the oscillator. It selects the wavetable entry used. The function alters the value of this argument so that the variable in the main program that stores the argument will have a different value after the function is called. Therefore, when using multiple oscillators, each oscillator should have a unique variable assigned to PHS in the main program.

```
            FUNCTION OSCIL(AMP,SI,NF,PHS)
C
C   TRUNCATING OSCILLATOR
C   FREQUENCY OF OSCILLATION (F0) IS RELATED TO SI BY: F0=SI*SR/512
C
            COMMON F(512,1)
C THE NEXT 6 STATEMENTS ENSURE THAT THE PHASE DOES NOT EXCEED
C THE BOUNDS OF THE TABLE.
            IF(PHS.GE.512.) GO TO 5
3           IF(PHS.GE.0.) GO TO 6
            PHS=PHS+512.
            GO TO 3
5           PHS=PHS-512.
            IF(PHS.GE.512.) GO TO 5
C   K IS THE ADDRESS OF THE WAVETABLE ENTRY.
C
6           K=INT(PHS)+1
C
C   INCREMENT THE PHASE FOR NEXT TIME.
            PHS=PHS+SI
C   SAMPLE THE WAVETABLE.
            OSCIL=AMP*F(K,NF)
            RETURN
            END
```

The function OSCILI is similar to OSCIL, except that it implements interpolation to produce a more accurate waveform.

```
            FUNCTION OSCILI(AMP,SI,NF,PHS)
C
C   INTERPOLATING OSCILLATOR
C
            K=INT(PHS+1.)
C   MAP PHASE INTO THE RANGE OF 1 TO 512.
            L=MOD(K+1,512)
```

```
C  P IS THE FRACTIONAL PART OF THE PHASE.
      P=PHS-AINT(PHS)
      PHS=AMOD(PHS+SI,512.)
      OSCILI=AMP*(F(K,NF)+P*(F(L,NF)-F(K,NF)))
      RETURN
      END
```

An approximation to white noise is produced by the function RAND. The arguments are as follows:

AMP Sets the peak amplitude of the noise so that the function returns a value in the range ±AMP.

SEED The seed value for the random number generator. It is ordinarily assigned a value at the beginning of the main program. Then each time RAND is called, the algorithm assigns a new value to it. The random number generators on many systems do not use seed as an argument. In this case, SEED can be deleted as an argument of the RAND function.

The function RANDOM returns a value between 0 and 1. On some computer systems, the random number generator produces a different range of numbers. In that case, the function must be scaled accordingly.

```
      FUNCTION RAND(AMP,SEED)
C
C  WHITE NOISE GENERATOR PRODUCING SAMPLES IN THE RANGE OF +-AMP.
C                        .
C  FUNCTION RANDOM RETURNS A VALUE BETWEEN 0 AND 1.
      SEED=RANDOM(SEED)
      RAND=AMP*(1.-2.*SEED)
      RETURN
      END
```

The noise-generating function RANDH enables a rate of noise generation that is lower than the sampling rate. Its arguments are as follows:

AMP Sets the peak amplitude of the noise output in the range of ±AMP.

SI Sets the frequency at which the noise is generated. For consistency with the other algorithms, SI is expressed as a sampling increment that is specified as if the noise generator had a table of 512 entries. Thus, SI and the frequency of noise generation are related in the same way as SI and the frequency of oscillation are in the oscillator algorithms above.

A The first of two consecutive variables in an array that is used to store intermediate results.

```
      FUNCTION RANDH(AMP,SI,A)
      DIMENSION A(2)
C
C  HOLDS RANDOM NUMBER FOR 512/SI SAMPLES
C
C  A(1) IS IS THE EQUIVALENT OF PHASE.
C  A(2) IS THE SEED FOR THE RANDOM NUMBER GENERATOR.  IT WILL
C  NOT BE NECESSARY ON MANY SYSTEMS.
C
      A(1)=A(1)+SI
      IF(A(1).LE.512.)GO TO 5
      A(2)=RANDOM(A(2))
      A(1)=A(1)-512.
5     RANDH=AMP*(1.-2.*A(2))
      RETURN
      END
```

The function RANDI also produces noise with an independent rate of noise generation, but in addition, it interpolates sample values between the randomly selected points of the noise waveform. The arguments AMP and SI have the same meaning as in RANDH above. The argument, A, is the first of four consecutive variables in an array that is used to store intermediate results.

```
        FUNCTION RANDI(AMP,SI,A)
        DIMENSION A(4)
C
C   INTERPOLATES BETWEEN RANDOM NUMBERS THAT ARE DRAWN
C   EVERY 512/SI SAMPLES.
C
C   A(1) IS THE EQUIVALENT OF PHASE, BUT SCALED BETWEEN 0 AND 1.
        A(1)=A(1)+SI/512.
        IF(A(1).LT.1.)GO TO 5
C   OTHERWISE DRAW THE NEXT RANDOM NUMBER.
        A(1)=A(1)-1.
        A(2)=A(3)
        A(3)=RANDOM(A(3))
        A(4)=2.*(A(2)-A(3))
        A(2)=1.-2.*A(2)-A(4)*A(1)
5       RANDI=AMP*(A(2)+A(4)*A(1))
        RETURN
        END
```

Realizing an envelope generator requires two subprograms: EVSET and EVLOPE. EVSET initializes the data to be used by the function EVLOPE. These routines generate an envelope with three parts, (1) an attack segment which is described by a function stored in a wavetable, (2) a sustain segment during which the last value of the attack shape is held, and (3) a decay segment which is also described by a function stored in a wavetable.

When using the EVLOPE function in a program, the associated subroutine EVSET must be executed first (ordinarily before the beginning of a note) in order to initialize the data needed for the junction. The arguments of EVSET have the following meanings:

RISE Rise time in seconds.
DECAY Decay time in seconds.
DUR Overall duration in seconds.
A The first of seven consecutive variables in an array that is to be used to store intermediate results.

```
        SUBROUTINE EVSET(RISE,DECAY,DUR,A)
        COMMON SR
        DIMENSION A(7)
C
C   INITIALIZATION ROUTINE FOR EVLOPE.
C   ALL PARAMETERS MUST BE >0.
C
C   A(1) IS ATTACK SAMPLING INCREMENT.
C   A(2) IS ATTACK PHASE SCALED 1 TO 513.
C   A(3) IS DECAY POINT SAMPLING INCREMENT.
C   A(4) IS DECAY POINT PHASE SCALED 1 TO 513.
C   A(5) IS DECAY SAMPLING INCREMENT.
C   A(6) IS DECAY PHASE SCALED 513 TO 1.
C   A(7) IS LAST VALUE.
C
        TN=512./SR
        A(1)=TN/RISE
        A(2)=1.
        IF(DECAY.GT.DUR) DECAY=DUR
        DECPT=AMAX1(TN*.001,DUR-DECAY)
        A(3)=TN/DECPT
        A(4)=1.
        A(5)=TN/DECAY
        A(6)=512.9999
        RETURN
        END
```

The arguments of EVLOPE are:

AMP Peak amplitude of the envelope.
NF1 Number denoting the wavetable containing the shape of the attack.

NF2 Number denoting the wavetable containing the shape of the decay. However, the decay function is sampled backwards, and thus the decay shape is stored in retrograde. This convention enables the same wavetable to be used for both the attack and decay segments if desired.

A Same as in EVSET.

```
      FUNCTION EVLOPE(AMP,NF1,NF2,A)
C
C  GENERATES AN ENVELOPE.
C  IF THE ATTACK AND DECAY OVERLAP, THE DECAY TAKES PRECEDENCE.
C
      COMMON SR
      COMMON F(512,1)
      DIMENSION A(7)
      IF(A(4).LT.513.) GO TO 10
      IF(A(6).LT.1.) GO TO 30
      K=INT(A(6))
      A(7)=F(K,NF2)*F(512,NF1)/F(512,NF2)
C  DECREMENT PHASE OF DECAY.
      A(6)=A(6)-A(5)
      GOTO 25
10    IF(A(2).GE.513.) GO TO 20
      K=INT(A(2))
C  INCREMENT PHASE OF ATTACK.
      A(2)=A(2)+A(1)
      A(7)=F(K,NF1)
      GO TO 25
C  SUSTAIN.
20    A(7)=F(512,NF1)
25    A(4)=A(4)+A(3)
30    EVLOPE=AMP*A(7)
      RETURN
      END
```

The BUZZ unit generator produces a band-limited pulse waveform as described in section 5.1. It produces the waveform by means of a discrete summation formula (section 4.3A). To improve computational efficiency, the function references a wavetable in which a sinewave has been stored. A table length of 1024 entries is needed for sufficient accuracy. Therefore, in the following algorithm two adjacent tables with 512 entries each are used. The first table stores the first half of the sinewave, and the second half is stored in the next table. FORTRAN allows concatenation of arrays in this way, but when translating this algorithm to other languages, a single wavetable with 1024 places may have to be used.

The arguments for BUZZ are as follows:

AMP Sets the peak amplitude of the pulse equal to AMP.

SI A sampling increment which determines the frequency at which pulses are generated. For consistency with the other algorithms, the sampling increment is related to the fundamental frequency as if this generator were an oscillator with a 512-entry wavetable.

HN Specifies the number of harmonics contained in the pulse.

NF1 Designates the wavetable in which the first half of the sine wave is stored. The algarithm assumes that the second half has been stored in table NF1+1.

PHS Holds current value of phase in the same way as in the OSCIL algorithm.

```
      FUNCTION BUZZ(AMP,SI,HN,NF1,PHS)
C
C  GENERATES A BAND-LIMITED PULSE WAVEFORM.
C
      COMMON F(512,2)
      J=INT(PHS)
      PHS=AMOD(PHS+SI,1024.)
      D=F(J+1,NF1)
      IF(D.GT..00001)GO TO 2
      BUZZ=AMP
      GO TO 3
```

```
2       H2N=2*HN
        K=MOD(INT(H2N+1.)*J,1024)+1
        BUZZ=AMP*(F(K,NF1)/D-1.)/H2N
3       RETURN
        END
```

The algorithm for a first-order recursive filter consists of an initialization subroutine, TONESET, and a function, TONE. During initialization, the filter coefficients are determined from the cutoff frequency and stored in the array A. It is assumed that in the main program the value of the sampling rate, SR, has been assigned and stored in common memory. The arguments used are:

FC The cutoff frequency in Hz. If FC is negative, TONE realizes a high-pass filter. Otherwise, TONE has a low-pass characteristic.

XINIT Determines the disposition of the previous output sample stored in memory. XINIT=0 sets this sample value to zero. Any other value of XINIT retains the stored sample intact.

A The first of three consecutive variables in an array that is to be used to store intermediate results.

```
        SUBROUTINE TONESET(FC,XINIT,A)
        COMMON SR
        DIMENSION A(3)
C
C       INITIALIZES TONE AS A FIRST-ORDER RECURSIVE FILTER.
C
        B=2.-COS(6.283185*FC/SR)
        A(2)=SQRT(B*B-1.)-B
        A(1)=1.+A(2)
        IF(FC.LT.0.)A(2)=-A(2)
        IF(XINIT.EQ.0.)A(3)=0
        RETURN
        END
```

The arguments of TONE are:

XIN The digital signal appled to the filter.
A Same as in TONESET.

```
        FUNCTION TONE(XIN,A)
        DIMENSION A(3)
        A(3)=A(1)*XIN-A(2)*A(3)
        TONE=A(3)
        RETURN
        END
```

Realizing a second-order, all-pole filter (see section 5.3) is a two-step process. First, the subroutine, RSNSET, must be executed to calculate the coefficient values. Then the function RESON can be used as a filter during the synthesis process. The arguments are as follows:

CF The center frequency of the filter in Hz.
BW The 3-dB bandwidth of the filter in Hz.
SCL Specifies amplitude scaling method as described below and further in section 5.5.
XINIT Determines whether the memory locations that store previous output values are cleared. Setting XINIT=0 clears them, otherwise they remain untouched.
A The first of five consecutive variables in an array that is to be used to store intermediate results.

```
        SUBROUTINE RSNSET(CF,BW,SCL,XINIT,A)
        COMMON SR
        DIMENSION A(5)
```

```
C
C    INITIALIZES RESON
C
      IF(XINIT.NE.0.)GO TO 1
      A(5)=0.
      A(4)=0.
1     A(3)=EXP(-6.283185*BW/SR)
      C=1.+A(3)
      A(2)=-4.*A(3)/C*COS(6.283185*CF/SR)
C
C    SCL=1 SETS GAIN=1 AT CF
C    SCL=2 SETS GAIN=1 ON WHITE NOISE INPUT
C    SCL=0 MEANS NO SCALING
C
      IF(SCL-1.)30,20,10
10    A(1)=SQRT((1.-A(3))/C*(C*C-A(2)*A(2)))
      RETURN
20    A(1)=(1.-A(3))*SQRT(1.-A(2)*A(2)/(4.*A(3)))
      RETURN
30    A(1)=1.
      RETURN
      END
```

The argument of RESON are:

XIN The digital signal applied to the filter.
A Same as in RSNSET.

```
      FUNCTION RESON(XIN,A)
      DIMENSION A(5)
C
C    SECOND-ORDER, ALL-POLE, BAND-PASS FILTER
C
C    A(4) HOLDS Y(N-1).  A(5) HOLDS Y(N-2).
C
      YI=A(1)*XIN-A(2)*A(4)-A(3)*A(5)
      A(5)=A(4)
      A(4)=YI
      RESON=YI
      RETURN
      END
```

A second-order filter "zero," as discussed in section 5.12, is realized by the initialization subroutine ZROSET and the function ZERO. The arguments are as follows:

CF The center frequency of the filter; i.e., the frequency at which the maximum attenuation occurs.

BW The bandwidth of the filter. In this case the bandwidth is defined as the frequency difference between the two points which have 3 dB less attenuation than at the center frequency.

SCL If SCL=1, the filter is scaled for a gain of 1 at 0 Hertz. Otherwise it is left unscaled.

XINIT Determines whether the memory locations that store previous output values are cleared. Setting XINIT=0 clears them, otherwise they are not altered.

A The first of five consecutive variables in an array that is to be used to store intermediate results.

```
      SUBROUTINE ZROSET(CF,BW,SCL,XINIT,A)
C
C    INITIALIZATION ROUTINE FOR THE FUNCTION ZERO.
C
      COMMON SR
      DIMENSION A(5)
      C2=EXP(-6.283185*BW/SR)
      C1=-4*C2/(1+C2)*COS(6.283185*CF/SR)
      D=1.
      IF(SCL.EQ.1.) D=1+C1+C2
      A(1)=1/D
      A(2)=C1/D
```

```
             A(3)=C2/D
             IF(XINIT.NE.0.) GO TO 5
             A(4)=0.
             A(5)=0.
        5    RETURN
             END
```

The arguments of ZERO are:

XIN The digital signal applied to the filter.
A Same as in ZROSET.

```
             FUNCTION ZERO(XIN,A)
             DIMENSION A(5)
        C
        C    SECOND-ORDER, ALL-ZERO, NON-RECURSIVE FILTER.
        C
        C    A(4) HOLDS X(N-1); A(5) HOLDS X(N-2)
             Y=A(1)*XIN+A(2)*A(4)+A(3)*A(5)
        C    SHIFT THE INPUT SAMPLES DOWN ONE.
             A(5)=A(4)
             A(4)=XIN
             ZERO=Y
             RETURN
             END
```

A second-order, Butterworth high-pass filter of the type discussed in section 5.13 can be implemented as follows. The initialization of the coefficients of the filter is accomplished by means of the subroutine HPSET. Then, the function BIFIL can be called to perform the filtering. The arguments are as follows:

FC Cutoff frequency in Hz.
XINIT Setting XINIT=0 clears the previous samples stored in memory. Otherwise, these samples retain their value.
A The first of seven consecutive variables in an array used to store intermediate results.

```
             SUBROUTINE HPSET(FC,XINIT,A)
             COMMON SR
             DIMENSION A(7)
        C
        C    INITIALIZES BUTTERWORTH HIGH-PASS FILTER.
        C
             IF(XINIT.NE.0.)GO TO 1
             A(6)=0.0
             A(7)=0.0
        1    ROOT2=SQRT(2.0)
             C=TAN(3.141593*FC/SR)
             A(1)=1./(1.+ROOT2*C+C*C)
             A(2)=-2.*A(1)
             A(3)=A(1)
             A(4)=2*(C*C-1.)*A(1)
             A(5)=(1.-ROOT2*C+C*C)*A(1)
             RETURN
             END
```

This algorithm scales the filter coefficients for a gain of one on signals at the Nyquist frequency.

The function, BIFIL, realizes a filter with two poles and two zeros. It can be used to implement any of the bilinear filters of section 5.13. Using the subroutine HPSET to set the coefficients results in a high-pass filter. However, modifying HPSET to use other equations to calculate the coefficients (such as those described in section 5.13) can enable BIFIL to implement low-pass, band-pass, and band-reject filters as well. The arguments of BIFIL are:

XIN The digital signal applied to the filter
A Same as in HPSET

```
                    FUNCTION BIFIL(XIN,A)
                    DIMENSION A(7)
         C
         C    REALIZES FILTER WITH TWO POLES AND TWO ZEROS.
         C
                    T=XIN-A(4)*A(6)-A(5)*A(7)
                    Y=T*A(1)+A(2)*A(6)+A(3)*A(7)
                    A(7)=A(6)
                    A(6)=T
                    BIFIL=Y
                    RETURN
                    END
```

This algorithm does not directly implement the equation given in section 5.13 for such a filter. The form of the equation has been manipulated into its most efficient computational form.

The balance function, described in section 5.5, modifies the amplitude of a signal (XIN) in an attempt to equalize its power with the power of a reference signal (YIN). The purpose of the subroutine BLNSET is to initialize the two low-pass filters used in the balancing process. The arguments are:

FC The cutoff frequency of the filters in Hertz. The default value of each is 10 Hz.
XINIT Determines whether the memory locations that store previous values in the low-pass filters are cleared. Setting XINIT=0 clears them, otherwise they remain untouched.
A The first of ten consecutive variables in an array that is to be used to store intermediate results.

```
                    SUBROUTINE BLNSET(FC,XINIT,A)
                    DIMENSION A(10)
         C
         C    INITIALIZES BALNCE WITH DEFAULT FC=10.
         C
                    IF(FC.EQ.0.)FC=10.
                    CALL RSNSET(0.,FC,1.,XINIT,A(1))
                    CALL RSNSET(0.,FC,1.,XINIT,A(6))
                    RETURN
                    END
```

The arguments of BALNCE are:

XIN Input signal that is to be equalized.
YIN Reference signal.
A Same as in BLNSET.

```
                    FUNCTION BALNCE(YIN,XIN,A)
                    DIMENSION A(10)
         C
         C    BALANCES THE POWER OF XIN TO THAT OF YIN.
         C
                    D=RESON(ABS(Y),A(6))
                    IF(D.EQ.0.)D=.0000001
                    BALNCE=Y*RESON(ABS(X),A(1))/D
                    RETURN
                    END
```

The realization of a comb filter requires an initialization procedure, CMBSET, which uses the value of the loop time in setting up the circular queue that forms the delay line. The following arguments are used:

XLOOPT Loop time in seconds.
XINIT Determines whether the delay line is cleared during initialization. Choosing

XINIT=0 causes the delay line to be filled with zero-valued samples. Otherwise the delay line retains the previous data.

A The first of 1005 consecutive variables in an array that holds the delay line and stores intermediate values. This provides for a delay line with 1000 cells and so the maximum loop time available is 1000/SR. Longer times can be obtained by increasing the dimension of A.

```
      SUBROUTINE CMBSET(XLOOPT,XINIT,A)
      COMMON SR
      DIMENSION A(1005)
C
C    INITIALIZES THE FUNCTION COMB.
C
C  THE FIRST 5 LOCATIONS IN A HOLD DATA DESCRIBING THE QUEUE.
C  A(1) IS THE ADDRESS OF THE LAST LOCATION IN THE QUEUE.
      A(1)=5.+AINT(XLOOPT*SR+.5)
      IF(A(1).GT.1005.)A(1)=1005.
C  A(2) IS THE LOOP TIME.
      A(2)=XLOOPT
      IF(XINIT.NE.0.)GO TO 1
      LE=INT(A(1))
      DO 2 L=3,LE
2     A(L)=0.
C  A(5) IS THE POINTER TO THE QUEUE.
      A(5)=6.
1     RETURN
      END
```

The function COMB, which performs the actual filtering, enables the value of the reverberation time to be varied on each sample, if desired. However, it calculates a new value for the feedback gain factor, g, only when the reverberation time has changed from the previous sample. The arguments for COMB are:

XIN Input signal to the comb filter.
RVT Reverberation time in seconds.
A Same as in CMBSET.

```
      FUNCTION COMB(XIN,RVT,A)
      DIMENSION A(1005)
C
C    COMB FILTER WITH REVERBERATION TIME = RVT.
C
      L=INT(A(5))
C  A(3) IS THE PREVIOUS VALUE OF REVERB TIME.
      IF(RVT.EQ.A(3))GO TO 2
      IF(RVT.EQ.0.)GO TO 20
C  A(4) IS THE FACTOR g.
      A(4)=.001**(A(2)/RVT)
      GO TO 30
20    A(2)=0.
30    A(3)=RVT
C  INCREMENT POINTER.
2     A(5)=A(5)+1.
      IF(A(5).GT.A(1)) A(5)=6.
      COMB=A(L)
      A(L)=A(4)*A(L)+XIN
      RETURN
      END
```

An all-pass network is initialized by calling the CMBSET subroutine above. This enables the function ALPASS, below, to perform the filtering. The arguments of ALPASS are identical to those of COMB except that the dimension of A is 155. This provides for a maximum length of the delay line of 150 cells, limiting the longest loop time to 150/SR.

```
      FUNCTION ALPASS(XIN,RVT,A)
C
C    ALL-PASS NETWORK  (INITIALIZED BY CMBSET).
C
      DIMENSION A(155)
      X=COMB(XIN,RVT,A(1))
```

```
L=A(5)
ALPASS=X-A(4)*A(L)
RETURN
END
```

The subroutine RVBSET initializes a Schroeder-form reverberator consisting of four comb filters in parallel followed by two all-pass networks in cascade. The loop times were chosen to imitate a moderate-sized hall. Notice that each of the all-pass filters has its own fixed, relatively short reverberation time that is independent of the reverberation time of the overall unit. The arguments are as follows:

XINIT Determines whether the delay lines are cleared during initialization. Choosing XINIT=0 causes the delay lines to be filled with zero-valued samples. Otherwise they retain the present data.

A The first of 3194 consecutive variables in an array that forms the delay lines and stores values that define characteristics of the unit reverberators. This dimension is chosen for a sampling rate of 20 KHz and the loop times given in the DATA statement. Doubling the sampling frequency should approximately double the size of the array. Lengthening the loop times by changing the values in the DATA statement may require the dimension of A to be increased. In some cases the dimensions on the arrays in the comb filter and all-pass network routines may also have to be increased.

```
          SUBROUTINE RVBSET(XINIT,A)
          DIMENSION XL(6),A(3194)
C
C     INITIALIZES REVERB.
C
          DATA XL/.0297,.0371,.0411,.0437,.005,.0017/
C
C     THE ARRAY XL HOLDS THE LOOP TIMES FOR THE 4 COMB FILTERS
C     AND THE TWO ALL-PASS NETWORKS.
C
          J=1
          DO 10 I=1,6
          CALL CMBSET(XL(I),XINIT,A(J))
10        J=J+INT(A(J))
          RETURN
          END
```

The arguments of REVERB are:

XIN Signal applied to the reverberator.
RVT Reverberation time in seconds.
A Same as in RVBSET.

```
          FUNCTION REVERB(XIN,RVT,A)
          DIMENSION A(3194)
C
C     REVERBERATES INPUT SIGNAL, XIN.
C
          X=0.
          J=1
          DO 10 I=1,4
          X=X+COMB(XIN,RVT,A(J))
10        J=J+INT(A(J))
          X=ALPASS(X,.096835,A(J))*.25
          J=J+INT(A(J))
          REVERB=ALPASS(X,.032924,A(J))
          RETURN
          END
```

The subroutine VDSET initializes the circular queue used in implementing a variable delay line. The arguments are as follows:

DLYMAX The maximum amount of delay in seconds to be used.

XINIT Determines whether the delay line is cleared during initialization. Specifying XINIT=0 fills the delay line with zero-valued samples. Otherwise the current contents is retained.

A The first of 1004 consecutive variables in an array that forms the delay line and stores values that define characteristics of the variable delay unit. This allows a maximum of 1000 cells in the queue—a maximum delay of 25 msec at a 40 KHz sampling rate. For a longer delay, increase the dimension of A.

```
      SUBROUTINE VDSET(DLYMAX,XINIT,A)
C
C  INITIALIZES VARIABLE DELAY LINE FUNCTION, VDELAY.
C
      COMMON SR
      DIMENSION A(1004)
C
C  A(1) IS ADDRESS OF LAST POINT IN THE DELAY LINE.
C  A(2) CURRENT POINTER TO THE DELAY LINE.
C  A(3) IS CURRENT AMOUNT OF DELAY.
C  A(4) IS CURRENT TAP DISTANCE FROM INPUT.
C
C  DELAY LINE HAS ONE EXTRA CELL TO ENABLE DELAYS OF ZERO.
      A(1)=4.+AINT(DLYMAX*SR+1.5)
      IF(A(1).GT.1004.) A(1)=1004.
      IF(XINIT.NE.0.) GO TO 1
      LE=INT(A(1))
      DO 2 L=5,LE
      A(L)=0.
2     CONTINUE
      A(2)=5.
1     RETURN
      END
```

The function VDELAY realizes a variable delay line using the queue set up by VDSET. It has the following arguments:

XIN Signal applied to the delay line.
DELAY Amount of delay in seconds. It must be a number between zero and DLYMAX.
A Same as in VDSET.

```
      FUNCTION VDELAY(XIN,DELAY,A)
C
C  IMPLEMENTS VARIABLE DELAY LINE.
C
      DIMENSION A(1004)
      COMMON SR
      IF(DELAY.EQ.A(3)) GO TO 1
      A(4)=AINT(DELAY*SR+.5)
C  IF THE DELAY IS TOO LONG, SET IT EQUAL TO THE MAX DELAY.
      IF(A(4).GT.A(1)-4.) A(4)=A(1)-4.
      A(3)=DELAY
1     IF(A(2).GE.A(1)) A(2)=4.
      A(2)=A(2)+1.
C  L IS THE CURRENT POINTER IN THE CIRCULAR QUEUE.
      L=INT(A(2))
      A(L)=XIN
C  K POINTS TO THE TAP POINT.
      K=L-INT(A(4))
      IF(K.LT.5) K=INT(A(1))+K-4
      VDELAY=A(K)
      RETURN
      END
```

The function NLPROC implements a non-linear processor. The transfer function has previously been stored in the 512 place table designated by F(I,NF). The arguments of the function are as follows:

XIN The input signal to the non-linear processor. It selects the wavetable entry used for output. The value of XIN must be scaled to assume values between 0 and 511. For example, suppose an oscillator producing a cosine wave is to drive the function NLPROC. An unscaled cosine wave takes on values between −1 and +1. Thus, the maximum amplitude of the oscillator could be set to 255 and the constant 256 would be added to the output of the oscillator in order to drive NLPROC in the proper range.

NF Designates the wavetable to be used.

```
      FUNCTION NLPROC(XIN,NF)
C
C   NON-LINEAR PROCESSOR
C   USES A TABLE OF 512 ENTRIES TO STORE TRANSFER FUNCTION.
C   EXPECTS A VALUE OF XIN IN THE RANGE FROM 1 TO 512.
C
      COMMON F(512,1)
      K=INT(XIN)
      IF(K.GT.512) K=512
      IF(K.LT.1) K=1
      NLPROC=F(K,NF)
      RETURN
      END
```

As an example of how the routines above can be linked into an instrument algorithm, consider the instrument design of figure A1. The instrument algorithm is expressed as the following subroutine. The argument A is the first of 1019 places in an array that is to be used to store intermediate results. The meaning of the other arguments may be seen by looking at the figure.

```
      SUBROUTINE EXAMPLE(AMP,FREQ,DEV,FR,RVT,A,OUT)
C
C   IMPLEMENTS FLOW CHART SHOWN IN FIGURE A1.
C
      DIMENSION A(1019)
      COMMON SR
C   THE NEXT STATEMENT CONVERTS FR TO A SAMPLING INCREMENT.
      RSI=512.*FR/SR
      VIB=RANDI(DEV,RSI,A(1))
      F=FREQ+VIB
C   THE NEXT STATEMENT CONVERTS F TO A SAMPLING INCREMENT.
      SI=512.*F/SR
      Y1=OSCIL(AMP,SI,1,PHS)+256.
      Y2=NLPROC(Y1,2)
      Y3=RESON(Y2,A(5))
      Y4=RESON(Y3,A(10))
      OUT=COMB(Y4,RVT,A(15))
      RETURN
      END
```

The array A holds coefficients and values for the routines that require storage of results between samples. The number of places needed for a given routine can be found by examining the dimension of A in the function. For example, the function RANDI contains the dimension A(4) indicating that four places are to be reserved in the array for RANDI. The RESON function uses five so that each RESON unit generator used must reserve five places. Finally, COMB needs 1005 places.

In the subroutine above and the program outline that follows, the array has been partitioned as:

A(1)−A(4)	RANDI	
A(5)−A(9)	RESON	(First filter)
A(10)−A(14)	RESON	(Second filter)
A(15)−A(1019)	COMB	

Three of the unit generators, the two RESONs and COMB, require initialization subroutines to be executed prior to synthesis. Therefore the main program must call these subroutines before calling the instrument algorithm above. In addition, the

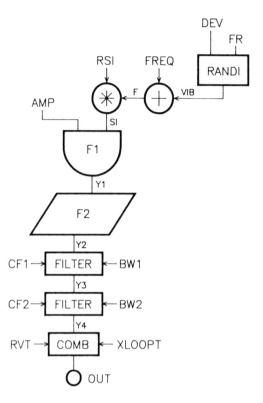

FIGURE A1   Example Instrument Design

main program must fill the wavetables: F(I,1) and F(I,2). The outline of the main program that accomplishes these tasks would be along the lines of:

```
C   OUTLINE OF MAIN PROGRAM
C
        DIMENSION A(1019)
C   A LARGER DIMENSION WILL PROBABLY BE NECESSARY DEPENDING ON THE
C   NUMBER OF OTHER INSTRUMENTS AND THEIR MEMORY REQUIREMENTS.
        COMMON SR
        COMMON F(512,2)
        SR=40000.
C     40 KHZ SAMPLING RATE
        .
        .
        .
C   IN THIS SECTION THE PROGRAM WOULD ASSIGN THE VALUES TO THE
C   VARIABLES USED IN THE INITIALIZATION STATEMENTS.
        .
        .
        .
C   INITIALIZATION STATEMENTS
        CALL RSNSET(CF1,BW1,1,0,A(5))
        CALL RSNSET(CF2,BW2,1,0,A(10))
        CALL CMBSET(XLOOPT,0,A(15))
        .
        .
        .
C   CALL THE ROUTINES TO FILL THE WAVETABLES HERE.
        .
        .
        .
C   AT THIS POINT THE PROGRAM WOULD INVOKE A SCORE INTERPRETER
C   WHICH WOULD DETERMINE THE ARGUMENTS FOR THE INSTRUMENTS AND
C   WHICH INSTRUMENT IS TO PLAY WHEN.
        .
        .
        .
```

```
        CALL EXAMPLE(AMP,FREQ,DEV,FR,RVT,A(1),OUT)
C  OTHER INSTRUMENTS MAY ALSO BE INVOKED IN THIS REGION.
        .
        .
        .
C  CALL ROUTINE TO DIRECT THE OUTPUT OF THE INSTRUMENTS TO A
C  D/A CONVERTER OR STORAGE DEVICE.
        .
        .
        .
C  GO BACK TO SCORE INTERPRETER AND OBTAIN DATA FOR NEXT EVENT.
```

GLOSSARY

Acoustics The study of the physics of sound.

A/D converter See data converters.

Additive synthesis Production of sound by direct summation of component frequencies. Generally, each component is produced by a separate sinusoidal oscillator.

Address A number that designates a particular location in a computer memory.

Aliasing In a digital sound system, the reflection of frequencies higher than the Nyquist frequency to lower frequencies. An "aliased" frequency is one which, after reflection, is indistinguishable from a lower, unreflected frequency.

Algorithm A step-by-step procedure for accomplishing a task. Each step must be defined unambiguously and there must be a clear path to the completion of the algorithm. Most algorithms can be translated into a programming language and executed on a computer.

All-pass network A device that recirculates a signal through a delay line. It is used as an element in a reverberator. The steady-state amplitude response of an all-pass network is flat.

Amplify To increase the amplitude of a signal. In computer music, amplification is normally accomplished by means of multiplication by a constant.

Amplitude In acoustics, the peak amount of atmospheric displacement of a sound, measured in units of pressure (Newtons per square meter). In computer music, amplitude describes the value of the largest sample of a signal.

Amplitude response In a filter, the ratio of the amplitude of the output signal to that of the input signal. The amplitude response most often varies with frequency.

Analog signal An electronic signal which varies continuously; that is, it has a value at every point in time.

Argument A value applied to a function which determines the output value of the function.

Array A collection of values stored in the computer in tabular form. An array can have one or more dimensions.

ASCII American Standard Code for Information Interchange. One standard convention for representing alphanumeric characters in binary form.

Assembly language A low-level language that enables the programmer to express an algorithm as a sequence of specific machine instructions.

Attack The segment of the envelope of a tone in which the amplitude increases from zero to its peak. This segment is also called the rise.

Attack time A term used to denote the starting time of a musical tone.

Attenuation The reduction of the amplitude of a sound or a component of the sound.

Band-pass filter A filter that passes frequencies in a specified region and attenuates frequencies both above and below that region. Its passband is characterized by a center frequency, a bandwidth, and a midband gain.

Band-reject filter A filter that attenuates frequencies in a specified region and passes frequencies both above and below that region. Its stopband is characterized by a center frequency, a bandwidth, and the maximum amount of attenuation.

Bandwidth   (1) A measure of the width of the passband or stopband of a filter. (2) A measure of the width of the frequency region occupied by the spectrum of a signal.

Beating   A noticeable and periodic reduction in the amplitude of a sound caused by the interference of closely tuned frequency components.

Binary number   A number whose digits can assume one of two states: 0 or 1. Each digit position has a value two times the value of the position to its right.

Bit   A single binary digit. It can assume one of two states: 0 or 1. It is the smallest unit of information recognized by a digital computer.

Byte   In most computer systems, a group of 8 bits. A byte is capable of assuming 256 unique states. It is the most common measure of the size of a computer's memory.

Carrier wave   The wave to which modulation is applied. The carrier wave is altered in sympathy with the modulating signal.

Cascade connection   The relationship between two devices where the output of the first is applied to the input of the second.

Cent   A unit of measure used in tuning to compare the ratio of two frequencies. One cent corresponds to a frequency ratio of $1:2^{1/1200}$ or $1:1.0005778$. There are 1200 cents in an octave.

Center frequency   The frequency about which the passband of a filter is symmetrically disposed.

Chorus effect   The creation from a single voice of the percept of multiple voices in unison.

Clavier   A keyboard of the type found on a piano or organ.

Code   Text for an algorithm written in a programming language.

Coefficient   A constant used to multiply a variable. In a filter algorithm, a set of coefficients determines the characteristics of the filter. In the algebraic expression of a transfer function for a waveshaper, a set of coefficients determines the spectrum of the shaped waveform.

Comb filter   A device that recirculates a signal through a delay line. It is used as an element in a reverberator. The amplitude response of a comb filter exhibits peaks and valleys that are equally spaced in frequency.

Component   A single frequency element found in a spectrum.

Composing program   A program that generates a musical score using algorithms and parameters supplied by the composer.

Computer-aided composition   One of a number of approaches in which the mathematical and logical powers of the computer are enlisted to assist in the expression of a composer's musical ideas.

Constant   A numerical value which does not change during the course of a program.

Continuous   (1) Characteristic of a signal in which every point on the waveform is smoothly connected to the rest of the waveform. (2) Characteristic of a random process where the results can fall anywhere within a range of values.

Cosine wave   A sinusoidal waveform whose phase relative to a sine wave is 90°.

CPU (Central processing unit)   Controls the operation of the computer by interpreting instructions and executing them.

Critical band   A measure of the ability of the ear to discriminate adjacent tones. Critical band plays an important role in masking of tones, and in the perception of loudness and timbre. The width of the critical band varies with frequency.

CRT (Cathode ray tube)   A device most often found in a data terminal for the visual display of information.

Cutoff frequency   The frequency that marks the transition from passband to stopband in a filter. It is normally defined as the frequency at which the signal is attenuated by 3 dB.

Cycle   One repetition of a periodic waveform.

D/A converter   *See* data converters.

Data   A collection of information.

Data converters   Devices that transform analog signals to digital form and the reverse. They are known as A/D and D/A converters, respectively.

Decay   That portion of the envelope of a tone in which the amplitude decreases from its steady-state value to zero. In an ADSR envelope (see section 3.5), the decay is from the peak amplitude to the steady-state value.

Decibel (dB)   A unit of relative measure used to compare the intensities of two signals on a logarithmic scale. Under certain conditions the decibel can be used to compare the amplitudes of two signals, as well.

Diatonic   The collection of pitches in a major scale.

Digital   Characteristic of a system or device that handles information in numerical quantities.

Discrete   Discontinuous. For example, a digital signal is discrete in that it is comprised of values at specific points in time.

Discrete summation formula   In sound synthesis, a mathematical relationship that expresses the sum of sinusoids in a compact form.

Disk   A peripheral device for storing large quantities of information. A disk consists of a rotating platter coated with magnetic material and a device for "reading and writing" the pattern of the magnetism.

Distortion index   A control on the amount of distortion, and hence the spectral content, produced by a waveshaping instrument. The distortion index generally has a large effect on the amplitude of the signal, as well.

Distortion synthesis   A class of sound synthesis techniques, including frequency modulation, nonlinear waveshaping, and the explicit use of discrete summation formulae, in which a controlled amount of distortion is applied to a simple waveform. All distortion synthesis techniques have an index which controls spectral richness.

Doppler shift   The perceived change in frequency observed when a sound source and a listener are moving relative to each other.

Dynamic range   The range of amplitudes that can be represented in a system. Dynamic range is limited on the low end by the noise of the system and on the high end by distortion.

Dynamics   The various indications in music notation for change of loudness level in a musical passage.

Editor   A computer program that enables the entry and modification of program text and data files in the computer.

Envelope   The shape of the amplitude variation during the course of a tone. A simple envelope consists of three segments: attack (rise), steady-state, and decay.

Envelope generator   A device for imparting an amplitude envelope to a tone.

Execution   The actual performance by a computer of a program instruction.

Exponential   Characteristic of a phenomenon that changes by the same ratio in a given time. For example, an exponential decay diminishes by a factor of two every time a fixed interval of time passes.

FFT (Fast Fourier Transform)   A numerical technique, optimized for rapid computer execution, for determining the spectrum of a digital signal.

File   A collection of information stored in the computer's external memory. A file may contain a program, data, or both.

Filter   A device that passes certain frequencies and attenuates others. The four principal types of filters are: low-pass, high-pass, band-pass, and band-reject.

Flanging   The process of adding a signal to a delayed image of itself where the amount of delay is swept from a maximum amount to zero.

Flow chart   A graphical representation of the logic in an algorithm or a program. In instrument design, a flow chart shows the interconnections among the unit generators.

Foldover   See aliasing.

Formant   A peaking in the spectral envelope of a tone. A formant is caused by resonances in the instrument or voice. Formants make an important contribution to our perception of timbre.

FORTRAN (FORmula TRANslation)   An algebraically oriented programming language suited for tasks that require a great deal of numerical calculation.

Fourier analysis   The process of breaking down a waveform into its component frequencies.

Fourier transform   The mathematical technique for changing the time-domain representation of a signal (its waveform) into a frequency-domain representation (its spectrum).

Frequency   The rate of repetition of a periodic waveform. Frequency is measured in Hertz (Hz).

Frequency domain   A way of characterizing a signal in terms of its frequency components. The representation of a signal in the frequency domain is called its spectrum.

Frequency modulation (FM)   The alteration of the frequency of a carrier wave by another signal called a modulating wave.

FM synthesis   The alteration or distortion of the frequency of one oscillator by a signal from a modulating oscillator. This produces a waveform with many more spectral components than the presence of only two oscillators might seem to imply.

Frequency response   In a filter, the ratio of the output signal to the input signal versus frequency. The frequency response consists of two parts: amplitude response and phase response.

Function   In mathematics, a way of expressing the dependence of the value of one quantity on the values of other quantities. In computer languages, a function is an algorithm that is passed parameters (arguments) and returns a result.

Fundamental   Ordinarily the lowest component in a harmonic spectrum. Under most conditions, the perceived pitch of a tone is at the frequency of the fundamental.

Fusion   The perception of a group of tones or spectral components as a single acoustic entity.

Gain   In a device, the ratio of output amplitude to input amplitude. When the gain is larger than one, amplification exists.

Glissando   A tone that exhibits continuous change of frequency, either up or down.

Graphics terminal   A data terminal with a CRT for display of line segments as well as alphanumeric characters. Graphics display often enhances the clarity of presentation of information to the user.

Hardware   The electronic equipment that forms a computer system.

Harmonic   A spectral component that is an exact integer multiple of the fundamental frequency.

Hertz (Hz)   A unit of measure for frequency. It denotes the number of repetitions per second of a periodic waveform.

High-pass filter   A filter that passes frequencies above a specified cutoff frequency and attenuates frequencies below that point.

Index of modulation   A measure of the amount of modulation, and thus the spectral richness, produced in a frequency-modulated instrument.

Initialization   In a sound synthesis program, the setting of parameter values prior to the actual process of calculating sample values.

Impulse response   The waveform produced when a filter is excited by a single positive input sample with all preceding and following samples equal to zero.

Instruction   In a computer, a numerical code stored in memory that represents an operation for the computer to perform.

Instrument design   A synthesis algorithm for realizing a particular class of sounds.

Intensity   A measure of the power in a sound, expressed in Watts/m^2. Intensity is the primary physical correlate with the perceived loudness of a sound.

Interactive   Characteristic of a situation where the user and the computer program respond to each other's actions on an approximately real-time basis. Any live-performance situation is, by definition, interactive.

Interface   The boundary or means of connection between two or more elements in a computer system. An interface can be between hardware devices, pieces of software, or a user and a computer system.

Integrated circuit   A large number of electronic devices fabricated on a small piece of silicon.

Interpolation The process of finding values intermediate to specified values. The two most common methods of interpolation are linear and exponential.

Interval The musical name for the ratio in frequency between two tones. Pairs of tones separated by the same musical interval share a similar quality.

Inversion The reversal of direction of a musical interval. For example, the inversion of the interval C/E♭ is C/A.

I/O (Input/Output) (1) A class of devices that provide the means for communication between the computer and its users or other computer hardware. (2) The process of communication between the computer and its users or other computer hardware.

Karplus–Strong algorithm An instrument design in which a signal is recirculated around a delay line through a low-pass filter. The algorithm is relatively efficient and quite successful at simulating the sound of a plucked string.

Kilohertz (kHz) 1000 Hertz.

Language (computer) A rigidly defined set of conventions for expressing algorithms. Once transmitted to the computer, the encoded algorithm is translated into machine instructions.

Linear (1) Characteristic of a phenomenon which changes by the same amount over a given interval of time. (2) Characteristic of a signal processor in which a change in amplitude of the input signal produces a similar change in the amplitude of the output signal.

Linear prediction In a sampled data system, the process of determining the relationships that enable the value of the next output sample to be calculated as a combination of previous output samples.

Localization The process of synthesizing cues that create the auditory illusion of the placement in space of a sound source.

Logarithmic Characteristic of a phenomenon where changes are perceived on the basis of the ratio of the change.

Lookup table An array, such as a wavetable used by an oscillator, containing precomputed values of a mathematical function. Its use can save a great deal of computer time because a program can simply retrieve values from the table instead of performing extensive calculations.

Loudness The subjective response to the amount of acoustical power received by the ear.

Low-pass filter A filter that passes frequencies below a specified cutoff frequency and attenuates frequencies above that frequency.

Machine language The actual numerical code for specific computer instructions.

Markov process A conditional random process in which the higher-order probabilities can be calculated as products of the first-order probabilities.

Masking The reduction in sensitivity to amplitude due to the fatigue of neurons on the basilar membrane. This often causes softer tones to be "covered up" by louder ones.

Matrix *See* array.

Memory The repository of both programs and data. It is divided into discrete units or locations which are distinguished by unique numerical addresses.

Microsecond (μsec) One-millionth of a second.

Midband gain The ratio of output amplitude to input amplitude for a signal at the center frequency of a band-pass filter.

Millisecond (msec) One-thousandth of a second.

Mixer A device for combining signals by adding them together.

Modulating wave The signal which alters the carrier wave in some way.

Modulation The alteration of the amplitude, frequency, or phase of a carrier wave in accordance with a modulating signal. The signal resulting from the modulation has a more complex spectrum than would be obtained by the simple addition of the carrier wave and the modulating wave.

Motive A characteristic melodic/rhythmic fragment in a piece of music, out of which larger units such as phrases are made.

Musique concrète A form of tape or electronic music made from "concrete"—i.e., recorded—sounds. In most musique concrète the recorded sounds are modified electronically from their original form.

Music 4   An influential language for sound synthesis created by Max V. Mathews at the Bell Laboratories in the early 1960s and exported to several other institutions.

Noise   Sound with a distributed spectrum. The most common form, white noise, has a "hissing" sound.

Non-linear processor   A signal-processing device in which a change in the amplitude of the input signal does not produce a similar change in the amplitude of the output signal. This alters the waveform, and hence the spectrum, of a signal passing through it.

Non-linear synthesis   *See* waveshaping.

Nyquist frequency   In a digital sound system, the frequency at one-half the sampling rate. It is the theoretical upper limit to faithful representation of frequency components in the system.

One-over-f (1/f) noise   Noise with a spectrum that rolls off directly with frequency.

On-line   Attached directly to a computer and operational. In computer music, it generally is used to indicate that the data converters can be accessed directly from the computer that calculates the sample values.

Onset   The time at which a tone begins.

Operating system (OS)   An organized collection of software which provides many useful services to the users of a computer. It also controls the flow of work in the system.

Orchestra   A collection of computer instrument designs.

Oscillator   A device for generating a periodic waveform. Its two principal controls are amplitude and frequency of repetition of the waveform.

Overflow   The condition that occurs when the result of a mathematical operation exceeds the capacity of the format used for number representation.

Overtone   A spectral component above the fundamental.

Parallel connection   The relationship among devices where the same signal is applied to the inputs of all devices simultaneously. The outputs of the devices are combined to form a single signal.

Parameter   A value input to an algorithm which is used in calculating the output. In computer music, a parameter in the score can control an attribute of the sound produced by a computer instrument.

Partial   A spectral component of a sound. It may or may not be harmonic to the fundamental.

Passband   The frequency region in which a filter passes signals with little or no attenuation.

Period   The time occupied by one repetition of a periodic waveform.

Periodic wave   A signal comprised of repetitions of a waveform at a particular, fixed frequency.

Peripheral   A device connected to the CPU in a computer system. Peripherals are usually for user communication (data terminals, printers, etc.) or external memory (disks, tape drives, etc.).

Phase   A means of comparing the relative position in time of two waveforms or of marking a specific point on a waveform.

Pitch   The subjective response to frequency.

Pole   A resonance. A filter that implements a pole causes a peak in the spectral envelope of a signal passing through the filter.

Polynomial   An algebraic expression that takes the form of the sum of a series of terms where each term consists of a coefficient multiplying a variable raised to a power.

Precedence effect   In the presence of the same sound from several sources, the phenomenon by which a listener attributes the location of the source on the basis of the sound that arrives first. This occurs even when subsequent sounds have higher amplitudes.

Probability   The likelihood of obtaining a given outcome of a random process. It is expressed as the ratio of number of occurrences of that outcome to the total number of results of the random process.

Probability density function   A mathematical expression that indicates the likelihood of a continuous random variable occurring within a range of values.

Program   A sequence of instructions to accomplish a specific task which can be executed by a computer.

Psychoacoustics   The study of the way humans perceive sound. It includes such subjective responses to sound as pitch, loudness, duration, timbre, and apparent location.

Pulse   A waveform with significant amplitude only during a relatively brief portion of its period. A pulse has a very rich spectrum.

Q   A measure of the selectivity of a filter. A filter with a high Q has a narrow bandwidth.

Random   Characteristic of a process that, under repeated observations with the same set of conditions, does not always produce the same results.

Random variable   A variable which takes on a value as the result of a random process. A random variable is discrete when it can take on only specific values; it is continuous when it can assume any value within a range.

Real-time   Characteristic of a process in which data is processed at the same rate as it is taken in or used. For example, a digital synthesizer is said to operate in real time when its calculation rate equals the sampling rate.

Recursive filter   A digital filter that determines the value of its current output sample on the basis of past output samples.

Resolution   The fineness to which a quantity can be represented in a digital system.

Resonance   A spectral peak, such as a formant.

Reverberation   The multiple reflections of sound in a room causing sound to be heard after all sources have ceased.

Ring modulation   The process of combining two signals by multiplication. Ring modulation produces sidebands but suppresses both the carrier and modulating frequencies.

Rise time   The duration of the attack segment of the envelope of a tone.

Rolloff   (1) The rate at which a spectral envelope of a tone decreases with frequency. (2) The rate at which the attenuation of a filter increases in the stop band. Both are expressed in units of dB/octave.

Sampling   The process of representing a waveform by measuring its value at discrete points in time.

Sampling increment   In a digital oscillator, the amount added to the current phase to determine which location in the wavetable to use next. The sampling increment is directly proportional to frequency.

Sampling rate   The frequency at which samples are generated (D/A) or taken (A/D) in a digital sound system.

Score   A list of musical events. Each event has attributes, or parameters, to describe it. Common parameters include designation of instruments to play, starting time, duration, frequency, and amplitude.

Score editor   A computer program that enables entry and modification of scores.

Score preprocessor   A computer program that enables the encoding of scores in a syntax that is easy to read and bears a strong, intuitive relation to the encoded music. The score pre-processor translates the code into the parameter list score format required by the music-synthesis language.

Serialism   A kind of music based on an ordered set of elements, such as a twelve-tone row. It often includes serialization of other elements, such as rhythm, as well.

Series connection   *See* cascade.

Sideband   A product of modulation whose frequency depends on the frequencies of both the carrier and modulating waves.

Signal   A temporal phenomenon, whether electrical or digital, that carries information.

Signal processor   A device that modifies a signal passing through it.

Signal-to-noise (S/N) ratio   A numerical comparison of the signal level to the noise level in a system.

Sine wave   A sinusoidal waveform whose phase is taken to be zero.

Sinusoid   A smooth waveform whose spectrum contains only one component frequency.

Software   Programs that can be executed by a computer.

Spectral envelope   The outline showing the distribution of acoustical energy with frequency. A spectral envelope can exhibit formant peaks.

Spectrum   The representation of a signal in terms of its frequency components.

Steady-state   The portion of the envelope of a tone in which the amplitude remains relatively constant.

Steady-state analysis   The characterization of the response of a device, such as a filter, to a sinusoid that has been applied to the device long enough for the output of the device to settle to a constant response.

Steady-state response   The response of a filter to a constant periodic signal.

Stochastic process   *See* random process.

Stopband   The frequency region in which a filter provides the greatest amount of attenuation.

Subscore   A part of a score, such as a group of proximate notes. Some score editors enable operations on subscores.

Subroutine   A subprogram invoked from the main program or from another subprogram.

Subtractive synthesis   A technique that uses filters to alter the spectral content of a sound.

Synthesis   The realization of electrically-generated acoustical elements.

Synthesizer   A device that implements synthesis algorithms, most often in real time.

Timbre   The characteristic tone quality of a particular class of sounds.

Time domain   A way of characterizing a signal in terms of its amplitude fluctuations versus time. The representation of a signal in the time domain is called its waveform.

Transducer   A device that converts mechanical energy, such as a sound wave, into electrical signals. All manual input devices, including claviers, digitizing tablets, sliders, etc. are transducers.

Transfer function   In a non-linear processor, an expression that determines output values on the basis of input values.

Transposition   The raising or lowering, by a specified musical interval, of the frequency of musical tones.

Tuning   Any one of a number of systems for distributing, or mapping, musical intervals into frequency.

Twelve-tone music   Music based on a twelve-tone row; that is, on an ordering of all twelve tones and permutations of that ordering (see serialism).

Underflow   The condition that occurs when the result of a mathematical operation is too small to be accurately represented in the data format that is used. This phenomenon can occur, for example, when two nearly equal numbers are subtracted from each other.

Unit generator   An algorithm that performs a particular function of sound generation, modification, or combination. It is controlled by parameters obtained from a score or transducer.

Variable   In a computer program, a reference to a memory location whose value can change during the course of the program.

Vibrato   A perceptibly slow, quasi-periodic excursion both above and below the fundamental frequency of a tone.

Waveform   In acoustics, the pattern of pressure variation versus time in a sound. The shape of the waveform can have a great effect on the perceived timbre.

Waveshaper   *See* non-linear processor.

Waveshaping   A technique of distortion synthesis which creates complex spectra from simple tones by explicitly altering the shape of the waveform.

Wavetable   An array in which sequential values represent the successive points in a single cycle of a wave.

White noise Noise with a uniformly distributed spectrum. White noise has a "hissing" sound.

Zero An anti-resonance. A filter that implements a zero causes a dip in the spectral envelope of a signal passing through it.

INDEX

Charles Dodge is an internationally known composer and educator. His accomplishments have been recognized with an award and citation from the American Academy and Institute of Arts and Letters, a Woodrow Wilson National Fellowship, and two Guggenheim Fellowships. Born in Iowa, Mr. Dodge attended the University of Iowa and Columbia University, where his composition teachers included Richard Hervig and Otto Luening. He studied computer music at Princeton University with Godfrey Winham and has composed extensively in this genre since the mid-1960s. Major performances of his computer music include those at the New York Philharmonic's Horizons '84 Festival, the Warsaw Autumn Festival, the Los Angeles Olympic Arts Festival, the American Composers Orchestra's inaugural concert, the Calarts Festival, and the Stockholm Festival of Electronic Music. Record labels featuring Mr. Dodge's music are Nonesuch, Composers Recordings Inc., Crystal, 1750 Arch, Fylkingen, and Folkways. Mr. Dodge is Professor of Music in the Conservatory of Music at Brooklyn College of the City University of New York, where he directs the Center for Computer Music.

Thomas A. Jerse is currently a Research and Development Project Manager with the Signal Analysis Division of the Hewlett-Packard Company. He leads a unit responsible for the system definition, design, and implementation of a family of spectrum analyzers. In addition to his work at Hewlett-Packard, Mr. Jerse has worked extensively in the development of hardware and software for musical applications. For example, he designed and built a 16-track mobile recording studio, as well as several synthesizers for which he also wrote the software. During the academic year 1979–1980, Mr. Jerse was Assistant Professor of Music and Technical Director of the Center for Computer Music at Brooklyn College of the City University of New York. Born in Michigan, Mr. Jerse received a BSEE degree from the University of New Mexico and an MSEE from Stanford University.